The Queen's People
A Study of Hegemony, Coercion, and Accommodation among the Okanagan of Canada

As the struggle of Canada's native peoples for self-determination intensifies, the media images of native life become more dramatic, more oversimplified, and more distant from the lives of non-natives. Peter Carstens counters those images with this book; he shifts the focus away from the high drama of armed confrontation to the realities of everyday life for Okanagan Indians on a reserve near Vernon, British Columbia.

The Okanagan came to live on reserves through no choice of their own. Carstens begins his study by analysing the process that brought them there, including the role of various governments in the control of Canadian Indians and the hegemonic influence on their lives of fur traders, missionaries, gold miners, and settlers.

He then presents a detailed and sympathetic study of the contemporary community, focusing on the local economy and band government, on poverty, factionalism, and education, and on the declining influence of the Roman Catholic church.

Finally, he offers new perspectives from which to consider the predicament of the Okanagan and other native peoples in Canada. He applies the peasant model to the study of reserve systems and finds significant correlations. Questions of class, status, power, and institutionalized inequality also come into play.

Throughout the book Carstens analyses the complex effects that confinement to a reserve has on people's lives. His findings add a new dimension to an understanding of the diverse problems facing Canada's first peoples.

PETER CARSTENS is Professor of Anthropology, University of Toronto. He is the author of *The Social Structure of a Cape Coloured Reserve* and co-editor of *The Anthropological Field Diaries of Winifred Hoernlé*.

The Queen's People

A Study of Hegemony, Coercion, and Accommodation among the Okanagan of Canada

PETER CARSTENS

University of Toronto Press Toronto Buffalo London

© University of Toronto Press 1991
Toronto Buffalo London
Printed in Canada

ISBN 0-8020-5893-0 (cloth)
ISBN 0-8020-6827-8 (paper)

Printed on acid-free paper

Canadian Cataloguing in Publication Data

Carstens, Peter
 The Queen's people: a study of hegemony, coercion,
and accommodation among the Okanagan of Canada

 Includes bibliographical references and index.
 ISBN 0-8020-5893-0 (bound) ISBN 0-8020-6827-8 (pbk.)

 1. Okinagan Indians – History. 2. Okinagan Indians –
Government relations. 3. Okinagan Indians –
Reservations – History. 4. Indians of North America –
British Columbia – Okanagan Valley – History.
5. Indians of North America – British Columbia –
Okanagan Valley – Government relations. 6. Indians
of North America – British Columbia – Okanagan
Valley – Reservations – History. I. Title.

E99.035C37 1991   971.1'00497   C91-093048-1

To All the Okanagan People
Past, Present, and Future

Contents

Part Three
THE WIDER FRAMEWORK

Illustrative Material

FIGURES

Okanagan Nation Declaration

On 23 August 1987 the following declaration of Okanagan aboriginal rights was signed by representatives of all seven Canadian bands: Okanagan, Westbank, Penticton, Osoyoos, Lower Similkameen, Upper Similkameen, and Upper Nicola (Douglas Lake):

> We, the Okanagan Nation make this declaration today as a sign for every generation to come. Therefore, we hereby declare that:
>
> We are the unconquered aboriginal peoples of this land, our mother;
>
> The creator has given us our mother to enjoy, to manage and to protect;
>
> We, the first inhabitants, have lived with our mother from time immemorial;
>
> Our Okanagan Governments have allowed us to share equally in the resources of our mother;
>
> We have never given up our rights to our mother, our mother's resources, our governments and our religion;
>
> We will survive and continue to govern our mother and her resources for the good of all for all time.

Foreword

I met Peter Carstens some twenty-five years ago when he made his first visit to our reserve community in the Okanagan Valley. The interest and attention he has given our community over the years, and now the publication of this book, are to be commended. Very little to date has been recorded of the life of the original inhabitants of our beautiful valley. Our presence has been somewhat reluctantly acknowledged, without full appreciation of the contribution our people made to the early settlers of the past and the continuing influence we could have for a healthier development in the future.

The government defined us as 'Indians' under the Indian Act and then set us apart by mapping our lands and restricting our movements. This attempt to dispose of us effectively removed our people from any major role in the development of the valley. As Peter discovered early in his study, the issues that arose as a result of this were never definitively resolved and remain, if anything, more obscure than ever. True recognition of the Okanagan people in their ancestral homeland continues to be avoided by the government and the larger community alike.

Although Peter has brought to life some of the characters of the past, and has made a concerted effort to lift out from the musty files some of the pertinent historical details which he thoughtfully interprets in the light of his experience in our community today, his contribution can be only a small part of the story. Unfortunately, the thoughts and the feelings of our forefathers, who were treated in such a grievous and insensitive manner by some of those whom they had welcomed to share their life, have not been recorded except in our bones. Some of these newcomers took what had not been given to them, and paid no heed to the Spirit that kept our world in balance.

This trauma is still part of our life and shapes much of our thought and action. Even now, these feelings find no words to express the distress and loss that was experienced. Perhaps when the time is right and we see each other as true brothers and sisters, with full respect for each other, the Mother Earth, and the Spirit that sustains us, the words will then be found or no longer needed. Then, there will be no distinctions between the 'Queen's People,' and we shall all be Okanagan.

Chief Murray Alexis
Okanagan Indian Reserve
Easter 1988

Preface

This book is a study of a small community of Canadian people who, through no choice of their own, live on a number of pieces of land set apart and reserved for them near the city of Vernon in the southern interior of British Columbia. These Okanagan, as they call themselves, were once part of a larger 'nation' whose territory extended over a wide area on either side of the lake with which their name is associated.

Although the Okanagan never signed a treaty with any government, they fall under the administrative umbrella of the Canadian Department of Indian Affairs in accordance with the provisions of the Indian Act of 1876, as it has been amended from time to time. The process whereby the Okanagan were incorporated into the Canadian state is complex, involving not only the hegemonic influences of alien people and subsequent coercion, but also their reaction and accommodation to these external forces.

The title of this book, *The Queen's People*, refers to the Okanagan people, many of whom still have faith in the power and authority of the Queen of England to rule that their traditional lands be returned to them. They have been faithful admirers of the British monarchy since the reign of Queen Victoria. For example, when King George V died in 1936 the chief at that time cabled the band's condolences to the royal family. It is therefore a mockery of that trust that from the colonial period onwards the lawmakers and administrators set in authority over native peoples of Canada were also the Queen's people. On the other hand, it should come as no surprise that the pacification of the Okanagan, the establishment of reserves, and the administration of people on reserves could never have taken place without those culture agents and administrators representing the British crown through the institutions established abroad in the name of the monarchy. In the latter instance these institutions appealed enormously to the Okanagan chief Nkwala in the mid-nineteenth century, and to his sister's son Chelahitsa, as they did to his grandnephews Alexander and Johnny Chelahitsa much later.

The book focuses on both the past and the present of these aboriginal people. First, I have attempted to explain how the Okanagan came to live on reserves. Second, I have presented a sociological picture of life in the reserve community as it emerged over the years. A third theme has been to consider some of the complex effects that the artificially created social environment of a reserve has had on the personal lives of these people.

The historical portion of the book emphasizes the interaction between the Okanagan and white intruders into their territory during the nineteenth century and onwards into the twentieth. The first seven chapters consider the influence of the fur trade, the gold rush, the role of the missionaries, the struggle for control and ownership of land, the creation of reserves, the advent of the Indian Act, and the process of Okanagan economic and political incorporation into the wider society.

The analysis of the Okanagan reserve as a Canadian community begins with chapter 8, and continues to the end of the book with discussions of factionalism, the local economy, political leadership, local government and administration, and to a lesser extent modern schooling and religion. In the final chapter, I discuss various themes relating to their socio-economic position in Canadian society: class and status, colonialism, and reserve culture as these emerge from the context of the study.

In spite of the artificial distinction made above between ethnohistorical and social anthropological and sociological dimensions, I have tried to integrate the two intellectual systems and to write from that particular epistemological perspective. I refer to this strategy as the diasynchronic[1] approach, because it involves coming to grips with both socio-cultural relationships in time (*diachronic*) and space (*synchronic*). In other words, I have attempted not merely to chronicle the events in Okanagan culture or simply to observe everyday events, but to come to terms with the Okanagan reserve community in both space and time *as one system*, also taking into consideration socio-

1 Readers used to Radcliffe-Brown's artificial distinction between synchronic and diachronic analyses (Radcliffe-Brown 1952: 4) might find the idea of a diasynchronic approach confusing. My only intention here is to avoid the false dichotomy between social anthropological and historical analysis, a legacy inherited from Comte's intellectual separation of social statics and social dynamics. The neologism 'diasynchronic' seems to have been used in linguistics, the discipline whence the terms diachronic and synchronic derive (Jakobson 1931; Lévi-Strauss 1963: 3, 21).

economic relations with the wider society. There is nothing new about the diasynchronic approach in the social sciences. In sociology and social anthropology, for example, the interpretation and selection of ethnographic data (facts) and the continuous process of interaction with them have always involved an unending dialectic which incorporates the present with the past and, by implication, with the future (see Aron 1985; Braudel 1980; Carr 1961; Hoernlé 1933).

No community study, however, is complete if viewed as a closed system, regardless of how far back local history is explored. I have therefore paid considerable attention to the continuing influence of, and reaction to, external socio-economic forces as these have impinged on the community over the years. It was this incorporation of a political economy paradigm into my work that enabled me to place the Okanagan community firmly within the context of the rest of Canadian society. Thus, apart from ethnic and cultural factors, the main structural difference between Indian reserve communities such as the Okanagan and any other contemporary Canadian community is the overwhelming fact that they are set apart from mainstream society according to the dictates of the Indian Act.

I have often been asked to indicate the extent to which this study is applicable and relevant to native people in Canada generally. Every Indian band under the administrative control of the Indian Act and the Department of Indian Affairs operates under an imposed system which defines not only the limits of social and economic expression, but also many of the internal structural arrangements and contradictions within those communities. All Indian reserve communities are encapsulated, as it were, by one common administrative system.

The importance of community studies can never be overestimated because it is in communities, however these are structured, that people perceive the 'outside world,' and are perceived by others looking in from the outside. The idea of community is further complicated by the fact that, contrary to popular usage, few if any communities are utopian havens of peace and good fellowship. And some communities such as Indian reserves are riddled with factions, dissension, quarrelsomeness, poverty, sickness, not to mention the frustration of political impotence.

Let me illustrate the reality of feelings of political helplessness from inside the community with an occurrence in the summer of 1982 while I was carrying out fieldwork. An Okanagan friend had written a letter to Buckingham Palace asking for an audience with Her Majesty the Queen to discuss Canada's violation of various informal agreements over land that were reached with Chief Nkwala in the mid-nineteenth century. The letter was never delivered to the Queen; it was referred by Buckingham Palace to the governor general's office, which in turn referred it to the minister of Indian and northern affairs in Canada. The reply to my friend's letter consisted of a rude legalistic form letter (unsigned) from someone who referred to himself as a 'Special Assistant.'

My friend was outraged and wrote an immediate reply in which he asked, inter alia, who had intercepted his letter to the Queen, and on whose authority did the special assistant reply to a letter he had sent to the Queen. Five weeks later he received a reply signed by the minister of Indian affairs who set the record straight:

> The authority of The Queen to deal with matters concerning Indians in Canada has lawfully been passed by Her and by the Parliament of the United Kingdom to the Parliament and Government of Canada. The Parliament of Canada, acting under these legal powers, has in turn enacted the *Indian Act* which entrusts to me, as the Minister of Indian Affairs, the responsibility of administering that Act. It was for this reason that your letter of March 4 was referred to me from the Governor General's Office on April 27, and was in turn referred by me to my Special Assistant. It had been referred by Buckingham Palace to the Governor General's Office on March 31.
>
> The legality of this transfer of authority over Indian Affairs matters in Canada was upheld by the English Court of Appeal and by the House of Lords during the winter of 1981–82. It was therefore not only legally proper for your letter to be sent to me but I, with the assistance of my officers, am the only person to whom it could properly be sent.

We discussed the minister's letter, and eventually my friend said, 'Well, Pete, I guess that's it. That Ottawa *tyhee* [big shot] has got all the power now, and the Queen and I have none.'

Visitors to the land of the Okanagan today are hard pressed to observe at first hand even the vestiges of traditional Okanagan society and culture. In the first place the majority of the people (numbering 1074 in 1987) live on the small parcels of land reserved for them by the governments of British Columbia and Canada between about 1861 and 1876 onwards. In the second place they control neither their political nor their economic destinies, while the formal education of their children and the ministering of 'approved' religion have been in the hands of non-native institutions for well over one hundred years. Superficially speaking, the Okanagan of today appear to have lost not only their territory and their power to control that territory, but also their cultural and structural identity. Their language is not dead, but few people speak it. There are few vestiges of traditional material culture. There are no war parties, no summer camps, nor apparently many of the manifestations of the old culture.

But such exercises in comparative trait analysis achieve very little, and even misrepresent and distort reality, because they make no attempt to comprehend the processes of change. Nowadays the people still view themselves as Okanagan 'Indians,' and the majority have quite specific ideas about their past. Local historians, moreover, through the medium of the oral tradition, articulate a lively knowedge of the past through their understanding of the networks of time in their own world-view.

It is true that the private thoughts and feelings of local ancestors went with them to the grave, but the world of the early Okanagan did not come to a sudden demise with them. The patterns of change and transformation, the resistance and acceptance of new values, technology, and institutions, and the dialectic between all of these, reveal a different and more complex picture of conquest and reaction of that conquest. When we speak of the Okanagan people in the 1980s we have inevitably to focus on what might be called an Okanagan reserve culture. But we should never lose sight of their traditional culture, their institutions, or their territorial boundaries as these were before the advent of the fur trade. Reserve life can only make sense if it takes that past, and the forces that changed it, into consideration.

The enormous power differential between the Okanagan and those who administer them can be observed in many different contexts in people's lives. Struggles for and over power loom large also at the local level within the community. These are evident in rampant factionalism and status differentiation, as well as in kinship and friendship networks.

Detailed community studies are indispensable to the disciplines of social anthropology and sociology because as ethnographies they provide material for further comparative research. Thus my hypothesis regarding the primacy of the Indian Act and its administration remains to be tested by comparing a representative sample of detailed community studies; and critics of this and other hypotheses and generalizations presented in the chapters that follow will inevitably use the comparative method to support or refute my analysis.

My interest in the Okanagan people goes back more than twenty-five years to when I visited Canada from South Africa and was afforded the opportunity to consider the impact of reserve systems in a very different part of the world where a colonial establishment had imposed its will on indigenous people. Concern with that specific problem grew out of research I had carried out in certain Coloured reserves in South Africa and Namibia between 1956 and 1961 (Carstens 1961, 1966), and after reading *The Indians of British Columbia*

(Hawthorn, Belshaw, and Jamieson 1958) while I was still in the field. Actually, Professor Harry Hawthorn himself must take additional responsibility for my interests. Not only did he take time to answer my probing and irreverent letters, but he also recommended me for a Koerner Foundation Fellowship at the University of British Columbia, thereby making it financially possible for me to visit Canada for the 1962–3 academic year.

During that year I spent about four months in the southern interior of British Columbia. How I came to be interested in the Okanagan in particular, and not in their Shuswap, Lillooet, or Thompson neighbours, was partly fortuitous. I was intrigued by their accounts of the past, their internal factionalism, their external rivalries (particularly those expressed about the Shuswap), and their apparent indifference to the outside world. I also made some good friends with whom I corresponded after my return to South Africa.

There are many people who object to making comparisons between Canadian and South African native reserves, either because they dislike cross-cultural comparison or because they cannot bring themselves to consider the possibility that similar principles and processes might be rooted in colonial systems past and present. It is, however, sometimes forgotten (or not known) that South Africa and Canada have in the past shared information on the administration of reserves. As Tony Hall (1990) has pointed out, 'the South African Department of Native Affairs maintained important official links with the Canadian Department of Indian Affairs until about 1962' (see also NAC, RG 10, vol. 8588, file 1/1-10-4).

I came back to Canada in 1965 to take up an academic position at the University of Toronto, but it was not until the summer of 1978 that I was able to return to the Okanagan reserve and begin the research that led to the writing of this book. I spent a total of twelve months in the field, and when I was not able to be in the field I kept in regular touch with friends, informants, and the band council. I received memoranda, copies of council meetings, official and unofficial reports, and on several occasions, I telephoned people to clarify items of data – a luxury I would never have believed possible when I did my first field research as an anthropologist. During fieldwork I lived on the reserve with friends or in a rented trailer.

This research, staggered over such a long period, afforded me the opportunity of observing the many changes that took place over a generation. I was also fortunate in obtaining a copy of the field notes that James Hirabayashi had recorded in 1954 while he was working at Six Mile Creek and the Head of the Lake as a researcher for Hawthorn's Indians of British Columbia project. In addition to fieldwork I spent a great deal of time undertaking very detailed archival and library research. My ability to interpret the archival material owes a great deal to inspiration from Rhys Isaac (1982), whose discourse on method in historical ethnography helped me to put the two kinds of research together.

Quite apart from the academic interest this book might have for social anthropologists, sociologists, and historians, I hope that the Okanagan and other native people will find it useful as they continue to plan for the future from their present vantage point in contemporary Canadian society.

Peter Carstens
Toronto
25 June 1990

Acknowledgments

I could never have written this book had it not been for the assistance of many Okanagan people over the years, and I must thank them all collectively for putting up with me and my research for so long. I am especially indebted to those several Okanagan critics whose devastating scepticism of the value of any research by outsiders helped erase some of my academic philanthropy.

There is no way that a social anthropologist can ever repay the members of a community except by hoping that publication of the research may be of some use to them in the future. But scholars also have an obligation to keep in touch with 'their' people after their research is complete, for who else in the outside world is better qualified and equipped to act as advocates in crucial matters relating to socio-economic and political issues? Advocacy must surely extend beyond the publication of research.

I would like to extend my formal appreciation to the members of the Okanagan Band Council and the office staff for their assistance, especially for giving me access to their archives and records, and making me feel at home at office parties and luncheons. Their 'farewell' lunch for me included fresh salmon, deer meat, and all kinds of vegetable dishes, desserts, and pies. The Okanagan don't like saying goodbye, and a luncheon such as this is designed to make you return. As one councillor put it: 'The Okanagan are difficult people [to get along with], but if visitors stay here long enough we don't always let them leave easily.'

Chief Murray Alexis has honoured me by writing the foreword to this book, and I am especially grateful to him for his kind words and critical insights.

Albert Saddleman read the whole of my manuscript, offered valuable comments, and pointed out some errors in the text. I am extremely grateful

to him. I must also thank Lyle Brewer, the band manager, for his concern
with accuracy, and his patience with my constant badgering when he was busy
with band affairs. Josephine Saddleman, receptionist in the office and key
person in band affairs, decided early on in my research that my work was
possibly of some interest and value. I am enormously grateful to her, and
cannot imagine what life might have been like if she had taken the opposite
view.

There are many other individuals to whom I am indebted for giving their
support and friendship over the years: Tommy Gregoire, a remarkable
political historian; the late Jimmy Bonneau, his son Wilfred Bonneau, and his
grandson Reynolds Bonneau – all of whom were elected chiefs for short
periods of time; Mary Abel and Mary Powers whose exhaustive biographical
knowledge spanned at least seven generations; the late Ella Alexis who always
believed that things were a little better than they appeared; Jenny Marchand
and the late Louie Marchand; the late Chief Pierre Louis and Mrs Louis;
William and Peggy Brewer; Lucy and the late Emery Louis; Phyllis Bonneau
and Tim Isaac who worked as research assistants and remained good friends;
Martin Wilson, especially for letting me loose among his four boxes of
photographs; Brett Alexis who located every dwelling house on the reserve
for me; Ray Williams; Anna Marchand; Madeline and Ziggie Gregoire; Mary
Gregoire; Thelma Marchand; John Spotted Eagle; Mr and Mrs William
Louie; Richard and Pam Louis, and many others.

My gratitude to one band member has to be acknowledged separately. I met
Dan Logan in 1962 and we remained close friends up to his sudden death in
May 1988. Over the years I stayed in his home on occasions, and he
permitted me to live on his property near the lakeshore. He used to go out of
his way to introduce me to people, acted as interpreter on occasions,
encouraged me not to give up when my critics had upset me, and much more.
What is so surprising about our relationship is that he pretended to attach
very little value to my work because, as he used to say, I did not take
seriously 'spiritual things like religion.' Dan Logan had a superb knowledge
of the Okanagan language. He was the most talented genealogist in the
community, and for me he became an important chronicler of family and kin
relationships, especially in the context of reserve factionalism and stratification. In acknowledging my enormous debt to Dan Logan I have also to
apologize to a friend for not writing this book the way he would have wanted.

In addition to the Okanagan people themselves, I would like to thank
Robert de Pfyffer of Vernon, a meticulous researcher and chronicler, and
Duane Thomson of Okanagan College, Kelowna, for sharing their scholarly
work with me. Dr Thomson's doctoral thesis, 'A History of the Okanagan'

(1985), was of great value to me while I was preparing the final drafts of this book.

The staff of the Greater Vernon Museum and Archives were always generous with their time, and I am especially grateful to John Shephard and Judy Gosselin for their interest and assistance, notably for allowing me to photocopy Dr D.A. Ross's notes on the history of Okanagan culture as told by the late Chief Pierre Louis and others. I must also thank the staff of the Kamloops Museum, especially Ken Favrhold, for granting me access to some Hudson's Bay Company records I had not yet seen. The staff of the Kelowna Museum kindly gave me access to their collection, for which I am most grateful.

I am especially indebted to Reuben Ware and David Mattison of the Provincial Archives of British Columbia for assistance in locating documents and manuscripts in Victoria. The staff members of the National Archives of Canada were always generous with their time, but my special gratitude must go to Dr David Hume for educating me with respect to the RG 10 series. In Winnipeg I was introduced to the Hudson's Bay Company Archives by the keeper, Mrs Shirlee Anne Smith, and taught the rules of handling original documents. I wish also to thank Judith Beattie for her help. The staff of the Department of Indian Affairs in Ottawa and Vancouver were always helpful. In particular I want to thank Dennis Madill for going out of his way to ensure that I received every piece of information and every document I asked for. Colleagues at the Canadian Museum of Civilization (formerly The National Museum of Man) were very tolerant of my Okanagan ethnocentricity. In particular I wish to thank Garth Taylor, Andrea Laforet, and Louise Dallaire.

Ken Mather, manager-curator of the O'Keefe Historic Ranch, provided valuable information on Cornelius O'Keefe, for which I thank him. Gary Yabsley and Harry Slade of Ratcliff and Company, North Vancouver, provided advice on legal matters concerning Okanagan land. As members of the band's legal council they were always very supportive of my work. Jill Torrie worked as a research assistant in the summer of 1983. She concentrated almost entirely on historical and archival work in the National Archives of Canada and the Archives of the Oblates of Mary Immaculate.

My colleagues at the University of Toronto, especially R.W. Dunning (emeritus), Shuichi Nagata, and Tom McFeat, gave encouragement over the years. I wish also to thank my many students for their interest and critical evaluation of my work and method of analysis. Albert Schrauwers read an early draft of the book and offered valuable criticism.

Yngve Georg Lithman of the University of Stockholm read parts of the manuscript and volunteered many refreshing comments. Robin Fisher of

Simon Fraser University gave me special help and encouragement during the early stages of my historical research. Toby Morantz generously gave me invaluable advice about the historical material likely to be available in the Hudson's Bay Company Archives, thereby saving me a lot of time. Ernst Klassen, a former social worker for the Okanagan and other Indian bands, kindly read my draft manuscript, made suggestions, and drew my attention to several egregious errors. Kenneth Coates, Department of History in the University of Victoria, read the 'final' manuscript and made suggestions which I could not ignore. I am extremely indebted to both of them.

Chantal Matthews Carstens helped sort and analyse the census data, deciphered some of the Oblate Archival Records, and helped me establish a chronology of Okanagan chiefs. I also benefited enormously from our theoretical discussions, especially in the fields of kinship and factionalism.

I must gratefully acknowledge the research grants received over the years – a research fellowship from the Leon and Thea Koerner Foundation at the University of British Columbia (1962–3), various Humanities and Social Sciences Research grants (1978, 1982, 1984) from the University of Toronto, and grants from the Social Sciences and Humanities Research Council of Canada (1983–4, 1986–7). I must also thank the University of Toronto and my department for granting me periods of leave to complete this work.

Cyrilene Beckles in University College typed the various drafts of the manuscripts, for which I am grateful.

A draft of this book was first completed in May 1987 but it has required a lot of rethinking and rewriting in response to constructive criticism from a number of people to whom I am especially grateful. Naturally, I have to take responsibility for the final formulation of arguments presented here.

It has been a great pleasure working with the staff of the University of Toronto Press; in particular I would like to thank the managing editor, Virgil Duff, for his advice. I would also like to thank Diane Mew for her editorial guidance.

This book has been published with the help of a grant from the Social Science Federation of Canada, using funds provided by the Social Sciences and Humanities Research Council of Canada. Publication was also assisted by a generous grant from the University of Toronto Women's Association.

PHOTOGRAPHIC AND MAP CREDITS

Plates 1 and 3 are from the Canadian Museum of Civilization (Neg. Nos. 18416 and 23855). Plate 2 is from the O'Keefe Historic Ranch and Interior Heritage Society of British Columbia. Plate 9 is from the Greater Vernon

Museum and Archives. All other photographs were taken by the author, except Plate 10, for which the photographer is unknown, and Plate 12, which comes from the Bonneau family's collection.

Grateful acknowledgment is made to the Hudson's Bay Company for permission to redraw 'A Sketch of the Thompson's River District' (HBCA B 97/a/2 fo. 40), included as Map 1. The other four maps were professionally drawn by Susanne Cheesman. The author is grateful to Duane Thomson for providing the idea and the model on which Map 3 is based. Map 4 was similarly inspired by one of Robert E. Cail's maps in *Land, Man, and the Law* published by the University of British Columbia Press in 1974. Map 2 was influenced in part by one of D.W. Meinig's maps in *The Great Columbia Plain: A Historical Geography, 1805–1910*, published by the University of Washington Press in 1968.

PART ONE

The Creation of a Reserve

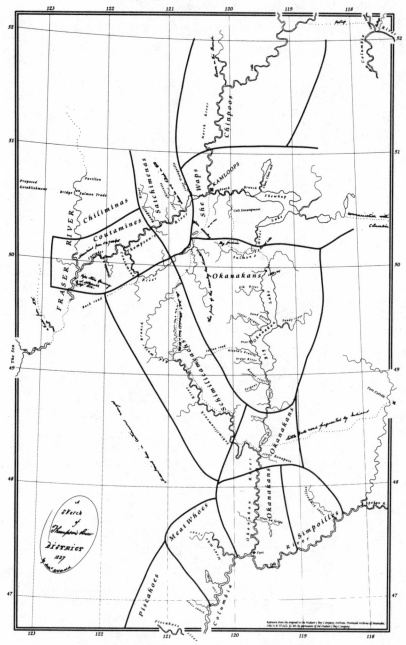

'A Sketch of Thompson's River District 1827' by Archibald McDonald; redrawn from the original

Chapter One

Traditional Okanagan Society and Institutions

This book is concerned with three closely related themes: the historical processes whereby the Okanagan Indians of British Columbia, through no choice of their own, came to live on reserves; social life in a reserve community at the present time with reference also to relations with the outside world; and the complex effects these historical processes and confinement to a reserve have had on the lives of the Okanagan people in general.

First it is necessary to establish an ethnographic base from which analysis can proceed, to find out what sort of lives the Okanagan led in the early nineteenth century when, together with their Salish-speaking neighbours, they still had control over their own destinies. This chapter, therefore, will provide a short account of Okanagan social structure and culture as it seems to have been early in the nineteenth century. This brief interpretive ethnography is based on certain published works, historical and archival research, and the oral tradition. It makes no claim to providing a detailed account of Okanagan institutions, and should be seen as an effort to understand the structural base in the past from which historical analysis can proceed. Given the paucity of published material on the Okanagan, my conspectus of their early traditions is inevitably rooted in Teit's ethnography and ethnology (see especially Teit 1914, 1928, 1930). However, it was only after I had received some instruction in the traditions of the Okanagan from the people themselves, and generally immersed myself in Okanagan life, that Teit's often unimaginative ideographic writing began to provide the inspiration of enlightened ethnography.[1]

1 For another little conspectus of Okanagan culture written from a somewhat different perspective and with different emphases, see Hudson (1986).

Traditionally[2] the Okanagan hunted, gathered, and fished for subsistence, producing a small surplus on occasion and trading with their neighbours. In the early nineteenth century they numbered about three thousand and occupied the territory around Lake Okanagan and southward to the confluence of the Columbia and Okanagan rivers.[3] This domain was given immediate recognition by the early fur traders, as illustrated by Archibald McDonald in his sketch map of the area in 1827 (HBCA B.97/a/2 fo. 40 1827). They spoke a dialect of the Interior Salish language, although some fluent speakers of the language today insist, largely for ethnocentric and political reasons, that the Okanagan tongue is quite different from the languages spoken by their Shuswap, Lillooet, and Thompson neighbours. The political and socio-linguistic implications of this ethnocentric perspective of their language are of special interest, because they are not at variance with informed opinion regarding speech and community (cf Elmendorf 1965).[4]

2 The term 'traditional' as used here refers simply to the period early in the nineteenth century when the Okanagan and other Interior Salish–speaking people still had control over their own destiny. My analysis does not deal, therefore, with the effects of the fur traders, missionaries, gold miners, settlers, and assorted alien administrators on traditional Okanagan institutions. But it must be noted that the Okanagan did *not* lose control over their destiny through culture contact and interaction with newcomers alone and in themselves. Rather it was the expanding frontier of the white man's economic ventures and the institutions which supported those ventures that placed the Okanagan in a disadvantagous position leading to loss of former power.

3 It is difficult to estimate the Okanagan population in the early nineteenth century. Teit (1930: 211–12) suggests that it was between 2500 and 3000. However, when he appropriately includes the Sanpoil, Colville, and Lake people together with the Okanagan, the figure rises to about 9000. Fur trade statistics derived from the Hudson's Bay Company population census for 1827 provide an estimate only of those people living in the three head villages where the three 'Chiefs or Principal Men' of the Okanagan resided at the time, and the clusters of peripheral villages nearby. Archibald McDonald, the author of the Kamloops report containing these details, refers to the 3477 souls occupying a 30,000-square-mile territory, and indicates that 578 of those were Okanagan with whom the Hudson's Bay Company traded (HBCA B. 97/e/1 1827 fo. 6 1827). Clearly these do not include all Okanagan inhabitants of the forty-five or so villages comprising the seven 'confederacies' identified by James Teit. If each Okanagan village supported an average of between 50 and 100 people (head villages sometimes accommodated 200 people) then Teit's figure of 3000 is a reasonable estimate of the Okanagan proper early in the nineteenth century.

4 Nowadays there are probably no more than five hundred fluent speakers of the Okanagan language in British Columbia and half that number in Washington State. There are still lively clusters of people who speak the language at home and with friends.

SETTLEMENT PATTERNS

In political and ecological terms Okanagan society was characterized by groups of people living in villages or camps under the tutelage of a headman. These bands were linked to each other through cross-cutting ties of kinship and bonds of friendship and association, and they often joined forces for communal hunts, warfare, and on ritual occasions. In the absence of any formal central authority, clusters of bands often coalesced, giving rise to what I have called band confederacies – incipient socio-political formations that took on more formal characteristics during the peak of the fur trade. In the early nineteenth century fur traders identified certain of these confederacies with the observation that in each case a prominent 'head chief' spoke or made decisions for the confederacy over which he was afforded limited authority by each band.

Following Teit's (1930: 203–11) identification of villages (and reinterpreting that material with the aid of oral tradition), I have established that there were seven such confederacies each comprising clusters of villages and camps:

1 The Head of the Lake (Nkamapeleks) confederacy with its nine or ten villages. Some might want to make a clear distinction between those villages constituting what is now called the Okanagan band and those constituting the Westbank band on the grounds that by 1877 each claimed its own chief.
2 The Douglas Lake (Upper Nicola) confederacy with its four or five villages, including the village at Fish Lake on the headwaters of the Upper Nicola River.
3 The Penticton confederacy with its two or three villages.
4 The Nkamip confederacy with its three villages.
5 The Okanagan River confederacy (south of what is now the Canadian border) with its five villages.
6 The Upper Similkameen confederacy with its six villages.
7 The Lower Similkameen confederacy with its twelve villages, including those in what is now Washington State.

Many of the descendants of the people who once lived in these villages and occupied Okanagan territory reside nowadays on reserves. The later chapters of this book focus on the lives of those people whose ancestors lived at Nkamapeleks and Sntlemuxten, the two chief villages among those comprising the Head of the Lake (Nkamapeleks) confederacy. Nkamapeleks ('the bottom,' i.e., 'the neck' of Lake Okanagan) was actually a village complex at the head of Lake Okanagan about 18 kilometres north of present-day Vernon. It became the seat of Okanagan power during the nineteenth century after the Okanagan people had directed their attention to their northern territory. Sntlemuxten ('place where slaughtered') constitutes the Six Mile Creek part of the same reserve located to the south of Nkamapeleks on the west shores of Lake Okanagan.

The location of villages and settlements provides us with crucial markers for establishing the various cores of Okanagan territory. Thus, the nearest permanent Shuswap villages were far to the north of the Okanagan near what is now Kamloops Lake, the South Thompson River, and at Salmon Arm. It is quite erroneous, therefore, to say as Hill-Tout (1911) did, that Enderby village was Okanagan. This was a Shuswap village and represents the most southerly stronghold of those people, and is an important territorial marker of the frontier between them and the Okanagan. The actual boundary was a little to the south of the village itself.

Okanagan territory in the traditional sense might be defined in terms of four components: the location of permanent and less permanent villages, the terrain used for hunting, fishing, gathering, and similar activities, their own perception of their territory, and the perception that other people had of Okanagan territory. The Okanagan had their own names for the Shuswap, Thompson, Lillooet, and twenty-three other people, including the Blackfoot. Their neighbours in turn had various names for them (cf Teit 1930: 199–203). Teit's conclusion that the Okanagan 'did not range back more than a few miles' from the lake is quite misleading and contrary to all the evidence (see Teit 1930: 213). Teit, it must be remembered, had married into the Thompson Indians, the Nekeleme'xu as the Okanagan called them, and shared certain of their prejudices against the Okanagan. The Thompson called the Okanagan TsawanEmux, 'the back country people,' 'the people down there.'

Okanagan villages were residential bases from which to set out on hunts, berry-picking excursions, fishing trips, wars, trade, and so forth. The Okanagan were thus never casual occupiers of land. They dispersed and moved around a great deal in summer, but most people returned to their home villages in the fall and lived together during the winter. But within this pattern there was always flexibility, so that some families (and individuals) could winter with one village and summer with the members of another, after which they were free to change their winter allegiance and settle with another band. This practice of changing social and residential formations mitigated against a static reproduction of social relations, providing an important example of the dynamics of Okanagan culture. Another consequence of this practice was the opportunity it afforded families and individuals to sever close ties when disagreements occurred, enabling them to avoid serious conflict by changing local affiliations (see also Ray 1936; and Ray et al. 1938).

ECONOMIC AND SOCIAL LIFE

Okanagan subsistence activities revolved around hunting, gathering, and fishing. On occasion there was a small surplus which could be used to cover the cost of premeditated war, to promote leisure, and for the production of items of material culture which in turn became items for trade.[5] The Okanagan made tools of stone, bone, and wood, household utensils, and a variety of paints and dyes. Their leather work was excellent, as were their mats, woven bags, blankets, and especially their coiled baskets, though the latter never equalled those of the Thompson Indians in design. They wore tasteful clothing and ornaments and their northern neighbours considered them to be well-dressed, stylish people. Differences in wealth and rank figured prominently in their designs and fashions.

For travel and transportation they made canoes and rafts. For carrying they made tump-lines of buckskin and rawhide, and in winter snowshoes were used regularly. Horses were introduced from the south early in the eighteenth century; dogs seem never to have been used for hauling purposes. Okanagan weaponry consisted of long spears pointed with stone, bone, and antlers. After the fur trade began on the coast, iron soon took their place. Tomahawk clubs were common as were bows and arrows. They also made a variety of war clubs and cuirasses and shields; and in general they were as well equipped for battle as they were for the hunt.

The spread of firearms and their aquisition by the Okanagan and other native peoples in the region is not easy to trace, but there is some evidence that both gun and horse converged in British Columbia at roughly the same time (Secoy 1953; Haines 1938). It is difficult to argue that the early smoothbore muskets were superior weapons to the traditional bow and arrow, especially when fired from horseback (Fisher 1977:17). What is significant is that guns were incorporated into the culture at an early date and became more and more important for defence and attack in war, and for hunting. Taken together, horse and gun revolutionized Okanagan society and eventually rendered traditional means of transportation and weaponry obsolete.

For carrying the berries and nuts gathered they used woven baskets and bark trays. Root-digging sticks were made of hardwoods. Hunting weapons included bows and arrows, knives, clubs, and spears. But they also drove animals in corrals of nets or entanglements and over cliffs and also used their

---

5 Thomson (1985: 195) argues that the Okanagan did not produce enough to collect a regular surplus, but his detailed account of their technology, subsistence patterns, and social relations of production seems to support the opposite conclusion.

dogs for hunting. In addition to regular hunting by men as individuals and in small groups, the Okanagan engaged in four great hunts every year; and on these occasions women helped the men to drive the game, and some women engaged in shooting. The Okanagan also developed technology for fishing which included nets of different kinds, single- and double-pointed spears, and weirs and traps.

Okanagan dwellings were basically of two kinds, the underground winter 'earth lodges' and the summer lodges. The kikuli or underground houses (*kwts'i*) were dug out to the depth of about four to six feet in well-drained sandy soil. They were covered with a low conical roof made of a wooden frame covered with bark, grass, and soil, and the entrance was through an opening on the roof. Summer lodges consisted of both circular and oblong dwellings constructed out of a framework of poles covered with tule mats. The circular style was most common, and these huts were looked upon as the main domestic family dwellings.

Various other architectural styles existed to accommodate people for special occasions. The long lodge, for example, was a lean-to construction often of considerable length, erected as a temporary shelter at fishing places or for social gatherings in the summer. (For a more detailed discussion of Plateau habitations and architecture, see Teit 1930: 226ff.)

Okanagan domestic life was thus closely tied to the annual round of fishing, hunting, and food-gathering activities, which followed a cycle beginning in spring 'with the reappearance of migrating birds and hibernating mammals' (Miller 1985: 12). Now people left their underground winter houses as the village inhabitants split up to perform their numerous tasks. In summer the pattern changed as men concentrated more and more on hunting while the women gathered all kinds of berries and wild fruit for immediate consumption. The women also dried and stored part of the berry and root crop while they were cooking and drying fish and meat for use in the winter. Thomson (1985) provides details of food-gathering operations by women and children, demonstrating the enormous value of wild crops to the band. He gives a similar analysis of hunting and fishing carried out almost entirely by men, and draws attention to the menstrual taboos that prevented women from participating in these activities, especially those disallowing contact with fish traps and the hunt, although women were often required to hustle the game on one flank. After the hunt, or the catch, women took charge of the animals and fish, and prepared them for eating, distribution, curing, smoking, and storage.

In fall the summer villages prepared to break up and there was a concerted effort by the women to dig roots, while the men were involved in intensive hunting of game and birds. By late fall (the Okanagan's fifth season) people began the process of moving back to their permanent winter villages while they carried out last minute foraging before the winter. The more food stored, the more comfortable the cold months were, enabling people to concentrate better on general education and special instruction in myth, legend, and the details of communal ritual.[6]

While co-residential families constituted primary production units they could only function as part of larger complexes such as a village or band. Some families assumed specialized economic functions (e.g., fishing, tanning, berry-picking) within the context of these wider production units. Individuals also acquired specialized knowledge and skills in hunting, fishing, basket-making, leatherwork, and so on. Some were recognized for their magical and medical knowledge which was highly valued in many facets of life. All these diverse aspects of production, together with age and gender divisions of labour, made for a complex domestic economy.

Vast tracts of land were regarded as commonage but some parts seemed to have become the preserve of local people. At times certain bands, and sometimes villages, claimed much more than usufructory rights over fishing grounds, particularly weirs where fish were trapped. Ownership of private property was, however, widespread, ranging from slaves to numerous items of moveable property, such as snares, deer fences, deer nets, weapons, tools, baskets, and dogs. Even Okanagan songs were considered the property of their owners.

Leisure and Feasts
The labour involved in maintaining acceptable standards of nutrition, housing, and clothing was always considerable and further effort was required to reproduce the full range of activities beyond mere primary needs. Nevertheless, the Okanagan often enjoyed considerable leisure, especially during those winters when plenty of food had been stored during the fall. It was in winter that story-telling and recounting of myths reached their peak. This was a time for learning (school, as the old people still call it) when the achievements of the past were recounted and plans were made for the future. The tasks of clothes-making and basket-weaving were always undertaken with creativity and artistry and some of their special costumes were worn during feasting, singing, and dancing. Winter was also a time for the giving and receiving of gifts, gambling, curing

6 Miller's (1985: 7–21) interpretation of the annual cycle of the Plateau people is of great value despite its ethnographic paucity.

of sickness, communing with guardian spirits, and finally greeting the sun which would eventually triumph over winter with the onset of spring.

The Winter Dance, as distinct from other dances, was a highly developed symbolic ceremony (Lerman 1950–6: 35–6) expressing both secular and sacred spheres of life. These dances, which lasted for several days, were hosted by people who possessed guardian spirits. They formed an integral part of the guardian spirit complex on the Plateau, thereby linking band with band, ethnic group with ethnic group. From the point of view of the participants, each dance reinforced ties of both kinship and friendship, drew attention to the realities of life with its changes and chances, and generally prepared people for the next cycle of life. Teit (1930: 293), referring to the guardian spirit dances which constituted part of the Winter Dance sequence, writes: 'each person sang the song he had received during his puberty training, showed his powers, and imitated his guardian spirit by cry and gesture while dancing.' For those individuals who had found their guardian spirits, Winter Dances reminded them of the need to fulfil their obligations to the metaphysical world and reinforced the moral codes of the social worlds.

The Okanagan were also great gamblers and loved games of chance and skill, foot racing, and horse racing. *Sla hal*, also called *tsillallacome* (cf Ross 1849: 331–6), was a game of chance involving players, gamblers, and spectators. It attracted large numbers of people and lasted a week or more. While the gamblers were involved in sleight-of-hand and guessing which fist held the bone, most of the spectators would be engaged in dramatic singing, drumming, and dancing (see Appendix 6).

Meals were frequently given in the wintertime by commoners who later enjoyed return feasts in an informal system of reciprocity. Chiefs and other members of the élite also gave feasts and gifts from time to time, and all these occasions were seized upon by people as appropriate opportunities for dancing and singing. Potlatches (*wau'Em*) do not seem to have been common.

Domestic Groups and Kin Relationships

Okanagan domestic units consisted of small independent families. Polygyny carried social prestige and occurred among chiefs and other high-ranking persons, but in practice few men had more than one wife. In the few compound families that did exist co-wives rarely shared common or contiguous households because of the 'brawls and squabbles [that] constantly ensue[d] when several wives [met]' (Ross 1849: 317ff). Polygynous households were therefore rare and chiefs had to go from camp to camp to visit their wives. There were no residence rules, but actual residence patterns suggest a preference for uxorilocality which enabled chiefs to take foreign wives and establish political alliances abroad.

Because marriage was proscribed between first or second cousins, the constant need to search for potential spouses beyond the extended family group gave rise to exogamous villages. Although elopements did occur, marriages were greatly influenced by parental attitudes towards prospective spouses. Many marriages were arranged by go-betweens who represented both families, negotiated the conditions of the marriage, and judged the status and compatibility of the couple. Many Okanagan marriages were political, and families were obsessed with guarding their positions in the status hierarchy. Social compatibility was a prime consideration before the formal, but simple, marriage ceremony, *okawa'it*, took place, especially when wives (and husbands) came from other bands and distinct villages. Contemporary Okanagan social historians often speak of particular wives being 'brought in' (sometimes 'bought') from another place. These were arranged marriages and a wife's family might receive a substantial material consideration when their daughter left home.

The complexity of Okanagan marriage rules and residence patterns necessitated a high degree of mobility, all of which are manifest in the idiosyncratic relationships and attendant attitudes that mould kin networks. Okanagan kinship terminology reflects many facets of those behaviours, the main features of which are outlined below.

1. Males and females use different terms and observe correspondingly different behaviour patterns towards many of their kin. For example, my (man speaking) father is my *lEē'u*, but my sister addresses him as *mistm*. My mother is my *sk'ō'i*, but to my sister, mother is *tom*. The precise meaning of these terms is unclear except *tom* ('to suck') refers to a woman's breasts and acknowledges one of the superior and special qualities shared by women.

2. Although different kinship terms were always used for specific brothers and sisters, and first and second cousins of all kinds, all were considered members of one generational category of 'siblings,' indicating that marriage could not take place between them. Collectively they were referred to by the term *sntc'oitl* or *skwaytlem* (sometimes *skuitlem*; cf Hudson 1986: 454) meaning 'people born together [from the same family].' This typical Hawaiian principle is not reflected in the terms of address, but it is extremely important because it established the exogamous principle which encouraged the formation of marriage alliances with neighbouring people.

3. (a) Another significant use of the generational principle occurs in the third ascending generation where all pairs of great-grandparents are treated

terminologically as equals by the term *tat'ō'pa*, a term which is reciprocally applied to great-grandchildren.

(b) As well as the *tat'ō'pa* classification, there is some evidence that my (man speaking) wife's brother, *stsiot*, was the terminological equivalent of my younger sister's husband. The other term of affinity having some semblance of classificatory equivalence is *sēastā'm* for wife's sister, brother's wife, husband's brother, but this is complicated by the somewhat unusual form of the levirate/sororate among the Okanagan, which I will mention separately below.

4. When a husband or wife dies the derived affinal relationships cease except the one corresponding to *sēastā'm* which is then transformed into *nEk'oi'tstEn* for deceased wife's sister, deceased brother's wife, deceased husband's brother. Thus, a man could marry his deceased wife's sister or his deceased brother's wife. And a woman could marry her deceased husband's brother. The *nEk'oi'tstEn* principle was a very practical one because it increased the chances of remarriage in the local community where first and second cousin marriages were not allowed.

POLITICS AND CHIEFSHIP

Chiefship
At the core of Okanagan life was the vacillating institution of headmanship or chiefship involving a complex of relations between people with influence and prestige and commoners and slaves. Okanagan preoccupation with status hierarchies flourished in colonial times during the heyday of the fur trade with its imperial base and the trappings of pageantry and power of British royalty.

Traditionally the Okanagan had no chiefs in the sense of political leaders with coercive authority backed by formal courts, councils, and other law-enforcing institutions. But they did have an institution of headmanship with its attendant high-ranking status and prestige. The term used by the Okanagan for their political leaders in traditional times was *Ilmexum*, meaning headman. Ideally, then, we should not speak of Okanagan chiefs at all, but this poses a problem because of the recurrent use of this term in the literature and by the people themselves at the present time. If I use the terms chief, headman, and *Ilmexum* somewhat interchangeably it is because I am at the mercy of both written records and the oral tradition. Thus, I will sometimes use the term chief in a non-institutionalized sense, and sometimes the term will also be applied to a variety of leadership roles outside the strictly political sphere.

The size of each band varied during the course of the year, because some families would winter with one band and summer with another. Band membership, therefore, could never be defined as a group of people who owed obligatory allegiance to a particular chief. Most bands consisted of several villages scattered over a fairly wide area. Some versions of the oral tradition, however, state quite emphatically that each of these villages once had its own headman. But, as Teit argued, it was only in quite recent times that 'people of some minor villages began to consider themselves as distinct bands, with chiefs of their own' (Teit 1930: 261–2).

Teit asserts that ideally accession to the office of chief followed hereditary principles, although he concedes that some chiefs did acquire office through their personal qualities. The latter, he says, became chiefs through prowess in war, by accumulating wealth and distributing it in feasts, by giving presents or entertaining strangers, and through their wisdom in council especially if combined with good oratory. But Teit provides no precise rule for hereditary succession to office. After analysing two genealogies of Okanagan chiefs, I am inclined to the view that hereditary chiefship did not exist. The fact that sons often succeeded their fathers to office suggests hereditary principles but does not demonstrate an inflexible rule. When a son did succeed his father to chiefship, he did so largely because of his social prestige, which he derived from membership in the band including particularly the status of his mother. It is surprising that there were no women chiefs traditionally, given the high status of women generally and the enormous prestige acquired by some.

Of the actual powers, duties, expectations, and obligations of band chiefs Teit writes:

The hereditary chiefs of bands were looked upon as fathers of the people, and gave advice on all internal matters of the band. They exhorted the people to good conduct, and announced news personally or through criers. To some extent they regulated the seasonal pursuits of the people. They looked after the maturing of the berries, personally or by deputy, in their respective districts. They kept time by notching sticks, and occasionally made records of notable events. They were often referred to, in case of dispute, regarding dates, the name of the month, etc. They gave decisions and admonitions in petty disputes and quarrels, and some-times, when asked to arbitrate, they settled feuds between families. They had little power to enforce any decrees. This was done by public opinion. Some of them had messengers or helpers, who acted generally in a persuasive way as peace officers … [all chiefs were expected to] help the poor, show a good example, and give small feasts or presents to the people from time to time. (Teit 1930: 262–3)

In addition to the regular chiefs who were recognized as 'political' leaders in most bands, there were also temporary subsidiary chiefs who seemed to have been appointed for the many war parties and hunting parties. Both war and hunting enterprises also made use of the powers of shamans. For example, large war parties had a war shaman whose duty it was to know the disposition of the enemy, to assist in victory, and to prevent defeat. Similarly, large hunting parties had their shamans who were believed to have special sway over game, placating the animals and drawing them to the hunters. Other duties of shamans on these occasions included protecting both the animals and the hunters from sorcery emanating from hostile competitors for these precious fruits of the hunt.

As individuals who wielded power in the band, shamans assisted the war chiefs in their duties by reinforcing secular power with supernatural power. There is no indication that shamans ever aspired to political office. This division of labour and power in the authority system points to the limitations of the power of the band chief, whose duty it was to lead rather than to rule; in those areas where his leadership was weak he relied on other individuals for assistance. Thus, a successful Okanagan chief was a person who, through his ability to manipulate social relationships, was able to maintain his office without falling foul of his rivals and lieutenants. There are no surviving accounts of the actual areas of conflicts in the system but one must assume that the position of *Ilmexum* was a precarious one, maintained largely by personal esteem, skill at manipulating human relations, wealth, and the ability to distribute surpluses in an acceptable fashion. Many chiefs forged alliances with other bands and ethnic groups through marriage to high-status women, and some successful chiefs had as many as seventeen wives which their wealth and personal esteem made possible. Chiefs had to take care to protect their élite status which, when reproduced over several generations, created the illusion that chiefship was a hereditary institution when in point of fact its exclusiveness rested on the preservation (rather than the circulation) of élites. A band chief had few additional ascriptive roles to strengthen his office. He was not necessarily a shaman, or a priest, or a leader in war, or a ritual dancer; therefore he had to rely on others to assist him, especially in those areas where his leadership was weak. In the mid-nineteenth century some chiefs attempted to use their association with the Hudson's Bay Company to routinize their charisma in a variety of ways. Others, Nkwala for example, strengthened their position by recruiting a personal bodyguard of young men to accompany them on their travels. But such action was a departure from convention and represented a reaction to a new era.

In addition to those shamans who assumed positions of importance in the supernatural sphere were dance chiefs in charge of the religious dances that were intrinsic to the religious tradition. There were also secular dance chiefs whose office was ad hoc, being appointed for special occasions involving local secular celebrations and the songs addressed to specific events.

There were no permanent councils among the Okanagan. Informal councils were called from time to time by chiefs or other prominent men if important news had to be communicated. It was the band chief who 'called [together] the councils in his own band.' Such meetings and ad hoc moots were open and anyone could attend and speak his mind.

Theoretically all bands enjoyed equal status, but some bands were larger and more prestigious than others. Thus, the Head of the Lake band laid claim in fur trade times to political superiority over all other bands, even those outside the Nkamapeleks confederacy. Teit was quite convinced that 'there was one recognized head chief of all the tribes,' but there is probably no way of discovering whether these distinctions were made earlier, and if so, how important they were. The senior chief of the Okanagan in the south, however, had his own 'royal insignia.' The emblem was 'a white wolf skin, fantastically painted with rude figures of different colors, the head and tail decorated with the *higua*, bears' claws, and the teeth of different animals, suspended from a pole in a conspicuous place near the chief's lodge' (Ross 1849: 313–14). Whatever hierarchy of chiefs existed at any time in the past, a band headman was never answerable to any head chief in local matters solely affecting the members of his band. This fact, together with the ill-defined area of authority claimed by the head chief, gave Okanagan politics a quasi-federal quality, reminiscent in social structural terms of the Khoi people of southern Africa with their political federation of clans with headmen enjoying autonomy in all local matters. Like the Khoi, therefore, Okanagan chiefs were very different from the powerful Nguni and Sotho chiefs in southern Africa who were at once, by ascription, rulers, judges, chief magicians, high priests, and military commanders of their subjects (see Schapera 1956; Carstens 1975).

Okanagan chiefs did sometimes attempt to boost their personal esteem by creating instant rituals and elaborating the procedures of smoking the ceremonial pipe, and by eloquent speechifying. But as Ross tells us, 'in all ordinary matters the chief is not more conspicuous than any other individual, and he seldom interferes with family affairs, or the ordinary routine of daily occurrences' (Ross 1849: 315–16).

In short, the Okanagan did not constitute a tribe in the sense of a coherently organized political unit, and their formal political structure as a population was no more than a network of bands each connected through their own institutions of chiefship. Whereas these political communities (bands) were for the most part autonomous units, clusters of bands quite often participated in joint hunts and communal rituals, and occasionally united against a common enemy in warfare. The traders, missionaries, and government officials brought with them the idea that every group was expected to be organized along tribal lines, and certainly the Okanagan as a whole were recognized by others as a distinct people, as indeed they regarded themselves. Thus, whether we call them an ethnic aggregation or a tribe matters very little, provided we see them politically in the context of chiefship as I have presented it. Particular headmen were able to manoeuvre themselves into positions of seniority over others, a dynamic process that made possible the incipient office of head chief, thereby providing support to Teit's conclusion which is corroborated by fur traders of the Hudson's Bay Company (HBCA B. 97/e/1 1827).

The Pelkamulox Family and Chief Nkwala

In order to place the institution of chiefship in its historical context I have included a brief account of the Pelkamulox family from whom Nkwala, the famous Okanagan chief, was descended.[7] Chief Nkwala (1793–1859) was a chief of the fur trade period and as such provides the political focus of the study of the transition of traditional Okanagan culture to the new society as it began to emerge.

Oral tradition informs us that the founding political ancestor of the Okanagan was Pelkamulox ('Rolls over the Earth'), probably born between 1675 and 1680. Pelkamulox was a chief of the 'salmon people' or Upper Spokan, and was said to be unrelated to the Okanagan. His son, Pelkamulox II, was born between 1705 and 1710, and was a headman among the same people.

Pelkamulox II left his own people and lived for periods among the Okanagan, Sanpoil, and Shuswap. He had four wives: the first was a Spokan; the second was a Shuswap whom he married at Kamloops; the third was a Sanpoil; and the fourth was an Okanagan, the daughter of the headman of the

---

7 I have drawn on several sources to piece together this interpretation of Okanagan chiefs before Nkwala. James Teit (1930) is the key source, but I have also used Marie Brent's (n.d.) version, and I have drawn on contemporary oral tradition (several versions) in my efforts to make sense out of quite sketchy material. A major technical problem is that Teit's work has become a source book for several Okanagan oral historians, while Marie Brent herself, although probably one of Teit's informants, tends to validate her account by referring to the work of Teit and others. Mary Balf's (n.d.; 1985) research on Nkwala has also proved very useful. Teit's genealogy of Okanagan chiefs is based on the preconception 'that there was one recognized head chief of all the tribes' (1930: 263). This idea was almost certainly fostered by Franz Boas under whose influence Teit conducted most of his work, and inevitably accounts for the selection of entries in the genealogy.

band located near the junction of the Similkameen and Okanagan rivers. As a young man he took part in several buffalo hunting expeditions on the plains and his band occupied a prominent position among the Okanagan generally, particularly with regard to military strength. It is said that during his life the Stuwi'x[8] were driven out of the lower Similkameen region. Pelkamulox II's importance in Okanagan political history derives mainly from his four wives, each of whom lived uxorilocally and retained her ethnic origin. Teit stresses Okanagan patrilineality, but the phenomenal influence of women (notably wives and mothers) illustrates the importance of cognatic kinship. These marital contracts gave rise to a Spokan, a Shuswap, a Sanpoil, and an Okanagan branch of the family. In later years the political significance of the first three families decreased as Pelkamulox II spent more time with his Okanagan family. Here we are largely concerned with the descendants of his Okanagan wife.

Teit's genealogy shows only one child in this marriage, a son who also bears his father's name of Pelkamulox, and I shall refer to him as Pelkamulox III. Teit calls him the 'head chief of the Okanagan.' He had two wives. The first was an Okanagan woman from the Head of the Lake, who does not figure prominently in Teit's analysis, largely, one suspects, because Teit did not appreciate her political significance. It is quite clear from the oral tradition, however, that Pelkamulox III acquired his political legitimation and power at the Head of the Lake through his Okanagan mother and his first (senior) wife, as well as through his sister who stayed in this household. The second wife was a foreigner to the Head of the Lake, being a Stuwi'x woman from Similkameen, who was probably part Thompson Indian. She bore seven children, one of whom was Nkwala, an only son.[9]

Pelkamulox III was the last of the traditional Okanagan leaders as far as the Head of the Lake was concerned. He was a great warrior in his day, and continued to be involved in the wars, feuds, and disputes that had preoccupied his father. He foolishly made his headquarters in the south at what is now Oroville, near the junction of the Similkameen and Okanagan rivers in Washington State. There he built a stone fort, and threatened to assert his authority over other Okanagan bands in the south as well as over neighbour-

---

8 The Stuwi'x were an Athapascan people who once lived to the west of the Okanagan in the region near the mouth of the Similkameen River. According to Teit (1930: 214) they were driven out by the Okanagan in the early eighteenth century.

9 The fur traders called him Nicola (Nicholas and various other spellings), which the Okanagan transformed into Nkwala which is spelt in many ways including N'uala, Unquoila, and N'Kwala. I have opted for Nkwala because it is simple and reasonably accurate.

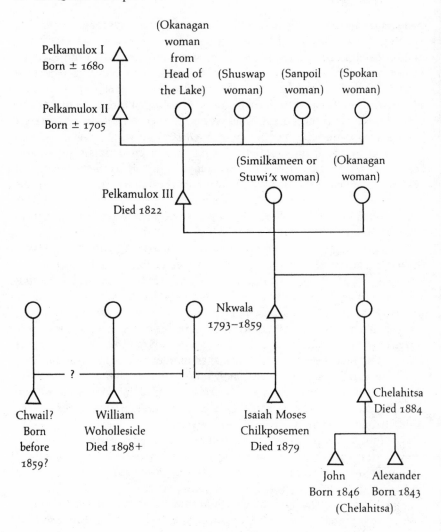

Figure 1

Genealogical connections between the Pelkamulox, Nkwala, and Chelahitsa families

ing peoples such as the Thompson, Shuswap, and Kutenai. But at no time during his life was he ever able to muster sufficient military strength to dominate other Okanagan bands or his foreign neighbours. Most of the opposition to Pelkamulox III's megalomania came from his own people in the south, and he was only spared the consequences of his folly by the timely intervention of his half-brother, Kwolila, who was head chief of the Kamloops Shuswap people in the north. Chief Kwolila apparently made the long and hazardous journey south where he successfully persuaded Pelkamulox III to leave the dangerous atmosphere of the south which he had created for himself and return to the Head of the Lake in the north.

It is too simple to attribute Kwolila's concern for Pelkamulox's safety purely to his love for a half-brother. Rather he saw this move as an opportunity to defuse the standing conflict and rivalry between the northern Okanagan and the Shuswap who had been at loggerheads for decades over the boundary between their respective territories. What was at stake was part of the interstitial no man's land between the two people, long coveted by the Okanagan. The Shuswap were tired of war and threats of war, and Kwolila took it upon himself after Pelkamulox III returned to the Head of the Lake to seal a peace treaty with his half-brother. I will call it the Fish Lake Accord. Teit (1930: 266) sums it up very well.

> Here at Fish Lake *Kwolī'la* made a lasting agreement with *PElkamū'lôx* giving him the perpetual use over all the Shuswap territory of the upper Nicola Valley, south, east, and west of Chaperon Lake, comprising Douglas Lake and Fish Lake ... *Kwolī'la* said [to PElkamū'lôx], 'You will have the country for yourself and your people as your own. I will live as your neighbour at ... [Chaperon Lake] and will retain all the country from there north. You will make Fish Lake your headquarters in the summer and I will summer at Chaperon Lake so that we may be close neighbours part of each year.'

At this time the area ceded to the Okanagan was rich in elk, deer, sheep, bear, prairie chicken, grouse, water fowl, and other game while the lakes teemed with fish. The Okanagan got a good deal out of the Fish Lake Accord, but Pelkamulox III paid a high price for the compact, being required to hand over his only daughter by his first (Okanagan) wife to Kwolila for adoption. Because this girl was born at the Head of the Lake, she became a political pawn in Okanagan-Shuswap relations, and a symbol of the Okanagan power. After the Fish Lake Accord, Pelkamulox III established his winter quarters permanently at the Head of the Lake which became the centre of north Okanagan life. His summer quarters seemed to have been at Fish Lake for some years.

He continued to strive for high office among the Okanagan people in general. He made a point of visiting all Okanagan bands and travelled extensively among neighbouring peoples, from the Shuswap in the north to the Wenatchi, Columbia, Spokan, and Kalispel in the south. He went buffalo hunting on the plains by way of Flathead country and got to know the political leaders of many different peoples, including the Blackfoot. He encountered white men for the first time very early in the nineteenth century when he met explorers and trappers from the North West Company near Helena, Montana. He was so impressed with them that he made a point of telling the Okanagan and others 'of the wonderful men he had seen on his recent trip.' He even made a special trip to Kamloops to report on these remarkable men *without* women (cf Teit 1930: 266–7; Balf 1985). Sometime during the third week of November 1822 Pelkamulox III was murdered by a group of Lillooet Indians on the Fraser River.

What is significant about Pelkamulox III is that although his ambitions and megalomania resulted in his assassination by a foreign enemy, he acquired more power and influence than any other Okanagan political leader before him. We cannot attribute his achievements to military strength but rather to his success in cultivating personal relationships among many different distinguished people. He got on the wrong side of the Lillooet people because he threatened Lillooet control over the salmon fishing industry on their section of the Fraser River. As an Okanagan chief, however, he made his mark by his willingness to resolve the rift that existed between his own people and the Shuswap. He was indeed the last of the traditional Okanagan leaders, and even if he too worked with the Hudson's Bay Company, he occupied his position in much the same way other Okanagan chiefs had before him, enjoying traditional influence and authority regardless of his new associations.

Pelkamulox had designated his son Nkwala his 'successor' a decade before he died. Nkwala's Okanagan name was Hwistesmetxē'qEn ('Walking Grizzly Bear') and his Shuswap name was Shiwelean. In fact, Nkwala had been acknowledged political leader of the Head of the Lake Okanagan band since the winter of 1811–12. He became an influential headman-chief within traditional Okanagan spheres of interaction, but it was the historical intersection of his remarkable personality, his strength in the traditional political arena, and the advent of the fur trade in which he was to figure prominently that effected a major change in the nature of Okanagan chiefship. Once the fur trade had been established in the area, Nkwala divided his allegiances between his own people at the Head of the Lake and the personnel of the Hudson's Bay Company. I will expand on the nature of this political power and the duality of this chiefship in the next chapter.

Feuds and Warfare

Feuding between families was common and these were sometimes settled by chiefs who acted as arbitrators, especially when blood money had to be paid. Teit cites the case of Nkwala's son, Kesakailux, who killed his wife and her paramour near Douglas Lake and then took refuge with his sister who lived in a band to the south. The members of the families of the two murdered people threatened to kill members of the chief's family and a bloody feud was imminent. Chief Nkwala then acted in two capacities: as chief and as a member of the guilty family. As chief he considered the case with the aggrieved parties and determined the blood money to compensate for his son's deed, paying 'a lot of horses, some cattle, and a number of robes' out of his own pocket (Teit 1930: 259–60). This feud, which took place in the 1850s, indicates a complete absence of courts for resolving disputes and offences of this kind. Nkwala was a wealthy man at this time and could afford adequate blood money to appease all parties and make it possible for his son to enter his band's territory again. In this regard it is interesting that the guilty party appears to have been safe among the members of another band.

Whereas feuds took place between parties within bands and between parties from different bands, warfare involved conflicts and rivalries between much wider associations. It was during warfare that Okanagan bands demonstrated their greatest unity, taking on a 'tribal' character when they united against a common enemy. War was in fact the only occasion when bands formed common associations of a political nature (Ross 1849: 311–12), and it is from this perspective that warfare is important in understanding the range and dimensions of political life and potential authority of an Okanagan chief.

There does, however, appear to have been a more small-scale kind of warfare – raiding parties consisting of two or three canoes full of adventurers 'who [were] bent on personal gain and whose actions [were] not representative of the attitudes of the tribes from which they [came]' (Ray 1939: 36). The prevalence of these raiding parties among the Interior Salish in general certainly reflected their lack of centralized authority, which would give rise to a sort of patterned disorder.

However, the most important wars the Okanagan fought were against the Shuswap people from the early 1700s until the signing of the Fish Lake Accord in the nineteenth century. The wars began after the Okanagan asserted exclusive claim to that territory as part of an expansionist plan in the eighteenth century. The economic and military status of the Okanagan was strengthened by the introduction of the horse before it reached other northern Salish people. The horse made travel easier and quicker than by foot or by canoe, and facilitated Okanagan expansion not merely to the north, but to the east and west as well. Without the horse it is doubtful whether the Okanagan would have won the Great Shuswap War and permanently secured the northern corridor between them and their enemies (Teit 1914: 295–6 and 1930: 214–17, 249ff; Haines 1938: 429ff).

Among the more important earlier battles between the two people in pre-equestrian days was the Battle of Sntlemuxten ('place where slaughtered') when practically the whole Shuswap war party from Savona was killed in retaliation for earlier skirmishes. Another victory over the Shuswap occurred in the Penticton area when the Okanagan contingent cut off the enemy and tricked them into advancing towards the hidden bluffs over the valley where large numbers of enemy troops fell to their death at night, while others, including the Shuswap war chief, were cut off by the steep cliffs and shot. Only a few escaped.

With most tribes in possession of horses and firearms, as we have seen, warfare between Indian groups now took on a different form, and in later years relations between Indians and European settlers were patterned with the knowledge that both parties had similar weapons. As late as 1877 both the Okanagan and Shuswap were perceived by white settlers in British Columbia to be a serious threat to their existence, and an uprising by the Indians related to their grievances over losing their land was taken seriously by all whites in the Okanagan Valley.

There were also times when the Okanagan enjoyed favourable relations with the Shuswap, who once united with them and the Thompson Indians to defeat the Lillooet forces in the 1830s to avenge the death of Pelkamulox III at the hands of the Lillooet in 1822. Generally conflict between rival peoples and the formation of lasting animosity towards one another was a result of disputes over land, especially over foraging and hunting grounds. Yet even the most intense inter-tribal conflict did not rule out the forging of kinship ties and friendship links between ethnic and tribal groups, and over the years the northern Okanagan established significant affinal ties with their Shuswap enemies.

The Okanagan never fought a full-scale war against whites for intruding into their territory but they came very close to serious conflict on a number of occasions. During the early days of the fur trade oral tradition relates of minor skirmishes with traders and at the Head of the Lake over trespass, and much later, in 1858, whites passing over Okanagan territory on their way to the Fraser River gold-diggings met with hostile opposition. Several whites were killed and horses were stolen, before peace was eventually established.

The last time the Okanagan, still possessing a modicum of political and military power, threatened whites with war was between 1875 and 1877 when the Indians of the interior of British Columbia were displeased with the treatment they were receiving from both the provincial and federal governments regarding access to their former land. At this time, the Okanagan planned to join forces with their former Shuswap enemies to drive the whites out of their territory. The scheme was aborted at the last moment largely because of disagreements between rival factions. Nkwala's sister's son, Chief Chelahitsa, from Douglas Lake betrayed the Okanagan cause because of the respect he had for white men and his confidence in their institutions. There was also strong pro-white influence from one Catholic priest at Kamloops (Teit 1930: 259; Fisher 1977: 190–7).

While these examples do not always apply to traditional Okanagan society, the whole question of Okanagan land continued as a political issue well into the nineteenth century. Present-day land issues, however, relate to a very different tradition which, although resembling those of the past, has its base in the new legal and political systems which were imposed on native peoples in Canada generally. Reserve land is determined by theodolite and surveyor, the bane of traditional life. Aboriginal land was measured by convention and traditional usage. Thus the whole of British Columbia (and the State of Washington) was 'formerly within the owned and recognized territory of one or other of the Indian tribes' (Duff 1964: 8)

The part played by band chiefs in warfare is not at all clear given the specialized roles of war chiefs and shamans. In 'true' warfare between the Okanagan and neighbouring peoples band chiefs did seem to play a political role in mobilizing support among federations of bands. In times of war (and in negotiating with foreigners), therefore, some band chiefs emerged, through their prestige, wealth, and personal esteem, to positions of superiority over others. Inevitably the advent of the fur trade and other external forces enhanced the status of some chiefs rather than others. If contemporary oral tradition can be taken at its face value, the potential for a head chief emerging at certain times was always a possibility in traditional Okanagan society.

STRATIFICATION

This discussion of Okanagan chiefs illustrates how individuals could achieve higher political status over others through various manoeuvres designed to enhance personal esteem. Thus, far from shunning élitism, the Okanagan fostered it with great fervour in the absence of any 'hereditary nobility' (Teit 1930: 261, note by Franz Boas). Both upward and downward mobility took place and there was no guarantee that high office or high status would last for life. Status was something that had to be constantly nurtured, and ineffective leadership on the part of a war chief or unsuccessful activities of a shaman, for example, could lead to a change in social position, and modifications were constantly taking place within the hierarchy.

Although slavery was neither an elaborate nor an extensive institution among the north Okanagan, women slaves do seem to have been important for marriage and hence in the biological reproduction of the population. (The south Okanagan do not appear to have had slaves at all [Ray 1939: 30].) Most slaves were young women captured in war, although sources do not specify which wars or where the women came from. Slaves were also procured through trade from the south and some came from as far away as the Snake country in Oregon. The Okanagan seem also to have obtained a few Lillooet and coastal slaves from their Thompson neighbours. Whatever their origin, women slaves were well treated and their children were incorporated into Okanagan society (Teit 1930: 277; Ray 1939: 31–2). Only in quarrels were they reminded of their origins, and in this regard I did occasionally hear uncharitable comments during fieldwork about certain people who were looked down upon by others because 'they were probably not true Okanagan, but Lakers or slaves or something like that.'

Women never became chiefs of any kind, but they were enormously influential in everyday affairs, and affinal ties were crucial in determining the rank and status of males and other social relationships. Men held office but it was on the basis of cognatic principles that their social position was determined. All upward mobility was essentially a synthesis of a person's parental statuses, affinal connections, and personal achievement. But rather than emphasize individuals moving up or down the social scale, Okanagan mobility is best interpreted in terms of domestic family status. Alexander Ross, who was married to an Okanagan woman, sums up the importance of the domestic family when he draws attention to the position of wives: 'Each family [was] ruled by a joint will or authority of the husband and wife, but more particularly by the latter' (Ross 1849: 318). The high status of women in the domestic arena and their influence in local political affairs, warfare, hunting, medicine placed them at the hub of all the important social and economic issues in Okanagan society, while being spared the ordeals of chiefship.

Although a stratified society, the sharing of food was common in the sense that game, for example, was divided and shared among all the people who hunted, and the individual who killed the game had no special rights over the property. Some meat would even be given to those who had not taken part in the hunt. But the prestige and kudos for obtaining the meat always went to the hunter and his lieutenants. In a big hunt these would consist of the hunting chief, the hunting shaman, and their helpers in that order. Thus, while the commodity (meat) was shared, its value was derived from the skills and labour that went into the hunt and not from the fact that the hunt took place on communal property (land). It is crucial, therefore, to distinguish between commodities such as a hunted deer and land. Both are commodities, but in the Okanagan context land was fixed communal property over which there was corporate control, a deer killed by shooting or trapping was not. The manner in which the meat of an animal was distributed involved communal expectations, but these were not fixed because there was always an element of flexibility and uncertainty as to how it might be distributed. It was in the actual process of distribution that the skill of the hunter was recognized. Snares, deer fences, deer nets, traps, weapons, dogs, and horses were all private property. The manner in which they were used enhanced the prestige and esteem of their owners while allowing various members of the band to benefit from other people's private property, personal skill, and initiative.

Teit has suggested that festivals and other socio-economic ceremonies such as potlatches (*wau'Em*) were held infrequently among the Okanagan, implying erroneously that the latter were introduced by their Thompson neighbours but never took a strong hold. 'Only about six men are known to have given potlatches, and now the custom seems quite dead' (Teit 1930: 277). Potlatching does not appear to have been a major preoccupation among affluent Okanagan who avoided the ostentatious excesses of inter-tribal ceremonies for political reasons. Archibald McDonald, who later became chief factor of the Hudson's Bay Company at Kamloops, gives a detailed account of a political 'grand banquet,' sponsored by a senior Shuswap chief and to which neighbouring peoples (including Hudson's Bay Company staff) were invited. Preparations for the occasion took several months and three hundred men from various tribes showed up. The Shuswap chief, Court Apatte, provided enormous quantities of food for the occasion, and dancing went on for two full days. During the dancing, gifts were exchanged between the various groups and the celebrations enabled 'them to pledge their friendship with each other' (HBCA B. 97/a/2 1826–27).

The occasion, with its 'international' entourage of guests, focused on the efforts and wealth of the Shuswap chief. It also cemented alliances of friendship between other peoples including the fur traders. McDonald specifically states in his text that 'None of the Okanakans attended,' suggesting that it was boycotted by the Okanagan for political reasons, given the animosity existing between them and the Shuswap.

Whereas Okanagan chiefs and other leading people gave feasts and presents to others from time to time, ordinary people were involved in a system of reciprocal meals or small feasts. The custom was quite different from the feasts given by high-ranking people because the latter drew attention to the superior social position of the giver, while reciprocal meals maintained a system of symmetrical exchanges in which the return gift was roughly equal to the gift it was repaying. In short, it acted as a levelling mechanism among commoners thereby setting them apart from those who had achieved high rank. There are virtually no detailed accounts of how upward mobility occurred, how individuals and their families actually broke with the network of social relations that held their status category together. The acquisition of wealth alone was never sufficient for a man to achieve a high-ranking status (cf Riches 1984). Upward mobility was frequently facilitated by marriage to a woman from a prominent family, and marriage with an appropriate foreigner could be used as a strategy to acquire more prestige as a concomitant to wealth. Linked with these marriage principles was polygyny. Plurality of wives was always associated with chiefs and other important people, a practice that demonstrated not only their wealth but their propensity to form prestigious relationships (Ross 1849: 318–19; Teit 1930: 263–76).

My analysis and interpretation of Okanagan social stratification differs somewhat from Ray's comparative study of the Plateau as a culture area (Ray 1939: 24–35). Ray takes the diffusionist view that there is an emphasis on equality for all Plateau peoples and that 'ideas of class and rank' were the result of superficial adoption of ideas from outside. It is not my intention to dismiss Ray's important work, but to emphasize that the Okanagan did have more complex social and economic systems than he and others are prepared to concede. This complexity is reflected also in Okanagan chiefship, an institution which permitted negotiation in all spheres of leadership. In many respects chiefship was flexible enough to accommodate the demands of the fur trade without losing its central character. The same could not be said of the effects of later external demands and commands that culminated in the enforcement of the Indian Act of 1876, a theme which is discussed later.

THE OKANAGAN AND THEIR NEIGHBOURS

In this synopsis of traditional Okanagan social structure and culture I have made very few comparisons with neighbouring peoples largely to avoid some of the problems inherent in macro-social analyses especially when the quality of available data is uneven. Another important reason was to ensure that in this particular study Okanagan culture and society always remained in sharp focus and not obscured by others.

There are, however, some significant differences between the Okanagan and their immediate neighbours. Ray (1939) highlights the importance of ethnic

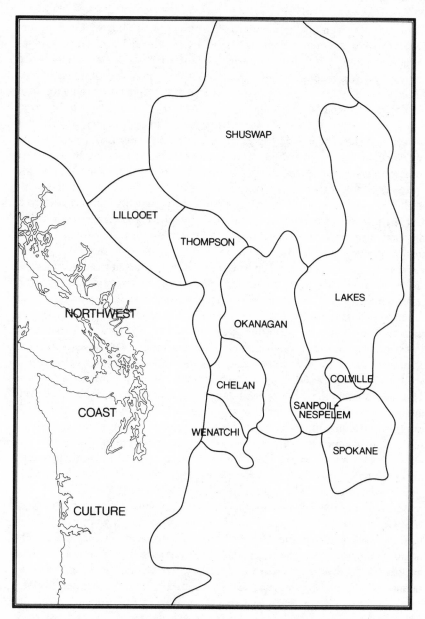

Okanagan and their neighbours before 1800

differences between all the northern Plateau people – Shuswap, Thompson, Lillooet, Lakes, Wenatchi, Sanpoil, and so on. He also shows the near absence of slavery among the northern Okanagan in sharp contrast to the Thompson and the Lillooet peoples. And he provides insights into the complexities and variation in such cultural aspects as winter guardian spirit dances, concepts of disease, and shamanism.

Teit (1930: 215–17, 248–60 et passim) writes in some detail of relations between all these people with particular reference to intermarriage, warfare, and trade illustrating the extent of the interaction between them. Warfare was common between all groups, but the battles between the Okanagan and the Shuswap were the most notorious and violent. The Thompson Indians (Nekeleme'xu) and the Okanagan seem to have enjoyed peaceful relations by and large and intermarriage was common. But the Okanagan at the Head of the Lake also married their enemies, the Shuswap, for reasons which, other than proximity to each other, are not always clear.

Two factors seem to have contributed to setting the northern Okanagan apart from their neighbours. First was their dependence on others for ocean salmon to which only the southern Okanagan had access. The other factor was the early acquisition by the Okanagan of the horse, which improved not only their hunting ability but also their offensive strategies in war, and especially their trade relations through efficient transportation. Teit gives a detailed account of the changes that took place in Okanagan trading patterns after the acquisition of horses. For example, before the horse they could not offer their Thompson Indian neighbours much more than Indian hemp and dressed skins in exchange for salmon pemmican and dentalia. The use of the horse helped to expand the inventory of trade goods by adding dressed buffalo skins and robes, dressed moose skin, painted buffalo hide bags and parflêches, and woven bags from the south. The addition of these commodities to their trading package also enabled the Okanagan to acquire salmon oil, salmon pemmican, and coiled baskets for which the Thompson are renowned.

As late as the 1820s the Okanagan were still distinguished from their neighbours by their equestrian hunting techniques and their lack of involvement in fishing. McDonald of the Hudson's Bay Company wrote in 1827: 'The Schimilicumruchs (Similkameen) and the Okanakuns of both sides[s] [of] the big Lake are tribes that resort most to the chase ... [and] are what may be called inland Tribes, being not quite so contiguous to the salmon fishery' (HBCA B. 97/e/1 1827 folio 7(4)). By the middle of the nineteenth century Okanagan equestrian culture provided an ideal base to incorporate cattle ranching and farming in their lives.

Chapter Two

The Beginnings of White Hegemony

Okanagan institutions and power did not fall immediate victim to the presence of the white man west of the Rocky Mountains, but it did not take long for the balance of power to be tipped in favour of the newcomers. The white man's cultural baggage, however, had made an impact on the Indians in the interior before his actual arrival. Guns and other trade goods, for example, passed from group to group from both the south and east, disrupting the balance of indigenous trade; certain features of European religious beliefs, not to mention European diseases such as smallpox, followed similar routes; and 'stories of strange ships and men and some trade goods filtered to them from the coast' (Duff 1964: 55). But none of these items, events, or ideas were of the same order as the developments that were to dominate the first sixty or so years in the nineteenth century, marking the beginnings of white hegemony[1] among the Okanagan: the land-based fur trade, the gold rush in the interior of British Columbia, and the arrival of Christian missionaries. The land-based fur trade and the gold rush both forged economic, political, and social ties between the Okanagan and the worlds of colonial and settler power, incorporating the Okanagan into a wider economy and society for the first time in their history.

---

1 In seventeenth-century English, the term 'hegemony' often conveyed the meaning of 'master principle.' Thus extension of its meaning from political dominance to include asymmetrical class relations or cultural imperialism is not out of line with accepted usage, which is the sense in which the term is used here. Hegemony might be understood, then, as the general direction given to any complex societal situation by the dominant or potentially dominant group. In hegemonic situations the values and will of one group permeate the whole society and lead the way for eventual domination (cf Gramsci 1971: 12–13, 57–8, 161, 258–64 et passim; Williams 1976: 117–18).

The negative impact of those worlds on the Okanagan soon rendered their institutions, often unwittingly, subordinate to foreign values and aspirations. My interpretation of the early years of contact between natives and colonists differs radically from that put forward by Francis and Morantz (1983) writing on the fur trade in the James Bay area. The latter argue that the fur trade created relations between traders and Indians that made both parties equal partners in their new economic and social transactions. Robin Fisher, writing on the impact of the fur trade in British Columbia, offers similar erroneous conclusions:

> With the decline of the maritime fur trade and the establishment of land-based operations, trading methods changed, but the essential nature of the contract between the races remained the same. The fur trade continued to be a reciprocal relationship between Indian and European. The Indians still to a large extent controlled both the trade and their culture, and European traders did not attempt any major interference with their way of life. The mutually beneficial nature of the land-based fur trade was indicated by the continued absence of major inter-racial conflict. (Fisher 1977: 24)

It is true that there was an absence of major conflict in that the fur traders did not necessarily report such conflicts as major; but the fur trade did in fact radically alter both the internal nature of Okanagan society as well as Okanagan relations with the outside world. Indeed, the fur trade began the process which made the Okanagan subservient to the white man not just economically, but politically as well. Similarly, the local gold rush which began in 1858 and the active penetration of Christian missionaries from 1839 onwards were to involve the Okanagan in a much wider network of relations than they had experienced before. But my concern here is not so much with these phenomena or even the changes they brought, but with the new social and economic relationships they created.

In spite of the obvious differences between the activities related to the fur trade, the gold rush, and missionary endeavour – especially the last – their agents were all in pursuit of 'commodities' whose nature and value were predetermined: furs, gold, and souls. Furs and gold were exported for economic profit. Missionaries were not directly concerned with material profit, and their aim was to convert les sauvages thereby removing them, symbolically, at least, from their traditional context. Perhaps the comparison between fur traders, gold miners, and missionaries makes better sense if they are portrayed as culture agents (Fortes 1938) forging links between European society and the Okanagan through social and economic interaction: the interaction between fur traders and band headmen; gold miners and native owners of territory; missionaries and headmen and shamans.

The proposition accepted here is that although there was negotiation between the two parties, the relationships were nearly always asymmetrical and skewed by potential white hegemony and power in favour of the newcomers, on whose terms negotiation was initiated and proceeded. The Okanagan could not predict the effects and outcome of the fur trade, or the demands and consequences of the gold rush, any more than they could fathom the implications of 'signing up' with the Roman Catholic church. For the Okanagan, therefore, it is impossible to accept uncritically Robin Fisher's belief that, although the fur trade brought change to Indian society, 'it was change that the Indians directed and therefore their culture remained intact' (Fisher 1977: 47).

THE FUR TRADE

The fur trade in the Okanagan Valley and southwards to the confluence of the Okanagan and Columbia rivers was relatively short lived, lasting less than forty years from 1811 to about 1847, when the Old Brigade Trail was abandoned and the last brigade came down 'with all its noise and colour' from Fort Kamloops past the Head of the Lake to Fort Okanogan. The occasion marked the end of British trade with the south after the border settlement with America had been achieved (Ormsby 1931: 20–1).

The south Okanagan were introduced to the fur trade by the Pacific Fur Company, but by 1813 the North West Company had established its men at Fort Okanogan after purchasing the existing furs and merchandise for little more than $80,000 from the American company. The north Okanagan were introduced to the fur trade by the North West Company through its operations from Fort Kamloops which it established in 1812, although they would also have had some contact earlier with the Pacific Fur Company.

Despite its short duration, the fur trade had devastating effects. Not only did it wipe out most fur-bearing animals in the area and deplete the supply of salmon, but it altered the nature of Okanagan chiefship and leadership, fostered the growth of factionalism, and undermined many facets of Okanagan culture and values to the extent to which they could never recover.

Commenting on his arrival in 1811 at what was to become Fort Okanogan, trader Alexander Ross wrote: 'Here the Indians assemble in friendly crowds, according to their usual habit – presented us with abundance of salmon, offered many horses for sale, and were in all other respects exceedingly kind. Here also they invited us to remain, to build, and to winter among them: they said their country abounds in beaver, nor should we want for provisions' (Ross 1849: 140–1).

In May 1813 Ross and two men with sixteen horses set out to the north from Fort Okanogan (which had recently been completed) to Shuswap country. He camped at 'Cumcloups' (Kamloops) and found about two thousand Indians assembled to exchange goods. He reports that the Indians were very anxious to trade; in one morning he bartered 110 beaver before breakfast for the price of five leaves of tobacco per beaver skin. Later during his visit, after his basic trade goods were depleted, he secured twenty prime beaver skins for one yard of cloth (Ross 1849: 200).

Two important issues are reflected in these reports: the difference between south and north in terms of the commodities that interested the traders; and the willingness on the part of the Okanagan and other Interior Salish Indians to obtain trade goods. There were plenty of fur-bearing animals in the south in the early years of the fur trade, but the companies were equally interested in the salmon and horses. Salmon constituted the main source of protein for the traders and their families in the Okanagan and over the years enormous quantities were taken during the annual summer runs. For example, about one thousand salmon were caught daily at Colville alone during the run in 1823–4 (Dolby 1973: 143). Even this seems to have been insufficient because on 1 March 1823 John MacLeod reports in the Thompson's River Journal that 4600 dried salmon were shipped to Fort Okanogan to support the traders and their families in the summer (HBCA B. 97/a/1/1822-23 No. 184 F.). Although Kamloops did have an independent supply of salmon, a good deal of their dried salmon came from the Fraser River. McDonald writes in his report of 1827:

> Dried Salmon is the Staff of life, and fortunately seldom fails ... Every fall and winter four or five trips are made to Fraser's river ... From the beginning of August till our return to the depôt the ensuing June about 12,000 Salmon are consumed exclusively for the district, and last year, 1,500 of that number were taken at [Fort] Okanakan. Each fish from Fraser's river (those on the Columbia are larger) split and dried with the back bone out, weighs one pound and 200, the usual horse load, will cost on an average about 5/-. Three such salmon are allowed a man p. diem – two for a woman & one for a child when supplied out of the Company's Store. (HBCA B. 97/e/1 1827)

The other commodity of interest to the traders was the horse, and during the early years of the fur trade the south Okanagan were active in supplying horses to all three fur companies. A decade later the centre of horse-trading shifted northwards to Kamloops and the Head of The Lake with the entrenchment of an equestrian culture among the north Okanagan (Dolby 1973: 142–3; Dawson 1891: 14).

The importance of the horse to the fur traders in the Okanagan Valley can only be appreciated when it is realized that not only furs but trade goods and food had to be transported long distances over rocky terrain, and that water transportation was not always possible, and certainly not as quick. For example, the Brigade Trail from Alexandria to Kamloops and Fort Okanogan, roughly 620 kilometres, was used to transport furs by pack-horse. At Fort Okanogan the packs were transferred from the horses to canoes for the journey to Astoria, later renamed Fort George (Brown 1914: 19). On the return journey trade goods were carried back to Fort Kamloops.

The motivation for the Okanagan to enter the fur trade during its early stages seems to have been unconnected with an interest in profit or the exchange of fur for commodities to improve their usual lifestyle. From a materialist point of view, the Okanagan were mainly interested in luxury goods, an interest consistent with their traditional preoccupation with status and achievement among themselves. Tobacco, beads, guns, and ammunition were highly desired, and they seem to have been little interested in blankets and iron (Dolby 1973: 140–1; Simpson 1931: 94 and 1947: 232). Tobacco especially was in great demand for its assumed magical and medicinal qualities quite apart from the pleasure it produced. The Okanagan had no apparent interest in alcohol up to the 1820s, as the Hudson's Bay Company records illustrate so conclusively.

By the early years of the fur trade the Okanagan had no great need for trade goods, a reality that often irritated the officials of the Hudson's Bay Company. This annoyance was exacerbated by the fact that the territory occupied by the Okanagan, especially in the north, never produced furs in great quantities by comparison with the area to the north of what is now Kamloops. Both the North West and Hudson's Bay companies report relatively small returns from the Okanagan people, and there are even complaints attributing this to indolent habits. 'I have not yet made a pack of beaver. The lazy [Okanagan] Indians won't work' writes the trader in charge at Fort Okanogan in 1814 (quoted by Dolby 1973: 141). Clearly the Okanagan had confidence in their own way of life in the early part of the nineteenth century when the fur trade began in the area.

During the 1820s the complaints and observations about the Okanagan changed. In the spring of 1823 John MacLeod, reporting on the various tribes between Fort Kamloops and Fort Okanogan, writes of the Okanagan people:

· This nation is very numerous say 250 to 300 Men, exclusive of adults [sic] women and children. They inhabit the whole of the banks of the Okanagan River from the Columbia river to Ok[anagan] Lake, and thence to Thompsons River, a distance computed to be about 400 miles. [T]hey frequent both the Okanagan and Kameloops Forts, they are such an indolent and improvident Set, that all tho' their Country in Summer abound with Trout and Salmon, yet are starving for the most part of Winter and Spring, living on no other food in the Spring of the year than roots and a kind of Moss that grows on the Fir trees and consequently give us a good deal of trouble and uneasiness attempting to steal our horses, when [we are] passing and repassing [them], but they bring us a share of their Trade. (HBCA B. 208/e/1 1822–1823)

A few years later Archibald McDonald notes incredible 'poverty' among the Okanagan, who are said to be starving. On 11 February 1827 he writes: 'Natives much alarmed by the disease among their children' who seem to have been suffering from malnutrition during the winter. On 9 March of the same year he reports: Two Indians arrived today all the way from the [Okanagan] Falls ... for a few leaves of Tobacco to enable them if possible to get rid of the evil Spirit now so fatal among the children – they have wonderful faith in Tobacco' (HBCA B. 97/a/2 1826–1827).[2]

On 16 January 1827 McDonald reports that Chief Nicolas (Nkwala) of the Okanagan and one of his friends 'are still hanging about our fireside – the fact is they are starving at home.' The latter, 'poor d---l [has been] starving four months of the year.' On 6 March he writes: 'About 30 Okanakan Indians ... have been living in this neighbourhood [i.e. Fort Kamloops] for some weeks,' and it is highly probable that their presence is related to lack of food in their territory.

There is good evidence that the beaver and other animals, including deer, were being rapidly depleted in Okanagan territory as a direct consequence of trapping and the other demands of the fur trade. As Archibald McDonald wrote to his superiors in the Hudson's Bay Company on 5 April 1827, 'A person can walk for days together without seeing the smallest quadruped, the little brown squirrel excepted' (HBCA B. 97/e/1 1827).

Most authors of Hudson's Bay Company reports saw no connection between the decline in fur-bearing animals and lack of food, in spite of the many references to the phenomenon. McDonald was an astute observer and is a notable exception. In his district report of 1827 he drew attention to the

---

2 It is possible that children were also afflicted by whooping cough which was reported at the 'lower part of the river' on 15 February 1827 (HBCA B. 97/a/2 1826–1827).

connection between the beaver's approaching extinction and the rapid disappearance of the food animals. Later in the same report he observes:

> The Chinpoos [Thompson Indians] of North River – the Schimilicameachs and the Okanakans of both side the big lake are the tribes that resort most to the chase – the two latter are what may be called inland Tribes, being not quite so contiguous to the Salmon fishery; however, even they are become dependant on that resource now, & after collecting what Berries & little fishes they can, they either remove to the Kettle falls on the Columbia or the lower part of the Thompson's river: but often they are reduced to roots – preparations from Pine Moss and such like to keep body and life together. (HBCA B. 97/e/1 1827)

In considering the question of starvation as a consequence of the fur trade, attention should be drawn to the main difference between the north and south Okanagan. The north Okanagan 'resorted most to the chase,' that is, they derived most of their protein from hunting. Oral tradition holds that they were meat eaters as opposed to fish eaters. Nowadays some Okanagan living at the Head of the Lake still regard themselves as superior and look down on people whom they regard as having come from a fishing tradition rather than one whose members lived by the chase.

The annual supply of salmon was not constantly plentiful. Occasionally the run was poor and starvation followed, although the effects of over-fishing in the area are not known. For example, the salmon run on the Fraser River failed in 1846, leading to starvation among the Lillooet people. Alex C. Anderson of the Hudson's Bay Company writes on 21 May: 'The Natives whom I saw amounting in all to about 50 men with women and children, were suffering from want of provisions, and were unable to supply us any. They ascribe the dearth to the state of the water which impedes the usual fishery. The inhabitants are very miserable, and exhibit every symptom of abject poverty' (HBCA B. 97/a/3 1846).

Dolby (1973) addresses herself to the theme of starvation among the Okanagan during the fur trade; her paper is of special interest because it throws some light on the growth of hostility, resentment, and anger among the Okanagan towards both the fur trade operations in their country and the Hudson's Bay Company itself. Accounts of their attitudes, which were often ambivalently expressed, are reported in the fur trade records of the time as well as in the oral traditions of the people.

I myself wish to suggest that these sporadic expressions of overt hostility by Chief Nkwala and his people towards the fur traders relate to their unconscious (sometimes conscious) feelings of resentment at their presence.

Most especially, though, their anger was a function of the unaccountable food shortages and those occasional periods of starvation associated with fur trade activity.

In his report to the Hudson's Bay Company head office John MacLeod records that on 5 September 1822 trader Montigny 'complains much of the insolent behaviour of the tribes he traded with ... they shot arrows at two of our Horses.' On 20 December in the same year he writes: 'There is a report in circulation that the Okanagan Indians intend to steal our horses on the way going out.' By 1 February 1823 relations with the Okanagan living near the Brigade Trail were so bad that he discussed the possibility of building a boat to take the property down the 'Big Okanagan Lake as there is great risk in carrying it on Horses along it.' And by 23 February 1823 '[Chief] Nicolas [Nkwala] and followers [are] angry about not getting ammunition and horses, and seem to have planned to ransack the Fort [Kamloops] since so many people were away.' It is surprising that Nkwala and the other Okanagan were short of horses, and it is possible that they had slaughtered horses for food. Horse meat was often eaten by the Okanagan at that time, although the idea is abhorrent to them now.

On 25 February, MacLeod started worrying about Nkwala's change in attitude. '[He] has rendered most aid to the whites and [is] undoubtedly the most manly and most to dread if he turned against us.' The cause of Nkwala's mood change turned out to be the jealousy and insecurity he felt when it was rumoured that MacLeod no longer recognized his title to chiefship. The misunderstanding was soon cleared up, but by 28 February, just as the brigade was preparing to leave Fort Kamloops for Fort Okanogan, MacLeod made sure he was on the right side of the Indians by giving powder, balls, tobacco, and flints to all three chiefs (including Nkwala) and their followers. The brigade reached Fort Okanogan safely on 18 March, but on the way there were several unsuccessful attempts by the Okanagan to steal their horses.

There are other references to the Okanagan which reflect hostility to the Hudson's Bay Company, and their demands for horses, guns, and tobacco. The company traders for their part also report the apprehension and uncertainty they experienced while passing through Okanagan territory. These events would seem to support my hypothesis regarding the depletion of game and tampering with the environment among the north Okanagan from about 1820 to 1850. The north Okanagan responded to these radical changes in their customary patterns of subsistence in a variety of ways, the most important of which was their aggression, both overt and covert, directed towards the employees of the Hudson's Bay Company. This indirect and accidental disruption of north Okanagan society and culture signalled the first major undermining of the autonomy of Chief Nkwala's people. In more general terms, though, it should be noted that the undermining of tradition began in different ways among different groups of native peoples. Thus the fact that the south Okanagan appear to have benefited materially in a way that the north Okanagan did not does not mean that the former escaped either the blatant or the subtle inroads of the commerce in furs, or the general influences of white presence.

CHIEF NKWALA (NICOLAS)

Chief Nkwala's political career and his role in the fur trade were inextricably bound up in two cultures – Okanagan, and that of the fur traders and the establishment they represented.[3] The influence of the latter was especially marked in his dress. Just before his death in 1859, '[He] ... wore a stove pipe hat and citizen's clothes, and had a lot of medals of good character and official vouchers of good conduct for several years' (Reinhart 1962: 129).

It is difficult to give an exact date when the fur trade became established in Nkwala's domain at the Head of the Lake. However, we know that two French Canadian traders, Pion and Montigny, were in charge of an 'outpost' located between the two northern arms of Lake Okanagan in 1811–12, Montigny having been sent north from Fort Okanogan for the Pacific Fur Company. One of the traders, probably Montigny, put Nkwala in charge of this post during a winter, asking him to keep it in good order and collect pelts for the company. In return for his work, Nkwala received ten guns and a good supply of ammunition (Teit 1930: 268; Dolby 1973: 146; Brent n.d.), and from that time on he earned a place in fur trade affairs. By the time the Hudson's Bay Company took over from the Pacific Fur Company, Nkwala was even further entrenched in the process of fur transactions. He began to be treated with respect and sometimes awe as his indispensability in commerce increased. Nkwala for his part made a point of ingratiating himself with company officials and white men in general.

By the 1820s the fur trade was in full swing, reaching its peak in 1822 among the north Okanagan, the Shuswap, and other neighbouring peoples in the general areas stretching out from Fort Kamloops, the headquarters of the Hudson's Bay Company in the area. It was during this period that a new kind of Okanagan political leader emerged, the double chief, of which Nkwala was

3 My intention here is to place Nkwala in the context of the fur trade. My main sources are: Balf (1985 and n.d.), Brent (n.d.), Hudson's Bay Company Archival Records (various), Teit (1930), and the oral tradition.

the prototype. I use the term double chief to show that economic and political leadership now took on a new dimension serving two kinds of societies, traditional Okanagan on the one hand, and the capitalist centred Okanagan, on the other (Carstens 1987).

Nkwala owed his growing success and reputation both to the personal esteem with which he was regarded by his own and neighbouring bands, and to his growing association with the Hudson's Bay Company. This duality enabled him to build two bases of authority, each of which he used to strengthen the other. As a prominent Okanagan, and through his seventeen foreign wives, he had access to potential supplies of furs (and probably fish from the south and west), which he was able to deliver to Fort Kamloops. As a friend and ally of the fur traders, he was in an ideal position to act as go-between and mediator between the company and the Okanagan and other native peoples to secure for his people the luxury items they desired.

Nkwala enjoyed far more influence, authority, and power than any Okanagan headman before him. He was crafty and a master broker, always able to enhance his status on both sides, while displaying remarkable independence when another posture suited his tactics (Tod n.d.). It would thus be inaccurate to characterize him as a mere stooge of the Hudson's Bay Company; in some instances he controlled the officials at Fort Kamloops almost as much as they controlled him. And his power over his own people increased because of the leverage he had over the fur traders and the access he had to trade goods and other commodities. This new order of authority is illustrated by the fact that Nkwala became the first headman-chief whose followers defined themselves through the allegiance that they owed him. Nkwala's leadership marked the transition from what Bertrand de Jouvenel (1957: 21) termed a *dux*, 'the man who leads into action a stream of wills,' to an incipient *rex*, 'the man who regularizes and rules.' The socio-political distinctiveness of traditional bands and villages declined but their autonomy continued to be expressed in the form of factions as authority moved from the local level to a more centralized position, though obviously the nature of structural change was more complicated than this. Nkwala was thus a special kind of charismatic leader who continued throughout his life as chief to play the game of broker, mediating between a rapidly changing culture and fur trade capitalism.

Throughout the 1820s Nkwala figures prominently in the reports and correspondence of the Hudson's Bay Company. The war against the Lillooet to avenge his father's death greatly perturbed the staff, largely because they feared that Nkwala would cease to be a broker-ally and encourage other groups to cut off their trade in furs, salmon, and horses. There was also apprehension about the safety of the Brigade Trail as the main transport route, especially in the Lake Okanagan region.

In general, the fur traders regarded Nkwala as an important ally and a trusted friend, and Archibald McDonald was able to write, '[Nicolas is] always acknowledged a staunch partisan of whites' after the Shuswap had taken umbrage because Nkwala had been given 'the key of the Fort [Kamloops] contrary to [Shuswap] custom' (HBCA B. 97/a/2 1826–1827). It is also on record that Governor George Simpson very much wanted to meet Nkwala in 1828 during his visit to the region. Unfortunately the 'favoured chief was off hunting' (Cole 1979: 139).

The fur traders held long conversations with Nkwala from time to time, and company men indicate that they knew where he slept and that he spent three days a week at his own lodge at the Head of the Lake. They even received detailed knowledge of war parties and tensions between ethnic groups and personalities from him. McDonald once reported on Nkwala's tendency to pay long visits to the fort and overstay his welcome, so that he and other 'gentleman chiefs ... not only become troublesome' but also 'lose the little dignity with which they arrive. They are immoderately fond of tobacco.' McDonald writes specifically of Nkwala on 6 December 1826:

> Nicolas very ingeniously maintains that he and those among them of any good sense smoak tobacco for a *much different* better motive [than other Indians] that which moves the white people to look in the Great Fathers Book: for the moment *he* takes his pipe, he cannot help thinking of the great question of the world and the number of good things done for their benefit the Indian cannot understand ... I never saw a savage that seems more concerned in the power of a Supreme being. (HBCA B. 97/a/2 1826–1827; emphasis in original)

McDonald's irony suggests that he had little control over Nkwala's actions and that the latter was merely using one of his many techniques for obtaining what he wanted from the white man.

In addition to his association with the Hudson's Bay Company and his role as chief political leader of the north Okanagan, Nkwala himself led important hunting parties. He crossed the Rockies on occasions in search of buffalo when game declined in Okanagan territory. 'He also organized elk drives in the upper Nicola country, to provide valuable meat, clothing and bone and antler tools. By the 1860s there were no elk left in the district' (Balf n.d.; see also Teit 1930: 242ff, 267). John Tod incidentally points out that by the early 1840s Nkwala and his family were poor, even begging a little bit, although they still brought in furs from time to time.

Nkwala became a close friend of Samuel Black, who was promoted to chief factor of the Columbia District in 1837, and later murdered in 1841 by Kiskowskin, the nephew of the Shuswap chief, Tranquille. Black's murder raised the alarm among the fur traders who feared that a general uprising was in the wind. Trading with the Indians was temporarily suspended and fur traders hurried to Kamloops from New Caledonia and as far afield as Fort Vancouver to support their fellows. No motive was ever discovered for the murder but it does seem to have been a Shuswap affair. Perhaps it reflected the Shuswap reaction to the depletion of game and increasing white hegemony. Fisher (1977: 38) accepts the view that Black was unknowingly the victim of the 'Indians' notions of revenge' (see also Morice 1904: 176).

Quite predictably in terms of his reputation and personal character, Nkwala saved the day and even delivered an oration at Black's funeral. Archibald McKinlay reports Nkwala's words:

A mountain has fallen! The earth is shaken. The sun is darkened to us poor miserable Indians, but we can blame no one for it but ourselves ... My heart is sad. I cannot look at myself in a glass ... He was kind, just and generous to us; and I know he loved us. Wherefore did we kill him? He is dead and we shall never see him again. Our wives and children will weep and wail for him. Indian men do not weep, but their hearts will be sore for a long time. You, my friends of the Shuswap tribe, the murderer is one of you. Justice calls on him to die, and die he must. (Quoted by Balf n.d.)

Mary Balf comments on Nkwala's words, saying: 'One can cynically suggest that such appeasement was necessary so that the Indians could again obtain ammunition for hunting.' Her interpretation is certainly appropriate, for it illustrates how cleverly Nkwala could perform his mediator's role, particularly in the interest of his own people. But the text also reflects Nkwala's growing marginality as his personality was transformed by the peculiar frontier colonial environment in which he was involved (cf Stonequist 1937; Dickie-Clark 1966). On the one hand, he mourns the loss of a friend; on the other, he deprecates himself and all the local native peoples – 'poor miserable Indians.' Only at the end does he point an incriminating finger at the Shuswap people.

Black's successor as chief factor at Fort Kamloops was Donald Manson. Manson immediately reversed the 'liberal' policy of his predecessors and, as Balf suggests, 'he certainly had no Indian friends.' Even the Nkwala family now received austerity treatment with regard to important luxury items such as tobacco. Manson writes on 28 January 1842: 'Received a visit from one of

Nicolo's sons who came to acquaint us that he was just going to start for his father's tent, and that he expected we should give him the usual present of tobacco' (quoted by Balf, n.d.). Instead of a foot or more of tobacco, the usual allowance given to members of the Nkwala family, Manson issued instructions to 'give the fellow two or three inches which I think is quite sufficient.' Nkwala was shrewd enough not to take offence at this discourteous act and before departing for the summer on 10 May 1842 he promised Manson that he would 'do all in his power to make the Indians exert themselves during the summer' (Balf n.d.; Manson 1841–).

In August 1842 Manson appears to have been replaced by John Tod, who similarly lacked friends among either the Indians or the Western Department of the Hudson's Bay Company. Balf suggests that he saw Nkwala 'as a threat or rival for supremacy and influence in the district where he wanted absolute rule,' which accounts for the many belittling remarks about Nkwala that occur in his journal, although in old age he did acknowledge Nkwala's importance to the company (Tod 1841–3).

Nkwala now paid fewer and fewer visits to the fort at Kamloops and eventually stopped coming altogether. 'Perhaps he resented being treated as a trouble-maker after all his years of peaceful co-operation' (Balf n.d.), but the times had changed, the heyday of fur trade was over in the district, and Nkwala had no place in that business anymore, although he was still on good terms with many individual white men. One of these friends, Chief Trader Angus McDonald at Fort Colville, claimed that Nkwala had in the presence of his sons deeded him Grande Prairie Valley during the 1850s. Nkwala had no right to part with communal land, and his action, if in fact true, reflects the enormous power and prestige he had acquired through his association with the fur trade system. It shows also that at least one white man had his eye on Okanagan farm and ranch land at this early date.

GOLD MINING

The fur trade in the area ended almost as quickly as it had begun, so that by the middle of 1858 'the dominance of the fur trade in Vancouver Island and British Columbia' had waned. The Okanagan and neighbouring regions were no exception. The decline in the fur trade in British Columbia was accompanied by a more general commercial change, namely the expiry of the Hudson's Bay Company's exclusive licence to trade with native peoples west of the Rocky Mountains, a concession which was becoming untenable anyway (Fisher 1977: 95).

It was almost by chance, therefore, that the year 1858 marked the end of one commercial era and the beginning another. For at roughly the same time as the fur trade collapsed news of the Fraser River gold discoveries reached California and an enormous influx of fortune-seekers began to arrive, first by the hundreds, later in thousands, as Sir James Douglas himself reported.

As far as the Okanagan were concerned it was not until 1859 when gold was discovered at Rock Creek that the influence of gold mining began to affect life in the valley directly. In October 1860 about five hundred miners, mainly Americans who had abandoned their claims in Oregon and Washington, were working in the Rock Creek area. By November, people were beginning to settle in the area to provide the miners with commercial services. Farming soon flourished to provide food. Prices were high at Rock Creek but in 1861 labourers on the gold claims were earning at least four dollars a day, and many miners were making excellent profits. In short, Rock Creek showed great promise for the merchants, and the anticipation of further expansion in gold mining began to have an impact on the lives of everyone in the region (Ormsby 1931: 28ff). But the Rock Creek gold deposits did not last, and when a prospecting party found grain and scale gold in all the streams flowing west into Okanagan Lake, many of the miners abandoned their diggings for Mission Creek and later Cherry Creek. The new finds literally proved to be no more than a flash in the pan, and the Okanagan 'gold rush' proved a complete flop.

Nevertheless, as Fisher points our, 'With the coming of the gold miners, Indians and Europeans were, for the first time, competing for the resources of the country,' and the gold miners were followed by settlers who wanted Indian land (Fisher 1977: 96). Fisher's statement is only partly correct because the fur trade also involved competition for resources that were closely related to the food supply in animals and fish.

In the interior, Indians objected to and were strongly opposed to the miners digging the soil for gold. The Fraser canyon seems to have been the location of a great deal of inter-racial hostility and violence in the summer of 1858 and there was even talk of an Indian war (ibid.: 99–100). Mining operations disrupted the catching and drying of salmon, and the miners interfered with Indian land holdings, village sites, fishing stations, and cultivated areas. The effect was especially hard on the Indians during the first winter of gold mining, 1858–9, and there are reports of Indian destitution and starvation. Many Indians themselves were involved in the gold rush, and as a result neglected their traditional summer rendezvous and preparations for winter. Some Indians became wage-earners and many congregated round mining towns (ibid.: 101; Knight 1978), but it is difficult to establish how many of these were Okanagan.

The discovery of gold in the Kamloops and neighbouring areas provoked the wild stampede of miners through the Okanagan up the Old Brigade Trail, and the Okanagan people had to put up with considerable interference in their daily lives and some brutal violence. In July 1858 a large party of American miners reached Lake Okanagan, and one of their number, H.F. Reinhart (1962: 125–6), reports that the white men saw some Indians moving away from their camp: 'The boys saw a couple of their dogs at their old camp ground, and shot them down, and they saw some old huts where the Indians had stored a lot of berries for the winter, blackberries and nuts, fifty or a hundred bushels. They helped themselves to the berries and nuts, filling several sacks to take along, and the balance they just emptied into the lake, destroying them so that the Indians should not have them for provision for the winter.'

Worse behaviour followed. After spending the night, all the miners appeared to have moved on and the Indians returned to investigate the campsites for left-overs, unaware that several miners were lying in wait for the unarmed Indians to arrive by canoe. The miners then opened fire on them: 'It was a great slaughter or massacre of what was killed, for they never made an effort to resist or fired a shot, either gun, pistol, or bow or arrows, and the men were not touched, no more than if they had shot at birds. It was a brutal affair' (Reinhart 1962: 127).

Some days later the same party captured two Shuswap men who were on their way to visit family in Okanagan territory. Execution was voted down, but the two people were held until the gold miners reached Kamloops (Balf n.d.). Here Chief Nkwala intervened. 'Old Nicholas the head chief of Indians around that country, came to see us about the two prisoners ... He was quite angry and said he was surprised to see 300 men take two Indians prisoners ... and did not show great bravery. And about the O[kanagan] Lake massacre, that it was brutal, and that he did not think much of Bostons, or Americans, that would do the like' (Reinhart 1962: 129). The prisoners were released.

It was Nkwala's personality and self-confidence no doubt that contributed towards his success in dealing with these American cutthroats. But he also 'had a bodyguard of young warriors who did his bidding and accompanied him on all important trips and visits to neighboring chiefs' (Brent n.d.). His bodyguard was well armed with guns and ammunition obtained from the Hudson's Bay Company in return for services rendered. He and his warriors would have been an intimidating group to the gold miners, who had no idea of what the combined strength of the Okanagan and Shuswap forces might be. It is true that Nkwala's political base was among Okanagan, but all the evidence points to his possessing much wider influence after the middle of the century, an influence that had grown out of his involvement – political and economic – with the fur trade. But it is evident that he occasionally used his influence to guarantee the safety of white miners as he had done with the fur traders earlier. He even prevented the Indians from making war on them. Marie Brent (n.d.) says:

> During the Fraser River trouble between the Thompsons (Indians) and the whites in 1858 and 1859, he advocated peace, although preparing for war had the affair not been settled. The Thompsons were against the miners and settlers. Although he was begged by the Spokanes and Thompsons to join them in war against the whites, he refused to allow his people [the Okanagan] to join them. He said that he was an ally of the whites, fur traders, King George and the Queen and that they were all good to him and his people.

The Okanagan for their part were understandably hostile to the gold miners who passed through their territory with little regard for Indian life and property. There are still many accounts in the oral tradition of Okanagan resistance to this white intrusion, although these tend to be played down nowadays. James Teit (1930: 259) refers to the white miners who 'were attacked and harassed by the natives, who opposed their passage at some points by erecting breastworks and shooting from them, setting fire to the grass, stampeding horses, picking off stragglers, and even attacking camps. In one instance a large white party was driven to the river and forced to cross. A number of whites were killed in these skirmishes.'

It is difficult to assess the direct influence of gold mining on the Okanagan people although oral tradition clearly reflects their conflicts with, and resentment towards, both gold mining and miners. The side-effects of gold mining were enormous and quite different from the fur trade, which tended to confine its centres of operation to specific areas. Gold mining attracted all kinds of white newcomers in addition to the miners; it stimulated the development of markets, the building of roads, and especially an interest in farming in the area. Margaret Ormsby concludes that the history of mining in the Okanagan Valley consisted of 'a series of discoveries, soaring hopes, and then disheartening failures.' But mining drew more white people into the district, and some turned to the land and became pioneer settlers. She sees the miners as a 'class of decent men who expected to improve their condition in life by their own honest endeavour.' Her account differs somewhat from the Indian experience but her interpretation is interesting because her perception of Okanagan history is essentially one seen through the eyes of the settlers, providing a sort of modernization view of the Okanagan Valley without the native. She highlights the importance of white occupation of land to the point of approving even of 'casual stragglers' who took up land. It should be noted here that land could be pre-empted under various acts, ordinances, and proclamations promulgated from 1859 onwards.

INCORPORATION INTO THE WORLD OF THE WHITES

In the early years of the gold rush, and within this changing socio-economic system, Nkwala was the one Okanagan chief who knew how to play his cards with the white man, and his extravagant matrimonial versatility with women from different groups illustrates his charismatic quality as an Okanagan Indian. As a key frontier figure in his day he contributed, perhaps unwittingly, to the process whereby the Okanagan were incorporated into the embryonic white society of the Hudson's Bay Company and the other fur trade companies. Nkwala's descendants were integrationalists and many tended to marry whites. His own daughter married Cyprienne Laurent, a Frenchman. His son's daughter, Sophia (b. 1870), married a British officer, Captain (later Colonel) Houghton, in 1868 or 1869. Sophia's daughter Marie married a Spanish American War veteran named William Brent. There are many other examples (see also Teit 1930; Brent n.d.).

The three fur trade companies themselves encouraged marriage and cohabitation with Indian women, and it is difficult to speak of fur traders without also noting that a general process of integration was taking place between the two groups, although these relationships were seldom symmetrical. Even Nkwala, in spite of his genius for manipulating both sides, was drawn into the world of the Hudson's Bay Company, which also meant his incorporation into the British Empire, an association which has made its mark on Nkwala's descendants up to the present day. These people still believe the testimony of Marie Brent, Nkwala's granddaughter, who recorded that 'Chief Nicola got his big beautiful lakeside reserve from King George III ... [who] gave [him] medals to seal the treaty that gave the Indians this land for themselves, his children and their descendants.' The reserve referred to is, of course, the Okanagan Reserve No. 1 at the head of Lake Okanagan. 'Her Majesty, Queen Victoria, also gave [Nkwala] recognition and medals' (Brent n.d.).

The impact that the idea of the British royal establishment had on Nkwala, his descendants, and the rest of the Okanagan people should not be underestimated. Similar sentiments and beliefs were generated in other parts of Canada and the British colonial empire, where the symbol of royalty was used in many parallel contexts to help incorporate native people through their chiefs, paramount chiefs, kings, and other people of high office. Native headman and chiefs were often treated regally in the name of the British monarchy. They were lavished with gifts and favours in the name of the king, or the queen, and on special occasions, they witnessed the flamboyant ceremony and pageantry which impressed upon them the uniqueness of these white monarchs. Symbols of office, moreover, were often bestowed on them – special garments, medals, flags, insignia, staffs of office, and so forth – and they became entangled in complex emotional ties which provided the raison d'être for maintaining good relations with colonial institutions. In 1858, a year before his death, when the gold rush was in full swing and the fur trade had lost its economic dominance in the area, Nkwala's influence in the north, but particularly in the south, had waned considerably. For example, there was near war in the south between the Okanagan and white miners en route to the gold diggings in British Columbia. It was at this time that a man by the name of Joseph Tonasket came into his own by cleverly tricking the white men into submission and then effecting a truce with them. This action impressed Nkwala so much that he (with the approval of the southern Okanagan) is said to have created a 'captaincy' for Tonasket. Although often referred to as Chief Tonasket in the literature, Tonasket was given the title of 'Captain' implying what might be characterized as a war and vice chiefship. Tonasket, incidentally, was an orphan who had been taken into one of Nkwala's southern households as a child and eventually married one of Nkwala's daughters.

I mention Tonasket in this context to remind readers of the north-south divisions among the Okanagan. The 'seat of power' was at the Head of the Lake during Nkwala's time, but he had always to contend with the weakening of his ties in the southern groups. It is quite clear that his declining authority in the 1850s made it necessary for him to delegate power to Tonasket.[4] After Nkwala's death Tonasket styled himself chief. Furthermore, it must be remembered that the Okanagan controlled an enormous territory, which, if it were to have been effectively governed, would have required an elaborate political structure which they did not have. Tonasket's influence and power were derived largely from the skill and tact he had for keeping white ruffians

---

4 The question of Nkwala's attempt to claim jurisdiction over the whole of Okanagan territory and to rule it with the help of sub-chiefs and a captain, whom he appointed, has many interesting parallels in nineteenth-century southern Africa where chiefs opted for expansionist policies, albeit quite unrealistically. In the northwestern part of the Cape Colony and beyond its borders, for example, chiefs who had claimed power unilaterally often asserted that they were putting such and such territory under the control of men they themselves appointed to high office (cf Marais 1939; Carstens 1966).

in order. He also became obligated to the white miners through the gifts they bestowed on him to ensure their safe passage through Okanagan territory on their way to the north. Teit (1930: 271) writes: 'In this way Tōnā'sqEt gained considerable influence and came to be called chief, but he was really no chief, although later the American Okanagan recognized him as such to some extent. Tōnā'sqEt himself, after Nicolas's death, claimed to be head chief of the Okanagon who lived on the American side of the line.'

Nkwala died in the late fall of 1859 at Grande Prairie at the age of sixty-six (Balf 1985)[5] 'on his way to Kamloops for a conference with the Hudson's Bay men.' His body is said to have been taken to Kamloops for burial at the Fort. It was exhumed in the spring 'and carried on horses to Nkamaplex [sic] (head of Okanogan Lake), where he was finally buried with his medals' (Brent n.d.). In 1959 a tombstone (see Plate 10) was placed on his grave to mark the hundredth anniversary of his death in the name of the 'Okanagan Indian Rights Defence League' bearing the inscription:

NO. 1 OKANAGAN

In loving Memory of
INQUALA

The Great Chief of the Indian Tribe of the Okanagans,
who was living and Ruling in 1838

Nkwala's claim to the paramount chiefship of all the Okanagan was largely a position bestowed on him by the whites and the colonial establishment of the time. The handsome granite monument was erected members of the Head of the Lake band during a period when Indian rights and pan-Indianism in Canada were being seriously discussed for the first time in this community. But Nkwala's monument tended also to reflect local loyalty to the descendants of those people whose reserve was said by Marie Brent to have been given to them by King George III, which is an interesting anachronism in itself.

MISSIONARIES

Religious beliefs and practices tend to have their own momentum, and unlike

---

5 There are some discrepancies over the exact date of Nkwala's death in the literature. Mary Balf's 1859 is accepted here.

trade goods can spread quite quickly through interaction with other peoples who have been exposed to alien systems of religious thought. Thus, some Indians imbibed the rudimentary notions of Christianity without any formal instruction from the traders themselves. Chief Nkwala is a very good example, as were the many other Indians who came in contact with Christianity through their association with Hudson's Bay Company staff and men, many of whom were French Canadian Catholics. There were also a number of Catholic Iroquois among them (Fisher 1977: 123).

Although both Roman Catholic and Protestant missionaries had been active on the coast since the early part of the nineteenth century, the first priest to visit the Okanagan people in the valley was probably Father Demers who travelled up the Okanagan River into British Columbia in 1839 'preaching, baptizing and giving instructions by means of a pictograph device.' In 1842 he made a second journey over the same route. He travelled with the Hudson's Bay Company supply caravan visiting Okanagan, Shuswap, and Carrier Indians (Ormsby 1931: 21; Morice 1904: 224). It is highly significant that the first formal missionary expedition among the Okanagan was identified with the Hudson's Bay Company.

Ross (1960: 59–61) has shown that the first missionary to sojourn among the Okanagan at the Head of the Lake was Father John Nobili, an Italian Jesuit, who founded the St Joseph's Mission in August 1846 at what is now called Bradley Creek. The mission station took about three months to build and consisted of a residence 'painted white' for the priest, a small chapel, and a garden with a forty-foot cedar cross at the entrance. The cemetery associated with the mission is still visible although I was not able to locate the foundations of either the chapel or the priest's residence. Gabriel (1958) argues that another Jesuit, Pierre de Smet, worked among the Okanagan between 1841 and 1844, but he was essentially an itinerant bush priest who worked largely among the Kutenai people to the east.

St Joseph's Mission was abandoned after two or three years because the Jesuits could not staff it. But it is also possible that they had difficulty in mediating between the two main village communities, one to the north, the other to the south of the mission. Oral tradition has it that the Jesuits introduced the first cattle to the area, in addition to gardening. The way for Roman Catholic teaching had therefore been paved by the Jesuits when three priests of the Oblates of Mary Immaculate arrived some years later to establish a mission near present-day Kelowna at L'Anse au Sable. The log mission buildings were constructed in 1859 and Okanagan Mission was founded by Father Charles Marie Pandosy with the assistance of Father Pierce Richard and Brother Richard Surel. Pandosy had been an ally of Indians south of the

American boundary and had worked among the Yakima from 1848 to 1855. He had been ordered to abandon his work during the three-year 'war' between American troops and the Cayuse Indians on the grounds of assumed complicity with the Indians (Ormsby 1931: 22–3).

Father Pandosy's years in the Okanagan were quite different from his American experience. He never involved himself with the politics of the local native people, his main secular concern being the cultivation of the soil. In a letter written in October 1859 to a priest at Esquimalt he mentions the possibility of starting a vineyard the following year if he could get some vine cuttings. By 1863 the priests were producing one thousand bushels of wheat, two hundred bushels of barley, and two thousand bushels of potatoes. They also kept a few hogs and sheep and grew a little tobacco. Ormsby remarks that it is a just tribute to Pandosy to call him the 'father of settlement in the Okanagan Valley' on the grounds that it was he who induced the first settlers to take up land and start farming! She gives several examples of Pandosy's influence over settlers, but tells us virtually nothing of his work with the Okanagan people (Ormsby 1931: 23–7).

In 1862 another Roman Catholic missionary, Father Paul Durieu, settled for about a year near the present city of Vernon and ministered to the natives. His most important contribution was teaching the Okanagan to cultivate the soil and grow crops of potatoes and wheat. The name Priest's Valley was given to the present site of Vernon in his honour (Gabriel 1958: 20–1).

The Okanagan Mission continued until 1912 when it was closed down and the last relic of the Oblates disappeared. Ormsby sums up the chief role of the mission and its connection with both the fur trade and the beginning of agriculture. She writes: 'Their work in the Okanagan Valley was made possible by the fur-trader's contribution in exploring the country and providing it with means of communication with the outside world ... Thus it happened that a mission was established on Okanagan Lake, and that white [sic] people began to settle nearby. From that time also dates the beginning of agriculture in the Okanagan Valley' (Ormsby 1931: 27). The Okanagan at the Head of the Lake seem to have accepted Catholic Christianity somewhat reluctantly if one can generalize from the Oblate records. Their main objections related quite specifically to Oblate policy rather than the theology itself. Duane Thomson's original analysis of the documents shows how the Oblates involved themselves in a system of indirect rule based on the [Bishop] Durieu system. This system of socio-religious control involved a hierarchy of appointed Okanagan officials – 'a chief, a captain, one or more watchmen, policemen, and a variety of lesser figures' (Thomson 1985: 52).

Thomson's account of the Durieu system in the area generally shows how

it conflicted with the Canadian system as laid down by the Indian Act, implying that the Oblates would have preferred to have taken over full control of
the Indian reserves and turn them into Oblate utopian communities. But even
if the Oblates had got their way with the Canadian administrators their plans
would have been curbed by a shortage of priests. In general, the priests were
no more than itinerant missionaries who seldom spent more than a few weeks
a year in each village. Yet the Oblates did establish church councils 'over
which the priest reserved the right to preside, although the chief was the usual
presiding officer' (ibid.: 54). Councils, according to Thomson, were made up
of the chief plus the captain, the watchmen, and a treasurer.

The whole question of the relationship between church councils and band
councils needs further research. Here I will merely draw attention to the title
of 'captain' which appears later in the context of the band council. Many of the
functions of the church council seem, moreover, to have been taken over by
the band council in the Okanagan. The court system which dealt with civil,
moral, and criminal cases towards the end of the nineteenth century and into
the twentieth century clearly had its roots in the Durieu system.

After St Joseph's Mission was abandoned in 1850, there was no church
building until 1876 when St Benedict's was built 'on the reserve plus a large
house for the priest' (ibid.: 59). Whatever else may be said about lack of
Okanagan enthusiasm for the Oblates at the time the Indian Act was being
enforced, Christianity had already made its mark in Chief Nkwala's former
domain at the Head of the Lake.

The Oblates were also involved in the formal education of the Okanagan,
but the early schools were both élitist and exclusive, giving preference to the
children from 'the best families.' The schools in the 1860s seem to have been
for boys only and the pupils had to leave home to enjoy this privilege at the
Okanagan Mission, which lay a considerable distance from home to the south
(see Thomson 1985: 96–109).

The Oblates never seem to have been particularly enamoured with the
Okanagan in general and the Head of the Lake in particular. Father Lejeune
summed this attitude up very well in a letter dated 23 November 1893. He
writes: 'the Indians of the Head of the Lake...are still quite backward' (Oblate
Archives HPK 5111 B86c 2. 1893).

AN EVALUATION OF THE HEGEMONIC PROCESS

Okanagan society as a traditional independent socio-economic formation was
weakened during the first half of the nineteenth century by three different,
yet related phenomena. First, there was the fur trade, that powerful capitalist

machine set on the trapping of animals (generally with support from native peoples) for the sole purpose of exporting furs for maximum profit. Second, there were the gold miners who poured into the interior of British Columbia constituting thousands of individual fortune-seekers. Lastly, there were the missionaries bent on saving souls not only by drawing natives away from their traditional beliefs and value system into the Roman Catholic Christian community but also by encouraging them to alter their mode of subsistence.

The Okanagan themselves could not know that the fur trade would draw them into a world of different habits and ideology, that it would both influence and eventually transform their subsistence system, create food shortages and at times starvation, alter their political system and positions of their headmen, and involve them in a sort of unconscious compact with the British crown on the latter's terms. For the Okanagan and other native peoples it is grossly misleading to assert that 'the fur trade was not an economic enterprise developed in the Old World and imposed on the New' (Francis and Morantz 1983: 41). Of course, trading practices were shaped by the environment and by the culture of the peoples involved, but from the earliest days of the fur trade throughout Canada the process of native domination by the colonizers began in both blatant and subtle ways.

Regarding the gold miners and their operations, the Okanagan could not foresee the consequences and side-effects of digging and panning for gold. On the whole, they opposed the gold-mining enterprise, but they could not know what was involved in the changes in the economy with the introduction of saleable commodities, the commercialization of horses, and the growing cattle market. Nor could they know that the decline in gold mining would create a surplus of white people, many of whom would become, together with other settlers, candidates for the pre-emption of land. Although they had experienced conflicts with whites during the heyday of the fur era, the conflicts which grew out of the movement of miners and gold-mining operations created new problems which were exacerbated by interference with land holdings, village sites, fishing stations, cultivated areas and so forth.

In all the conflicts arising out of the gold rush, the attitudes of Okanagan chiefs such as Nkwala and Chelahitsa were characteristic of the duality that was developing among the Okanagan as they were hegemonically incorporated or co-opted into many white institutions. In portraying Nkwala as a double chief I have pointed, *inter alia*, to his own characteristics of duality and marginality: on the one hand, he was always ready to ingratiate himself with the whites; on the other hand, he preserved the 'Indianness' of his people. The synthesis of the dimensions of this paradox was to facilitate Okanagan incorporation as dependent people into a wider society and economy, a status that was formally delayed until the second half of the nineteenth century.

Although it was not the intention of the missionaries to prevent Okanagan admission into the Christian society identified with their work, local mission stations were never established among the native people themselves. This had the effect of widening the gulf between the Okanagan and the settlers and other newcomers in the region, who always had easier access to the services of the church and the priests who served in it than the natives themselves.

The question so often asked is: Why were the Okanagan drawn to any form of Christianity in the first place? That there were no theological or spiritual reasons is abundantly clear, nor does John Webster Grant's general hypothesis that the Indians turned to Christianity in times of social and cultural stress ring true for the Okanagan. But as Grant also points out, chiefs often found advantages in Christianity as they sought to consolidate their power. Among the Okanagan, association with the Oblates soon became a symbol of high status and power, a detail that is reflected both in the election and appointment of chiefs and in the rise of local political factions as these developed from the 1860s onwards. By 1876 missionaries, white administrators, and chiefs were all involved in a common system, as will be illustrated later, missionaries being, as Grant phrases it, 'at once emissaries of Christ and associates of Caesar' (Grant 1984: 242, 258). Thus, whatever the reasons for their conversion to Christianity, the process entailed parallel and commensurate political accommodation to white administrative authority as happened in many other parts of Canada, Africa, and Australia (cf Trigger 1989).

When we consider both the socio-economic and the psychological effects of the fur trade, gold rush, and missionaries on the Okanagan people, we begin to get a glimpse of the deep-rooted changes that were taking place in Okanagan society. This period, lasting roughly half a century from 1811 to the early 1860s, produced structural and cultural changes which could never be reversed. In addition, radical and overwhelming changes took place in the personalities of individual Okanagan, and in the conscience collective of their society itself. The crux of these less obvious changes was the perceptions that the people developed of themselves. Whether they wished to accept it or not, they fell under the hegemonic spell of the white man and his institutions. At first they wanted trade goods; then they wanted his powers; then they identified with the alleged wishes of the monarchy, first King George III and later Queen Victoria; they learned about the mysteries of Christianity which required considerable rejection of their traditional beliefs and values; they observed the unruly behaviour of mining hooligans; and learned the pleasure and pain of alcohol. In short, they began to experience a dual or bifurcated culture and developed social personalities to match. The conscience collective had two parts, an Indian part which they were learning to despise, and an unreal fantasy part, based on their observations and misunderstanding of the strangers who came from afar, like white giants, with ideas that reflected an inversion of the old world with which the Okanagan were still familiar.

I do not wish to give the impression of supporting in its entirety the 'fatal confrontation' hypothesis which asserts that all native peoples were irrevocably doomed by the simple fact of contact (Wilbur Jacobs 1971). Yet by the 1850s in Okanagan history the stage had been set, and the mental sets had been prepared, to receive the new eras which were to follow.

Chapter Three

Reserving Other People's Land

The importance of land as territory claimed by, and *belonging to*, specific native peoples is sometimes unwittingly downplayed in anthropological writing about so-called hunter-gatherers by the emphasis that is placed on the importance of subsistence activities such as hunting, gathering, fishing, and trapping, rather than on the economic value of land itself (for example, Hudson 1986; Lee 1979; Murdock 1967). The Okanagan were never casual occupiers of land and in their seasonal movements they relied entirely on the understanding that they were the sole owners of their land. Moreover, their attachment to land and their jealous concern for territory were manifest in their boundary disputes with their Shuswap neighbours. The very presence of fur traders, miners, and missionaries in Okanagan territory undermined that tradition if only as a general foreboding of what was to come.

After the Hudson's Bay Company's exclusive monopoly to trade west of the Rocky Mountains lapsed in 1858, the whole territory reverted to the direct administration of the British Colonial Office. At that time the mainland of British Columbia came into existence as a separate colony from Vancouver Island, but it was not until 1866 that the two merged to form one unit, the colony of British Columbia. The new colony entered Confederation in 1871 as the province of British Columbia.

The brief transitional colonial period in British Columbia lasted from 1858 to 1871. It involved the transference of the main external force exerted on the Okanagan from the Hudson's Bay Company to the colonial government and its administration. Whereas the former was preoccupied with furs, the latter was to become obsessed with its settlers and their interest in land. British Columbia, therefore, like so many other colonies, was involved with 'clearing the land,' as it were, in preparation for its immigrants. Clearing the land has two meanings. It implies ways of moving or resettling, and then dominating native people, as much as it suggests clearing bush and forest, and building towns, roads and railways. The main focus here is on moving and dominating native people in a colonial context. Before we turn to that context for the Okanagan, however, it is necessary to provide a short summary of British Columbia's land and Indian policy.

LAND POLICY AND NATIVE PEOPLES

In presenting this material I have drawn heavily on Robert Cail's masterful work, *Land, Man, and the Law* (1974), partly because of his thorough examination of data, and partly because his interpretation of those data is so much more enlightened than that of most other writers. It was Cail who appreciated the power and influence that social systems and institutions wield over individuals, and that 'land policy' and 'Indian policy' are, in the final analysis, based on institutional decisions and are not merely a function of personalities, good, bad, or indifferent.

When local Okanagan politicians nowadays look back to the colonial period in their history they regard it with ambivalence. There is a good side and a bad side, virtue being identified with Governor James Douglas, evil with Joseph Trutch who was appointed chief commissioner of lands and works in 1864, the year Douglas retired from office. This dual perception certainly has some foundation, but it does not mean that Douglas 'had an amazingly enlightened attitude towards native peoples' (Thomson 1978: 43) or that Douglas's reserve policy allowed Indians to select as much land as they wanted (Ware 1974: 4). Nor would I agree with Ware that Douglas's policy was dramatically reversed in 1864–5 by Joseph Trutch, or with Fisher (1971–2) that Trutch's stereotyping of Indians as lawless and violent was simply a reflection of his own background. Okanagan perception of their colonial past has undoubtedly been coloured by what people have read. More accurately, the oral tradition has been tainted by non-Indian opinion. Here I wish to argue that the colonial period produced its own policy at an institutional level, and that shifts in policy were largely determined by changes in social and economic forces. Both Douglas and Trutch, therefore, merely reflected trends in the status quo, and it is from this vantage point that they are relevant to our understanding of the land question, not as independent personalities.

Let me begin with James Douglas, the first governor of British Columbia (1858–64). Douglas's policy towards the Indians was essentially paternalistic and colonial. He regarded them as the special wards of the crown, partly because he had been instructed to do so by the Colonial Office, since such a policy was good business, and partly because he felt it to be in the interests of humanity (Cail 1974: 173). It is important to draw attention to the roots of paternalism, for it was destined to continue to the present day and constitutes a major facet of contemporary Canadian attitudes towards native people. If the fur trade initiated white hegemony, then the colonial period sowed the fertile seeds of paternalism. Douglas, it will be remembered, had been chief factor of the Hudson's Bay Company's base on Vancouver Island, and for a time had held two positions when he was first appointed governor. His policy should therefore be seen as straddling two periods of history.

On 12 August 1856 in his address to the first Legislative Assembly on Vancouver Island Douglas announced that he proposed to treat the Indians 'with justice and forbearance, and by rigidly protecting their civil and agrarian rights.' He also stressed the importance of maintaining friendship with the Indians for the good of the colony. Two years later in response to a dispatch from Sir Bulwer Lytton, the colonial secretary, Douglas enlarged on his policy. He foresaw the creation of reserves for the Indians where they would be protected from the encroachment of white settlers. Having Indians on reserves, moreover, would lessen the possibility of vindictive warfare against white settlements. Any land on these reserves not being utilized would be leased to the highest bidder, and the proceeds used for the exclusive benefit of the Indians. 'On the reserves each family was to have a distinct portion for its own use, but Indians were to be denied the power to sell or alienate the land.' Reserves were to include the Indians' cultivated land as well as their village sites (Cail 1974: 173–4).

Cail asserts that these general principles were more or less adhered to by the colonial government for the next twelve years (1859–71), remaining in effect at Confederation. However, he points out that in assigning reserves 'Douglas and his officials followed no consistent pattern other than that of including within a larger reserve, if possible, all Indian settlements, graveyards, gardens, hunting lodges, berry patches, or fishing stations, or of making one or all of them separate smaller reserves' (Cail 1974: 175). Although these details are relevant to the policy at a more general level, the crucial issue so astutely brought out by Cail is that in this whole matter, 'The only principle adopted was to placate the Indians and keep them out of the way of incoming settlers by granting each tribe a definite reservation of land' (ibid.).

Thus the colonial period in British Columbia and its preoccupation with opening up the land for settlers also marked the beginning of reserving land for Indians. In practice this meant that settlers could pre-empt land while

Indians could not, unless they had written permission from the lieutenant-governor-in-council (Cail 1974: 177–8, 201–8). Both peoples were at the mercy of the law, but the law was essentially different for each group. This difference is clearly reflected in terms of land allocations. Settlers could pre-empt 160 acres of land in single blocks. Indians, however, acquired whatever they were allotted in terms of the reserves that were parcelled out for them, but the rights of Indians to hold land were still undefined. For example, on 14 April 1861 it was reported that land had been pre-empted in the names of Father Richard (a missionary), J.C. Larame, W.G. Cox, Gideon Pion, and J.C. Haynes, a justice of the peace (see Ormsby 1931: 29). Of special significance with regard to the acquisition of land for farming purposes is that missionaries, ex-miners, and government officials were among the first to occupy the territory of the Okanagan people as pre-emptors recognized by the Colonial government. The names of Cox and Haynes stand out prominently since they of all people were soon to become involved in setting out reserves for the Okanagan.

In spite of Douglas's so-called intentions in his early years of office regarding the adequacy of Indian reserves, by 1864 the 'policy' was being administered in a different way. In a sense we might say it had been transformed, but in practice it was still the same colonial policy. If there is a difference it is the difference determined by settler pressure and demands. When Douglas addressed the newly elected first Legislative Council of British Columbia at New Westminster on 21 January 1864, he was able to state:

> The Native Tribes are quiet and well-disposed. The plan of forming Reserves of land embracing village sites, cultivated fields, and favorite places of resort of the several Tribes, and thus securing them against the encroachment of settlers, and forever removing the fertile cause of agrarian disturbance, has been productive of the happiest effects on the minds of the natives.
>
> The areas thus partially defined and set apart in no case exceed the proportion of *ten acres for each family* concerned, and are to be held as the joint and common property of the several tribes, being intended for their exclusive use and benefit, and especially as a provision for the aged, the helpless, and the infirm. (British Columbia Legislative Council 1864: 2; quoted by Cail 1974: 175; italics in original)

Douglas's address brings out very clearly the purpose of reserves. They were created to keep the natives quiet, to prevent settler encroachment and thereby avoid conflict, to assure the settlers that natives were being allotted no more than ten acres per *family*, and to create social refuge areas for old and infirm Indians. In short, British Columbian Indian reserve policy was a sort of liberal apartheid. What is especially significant is that no reserves of land were made by official notice in the *Gazette* until 1866, after Douglas had retired, and only half of the surveyed reserves were gazetted (Cail 1974: 176).

In evaluating these trends the personality of Douglas should not be considered relevant, and we should look to the wider socio-economic implications of colonial rule for insights. Even Cail makes the error of asserting that 'so long as Douglas was governor, the Indians had only to ask to receive additional land' (Cail 1974: 179). But colonial systems do not work that way, and by the time Douglas retired in 1864 more settlers were demanding land, and the Indians had to pay the price. As we have seen, Douglas himself announced shortly before his retirement that ten acres of land for each Indian family on a reserve was to be a maximum. This was itself a reduction, and subsequent reductions made by Douglas's successors were merely part of a general trend.

It is true that Joseph Trutch was no friend of the Indians, but was it not Douglas himself who recommended Trutch for the position of chief commissioner of lands and works? (See Fisher 1971–2.) Trutch should therefore be seen as the bureaucrat who fitted the needs of the colony and its settlers best from 1864 onwards. He put into practice what the settlers wanted and what the Indians did not fully understand at the time, or what the latter were often misled into accepting. But Indians were not slow, especially in the Okanagan, in learning the deceptive methods of the white man and his colonial government. Unfortunately for them, the forces of an external alien administration were always several jumps ahead of them. Like the fur traders, gold miners and missionaries, the colonial administrators had a clear idea of what they wanted to achieve in advance. In short, colonial Indian policy, as an external set of principles, took the Indians by surprise. 'Policy,' moreover, is essentially a dual phenomenon. It aims at achieving its end, but it also has the means for achieving that end. The Okanagan today with their strong sense of history see Trutch as the villain because he symbolizes the realization of the goal – reducing the size of the land that had already been reserved for Indians. He also symbolizes the decision-maker and coercer. Douglas, in contrast, is perceived as the Queen's representative who 'did good things for the Indian,' thereby demonstrating the subtle and smooth strategies of paternalism.

It matters little to sociological analysis that Douglas generally referred to the Indians as 'Native Indians' while Trutch usually called them 'savages.' In the long run they were both involved in the same socio-economic system. So well matched were they in the eyes and minds of the settlers and colonial establishment that when Trutch's turn for high office came in 1871 he was appointed as the first lieutenant-governor of the new Province of British Columbia when it joined Confederation.[1]

The colonial period in British Columbia generally centred on the problems of land involving complex and comprehensive legislation as far as both settlers and native people were concerned. The Okanagan had very definite ideas on their relationship to their aboriginal lands. They enjoyed a system of communal land ownership, and, in some contexts, concepts of individual land tenure had begun to exist together with their traditional notions of individual private property ownership. The reserve system was totally alien to them and was imposed on them by a variety of techniques, including promise of protection by the British crown through the Queen and her representatives. The foundation for the reception of these ideas by the Okanagan and other native peoples had been laid by the fur trading companies, as we have seen in the previous chapter. Now we must turn to see how colonial land policy and the creation of reserves operated in the 1860s.

THE HEAD OF THE LAKE

Ware (1974: 4–5) has asserted that Douglas's reserve policy generally allowed Indians to select as much land as they wanted! His reasoning is based on some of the false assumptions we have already discussed, but particularly on the fact that Douglas directed the chief commissioner of lands and works to mark out Indian reserves distinctly, and to mark them out 'as they may ... be pointed out by the natives themselves.' In practice this meant that Indians were asked to indicate what land they were using *at a particular time*, and it was reserved for them, often in a modified form. Such was one of the strategies used for depriving people of the bulk of their land.[2]

Land at the Head of the Lake was reserved for the first time on 1 June 1861 by W.G. Cox who had been recently appointed assistant commissioner of

1 Robin Fisher's 1971–2 paper on Trutch's involvement in British Columbian Indian land policy is an important work since it places Trutch in a broad context, and shows his relationship to Douglas and other political figures. Although I disagree with certain of his interpretations, this paper facilitated the formulation of my ideas presented here. There is a wealth of detail in the Colonial Correspondence relevant to the matters discussed here. See especially files 363–377 and 732–767B in the Provincial Archives of British Columbia. These can be located quite readily on microfilm reels B-1320 and B-1333 respectively.
2 In this section I have drawn heavily on Duane Thomson's 1978 paper dealing with the Okanagan reserves during the colonial period. Without Thomson's detailed research into the topic my task would have been far more difficult. See also Thomson's excellent 1985 PhD thesis, especially chapter 4.

lands and works. The raison d'être for laying out the reserve appears to have been an attempt to ward off conflict between miners and the Indians (Thomson 1978: 45). The reserve boundaries were said to have been determined by the Indians. In a letter to the chief commissioner of lands and works dated 17 June 1861 Cox wrote that 'the Indians appeared well satisfied, having selected the ground themselves and also named the extent desired by them.' Thomson comments: 'The Indians chose good bottomland, at the head of the lake, in the valley leading to the east arm of Okanagan Lake and in the valley around Swan Lake from the debouchment of the present BX Creek around the west side of the lake to include the rich flatlands to the north' (Thomson 1978: 45).

In a separate letter Cox included a sketch map of the Head of the Lake Reserve. The map indicated village sites, garden plots, the fishery, and the creek where gold deposits were reported by the Indians (Thomson 1978: 45–6, 1985: 116). These details are significant because they draw attention to changes in Okanagan society, especially their involvement in agriculture as indicated by the existence of garden lots, where they cultivated corn, potatoes, and tobacco. The Okanagan owned large herds of horses and possessed a good number of cattle (Manson 1859–62; Brent n.d.; Thomson 1978: 46).

It is true that this reserve was 'an excellent one' (Thomson 1978: 45), but it established a precedent in the area by restricting the locality of the community of Indians living at the Head of the Lake to a piece of *their own land allocated for their use by the colonial establishment of the British crown.* The reserve, excellent though it was in relative terms, included only one small segment of the land used and claimed by the people. It was, first of all, the late Chief Nkwala's headquarters, and there is no evidence that Nkwala's people had relinquished any of the adjoining land before his death in 1859. Second, much of their usual range land is not shown, nor the hunting grounds. Third, the large settlement at Six Mile Creek is not even included. And lastly, there is no sign of berry-picking land and so on.

This first 1861 reserve was a reserve in the strict sense of the word – a piece of Okanagan land set aside for Okanagan use by the colonial government. The conditions under which the land was reserved are not entirely clear, but Cox reports that he had a lengthy discussion with Chief Chelahitsa while he was waiting for instructions from Colonel Moody, then chief commissioner of lands and works, regarding the land he was to reserve (British Columbia 1875: 21; Thomson 1978: 45, 50). Chelahitsa was consulted by Cox because of his pro-settler tendencies. It is true that he was Nkwala's sister's son who had been adopted by Nkwala and, according to Teit (1930: 268), designated by the latter to succeed him. However, the 'appointment' was never accepted by the majority of the Head of the Lake people. Whatever the case, there is no record of proper negotiation with the Okanagan in the creation of this 1861 reserve.

To argue that the Okanagan were given larger and better reserves than other native peoples in British Columbia is irrelevant in this discourse. If they received 'nearly all the agricultural lands situated about the head of the lake,' and if the Head of the Lake Reserve included roughly one thousand acres of rich tillable land independent of grazing and timber land (Thomson 1978: 46), it was because these were already part of more extensive traditional lands. Similarly, if this reserve gave each family a little more than the notorious ten acres, the land reserved still constituted an unbelievable reduction in Okanagan land as it had been recognized in the past.

As Thomson correctly points out, the Okanagan valued the land for the same reasons that the intruding settlers did, and over the years they had become quite experienced stock-raisers with a knowledge of the importance of good pasturage, including winter range. I must, however, disagree with Thomson's confident assertion that 'the lands that they chose would have supported them had they been allowed to retain them.' The members of the Okanagan band *as a whole* had still to establish themselves as ranchers and agriculturalists, and in 1861 only certain families were involved in cattle ranching and farming and horse breeding. If the population of the Head of the Lake (excluding Six Mile Creek) was about 120, the reserve was still inadequate for their future needs. In short, Cox's 1861 reserve, although quite adequate for the immediate needs of the small ranching and farming élite, did not make provision for the future or for those Okanagan who were still involved in gathering and hunting. Provision does seem to have been made for those engaged in fishing, but it excluded all the Six Mile Creek people living to the southwest close to the lake.

Cox held the office of magistrate at this time, and as such represented the Queen through the colonial government in the Okanagan district. In April 1863 he was promoted to assistant gold commissioner for Cariboo West and replaced by John Carmichael Haynes. Haynes knew the area well, having begun as a police constable. He quickly worked his way up the local colonial hierarchy and soon found himself appointed a member of the Legislative Council for British Columbia in 1864. He served for two sessions in New Westminister where he heard complaints from potential settlers that 'the Indians held nearly all of the best land in the Okanagan' (Thomson 1978: 46–7).

By the time Haynes took over from Cox more settlers were eyeing Indian land in the Okanagan, and Haynes was given considerable responsibility: he collected border revenues and mining fees, gave information on climate,

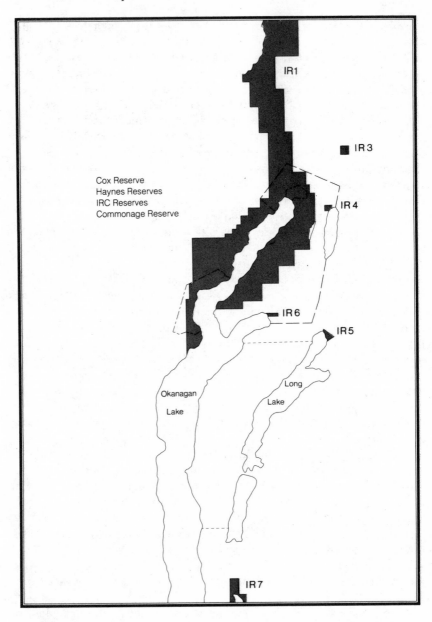

Okanagan reserves at the Head of the Lake showing the Cox Reserve (1861), the two Haynes Reserves (1865), and the approximate boundaries of reserves assigned by the Joint Indian Reserve Commission from 1876 onwards

immigration, and mineral discoveries, kept the peace, recorded pre-emptions, and dealt with Indians (ibid.: 47).

One of Haynes's tasks after taking over Cox's job was to investigate settler complaints in April 1865 that the Okanagan had had too much land reserved for them.[3] He travelled to the Head of the Lake (and other reserves) accompanied by 'Chief' Tonasket, a south Okanagan from the United States related by marriage to Nkwala. Tonasket had absolutely no authority to speak for the Head of the Lake people and had little interest in the northern branch of his ethnic group at that time. Haynes inspected all the Okanagan reserves and concluded that they were all 'much too large as the natives occupy land in several other places and remain on the reserves but for a short time in the year' (PABC file 741; Thomson 1978: 47).

Authority to reduce the size of the reserves was granted in 1865, with the proviso that such action did not produce too much dissatisfaction among the Indians. Haynes enlisted the help of Surveyor J. Turnbull, and together with Tonasket they proceeded to the Head of the Lake Reserve to carry out the task of reducing the reserve. Captain Houghton also accompanied them, being both a settler and married to Nkwala's granddaughter. It must have been an ominous group: two government officials and two relatives of Nkwala – all supporting wishes that were attributed to the British queen and speaking in her name. Thus the 1861 reserve was reduced, and Haynes informed the chief commissioner for lands and works that sections of the old reserve could now be listed in the *Gazette* as being available for pre-emption (PABC file 741). Turnbull prepared a map and forwarded it with his report. This map has been displaced but Duane Thomson (1978) ingeniously had it reconstructed and published it in his scholarly paper. He was then able to estimate that the *two* reserves replacing the 1861 reserve had a total acreage of only 1438 acres, not 2600 acres as Turnbull's estimate asserted. The Cox reserve of 1861 consisted of about one thousand acres of tillable land and about nine thousand acres of commonage (see PABC file 365 and Thomson 1985: 115–17).

The nature of these reductions of land in the Okanagan is very aptly summarized by Thomson:

> The lands of the Okanagan Indians had been reduced by the Queen's representative despite a previous agreement with an authorized magistrate acting under instructions from Governor Douglas. Haynes and the government that he

---

3 It is worth recording that the smallpox epidemic of 1862–3 had probably taken its toll at the Head of the Lake and reduced the population.

represented gave no thought to allowing the Indians to retain enough land to establish viable ranching operations. While white settlers began to acquire vast acreages the reserves were reduced drastically. No compensation was given and there was little perceived dissatisfaction, at least initially. (Thomson 1978: 48)

'Little perceived dissatisfaction' may have been reported initially, but repercussions and protest were soon to follow. Further, we should not underestimate the moral and psychological damage done to the people themselves as their homeland was tampered with. The new reserves would also revive the old rivalries between the two traditional village settlements at the Head of the Lake proper and Six Mile Creek to the south. Although the 1861 Cox reserve was decreased in size and some of the best land was cut off, recognition was given now for the first time to the Six Mile Creek people who constituted a separate but related village aggregate in the traditional sense. This is important because it confirms the Six Mile Creek people's oral history that they were never consulted by Cox, and that his decision was based entirely on representation from one segment of the Head of the Lake village cluster.

Thomson (1978: 49) attempts to determine the reasons why the Okanagan initially acquiesced to Haynes's reduction and modification of reserve boundaries at the Head of the Lake. Most of these are plausible enough. First, band organization was loose and there was no one effective vigorous chief. Chelahitsa was too preoccupied with his own reserve in the Nicola Valley, and Tonasket's loyalties were to the south across the American border. Second, the smallpox epidemic in 1862–3 had seriously affected the people and their group cohesion and morale, making them ill prepared to stand up to the colonial regime. Finally, was the view the Indians had of themselves 'as loyal allies under the protection of Queen Victoria.' Loyalty to the Queen was of crucial significance, as has already been alluded to. Thomson describes the coercive nature of this bond with the British crown: 'Haynes arrived with the full weight of the Queen's authority accompanied by two recently discharged imperial officers, Turnbull and Houghton ... It was undoubtedly difficult for [the Indians] to challenge Haynes' authority.'

Surveyor J. Turnbull helped to lay out the Haynes reserves of 1865, and his journal during this period provides an insight into the various problems at hand (British Columbia 1866: 11–35). Turnbull must have had some personal interests in surveying the area, since at this time he was not officially in the employ of the colonial government, and his authority to carry out the survey is not entirely clear.

From Turnbull's journal we learn that the Okanagan Indians who worked for him were 'unreliable' because they changed their minds so often and refused to continue with their contracts as couriers for Turnbull and his team; that the Okanagan were partly involved in the money economy at that time; and that Turnbull paid his men $2 a day for carrying equipment. On certain occasions, however, he was obliged to pay 'a most exorbitant price' in kind, that is, half of his own possessions. And once he found himself, after considerable negotiation, paying four bearers $2.50 each a day, plus presents for their wives amounting to fifty pounds of flour and some bacon!

Turnbull always asserted himself in typical colonial style, sending Indians off to look for a horse that had strayed and expecting them to carry extra baggage because one man had quit his job or to handle a canoe in difficult rapids. But he did not always get his own way because, as he complains, so many of his Okanagan servants refused to knuckle under, demanding their wages or equivalent in kind, and expecting to be paid immediately.

The journal also reveals the process whereby Haynes reduced the Cox reserve. Turnbull writes that he accompanied Haynes and Captain Houghton to the arm at the north end of Lake Okanagan where Haynes tried to palm off fifteen hundred acres on the Indians. But the Indians were very discontented with the locality, and the next day, 26 November 1865, Haynes ended up giving up the idea of reserving the arm, indicating that the Indians still had some power over the officers of the Queen at that time.

Thus, after his failure to negotiate, Haynes accepted the Okanagan's wish for land at the Head of the Lake and also the area now known as Six Mile Creek. On the third day, 27 November 1865, he laid out the reserve at the Head of the Lake, and on the following day he surveyed the second reserve (Six Mile Creek).

CONCLUSION

The establishment of the Haynes reserves in 1865 went a step further than the creation of the Cox reserve in 1861. Quite apart from its moral, sociological, and psychological effects, it deprived the Okanagan as a whole of land necessary for establishing large-scale ranching operations. From the point of view of the settlers, it released the bottom land necessary for the development of several pioneer ranches in the Head of the Lake area. In short, we might conclude that by 1865 the colonial establishment had quite unselfconsciously begun to yield to settlers' requests and their demands at the expense of the Okanagan. We may attribute this trend to the increase in the number of settlers in the area as well as to the growth of settler power and influence. It is related also to the routinization of colonial policy and the entrenchment of colonial values in British Columbia – the affirmation of the social and economic dichotomy that would become entrenched between Indians and settlers in the future.

Turnbull's journal is especially interesting because it brings out something of the Indians' disposition to the white man's regime and their willingness to negotiate. But most of all it demonstrates that the Okanagan were beginning to have similar aspirations to those of the white settlers with regards to ranching and agriculture. The Okanagan seemed to understand what their rights were although they were not able to withstand all the external forces that were operating on them. The brief colonial period, from 1858 to 1871, incorporated the Okanagan more and more into a wider system of socio-economic relations. Land and the control of land were the key issues for both the Okanagan and the settlers. As a result the Okanagan had parts of their own land reserved for them, a process which grew out of colonial paternalism and its concomitants – subversive trickery to destroy traditional rights and values, and embryonic coercion.

In the next chapter we will look at some of the settlers who pre-empted Okanagan land during the colonial period, and trace the way in which they established themselves later on. Settler interaction with the Okanagan also throws light on the impropriety and illegality of Haynes's reduction of the reserve at the Head of the Lake.

Chapter Four

The O'Keefe Syndrome

There is a close relationship throughout British Columbia, especially in the southern interior, between the establishment of reserves for Indians and the acquisition of land by settlers.[1] The same could also be said of reserves elsewhere in Canada, the United States, and other colonial countries such as South Africa. The Indian Act defines a reserve as a tract or tracts of land that have been set apart by Her Majesty for the use and benefit of a band. The key words here are, of course, 'set apart' because they imply the unequal power of the Indians and those who set tracts of land apart for them. Both the location and physical shape of reserves reflect this asymmetrical position of Indians in relation to settlers. Reserves in many parts of British Columbia were not carved out of the countryside; rather they consisted of residues of land that remained after pre-emptions and purchases by the settlers had been made, and after crown land had been established. Perhaps a more accurate depiction can be given in the language of theoretical ecology. Reserves stand in a subordi-

---

1 The research on which this chapter is based, and the spirit in which it has been written, were inspired by the work of Robert Cail. Much of the detail regarding settler appropriation of Okanagan land is drawn from correspondence and notes of the Joint Reserve Commission. These documents are in the National Archives of Canada (see bibliography). Additional information on the O'Keefe and Greenhow families was also culled from *A History of the O'Keefe Ranch, 1867–1978* (O'Keefe 1978) and from Okanagan and settler oral traditions. I also used *The History of the O'Keefe Ranch* by Stan McLean (1984) because it presents settler history entirely from a white perspective, which I found intriguing because the author is quite oblivious to the existence of the native people. Another important source was the personal communications from Ken Mather, curator of the O'Keefe Ranch Archives.

nate symbiotic relationship to the outside world, and their sizes and shapes have been determined by external forces largely through a process of invasion by settlers and newcomers.

The Okanagan never relinquished their land and signed no treaty, so here we are concerned mainly with the process of invasion by settlers in the Okanagan Valley. The presence of settlers and their demands were often the key factors in exacting the size, shape, and character of the Okanagan reserves, although it must be noted that government policy dictated impressionistic rules as to the number of acres each Indian required to live, however small these allowances might have been.

During the colonial period, then, the administration of Indians in British Columbia revolved almost entirely round the question of land and the tensions that stemmed from it. Both Indians and settlers had grievances. Indian grievances related to radical loss of land, settler grievances to their demands for more extensive and better land. Okanagan reactions to land reductions, notably the Haynes reserves, soon became evident once they began to challenge the rights of the white settlers who had intruded on their land.

When British Columbia joined Confederation in 1871, Indian affairs came, by and large, under federal jurisdiction. Part of clause 13 of the Terms of Union of 1871 states:

> The charge of the Indians and the trusteeship and management of the land reserved for their use and benefit shall be assumed by the Dominion Government, and a policy as liberal as that hitherto pursued by the British Columbia Government shall be continued by the Dominion Government after Union.
>
> To carry out such a policy, tracts of land of such extent as it has hitherto been the practice of the British Columbia Government to appropriate for that purpose, shall from time to time be conveyed by the Local Government to the Dominion Government in trust for the use and benefit of the Indians, on application of the Dominions Government; and in case of disagreement between the two Governments respecting the quantity of such tracts of land to be so granted, the matter shall be referred to the decision of the Secretary of State for the Colonies.

There is a certain irony in clause 13, since it assumes that the province of British Columbia had a liberal Indian policy which the dominion should follow. There is also the assumption that bona fide reserves had been established for native people in the province. In point of fact, provincial policy, in so far as one existed, was certainly not liberal, nor had appropriate reserves been set out, nor was there any generally accepted policy as to the amount or principles of compensation (Hawthorn et al. 1958: 52). Indians, moreover, had been excluded from all discussions relating to Confederation, and were given no role in government after 1871. In 1872 and 1875 legislation was passed which specifically excluded Indians from voting on the grounds of race (Fisher 1977: 178).

Matters did not go smoothly for any of the parties concerned, although several Indian groups had hoped that they would get a better deal after Confederation (ibid.: 175). They were soon disillusioned, and were driven to organize several incipient resistance movements which in turn threatened settler security. Many missionaries in the province, now also disillusioned with the way Indians were being treated, kept them informed of political events, much to the disapproval of the settlers.

In an attempt to control the Indians in the province, the federal government entrusted two men with the responsibility of administering Indian affairs. Dr I.W. Powell became Indian superintendent in 1872, and James Lenihan was appointed second superintendent in 1874. Lenihan was based in New Westminster and was responsible for the interior people including the Okanagan. Neither Powell nor Lenihan had any experience of Indian matters, and the latter's sole qualification seems to have been his Toronto business experience (ibid.: 180–1).

In 1875 the provincial and federal governments reached a dubious agreement by means of which a solution to the Indian land question could be found, and three joint commissioners were appointed. A.C. Anderson, an old Hudson's Bay Company man, represented the dominion. Another ex-company man, Archibald McKinlay, represented British Columbia. The third member was Gilbert Sproat, 'the pivotal and most energetic member of the joint commission' (ibid.: 189), and a prolific writer of reports.

The provincial government was never sympathetic to the joint commission, and from the beginning undermined its task, especially in the interior where the Okanagan and other native peoples were experiencing difficulties with settler pre-emptions and illegal occupation of land. It is to this issue that we now turn, focusing primarily on settler presence and their entrepreneurial expectations.

CORNELIUS O'KEEFE

The case of settler and pre-empter Cornelius O'Keefe can be used to illustrate the many facets of relations between settlers and Okanagan. O'Keefe's socio-economic profile is especially instructive. He had family ties with the

Okanagan band at the Head of the Lake; he pre-empted land, purchased land, intruded on Indian land, became a wealthy rancher, farmer, and businessman on whom many Okanagan people were later obliged to depend; and he became both hero and impertinent anarchist in the eyes of other settlers and government officials. O'Keefe made false moves and illegal moves, but he emerged triumphant, well off, and successful. Today his former ranch is recognized by the province as a historical monument and stands as a testament to his character and his social and economic status – admired by whites, treated with ambivalence or indifference by the Okanagan.

Cornelius O'Keefe was born in 1837 in the pioneer settlement of Fallowfield, now a suburb of Ottawa. His father, Michael O'Keefe, was a farmer of Irish stock, and his mother, Esther Demers, was a French Canadian. Cornelius is said to have been restless and ambitious as a young man, and he left home at the age of twenty-four to explore the West, especially the Cariboo goldfields. He travelled via New York by sea to Panama, crossed the isthmus by railway, and then by sea again to Victoria via San Francisco. He arrived at the Cariboo later in the year (1861). Like so many others, he was an unsuccessful miner, but he remained in the Cariboo for five years and managed to save $3000 from his earnings in a variety of entrepreneurial pursuits. He was involved in freighting supplies to the area, and worked on the road between Clinton and Bridge Creek. He was probably employed in the construction of the 151 Mile Stopping House on the Cariboo Wagon Road where he may have made extra money selling food to the miners (Ken Mather, personal communication).

In the spring of 1866, while on his way to Oregon to buy cattle, he met another settler named Thomas Wood. Wood was the son of an Anglican clergyman and a Newfoundlander, who had also failed to make his fortune in gold but had earned some money 'hauling freight on the Cariboo Road between Lytton and the mouth of the Quesnel River' (McLean 1984: 24–5). Wood travelled to California in 1865 with his savings to buy cattle to drive to the mines in British Columbia. On his return he and O'Keefe met.

O'Keefe and Wood combined their efforts and their business skills to become successful cattle runners. The following year they met Thomas Greenhow, another settler, who joined them in the cattle business, and the three men journeyed to Oregon together. The route followed in these cattle-running expeditions was the Old Brigade Trail on the west side of Okanagan Lake. They reached the Head of the Lake in June 1867, and decided to pitch their tents and remain there. The Cariboo market was now virtually non-existent, but they continued to supply the valuable Kootenay gold-fields, their main market into the 1870s (Ken Mather, personal communication).

The decision by O'Keefe, Wood, and Greenhow to remain at the Head of the Lake and occupy Okanagan Indian territory is a crucial event in Okanagan history. It marked the beginning of settler control of land and its resources, and the growth of settler wealth. The settlers fattened their cattle on the lush bunch grass of the Okanagan Valley and enjoyed the abundance of water and wild hay; and 'there were plenty of prairie chickens, grouse, deer and fish. There were no game laws, nor any fences. All their wishes seemed to have been fulfilled' (McLean 1984: 27).

The fact that the colonial reserve established by Haynes in 1865 was already in existence made the usurpation of Indian land easy for the settlers, and they immediately purchased breeding stock to improve their herds (O'Keefe 1978). It was not until 1868, however, that O'Keefe and Greenhow acquired land by pre-emption in accordance with the Land Ordinance of 1860 (Ormsby 1931: 171). In terms of the ordinance each would have been entitled to an initial holding of 160 acres of unsurveyed agricultural land (Cail 1974: 12–13).

Wood and O'Keefe remained partners in cattle raising and general farming until 1871 when Wood sold his interest to Thomas Greenhow. The Wood (Greenhow) property consisted of 160 acres near Irish Creek, roughly where the Okanagan band office stands today. There is some suggestion that Greenhow acquired other land from Wood (see Gabriel 1958: 23).

Thomas Wood moved south to what was to be known as Wood Lake and became a prosperous rancher after obtaining '3800 acres of land extending from the south end of Woods Lake to Long Lake' (Ormsby 1931: 47). O'Keefe went on to buy 480 acres at the Head of the Lake in October 1871 and another 162 acres in March 1872 for a total price of $642 – in other words, one dollar per acre (Cail 1974: 31). He also seems to have bought 'about 700 acres of the Houghton estate' which originally belonged to the Vernon brothers (Gabriel 1958: 23).

O'Keefe and Greenhow remained in partnership until Greenhow's death in 1889, and his widow continued the business association. In this connection it is relevant to point out that Thomas Greenhow had married O'Keefe's niece, probably in 1878. O'Keefe continued to be the senior partner, a position he had always held.

Cornelius O'Keefe's domestic life at the Head of the Lake began in the late 1860s when he invited an Okanagan Indian woman named Rosie to live with him in his log house. Rosie enjoyed the status of common law wife, and bore O'Keefe two children, a son and a daughter. She was a good homemaker, an excellent seamstress, and had a thorough knowledge of native medicine (Van Kirk 1980). Written records of this new family were lost in a fire, but the main details of the relationship are well remembered by the Okanagan themselves, and said to be acknowledged by certain members of the O'Keefe family. Several of my Okanagan friends insist that it was a bona fide marriage: 'You go and look in the Catholic church records and you will find it [the marriage certificate] right there.'[2]

As O'Keefe's finances and social standing improved, he sought what the Okanagan regarded as a second wife. This time he looked farther afield, to his birthplace in the Ottawa Valley. His choice was Mary Ann McKenna who, like O'Keefe, was descended from Irish settler stock. The marriage took place in 1877, creating an interesting domestic arrangement which now included the new bride, Rosie, and the two children in a compound family. Rosie O'Keefe apparently cooked for the newlyweds for a while before returning to her family at the Head of the Lake, where she lived until her death in 1910 (O'Keefe 1978: 12–14; oral tradition). Settler oral tradition holds that Mary first heard about Rosie when O'Keefe's Okanagan son purchased goods at the trading store one day and said, 'Charge them to my dad.'

Mary gave birth to nine children between 1879 and 1893, and the O'Keefe business enterprise continued to expand and flourish as the size of the cattle herds and the fields of grain increased. In 1891 O'Keefe threshed 575 tons of wheat from 565 acres; in 1898 he purchased a spectacular labour-saving threshing machine, and by 1899 O'Keefe and another farmer, C.J. Tronson, were reported to be shipping large numbers of cattle and making enormous profits. In addition to farming, O'Keefe became the first postmaster in the Okanagan in 1872, a position he held for forty years. The O'Keefe ranch also had a general store which supplied many Okanagan with groceries and other goods. O'Keefe, with donations from over fifty settlers in the valley, built a church named St Anne's as a monument to his little empire.[3] 'At one time [O'Keefe and Greenhow] also had a liquor licence and kept a stopping-place and store. Later their partnership was dissolved and both became general

---

2 I was unable to gain access to the relevant Catholic church records, and there is no mention of Rosie or her brother in Father J.M. Baudre's count made of '[Les] Sauvages de la Tête du Lac' in 1877, which supports the detail that Rosie remained with the family after O'Keefe's first marriage. The baptismal records of the diocese of Kamloops for 8 August 1900 refer to the marriage of Isaac Harris, a band member, to Cornelius O'Keefe's Indian daughter (personal communication, Ken Mather). O'Keefe was not the only settler to establish ties of blood and kinship with the Okanagan people. For example, there are many references in the oral tradition to Thomas Greenhow's 'unofficial' Indian family on the reserve.

3 Father Carion of the Oblates did all the painting and the church was consecrated on 25 December 1889. The Oblate correspondence about this church mentions that it was 'pour les blancs,' showing a conscious separation of the Okanagan from the white settlers (Ken Mather, personal communication).

merchants' (Ormsby 1931: 145). In the 1890s the O'Keefes and Greenhows built new houses which they expanded from time to time, illustrating how prosperous they had become.

Mary died of a stroke in 1899 at the age of forty-nine, and Cornelius once again turned to Fallowfield to look for an appropriate replacement. Within a year he had married Elizabeth Tierney, aged twenty-three. O'Keefe was then sixty-two. His new bride came from a wealthy Irish immigrant family and is said to have been a pampered young lady with expensive tastes and an artistic bent. But she proved to be a gracious hostess to new settlers in the district with the help of her white settler servants and the Okanagan women who did the washing and cleaning. Elizabeth's six children were all born between 1901 and 1913.

These were affluent times for the O'Keefes. By 1907 Cornelius had acquired an enormous acreage of agricultural land and was able to sell 5700 acres for $184,193 to a syndicate of Belgian capitalists. He continued to raise cattle and grow grain, but he now turned to construction in Vernon and Kamloops to compensate for the decline in their market value. However, by the time of his death in 1919, he had incurred serious debts, largely as a result of the decline in the real estate market during the First World War. But the O'Keefes had lived well by any standard and enjoyed the luxury of a large appropriately furnished home.

O'Keefe the entrepreneur, the land expropriater, and the foreign culture agent embodied for the Okanagan Indians the character of the British empire and the British crown of those days. If there are few overt conscious feelings of hostility towards O'Keefe today, it is because he provides the model of success to which many Indians have aspired for over one hundred years. O'Keefe, for his part, cultivated appropriate contacts in high office in Canadian society. For example, the first lieutenant-governor of British Columbia, J.W. Trutch, was his hunting guest in the early 1870s. And in 1882 the Marquis of Lorne spent four days at the ranch while he was governor general of Canada. O'Keefe, despite his Roman Catholicism, always had good connections with the largely Protestant establishment which, together with his success, impressed the Okanagan, whose anglophilia has already been noted. It must also be remembered that O'Keefe was regarded as a relative by 'marriage' by many Indians at the Head of the Lake through Rosie and her children. He may have been irresponsible but he was, after all, one of the family, although he was never admitted to membership.

Both Cornelius O'Keefe and his trading partner, Thomas Greenhow, obtained Okanagan land against the wishes of the Indians. Moreover, it was often obtained illegally according to the opinions of the joint commissioners who carried out an investigation of the land question at the Head of the Lake in 1877. What is of special interest is the manner in which these two settlers almost always got their own way even when it was contrary to Indian customary law and the laws of both the province and the dominion of Canada. Occasionally their behaviour was challenged, but it usually took years before action against them was contemplated, illustrating how the new legal system always worked against Indians. It also demonstrates how much power settlers were able to generate right from the start to further their economic and political interests.

Okanagan power was consequently defused by the system imposed on them through the incipient administration of the Indian Act, and the confusion generated by contradictory principles of authority. Here I have in mind the conflicts and misunderstandings created by the difference between British Columbian and dominion attitudes, and the contempt with which the joint commissioners were held by the settlers because they dealt with Indian interests. Another facet of governmental power relating to the joint commission also looms large: namely, its multiplex function to keep the Indians happy so as to prevent open confrontation, thereby weakening the Indians' control over their own destiny and defusing the threat to the settlers who had intruded into their territory. In this connection it should also be remembered that Okanagan territory, in the shape of reserves, had been defined for them by government decree through the services of the commissioners themselves. This contradiction between the perception of the joint commission as an institution designed to help the Indians and its pro-settler function was never resolved and led eventually to the commission's demise.

The brief colonial period from 1858 to 1871 prepared the way for the new entrepreneurial class of which O'Keefe is an example, destroying the political effectiveness of the Okanagan and reducing the size of their land. From an economic perspective the transformation from hunting, fishing, and gathering to stock raising, agriculture, and horse breeding was seriously curbed. The influence of the colonial period and its ramifications continued long after 1871, and never lost its momentum. The unequal balance of power between Indians and settlers turned out to be permanent in three arenas – political, economic, and territorial. To the hegemony of the fur trade was now added the bureaucratic power of the colonial period. The Joint Indian Reserve Commission must be seen diasynchronically as a function of that past.

SETTLERS, LAND, AND RESERVES

We have seen how the Haynes reserves, from the perspective of the settlers, opened up new lands and encouraged settler pre-emption in accordance with the Land Ordinance of 1860. Haynes's action, therefore, must be seen as the final cause of settler land-grabbing at the Head of the Lake and elsewhere, but it must also be seen in its colonial context. Thus Cox, who was the first official to proclaim a reserve for the Okanagan in 1861, was ordered by Governor Douglas in the following year to stake out an area ten miles square as a government reserve at the head of Lake Okanagan (Ormsby 1931: 142) just in case the land was needed for a town site or for pre-emption. Another interpretation is that Douglas intended the government reserve to be set aside for the Okanagan.

The earliest award of land to a settler in the northern Okanagan seems to have been made in 1863 to Captain Houghton by virtue of the military ordinance of 1861 granting retired officers free land. In 1866 the two Vernon brothers each pre-empted 160 acres, and on the same day one of the brothers applied to purchase an additional 160 acres. On 1 September 1867 Luc Girouard, a French Canadian who had arrived in the valley in 1860, registered a pre-emption in the same area, Priest's Valley, which was later to be called Vernon (Ormsby 1931: 142–4).

Although all these early pre-emptions were made on what was technically aboriginal territory, it was not until 1867 and 1868 that blatant pre-emptions occurred, which affected Indians at the Head of the Lake immediately. It was therefore with the arrival of Cornelius O'Keefe, Thomas Wood, Thomas Greenhow, and William Coulter at the Head of the Lake that the Okanagan had to face the reality that they were actually in competition with the settlers. Each of these settlers occupied land in 1867 (perhaps a year earlier). Wood chose 160 acres near Irish Creek, in the vicinity of the present band office. O'Keefe's first pre-emption was about half a mile north of the present O'Keefe ranch buildings, and Greenhow's immediately to the north of that. William Coulter's pre-emption (Coulter died shortly after his arrival) was also in the same vicinity. Coulter, O'Keefe, and Greenhow all registered their pre-emptions on 25 July 1868. Wood obtained a certificate of improvement for his land on 19 July 1870 and later sold the land to Greenhow on 10 August 1870 (NAC, RG 10, vol. 3612, file 3756-13). Wood then left to take up his extensive newly acquired land in the vicinity of the lake which later took his name.

Captain Houghton obtained the rest of his military grant in June 1872 when he took possession of a crown grant for Lot 25, Osoyoos District of Yale Division, naming it the Coldstream Ranch. It lay between the buildings of the present Coldstream Ranch and Long Lake (Ormsby 1931: 144–5), in the heart of Okanagan territory, and there must have been Indian opposition which was not recorded, though the protests may have been weak, because of the reduction of the population in the smallpox epidemic of 1862–3. But Houghton, it must be remembered, was married to Chief Nkwala's grand-daughter, which would have made some Okanagan more tolerant of his presence.

When the joint reserve commissioners arrived at the Head of the Lake in 1877 to settle the Indian protests and unrest that had their roots in the colonial period, it was to the land holdings of O'Keefe and Greenhow that their attention was immediately directed. Although neither occupied land 'awarded' to the Indians by Haynes, Indian protest was nevertheless powerful and militant, demonstrating that the Haynes reserves had never been accepted, or if they had been, only under protest or duress. The commissioners found that '2560 acres [were] claimed by these 2 gentlemen [O'Keefe and Greenhow], and for which they show some kind of papers' (NAC, RG 10, vol. 3612, file 3756-13).

I accept without question contemporary Okanagan Indian opinion that, in terms of aboriginal rights or traditional entitlement to land, *all* of these pre-empters and other settlers, from O'Keefe and Greenhow to Houghton and the Vernon brothers, owned their land unconstitutionally. Here I want merely to examine the articulation of views and attitudes between the Indians and the commissioners in the year 1877.

By 1877 O'Keefe and Greenhow had acquired at least 2522 acres[4] of land between them – an average of about 1261 acres each. The Okanagan living at the Head of the Lake at that time according to the commissioners included seventy-five men (heads of households) who had had their lands reduced by Haynes in 1865 to a total of 1438 acres (Thomson 1978: 48). This suggests that each Okanagan family or household had an average of only 19.17 acres of land at its disposal. According to the commissioners, each of these seventy-five adult men had less than ten acres of 'really cultivatable land.' They did enjoy 'pastoral rights, in common with white settlers, over unoccupied Crown lands, but had no actual pastoral reserves' (NAC, RG 10, vol. 3612, file 3756-22). Thus two settlers held an average of 1261 acres each, while seventy-five Okanagan Indian men and their families held an average of just over nineteen acres each.

---

4 Ken Mather, who is in the process of extensive research into the lives of O'Keefe and other settlers, disagrees with some of my findings, asserting that this figure should be 'more like 1920 acres' (personal communication). This discrepancy seems to lie in the fact that my figures are derived from Sproat's 1877 notes for the joint commission, while Mather derives his data from the land registers for British Columbia.

Commissioner Sproat, after settling some of the problems emerging from these inequities, wrote to the superintendent in Ottawa:

In advising you that the Commissioners have settled the Land Reserves for the Okanagan Indians living at the head of the Lake of that name, I beg leave to say that this place has been one of the most difficult places in which we have carried out our work. I found that the Indians were much dissatisfied, and that they had reasons for being so. Their reserves were insufficient, and they have been waiting for many years for an adjustment and have seen white settlers obtaining possession of adjacent lands which the Indians wished to get and considered were necessary for their comfort and welfare.

Indian objection was both general and specific. They found that land which they had always regarded as their own when they needed it was now controlled by the crown or settlers. But there were two specific objections which caught the eyes of the commissioners. The first was the 160-acre pre-emption that Greenhow had purchased from Wood in 1870 – the land at the Head of the Lake at Irish Creek. The second was O'Keefe's 1873 pre-emption of 320 acres at Meadow Creek at the northeast corner of the lake.

The initial reaction of the chairman of the commission, Gilbert Sproat, to both Greenhow's and O'Keefe's pre-emptions in general is interesting. Sproat's inclination was to rule that, in terms of current legislation, each successive pre-emption invalidated the previous pre-emption and that neither Greenhow nor O'Keefe should be allowed to continue to increase their land holdings the way they had been doing. Sproat writes in his notes of 1877: '[A]ll the acts distinctly forbid any person from holding two pre-emptions, and only enable a second pre-emption to be taken up when a settler has ceased to be a pre-emptor by abandoning, selling, or getting a Crown Grant for his first one.' Sproat concluded that O'Keefe and Greenhow did not fully acquire title to the portions of their lands held by pre-emption. They made records and payments in *part fulfilment only* of the conditions of the acts under which the lands were taken up. Moreover, much of the land which they regarded as their own was legally 'Crown land, and therefore at the disposal of the Commissioners for Indian purpose.'

Although sympathetic to the settlers for having 'placed themselves in an exceedingly uncomfortable position,' at least Sproat took his appointment as commissioner seriously and therefore attempted to address and solve Indian grievances. He carried out his work like a responsible administrator when dealing with the settlers and paid special attention to the law. He also showed a keen understanding of what might be called Okanagan customary law when dealing with Indian claims to traditional settlements. But he seldom got his own way when it came to rulings regarding the rights of the settlers because Alexander Anderson and Archibald McKinley, the two other commissioners, had views of their own. McKinley and Sproat, for example, crossed swords over the question of the confidentiality of the work of the commission, and their correspondence reveals that on at least one occasion McKinley discussed land issues with some of the settlers.

Let me now return to Greenhow's 1867 pre-emption and O'Keefe's 1873 pre-emption (both at the Head of the Lake) as illustrations of the relations between settlers and Okanagan over the question of land. Thomas Greenhow purchased Thomas Wood's illegal pre-emption at Irish Creek in 1870 and the commissioners made it their business to see that the land was returned to the Okanagan band. The details are set out in a letter dated 25 September 1877 to Wood from Sproat and Anderson. McKinley, the provincial representative, did not sign the letter, which stated that the 160 acres of which Thomas Wood was the original pre-empter was, according to local knowledge, an Indian settlement and continued to be an Indian settlement under clause 12 of the Land Ordinance of 1865. Consequently, it had never been open to pre-emption by a settler. Clause 12 made this quite clear with respect to both an Indian reserve and an Indian settlement. Furthermore, since this was the law, 'the Governor had no power to give instructions to Mr. Haynes contrary to it, nor could the Government subsequently to the passing of the above Ordinance throw it (?) open for pre-emption [as] an actual Indian Settlement.'

All the statements made to the commissioners indicate that this piece of land had been the principal headquarters of the important Okanagan group of which Chief Nkwala had once been the head. The members of this band were known as the people of 'Talle d'Epinettes,' referring to the grove of spruce trees situated on the village site which also contained several old Indian graves. A section of the land had, moreover, been cultivated by Indians ten years or more before it was pre-empted. Commissioner Anderson reported that the place had been an Indian settlement in 1835 when he first passed there, and that he knew it had been occupied by Indians up to 1849, the last of his many visits to the area while he was an officer of the Hudson's Bay Company.

An old Indian, Kisso-wee-luck, told the commissioner that he had lived on this land before Chief Nkwala's death in 1859 and that he had a cultivated enclosure railed off. In the spring of 1857 he removed these rails and used them to enclose a piece of land nearer the lake. He had cultivated that land, or had had it cultivated for him ever since, and the grain there now was his. Although he used a plough now, he and his wife used to break up the land with root sticks and a hoe. He also learned irrigation from the white man, and once employed Johnny McDougal to help him with a plough. Haynes appears to have dispossessed Kisso-wee-luck of this land on the grounds that he was encamped at Grand Prairie during Haynes's visit. Later a white man (assumed to be Wood) told Kisso-wee-luck that he was going to take the land, which he did, although Kisso-wee-luck continued to cultivate parts of it. The commissioner's interpreter, Antoine Gregoire, confirmed this evidence and pointed out that the area in general was once occupied by Chief Nkwala and his people.

The details supplied by Kisso-wee-luck were similar to those supplied by Wood himself to the commission – that an Indian had a piece of land under cultivation on the property when it was pre-empted and that he continued to use the ground until the certificate of improvement was sold to Mr. Greenhow. Wood wrote to the commission: 'The Indians do not now permit the use of the land by Greenhow. They say the land is theirs and that no one had the right to take it from them. The dispute over this land was one of the main causes of discontent among the Indians at the Head of the Lake.'

Why Sproat and Anderson wrote to Wood and not to Greenhow was never made explicit. However, it would appear that their decision was designed to prove that Thomas Wood had had no legal right to pre-empt the land in the first place. The commissioners were able to show that the land was, and always had been, Okanagan land and that no settler had any right to it. Wood accepted the ruling, as did Greenhow. Greenhow seems to have lost interest in his pre-emption in any case, concentrating his attention on his other land, and on his trading partnership with O'Keefe. Sproat pointed out in his memorandum of 20 January 1878 dealing with O'Keefe's 'land claim' that the commissioners solved the Greenhow case quite simply by telegraphing the local government (British Columbia), and after discussion with Greenhow himself.

Cornelius O'Keefe provided more of a problem for the commissioners. From the point of view of the Okanagan, his 320 acres at Meadow Creek had been illegally pre-empted in 1873, and recorded on 29 April of that year. After examining the grievances expressed by the Okanagan Indians, all three commissioners signed a letter to O'Keefe on 1 October 1877 informing him that his pre-emption had been cancelled, and that it was now illegal for him to occupy or use any portion of the 320 acres without the licence of the superintendent general of Indian affairs in Ottawa. The letter went on to inform him that the Indians had generously agreed not to interfere with his fences, houses, movables, and growing or stacked crops provided they were removed before twelve o'clock on the day of 1 March 1878.

Although the commissioners had other grounds to remove O'Keefe from this piece of Indian land, they gave as their main reason the fact that O'Keefe had not occupied this pre-empted land either himself or through an agent as required by the land ordinances of 1870 and 1873. But the letter also made it quite explicit that the land was being claimed by the Indians as 'their old place,' and in their judgment the commissioners considered it necessary to set this piece of land aside 'for the use and benefit of the Okanagan tribe usually residing at the head of the lake' (NAC, RG 10, vol. 3663, file 9801).

At the time of the commissioners' visit O'Keefe was in the Ottawa area making arrangements to marry Mary Ann McKenna. On receipt of the letter he handed the matter over to his lawyers, Messrs Drake and Jackson, who wrote to the chief commissioner of lands and works, George A. Walkem, on 20 December 1877. The tone of the letter reflects the attitudes of the white population towards the rights of settlers and their contempt for the Indian reserve commissioners. The lawyers asserted that 'Mr. O'Keefe had been in continuous personal occupation of the land' since 29 April 1873, that he had left to go to Canada [sic] in May 1877 leaving a man in possession of a large quantity of cattle, and that the Indian Reserve Commission had no right to override the rights of settlers and give their interpretation of current legislation.

O'Keefe's 'land claim' also sparked off discussion in the British Columbia Legislative Assembly. Sproat submitted a detailed memorandum on the case, and most of the relevant correspondence was made public. The memorandum made it quite clear that O'Keefe's lawyers were entirely in error and that the land claim had been cancelled by O'Keefe's own default and not by any act of the commissioners, since O'Keefe had never resided on the 320-acre lot in question. It is interesting that O'Keefe had extended an invitation to the commissioners to visit him when they were on their way to the Okanagan, but later changed his strategy by going to Ottawa both to marry and to avoid confrontation with the three officials.

Sproat's memorandum makes it abundantly clear that the three commissioners mistrusted O'Keefe's motives. In addition to the false declaration regarding residence, there was also the suggestion that he was attempting to prevent other settlers from acquiring the land themselves. O'Keefe knew that the land was claimed by the Okanagan Indians and he may well have been scheming to obtain 'compensation' for the 'surrender' of these 320 acres for Indian occupation. Sproat incidentally implies that O'Keefe may have been angling for a general land settlement relating to all his holdings at the Head of the Lake in the event that all his property were to be turned over to the crown for Indian use. In this connection it is tempting to speculate that O'Keefe would have welcomed a handsome sum as compensation for all his properties. Not only would such a settlement have pleased his new wife, who was reluctant to move from Fallowfield to the wild west, but it would also have facilitated the termination of his alliance with Rosie, his Okanagan wife. In this regard it is interesting that after considerable conflict between O'Keefe and Rosie's family, a 'divorce' was eventually said to have been granted by the Okanagan. O'Keefe was required to give the family a large herd of cattle by way of compensation or alimony. Some of my informants say that O'Keefe gave the family absolutely nothing.

There were never any attempts at litigation against the decisions taken by the commissioners, but the provincial government never gave positive support to their actions. For example, on 4 May 1878 Sproat complained to the chief commissioner of lands and works that O'Keefe's claim to the disputed 320 acres had still not been officially cancelled, pointing out that 'The delay has weakened the authority of the Commission in the minds of the Indians.' On 17 July 1878 Sproat wrote again asking whether O'Keefe's record had been cancelled. By 5 March 1879 the issue had still not been resolved, and Sproat, who had by this time become the sole commissioner, wrote the new chief commissioner for lands and works complaining respectfully that 'in preparing instructions for the Dominion Surveyors of Indian Reserves during the corning [coming?] season [he was] embarrassed by the position in which [he found] the adjustments of the Okanagan reserve owing to the Provincial Government not having taken the necessary steps to complete the adjustment.' The letter continued, pointing out that the dominion government wanted the Okanagan Indians to have 'such a reasonable portion of land as will afford no ground for complaint on their part, and will enable the Indian Department to subdivide the agricultural portion of the reserve into individual holdings secured to the occupiers.'

This reference to 'individual holdings' is of considerable significance to understanding Okanagan economy and society at the time, because it proves that there had been a move away from communal ownership, and that individual Okanagan agriculturalists, gardeners, and ranchers had been in competition with settlers since the early 1860s. Thus Sproat was able to write: 'This [subdivision into individual holdings] is the first step in the management of the [Okanagan] Reserves, and a step which must be taken to ensure contentment and progress on the part of the Indians.'

In order to achieve part of this goal for the Okanagan reserve, Sproat pointed out that three or four hundred acres of agricultural land was still required in addition to the other land – in other words, O'Keefe's 320 acres were needed forthwith. It was now up to the provincial government either to cancel O'Keefe's pre-emption record or to override the decision of the Reserve Commission. If the latter course was to be taken then 'there [would be] no other course open to the Provincial Government than to purchase the land from [O'Keefe] for assignment to the Indians.' However, in his letter Sproat was quite firm in sticking to the commission's earlier view that O'Keefe did not have legal title to the land, reiterating his view that O'Keefe 'had probably occupied [the land] mainly for the purpose of making terms with the Provincial Government.'

It seems clear that Sproat did not expect the provincial government to take immediate action, and five days later, on 10 March 1879, he wrote to the superintendent general of Indian affairs in Ottawa (John A. Macdonald) pointing out that a question had been raised in the House of Assembly in Victoria regarding O'Keefe's position with regard to the recommendation made by the commission some sixteen months back. He enclosed a copy of his letter to the provincial government, and hoped 'that the view which [he took] of the position of the two governments respectively may be found to be correct.'

The O'Keefe matter dragged on for another month until 11 April 1879 when Chief William, on behalf of his band, sent a letter to the Indian commissioner complaining about the state of affairs. The letter was translated from the Okanagan and Chinook languages and certified by Mr. Girod [Girouard?]. The text is as follows:

Mr. O'Keefe claims a parcel of land marked 28 on the map of the reservation allotted to us by the Commissioners two years ago and went on to plow on it spite of our protest. We beg to know for certain, if said land is his or ours.

When the Commissioners 'tyhees' gave us the land, we took it for granted it was ours. Since [then] two years vanished away and O'Keefes still comes on a choice spot to raise a crop.

As we were telling him you gave it to us, he answered you had no right to give his land away, that if he is paid for it he will give it up and if not, he won't.

We wish for(?) no trouble, but our heart grieves (nesika sick tum tum) to see our rights disputed, we wait for your answer to put a stop to our anxiety.

We wish to know also if we have right to the crop O'Keefe puts in, spite our protest.

As you were here you told us that if any white men come on our land to summon them twice to go and should they refuse to comply with our request to let you know. It is therefore, with confidence that we address you this request in order to redress our wrongs.

We have also another grievance against the same party. They [O'Keefe and Greenhow?] allow their cattle to graze on our reservation.

When we protest they tell us we have no fences. We thought the line you drew for our reservations were(?) fences 'ipso facto'.

Send word to us as soon as possible to settle our mind and soothe our grieve.

When Sproat received Chief William's letter he sent it on to Macdonald in Ottawa with a covering letter dated 26 April 1879.

I hardly know now what answer to send to these Indians, having so often said the same thing to them.

I am under the necessity of upholding the character and authority of the Provincial Government as well as the Government of Canada in the minds of the Indians, and yet I feel that in continuing to assure these Okanagan Indians that the matter which they complain of is receiving effective attention, I am stating what is probably not quite true, so far as the Provincial Government is concerned.

Although Chief William's and Commissioner Sproat's letters speak for themselves, it is important to draw attention to the chief's patience with O'Keefe and also his trust and confidence in the authority of the commission in general and of Sproat in particular. Chief William and the majority of his band really believed that they were dealing with the Queen's representative, if not her right-hand man, when dealing with Sproat. It was this trust, and the failure to understand the power structures of both the provincial and dominion governments, that undermined Chief William's authority and the power of his people.

Sproat must be seen as the mediator between Indians, settlers, and provincial and dominion authorities. His purpose (manifest function) was to give the Indians their due. Analytically, however, the subliminal part which he played (latent function) was to make the Indians subservient to the wills of the two governments and to the settlers. Even if he had been given the authority to force O'Keefe and others to comply with the law and the wishes of the commission, he would still have represented the antithesis of Okanagan interests. His frustration with the arrogance of the provincial government does not signal his support for Okanagan power. His frustration was merely a reflection of the job he had agreed to do – to settle Indian grievances during the transition from colonial to dominion rule. With the enforcement of the Indian Act, Sproat (and his two colleagues earlier) established the pattern by which Indians would continue to become more dependent on the dominion government. Chief William's letter was the epitome of deference to a higher authority, and he and some of his people wanted their minds settled and their grief soothed. They protested, but they did not wish to cause trouble and were content to wait for Sproat's answer with grieving hearts.

Fisher (1977: 192–9) has tended to portray Gilbert Sproat as a champion of Indian rights, basing his interpretation on Sproat's correspondence alone. It is perfectly correct to draw attention to his honesty and integrity and his 'great interest in the Indian way of life,' and his insistence that their way of life 'had to be understood before reserves could be satisfactorily assigned to them.' But my interpretation is that during the crucial years of manoeuvring the Okanagan and other Indians into the administrative framework that had been created for them, Sproat, by playing the role of benevolent administrator and amateur applied anthropologist, played an unconscious part in forging acceptance of the system by the Indians. Although he was at times severely criticized by the settlers for treating the Indians too generously, Sproat had nevertheless always tried to keep the peace by not interfering with the interests of those settlers (cf ibid.: 195).

To return to the O'Keefe problem, which had remained unresolved by 5 October 1879, Chief Chelahitsa of the Douglas Lake band wrote to Sproat: 'Yesterday the Okanagan Indians informed me that they would take forcible possession of [the disputed land], but, I advised them to take no steps in the matter and told them I would communicate it to you and told them to wait for your answer.' What is so interesting in this context is that a neighbouring chief is again consulted, presumably because Chief William's letter had achieved nothing. We have here an example of the growing confusion over the office and the authority of the new chiefs. We might even say that *certain* chiefs were being regarded as if they were government officials. Not only were the rank and file of the Indians taken in by Chief Chelahitsa's advice to wait for Sproat to reply, but the chief himself indicated his personal identification with Commissioner Sproat. Chelahitsa closes his letter thanking Sproat for his kindness, adding that he would like to be near to him to shake hands!

It is true that Chelahitsa was Nkwala's nephew, but the members of the Head of the Lake band did not all see him as 'the principal Indian chief in the Southern Interior of the Province,' as Sproat indicates in a letter to John A. Macdonald in Ottawa dated 10 November 1979. The friendship between Sproat and Chelahitsa illustrates how quickly chiefs and certain of their people were being drawn into the system of administration that had been consciously created for the native peoples of Canada. The Okanagan and neighbouring chiefs, almost without exception, from the fur trade onwards, allied themselves to some degree with the white establishment.

SOME REFLECTIONS AND CONCLUSIONS

Sproat continued to carry out his duty as a civil servant, communicating more frequently with Ottawa as 'the attitude and inaction of the settler government in Victoria' increasingly hampered his work. There was a constant struggle for land by the Indians as new reserve boundaries were created, and by the settlers as new pre-emptions were sought, with the dice nearly always loaded in favour of the latter. The Land Amendment Act of 1879 laid down regulations as to how reserves were to be surveyed, and in this regard the act seems to have been retroactive. 'In the end, not a single reserve laid out by the reserve commission was approved by the provincial chief commissioner of lands and works' (Fisher 1977: 197).

Early in 1880 Sproat resigned, partly out of frustration and partly because of the pressure to which he was subjected from both settlers and people in high office, including John A. Macdonald himself. Sproat's successor was Peter O'Reilly, who was Lieutenant-Governor Trutch's brother-in-law. As a magistrate during the colonial period, O'Reilly had had experience in laying out reserves to the detriment of the Indians and to the advantage of the settlers. He was thus a popular choice among the settlers whom he was to represent. But the real change was not O'Reilly replacing Sproat; rather it was the change in policy which gave the reserve commissioner less power. Fisher (ibid.: 199), for example, shows quite conclusively that 'Trutch advised Macdonald that in future the decisions of the reserve commissioner should be subject to confirmation by the Indian superintendent and the chief commissioner of lands and works, and this suggestion was accepted by the Department of Indian Affairs.'

This change in policy reflected an increase in settler power and a decline in Indian power. It also anticipated the increase in settler population and a decrease in Indian population. The change in population ratios was very definitely correlated with the relative power relations between Indians and settlers. While I agree with Fisher that population changes reduced the settlers' fear of an Indian uprising in the Okanagan area, I must reiterate the view that from the beginning Indians and settlers were involved in a process of manipulative negotiation over access to the Indian resource of land. While this negotiation was taking place the Indians were slowly being incorporated into the administrative structures of both the province and the dominion in much the same way as the settlers were. The Indians lost because both the law and the rules of the game discriminated against them. The Okanagan could not pre-empt land in the same way settlers could, and this placed them at a further disadvantage, especially when they had adequate means to do so. As matters turned out, many Okanagan later found themselves cast in the mould of wage labourers on the large settler estates, of which O'Keefe's was one.

Quite apart from the obvious economic exploitation of the Okanagan, we must also emphasize a theme that runs through the pages of this book – the social and psychological effects of colonial and post-colonial law, administration, and bureaucracy. If the colonial period was characterized by white hegemony, Confederation marked the beginnings of coercion at both the provincial and federal levels, which set the stage for a new system of administration.

Chapter Five

Rule by Notables

Max Weber, who was interested in the general question of domination, wrote: 'Every domination both expresses itself and functions through administration. Every administration on the other hand, needs domination, because it is always necessary that some powers of command be in the hands of somebody. Possibly the power of command may appear in a rather innocent garb; the ruler may be regarded as their "servant" by the ruled, and he may look upon himself in that way' (1968: 948).

While Weber did not intend these notions to apply to reserve systems or those other 'closed systems' where authority originates almost entirely outside the structure, he was nevertheless addressing himself to an ideal typical situation which makes a good deal of sense in the context of the administration of the affairs of Indians in Canada. Over the years, native peoples (the ruled) have come to regard bureaucratic rulers as their servants. Such a relationship involves a number of ingredients – paternalism, dependency, power, as well as a condition of symbiosis. This chapter will outline the nature of the new administration imposed on the Okanagan soon after 1871 and show how new reserves were laid out and in what localities.

With Confederation the administration of Indian affairs was placed under the office of the secretary of state in Ottawa. The Terms of Union laid down in article 13 that 'the charge of the Indians and the trusteeship and management of the lands reserved for their use and benefit' were to be assumed by the dominion.

British Columbia was the only province in Canada to have a commissioner for Indian affairs, an office that goes back to Dr I. W. Powell's appointment in 1872. In 1881 six agencies (one of which was the Okanagan) were established, and in 1883 two new ones were added. Still more agencies were added later and some subdivided (see Duff 1964: 62–4). An agency was essentially an administrative subdivision of the native population into districts under the jurisdiction of an agent whose job it was to administer the Indians, protect their interests, advise them on local matters, and, where possible, eradicate certain of their customs ranging from traditional supernatural beliefs to potlatches and ceremonial dances.

Over the years, agents (or superintendents) acquired enormous power, including the task of deciding matters pertaining to the scope of education. Hawthorn et al. (1958: 486) summarize the specific duties of a superintendent:

> The superintendent deals with property and with records, or with the recording of property. He registers births, deaths, and marriages. He administers the band's funds. He supervises business dealings with regard to band property. He holds band elections and records the results. He interviews people who want irrigation systems, who complain about land encroachments, who are applicants for loans. He suggests to others that, if they are in a common-law relationship, they should get married, for, among other reasons, this simplifies the records. He obtains information about persons applying for enfranchisement. He adjusts the property of bands when members transfer. He deals with the estates of deceased Indians. He obtains the advice of the engineering officers on irrigation systems, and the building of schools. He negotiates the surrender of lands for highways and other public purposes. He applies for funds to re-house the needy and provide relief for the indigent. He draws the attention of magistrates to factors which bear upon Indians standing trial on criminal charges.

Indian agents operated under the Indian Act as it was amended from time to time. They had the power to override traditional authority and provided the official link between the natives and the Indian Affairs Department. They were anxious that the Indians should become Christians and often worked closely with missionaries. Agents, as intermediaries, were key people in the system of 'rule by notables,' that is to say the system of administration generated by the federal government and staffed initially by Canadian whites who occupied key positions in directing those under their jurisdiction.[1] Native

---

1 The phrase 'rule by notables,' as used here, differs somewhat from Weber's meaning (Weber 1968: 948–52), but there are many similarities. Dunning (1959a) gives the impression that Indian agents lacked esteem, prestige, and financial standing, but in the Okanagan Valley at least this would not appear to have been the case.

peoples in British Columbia have thus lived for over a hundred years in the context of an administrative system which impinges either directly or indirectly on every aspect of their lives. It is crucial, therefore, if one is to understand the behaviours, attitudes, and values of the Okanagan at any time in their more recent history, to see them in this context: almost every facet of their existence has been conditioned by the Indian Act. Their social position in Canadian society has, so to speak, been moulded through time by an administrative design based on many of the ideas and practices of the colonial era. Some may even wish to argue that the Okanagan and other native peoples are involved in a routinized version of colonial hegemony.

THE INDIAN ACT

In 1876 the various laws respecting Indians were consolidated and amended to form the Indian Act of 1876. This act laid down who Indians were, who they were not, and where they fitted into Canadian society. Provision was made for the control and management of the people living on reserves together with their lands, their money, and their property. Indians were defined in terms of criteria created by administrators, and were categorized as being separate from 'persons.' Thus, in the eyes of the federal government, Canada consisted of two estates – Canadians (persons) and Indians. As far as the act was concerned, the distinguishing feature of Indians was not so much their race, but the fact that they lived on reserves which had been created for them. More accurately, reserves were tracts of land set apart for particular bands of Indians. Legal title to these tracts of land was held by the crown and included all the trees, wood, timber, soil, stone, minerals, metals, and so on, in spite of the fact that many native peoples, including the Okanagan and their neighbours, never relinquished their aboriginal rights.

The act allowed for individuals to be granted location titles to lots subdivided by survey. Initially these seem only to have been held by men. Upon death there were elaborate procedures as to how these holdings, together with goods and chattels, were to be devolved. Widows were entitled to one-third of the estate while the remainder was divided equally among the children. Provision for individual wills was introduced later.

The act contained clauses which aimed at protecting the reserves from outsiders, that is, non-band members who might attempt to settle, hunt, or cut wood. An elaborate system of fines was laid down, illustrating the assumption that all offenders would have access to cash in dollars.

All bands of Indians were bound 'to cause the roads, bridges, ditches and fences within their reserve to be put and maintained in proper order.' Even those Indians residing on reserves and engaged in agriculture as their principal means of support could be required to labour on public roads, but it is not quite clear from the act if or how labourers would be paid.

No reserve or portion of a reserve could be sold, alienated, or leased unless assented to at a special meeting by a majority of male members (twenty-one years of age and older) of the band. But such action had always to be approved by the governor-in-council or the superintendent general. Elaborate regulations applied to the management and sale of Indian lands as well as the management and sale of timber. Regarding the latter, the superintendent general or anyone authorized by him had the authority to grant licences to cut timber on reserves subject to certain provisions laid down in the act. All monies accruing from the sale of Indian lands or timber had to be made available to the Indians, together with any other monies or securities available for the support or benefit of the Indians. This money was to be paid to the receiver general to the credit of the Indian fund.

A most important aspect of the act was the provision made for the election of councillors and chiefs, and the appointment of agents (superintendents) by the superintendent general. Thus, when the first Indian Act of 1876 came into force, agents became the representatives of the federal Indian Affairs Department. Chiefs and councillors, in the words of Hawthorn et al. (1958: 35), were 'administrative devices, without forerunners in the pre-white cultures.' They were thus comparable to the agents, except that agents were external appointments while chiefs and councillors were supposed to be elected internally in the presence of an agent by men (twenty-one years of age) in accordance with the provisions of the act. All elections were subject to confirmation by the governor-in-council, and generally appointments were for a period of three years. However, a chief could be deposed at any time by the governor (but in practice by the agent) for 'dishonesty, intemperance, immorality, or incompetency,' but not by the electorate. Chiefs and councillors as federal government civil servants had to toe the line to keep on the right side of the agent since they were all part of the same system, a system which gave the agent the balance of power. There are several examples among the Okanagan of chiefs being deposed against the wishes of the majority of the people. Even the so-called 'life chiefs' (chiefs elected for life) could be removed from office for the same reasons as other chiefs.

It is difficult to gauge what exactly the duties of these early chiefs and councillors were, apart from assisting the agent in his task of administering the act. They were, however, entitled to frame rules and regulations (subject, of course, to the governor-in-council) relating to the following matters:

1 the care of public health
2 the observation of order and decorum at assemblies of the Indians in general council and on other occasions
3 the repression of intemperance and profligacy
4 the prevention of trespass by cattle
5 the maintenance of roads, bridges, ditches and fences
6 the construction and repair of school houses, council houses and other Indian public buildings
7 the establishment of pounds and the appointment of poundkeepers
8 the locating of the land in their reserves, and the establishment of a register of such locations

The early history of the Okanagan reserve suggests that chiefs and councillors were unimpressed with some of these items, regarding them as superfluous to life in the 1870s. They were, however, doubly concerned with others, notably those preventing settlers' cattle from trespassing on their reserves, and with locating and protecting reserve land. Disabilities and penalties were defined as were privileges. For example, any band member convicted of a crime punishable by imprisonment was excluded from receiving annuities, interest money, rents payable to the band, and so on. The agent could require band funds to be paid for relief of sick, disabled, aged, or destitute persons. Indians could not purchase or consume alcohol either on or off their reserves. They were granted certain financial privileges and were not taxed for any real or personal property unless these were located off the reserve.

The Indian Act of 1876 even contained a clause making it lawful for Indians 'destitute of the knowledge of God' to give evidence at inquests involving criminal (and other) charges. Such persons were cautioned that they would be punished if they did not tell the truth! There were also detailed clauses dealing with the enfranchisement of Indians and a number of 'miscellaneous provisions.' The procedures for enfranchisement were complex and drove home the enormous gap between *reserve Indians* and other *persons* in Canada at that time.

OKANAGAN RESERVES

The Setting
The main practical job of the Joint Reserve Commission's sojourn at the Head of the Lake in the summer of 1877 was to create permanent reserves as called

for in the Indian Act and arrange for the surveying of these reserves.[2] The task was not easy. It received little support from the provincial government, which even attempted to sabotage its work by delaying its visit to the Okanagan Valley for a year. In addition to this work for the federal government, the commission had to cope with the demands of both settlers and native peoples.

The commission's delay in reaching the interior angered both the Shuswap and the Okanagan at Head of the Lake, who had been planning some form of militant action against the settlers over the land question. Some settlers took the threats seriously, while others continued in their usual complacency, despite the fact that both the Shuswap and the Okanagan were arguing 'that armed force was the only way to extract concessions from an unresponsive government' (Fisher 1977: 191).

In early July 1877 a joint meeting of Okanagan and Shuswap councils was held at the Head of the Lake to discuss the form their resistance should take. Full details of these meetings were never recorded, but I have tried to reconstruct some of the social processes and issues involved from letters and reports written by Sproat and other members of the commission[3] together with some versions based on the oral tradition. At the outset let me make it clear that had Sproat, Anderson, and McKinlay *not* arrived in the summer of 1877 a serious outbreak of violence might have occurred. Moreover, had the Okanagan at the Head of the Lake been able to agree with their Shuswap neighbours, a very effective resistance movement could have been successfully formed to drive the settlers out of the valley. Both the Okanagan and the Shuswap had guns and ammunition, and a considerable number of superior horses for such action.

In a letter to the provincial government on 6 July 1877 Sproat writes of the 'great Okanagan meeting,' the principal aim of which was to force Indian demands for land upon whites. Some American chiefs were present, and this seems to have distracted the Shuswap and Okanagan from their main

2 In this section I have drawn to some extent on the oral tradition but mainly on written historical records. See especially: Joint Reserve Commission, 2nd Report dated 1 December 1877, PABC, GR 494, box 1, file 46; Joint Reserve Commission 2nd Condensed Report 1 January 1878 [6 February 1878] PABC, GR 494, box 2, file 53; Indian Reserve Commission Correspondence, NAC, RG 10, vol. 3653, file 8701; Joint Reserve Commission, 2nd Condensed Report, RG 10, vol. 3612, file 3756-16.

3 I have derived much of my data from the various correspondence and reports written between June 1877 and October 1879. See PABC, GR 494, box 1, files 30, 32, 33, 36; NAC, RG 10, vol. 3612, file 3756; ibid., vol. 3641, file 7571, and vol. 3653, file 8599$^1/_2$.

objective, as twenty to thirty of them went off to join the American insurgents supporting Chief Joseph and the Nez Percé across the line in the United States. Sproat implied that the Shuswap chiefs were the most militant, but local Head of the Lake historians (contemporary informants) argue that if the Okanagan had had their way, war would have surely broken out. Just how bad the situation was is borne out by the fact that Sproat and Anderson sent a telegram on 13 July 1877 to the minister of the interior in Ottawa as a consequence of the Head of the Lake meeting. The message stated: 'Indian situation very grave from Kamloops to the American border. General dissatisfaction – outbreak possible ... at least 100 mounted police should be secretly sent to Kamloops.'

The commission (with some help from the missionaries) used considerable guile to protect the settlers from Indian anger and aggression by exploiting the rivalries between the Shuswap and the Okanagan. They intensified the existing factionalism within each group and the divisions between young and old, and undermined what traditional leadership still existed. Father C.J. Grandidier, a missionary, persuaded the Adams Lake Shuswap to meet with the commission rather than attend the Head of the Lake meeting (Fisher 1977: 193). This exercise in colonial-style applied anthropology produced the necessary societal fragmentation. By preventing a unified force of Indians the commissioners could set about their task of creating new reserves which could be accepted without battle. In the process the commissioners, perhaps unwittingly, created further infighting among the chiefs when they assigned varying quality and quantity of land to each group. The effect of all these strategies and events was to erase all traces of Indian solidarity thereby dissipating much of the hostility towards the white settlers. Certain members of the Okanagan community, thanks to the pro-British Douglas Lake chief, Chelahitsa, were even beginning to look forward to the arrival of the commission as if it possessed messianic qualities.

By the time the commission reached the Okanagan community later in the summer both the Shuswap and the Okanagan had begun to accept Sproat, Anderson, and McKinlay as if they were Queen Victoria's personal envoys, and the threat the Indians posed to the settlers largely disappeared. The commission's policy was to speed up the establishment of reserve boundaries thereby pacifying each local group as they went along, trusting that conflicting rivalries and divisions would continue to solve matters according to the well-known effective principle of divide and conquer. But several serious tensions still persisted in the area. Having resolved the Kamloops crisis to their own satisfaction, they swept through the part-Okanagan part-Shuswap Spallumcheen area, undermining the authority of the traditional chief by siding with a rival faction while they decided on the reserve boundaries. In a letter to the provincial government dated 22 August 1877 Sproat notes how the government's reserve policies fuelled war feelings and increased the numbers of an 'army.' Although he admits some success with the Shuswap people in land allotments, he notes that Shuswap chief Loui was able to hold the Shuswap of the Kamloops area and environs together. He also points out that the Okanagan at the Head of the Lake were annoyed with the Shuswap for seceding from the 'league.' This move on the part of the Shuswap refuelled the old fire of bitterness between them and the Head of the Lake Okanagan, a rift that was widened by the Spallumcheen allotment.

Okanagan militancy stemming from their resentment over the land question and the nature of reserve boundaries subsided but did not disappear altogether. Sproat wrote to the chief commissioner on 13 September 1877 indicating that, although Father Pandosy had reported that the Indians were not too dissatisfied with the existing reserves, a speech had been made by an Indian at Okanagan Mission advocating war if certain boundaries were not given to the native people. (To this day the Okanagan are still questioning certain of their reserve boundaries which have remained unresolved for over a hundred years.)

Sproat's view had been that if settlement was made quickly and calmly in the Okanagan (where there were still considerable problems with the settlers), then the Indians would be appeased, and the good news would spread, preceding the commission as it travelled through the rest of the country, thus saving the reputation of the Canadian government and its new Indian policy! In many respects, therefore, the failure of the commission was inevitable.

The Indian Act of 1876 codified the status of Indians and set them apart from other Canadians. This act forced the Indians to resolve the questions of land, boundaries, and reserves. While it is true that Indian militancy loomed large for a while, the structure of interior British Columbia society, the forces of history, and greater involvement with the outside world placed the Okanagan in a socio-economic position above which they have never really been able to rise. The reserves which were created at this time froze the Okanagan spatially, while the Indian Act determined their future socio-economic position to an overwhelming degree. It is to the flawed handiwork of the commissioners and their surveyors in the creation of reserves to which we must now turn.

The Reserves at the Head of the Lake

On 3 October 1877, about two weeks before the reserves were officially described for the Indians at the Head of the Lake, Sproat submitted his general

TABLE 1
Head of the Lake Census, 1877

Adult males	64	Adult females	63
Young males	1	Young females	5
Child males	56	Child females	59
Total males	121	Total females	127

Total Head of Lake population = 248

Livestock		Farming implements etc.	
Horses	585	Houses – log and frame	16
Cattle	190	Stables	15
Work oxen	2	Outhouses	9
Pigs	125	Sets of harness	15
Fowls	178	Ploughs	14
		Harrows	7
		Wood trucks	2
		Corn mills	2
		Set of chains – yokes	1
		Scythes	12

SOURCES: Indian Reserve Commission, Second Condensed Report dated 1 January 1878 and census of 10 September 1877 (NAC, RG 10, vol. 10011, 1877 census – Okanagan Tribe.

report to the superintendent general in Ottawa. He pointed out that the area at the Head of the Lake had long been the chief home for this particular band and that it was especially valued at the present time now that farming and stock-raising were expanding among the Indians. He noted that the existing two Haynes reserves left seventy-five men (heads of households) with less than ten acres of cultivable soil per household and that pasture had to be shared with white settlers on crown land. The Head of the Lake people possessed 560 horses and 187 head of cattle. Roughly six to seven hundred acres had been fenced in and two hundred acres were under cultivation. Four men had a fence round three hundred acres. In short, these Okanagan were in desperate need of more land for agriculture, as well as for winter and summer grazing for their livestock.

In the Second Condensed Report of the commissioners dated 1 January 1878 Sproat and McKinlay provided details from an updated census taken at the Head of the Lake between June and November 1877 (Table 1). Sproat drew attention to the illegal pre-emptions by settlers such as Cox in 1865, Wood in 1867, Greenhow, and, of course, O'Keefe, stressing that the pre-emptions were not only illegal because the law prevented one man from holding two pre-emptions, but also because no settler could legally hold Indian land. Sproat thus claimed a legal victory over these settlers: 'They own a quantity of land, and in my opinion knowingly risked the dangers of non-compliance with the law, in the hope of getting more, and they have lost the game.'

In his dealings with the Head of the Lake people Sproat repeatedly made it clear to everyone that his work was limited to land problems. It was not his business to be concerned with local politics or social and individual problems. Even complaints by Chief Chelahitsa and other 'elders' regarding the relations between Indian women and white men created little interest for him, and he seemed quite unaware of O'Keefe's common law Okanagan wife and their two children. In the final analysis, Sproat and the other two members of the commission, whatever else they thought and said, were only intent on creating reserves for the native people.

The commissioners laid out ten reserves at the Head of the Lake and its environs to the north and south which were much larger than the existing Haynes reserves. These reserves were described and later surveyed. They were numbered but also acquired names, and constituted the pieces of land on which members of the Okanagan band were living permanently in 1877. The reserves were as follows:

	Acres
Okanagan Indian Reserve No. 1	25,539.00
Otter Lake Indian Reserve No. 2	62.00
Harris Indian Reserve No. 3	160.00
Swan Lake Indian Reserve No. 4	68.00
Long Lake Indian Reserve No. 5	128.00
Priest's Valley Indian Reserve No. 6	83.00
Duck Lake Indian Reserve No. 7	457.00
Mission Creek Indian Reserve No. 8	5.00
Tsinstikeptum Indian Reserve No. 9	1544.59
Tsinstikeptum Indian Reserve No. 10	768.34

(In 1963 the last three of these reserves seceded to form the Westbank band.)

Okanagan Indian Reserve No. 1 was identified by the commission in its Minute of Decision dated 15 October 1877. This is still the largest reserve of the Head of the Lake complex and is generally regarded as synonymous with the band itself. It comprised approximately 25,539 acres and capped the north arm of Lake Okanagan. Edward Mohun surveyed the reserve in 1881, but there are certain discrepancies between the boundary identified by the Joint Reserve Commission's Minute of Decision and Mohun's plan. Although the discrepancies do not alter the shape of the reserve significantly, the fact that changes were made at all is a serious indictment of the Department of Indian Affairs and a reflection of Mohun's irresponsibility for not following the instructions given to him by the commission. Mohun both added and removed some land, but overall the Okanagan suffered a sizeable loss of 1147 acres (Yabsley to Band, 13 January 1983). Mohun's motives are not easy to discern, but careful study of the map suggests that he was conscious of settler interests, particularly the pre-emptions that were contiguous to land being used by the Okanagan at that time. There is, moreover, considerable evidence that Mohun himself had interests in land – not at the Head of the Lake but elsewhere in the interior of British Columbia. Whatever his motive, by altering the boundaries Mohun acted illegally in terms of the Indian Act of 1876. Section 25 states: 'No reserve or portion of a reserve shall be sold, alienated or leased until it has been released or surrendered by the Crown for the purposes of this Act.'

The Okanagan Indian Reserve No. 1 was clearly a reserve at that time as defined by the Indian Act. To make any change or reduction in the boundaries Mohun would have had to have been instructed to do so by an Okanagan popular assembly consisting of the males twenty-one years of age and over (see section 26(1) of the Indian Act 1876). Quite apart from the legal implications of Mohun's work, there was the general dissatisfaction which still exists among the Okanagan regarding the sleight of hand of Edward Mohun and his theodolite.

In 1877 the population of Okanagan Indian Reserve No. 1 was about 250. The majority of people were living quite close to the Head of the Lake in areas that were also defined as reserves at this time. Detailed statistics regarding land use are not available for the 1870s, but a hundred years later agricultural surveys classified the land as follows: agriculture, 14,815; woodland, 6902; and wasteland, 3663 (Kerr and Associates 1975: 13; Indian Affairs 1971). These figures are somewhat misleading since only 5000 of the 14,815 acres could be classified as potential arable land, while the remainder is a mixture of commonage and land under hay. Furthermore, building sites generally form part of agricultural land, which reduces the size still further.

The Royal Commission of 1913 did not throw a great deal of light on land usage at that time, but the general impression conveyed was that cultivation of crops was in decline on the reserve and that more land was being used for grazing and being placed under hay than before. The main crops were oats, wheat, and potatoes. There was a shortage of good fertile land, and people were anxious to obtain more land. Many were not farming at all in 1913 because they did not have adequate land or capital to develop it. Only a minority were profitably involved in cattle ranching; because of insufficient land many Okanagan were employed, out of necessity, as labourers on white farms. These trends and their wider implications are discussed in the next chapter.

A brief discussion of the remaining Okanagan reserves associated with the Head of the Lake complex is given in Appendix 1. These smaller reserves were also created by the Joint Reserve Commission in its Minute of Decision on 15 October 1877, and surveyed by Edward Mohun in 1881 shortly after he had completed his survey of Okanagan Indian Reserve No. 1. The surveys were also poorly executed by Mohun, although Indian reserves 2, 3, and 4 would seem to coincide with the descriptions given. All the surveys were approved in April 1881 by I.W. Powell, commissioner for Indian affairs for British Columbia.

The Commonage Reserve

The creation of the reserves took place at a time when Okanagan economy and culture were in the process of being transformed from their traditional small-scale systems into a new social formation similar to that of the settlers. Both Okanagan and settlers were involved in agriculture and cattle ranching with some interest also in pigs and chickens. Both relied on horses as draught animals and for transportation, although Okanagan horse breeding was far superior to that of the settlers. Clearly, from the 1860s and 1870s onward the two groups were now consciously in competition for similar resources and commodities – land, water, cattle, and horses. The creation of reserves made the Okanagan even more aware of their land base, and the importance of having adequate agricultural land, irrigation, and commonage for pasture. All three were needed.

Important changes in Okanagan subsistence activities had therefore taken place since the middle of the nineteenth century. In the 1850s they were cultivating only a few potatoes for domestic use, but they also hunted and fished, bartered skins, and kept a few horses. By 1877 the joint commission reported that the Okanagan were growing grain, root crops, and vegetables. Similarly, stock-raising increased sufficiently for Commissioner Sproat to write on 1 December 1877 that stock-raising was the principal occupation, and that the area was well suited to this activity. Moreover, Okanagan who had worked as labourers on white ranches had learned to distinguish more clearly between useful and useless land, the differences between summer and winter pasturage, as well as how many acres were needed to make a profit out of ranching.

Just as there had been a change in agriculture since the 1850s and 1860s, so in the twelve years between 1865 and 1877 there was an increase in stock-raising; indeed, as the former had declined, so had the latter increased. By 1913 when the royal commission visited the Okanagan it was abundantly clear that more and more agricultural land was being put under hay partly to make up for shortages of pasture due to overgrazing by cattle and horses, and partly because of the decline in the wheat industry in the valley (Graham 1930; Ormsby 1931). The Okanagan were always reluctant to reduce the size of their horse herds to accommodate more cattle, because they had developed an equestrian tradition early in their history, and valued both for different reasons.

When the joint reserve commissioners were laying out the ten reserves in the Okanagan area they had to keep in mind the bare optimum needs of the Okanagan people – that is, the amount of land that would satisfy *immediate* Okanagan demands while not interfering with settler aspirations to develop their pre-emptions and even expand them. However, in the Minute of Decision of 15 October 1877 provision is clearly made by the commission for a significant tract of land to be set aside for pasturage to be held in common by the Okanagan Indians and the white settlers. The land was surveyed by Mohun in 1881 and found to contain an area of 24,742 acres.

The purpose of creating this commonage reserve was clearly to appease both the Okanagan Indians and the settlers. The Indian Reserve Commission had the interests of the Indians clearly in mind when they created it. The commonage reserve was described as:

> ... the unoccupied tract of land lying between on one side Okanagan Lake and on the other side Long Lake and the unnamed Lake from which Long Lake is separated by the natural causeway known locally as the 'Railway' the said tract to have its Southern boundary adjacent to the lands at Priest's Valley and head of Long Lake occupied by white settlers as may be determined by the Indian Reserve Commission on further information but the above pasturage right of the Indians on the said tract of land is to be enjoyed by them in common with those white settlers owning not less than 320 acres, actually resident on their farms or represented by actual resident agents, not Indians nor Chinamen, carrying on as such agents the business of farming bona fide on the farms of their employers ... If the Provincial Government can take the steps necessary to carry out this arrangement with the consent of the Indian Department and if further it can be arranged between the Provincial Government and the Indian Department that this tract of Common land is to be grazed in winter only the Commissioners believe that the arrangement will benefit both the white settlers and the Indians. *If the arrangement is not within the powers of the Commissioners or cannot be carried out, the said tract of land to be Indian Reserve.* (Italics added)

Given the fact that the arrangement did not work out, the commonage reserve should have become an Indian reserve with the same status as the other reserves surveyed at the time. This does in fact seem to have happened, because on 28 January 1888 the province protested to Ottawa the allotment of the commonages. Later it was blatantly asserted that the Okanagan commonage was unnecessary in view of the other 'extensive' reserves. In a letter from the dominion to the province on 26 November 1888 it was recommended that the commonage reserve be thrown open for sale after Peter O'Reilly, then Indian reserve commissioner, had visited the district himself. Inevitably a federal order-in-council soon followed, dated 5 January 1889, and the commonage reserve was illegally cut off (see NAC, RG 10, vol. 1109, folios 000977–8).

The full details of the commonage reserve cannot be discussed here but we must observe that its loss deprived the Okanagan of the additional grazing lands many people needed to compete with the white settlers.

By way of clarification, it will be recalled that article 13 of the Terms of Union with Canada required that the province 'convey' lands to Canada in trust for the use and benefit of Indians. Controversy as to the interpretation of article 13 developed immediately, particularly over the question of reserve size. Apart from the northeast area, no treaty had ever been negotiated in British Columbia before or after Confederation. The commission established in 1876 to fix the extent and locality of reserves based on *Indian needs* and *settler claims* created more than one thousand reserves by 1908, but these were never officially confirmed. The royal commission which reported in 1916 on Indian Affairs in British Columbia recommended that the Long Lake and Swan Lake reserves be cut off from the Okanagan band. By and large, the McKenna-McBride Report (as the lengthy published document came to be known) was accepted by the federal government, apart from some amendments made in 1920–3. It was only in 1938 that the Indian reserves in British Columbia, as these had been adjusted, were formally conveyed to Canada. The Long Lake–Swan Lake cut-offs in the Okanagan were never accepted by the band, but it was not until 1978 that legal action against Canada was contemplated. The Okanagan band council has only recently confronted the illegality of the commonage cut-off of 1889.

CONCLUSION

I began this chapter making brief reference to Weber's interest in the relation between domination and types of administration. Every administration dominates because it is necessary that some powers of command be in someone's hands. Often such power of command appears in a favourable garb from the perspective of the ruled, who may even see their ruler or administrator as their servant. Thus 'rule by notables' is often perceived reflexively as rule by 'servants,' an experience shared by native people throughout Canada.

The success the federal government had in implementing the Indian Act of 1876 and the package that went with it was achieved almost entirely by its own administration and the attitudes of the Okanagan towards it. The land question was surely the central issue of the Indian Act at that time for both the Okanagan and the settlers, but its temporary resolution was achieved through administrative strategies and negotiations which emanated from legislation.

From the Okanagan's perspective, the new era into which they were drawn focused them first of all on the personalities – culture agents if you will – of the Joint Reserve Commission. There were also the Indian agents who assumed control as the administrators of the Indian Act, and the surveyors who set the physical boundaries of the reserves. In the background were the senior officials of the Department of Indian Affairs, and over the waters was the Queen of the British empire, who was believed to be the benevolent monarch behind the new scheme of things. The irony of the situation is that all were the Queen's people: the Okanagan through their acceptance of the British monarch and her promises; the white rulers and officials as bona fide representatives of the crown.

Collectively all these personages were perceived by the Okanagan as *honoratiores* (notables), to use Weber's term. Relative to Okanagan standards all notables earned good incomes involving comparatively little labour, and they had a mode of life marked by prestige and honour. Weber distinguished between what he called direct democracy and the rule by notables. In the Okanagan both occurred as part of one general system which articulated two estates – Canadians of multiplex backgrounds and walks of life, and Indians as defined by the Indian Act. Thus the Okanagan were subjected to a system of administration that originated in the Canadian estate, and from the latter's perspective it *was* perceived as direct democracy. But the Okanagan, who had no part in that democracy, nevertheless established a cognitive link with it through certain administrators. Had this sentiment of positive affect not existed in the minds of the Okanagan towards the notables, there would surely have been a revival of hostility towards settlers and others as the Indian Act was being enforced.

Earlier I discussed the beginnings of white hegemony in the Okanagan Valley and its environs, showing that it was in the context of that frontier culture that the Okanagan and neighbouring native people developed their attitudes to the Queen and her agents in Canada. Thus the idea of rule by notables had its roots earlier in the century when the fur trade was in full swing. Now the Indian Act involved all the Okanagan in a formal institutionalized manner with a much wider world that included the settlers, the province of British Columbia, the dominion of Canada, and Great Britain. An important component of the new system was its rigidity, because it placed enormous limits on Okanagan expression and action as they became encapsulated into the segregated world that had been created for them. It marked the beginning of Indian domination by white notables.

Chapter Six

The Process of Economic Incorporation

We have seen how the Okanagan were incorporated into the political arenas of the province of British Columbia and the dominion of Canada, not as equal partners in Confederation, but as people of special status defined by the Indian Act. Here I want to examine some of the processes of economic incorporation of the Okanagan as people of special status which took place between the 1870s and the first two decades of the twentieth century, with particular reference to changes in modes of subsistence.

Relations of dependence in some form or other occur universally in human societies, but some groups, such as proletarians and peasants, stand in greater degrees of dependency to captains of industry, landlords, and the ruling class in general than do members of the petite bourgeoisie. The Okanagan and other reserve dwellers occupy socio-economic positions which are not unlike those occupied by many peasants and proletarians, although there were times in the late nineteenth century when some Okanagan appeared to do very well in their reserve-based economy when relying on their own resources. In fact, the success of these few Okanagan farmers, like many of the white settlers, was determined by their access to sufficient agricultural land. But the main difference between these two categories of farmers was that Okanagan land which could not be increased by pre-emption.

Yet in spite of their fixed boundaries and legal ascriptions, reserves are always part of wider political and economic systems whose influences impinge on these local communities. Similarly, the members of these communities extend their socio-economic boundaries beyond the lines marked out by surveyors when they seek employment in the world outside, and when they establish cultural alliances within that wider domain.

MAKING A LIVING AFTER THE COLONIAL PERIOD

The cultivation of crops by the Okanagan at the Head of the Lake had begun in a small way as early as the 1850s.[1] But the chief modes of subsistence for the majority of families continued to be hunting and gathering with some fishing. By the 1870s the number of people actively engaged in, and interested in, cattle ranching and/or farming and gardening had begun to increase. However, less than half of the domestic families had livestock and not more than six families were involved in profitable agriculture or gardening. By the time the Joint Reserve Commission arrived at the Head of the Lake in 1877 the majority of the population were eager to try their hands at ranching and farming, which explains their discontent over the land shortage that had been produced by the creation of reserves in the previous decade.

There are four important factors to be taken into consideration when comparing Indian and settler land. First, settler land was always good land, selected by the individual settler before pre-emption. Second, settlers could increase their land by further pre-emption, by purchase, and occasionally by receiving special military land grants (for example, Captain Houghton). Third, reserve land was often encroached upon by settlers who wanted extra grazing for their stock. And finally, only the settlers had access to loans for developing their holdings and the majority brought capital with them into their ventures.

In the second half of the nineteenth century the Okanagan could have become the social and economic equivalents of the white settlers. But they did not have similar economic aspirations, or similar social and cultural aspirations. Moreover, they had been incorporated into the new society in numerous ways. In spite of enormous prior conflict between the two ethnic groups, the process of integration between Indians and settlers had begun and intermarriage with settlers was common. At the same time the two groups were kept apart, both by the Indian Act which defined *people* differently, and by institutionalized unequal competition for common resources.

This does not mean that the Okanagan had first to adopt settler culture in order to succeed as agriculturalists and cattle ranchers. They did owe a great deal to the settler's technological baggage and to the information networks enjoyed by settlers. But Okanagan culture was quite capable of accommodating new ideas and innovations from without. On the other hand they could do

1 Much of the detail for this analysis comes from the Sessional Papers (Canada 1871–1912) in which the agency reports were published. The oral tradition was always useful to substantiate trends. Other references, where appropriate, are noted in the text. The interpretation of the data is my responsibility.

very little towards competing with the settlers without access to suitable land. And it was this deprivation (in addition to their new political position) which determined the shape of their incorporation into the new economy of the Okanagan Valley. It had nothing to do with their 'Indianness.'

If the Okanagan could not make ends meet in the new economy because of a shortage of land, how did they manage? The answer is that they were obliged to involve themselves in a complex mixed economy, in much the same way that reserve dwellers have done everywhere. The Okanagan as a whole, therefore, were to involve themselves for a long time in a composite of cattle ranching and agriculture; wage labour; and hunting, fishing, and gathering.[2]

Cattle Ranching and Agriculture

While the Okanagan were in the process of becoming ranchers alongside early settlers such as Wood, O'Keefe, and Greenhow, they were subjected to the same economic forces, and having been horse breeders from an early date, they possessed the requisite commodity and tradition for cattle ranching. The Okanagan owned at least 585 horses in 1877, while their cattle herds had grown to just over 190. They also kept pigs and fowls.

During the next few decades the Okanagan devoted a great deal of time attending to their livestock and improving the quality of their horses. Horses gave a man high status in the community, cattle gave him wealth and always had a good market value. Large quantities of hay were stacked in different parts of the reserve, as people hoped to increase their cattle herds. Some were even making the effort to reduce the excess number of horses to improve grazing.

As the agent pointed out in 1884, cattle had became the principal means of making money for some. But the general shortage of range land soon slowed down the cattle industry, and people were obliged to slaughter more animals than they intended, especially during winter. Some farmers turned to hog production for which there was a ready market.

In spite of the problems of cattle ranching in the 1880s and 1890s, the Okanagan as a whole did quite well, producing enough meat for local consumption. Some individuals were even producing a surplus which they sold on the British Columbia market. But it must again be emphasized that not all Indians had access to the much-coveted cattle industry, a fact that was deeply resented. This inequality in turn gave rise to serious factional divisions on the reserve, making it difficult for people to agree on a common policy for such matters as fencing and making improvements on the reserve.

---

2 For a somewhat different treatment of the Okanagan material, see Duane Thomson's scholarly work and rich historical data (1978 and 1986).

When we compare the scale of ranching of the Indians to that of the local settlers, the gap between the two groups looms large, and the effect of reserve boundaries on Okanagan expansion becomes obvious. It is true that, had reserves never been established, the Okanagan might have lost all their land (unless they had waged war against the settlers), but my intention here is merely to point to the wide economic gap that was formally and deliberately forged between the two peoples over the years.

The first cattle to be brought into the interior of British Columbia almost certainly came from south of the forty-ninth parallel in 1846 when the Hudson's Bay Company transferred animals to Kamloops, although Ormsby has argued that cattle were first introduced into the Okanagan Valley in 1859 when the priests at L'Anse au Sable established a permanent herd at their mission. Throughout the 1860s cattle poured in to the interior, largely to feed the miners in various parts of the country. During the first half of 1864 duty was paid at Osoyoos on 7720 cattle, 1371 sheep, 5378 horses, and 998 mules, and settlers were grazing about 300 cattle at the Head of the Lake on Okanagan land in 1867. By 1891 the number of cattle owned by a handful of settlers round the Head of the Lake was considerable. For example, Cornelius O'Keefe owned about 1000, Mrs Greenhow owned 800, there were 200 on the BX Range and 2200 on the Coldstream Ranch (Ormsby 1931: 46) – a total of 4200 head of cattle compared with the 1373 owned by the 925 or so Indians in the whole of the Okanagan Agency. Prorated and translated into local terms, a handful of settlers owned 4200 cattle while 165 Indians owned about 250 at the Head of the Lake and its environs.

Cattle ranching provided the sole source of revenue for the settlers in the Okanagan Valley for many years, and while some Indians also exploited that market, their involvement was quite meagre in comparison with settlers such as O'Keefe and Greenhow. During its heyday, cattle ranching was extremely profitable even when prices were low. Grazing was cheap and often stock were allowed to drift on to Indian land. However, ranching was slowly to become less attractive during the 1890s as the ranges became depleted of bunch grass, and as the railway led to fencing additional areas. There was also the fact that the Indian reserves were partly fenced in at this time, making encroachment more difficult. Gradually cattle ranching became a thing of the past for settlers, as the cost of the industry increased and the market value of animals declined. Coupled with this decline was an increase in the value of land as more settlers arrived in the area. Land at the turn of the century began to sell at $100 per acre rather than $5, and the old ranching estates were cut up into fruit lots of twenty and forty acres (Ormsby 1931: 56–8).

It is more difficult to assess the impact the external market had on

Okanagan cattle ranching because, although the Head of the Lake people were always affected by regional trends, they could not sell their land to fruit farmers. Nor could they switch from ranching to fruit farming in the absence of irrigation schemes and government subsidies. As far as ranching itself was concerned, the reserve commonage had also been overgrazed. In 1913 Chief Pierre Michel told members of the royal commission that there were 260 head of cattle on his reserve at the Head of the Lake, roughly the same number as there had been in 1891 when the herds had already declined after the heyday of the industry in the 1880s. Regarding the reserve's carrying capacity for cattle, the commission concluded that Indian Reserve No. 1 'could raise 1000 head of cattle without any trouble as far as pasture [was] concerned if the Reserve was fenced in,' an opinion shared also by the Indians.

The history of agriculture at the Head of the Lake followed a similar pattern to that of cattle ranching, reflecting the general trends in the valley and further afield. By 1877 several members of the reserve community were involved in agriculture. Potatoes were grown in huge quantities and some land was under wheat. By 1891 over 100 tons of wheat was raised, and one enterprising band member had installed a grist mill. The Department of Indian Affairs encouraged farming from the late 1870s onwards. For example, the report on agricultural implements and carpenters' tools supplied to the chief and his band for the year ending 30 June 1878 records the following items: one plough, one harrow, one harness, six spades, three shovels, six hoes, three rakes, two sychthes and snaths, one one-inch auger, one two-inch auger, one cross-cut saw, one hand saw, two hay forks, one grindstone, one hammer, one drawing knife, one frow, three axes, two socket chisels, one brace and bits, one square. These basic implements and tools were well received and good use was made of them, as indicated in the agent's reports between 1883 and 1904.

The reports also draw attention to the amount of energy the Okanagan put into their farming. They made good use of their land, and a number of farmers continued to produce large quantities of grain up to 1904. The peak years for agriculture, as for cattle ranching, were the 1880s. At this time the Okanagan also improved their houses, barns, stables, and fences. They built a fine council house and were reported to have been quite well off by the standards of the valley in general, in spite of the fact that they were suffering from a shortage of both arable land and commonage. As the Indian agent remarked in his 1886 report: 'The best proof ... of their prosperity, under many adverse circumstances, is the fact that they are self-supporting, and the amount of eleemosynary is certainly not more than would be dispensed among a similar population of white people.'

But not everyone was as well off as the chief's son, Joseph, who harvested twenty-six tons of wheat in 1888; or Chief William who worked 150 acres of land in 1883 with his four-horse team hauling wheat and selling surpluses. Many, as we know, did not have access to land to produce crops of grain, hay, and root crops with significant surpluses. And, as with cattle ranching, people were divided by their unequal access to resources. The productive group were farmers; the others were like peasants with strong aspirations but poor expectations to become farmers (see Wolf 1955). Okanagan farmers have never been characterized as being hoarders, but their self-proclaimed individualism, status consciousness, and factionalism were not conducive to supporting the romantic view associated with sharing in a diversified world.

The decline of Okanagan farming after 1890 paralleled that of the white settlers, and throws light on the plight of the reserve Indians at the time. The following sketch focuses on the wheat industry which gave the economy of the Okanagan Valley an enormous boost at the time.

White settlers in the region first began growing wheat in the valley during the late 1860s in the Enderby area, and large crop yields were realized as the industry expanded. Farming methods were generally primitive to begin with and it was not until about 1885 that the manager of the BX Ranch at Vernon bought a steam thresher. Flour for domestic use was ground in small coffee grinders, but by the 1880s O'Keefe and Greenhow had developed quite sophisticated methods of milling (Ormsby 1931: 61–3).

Wheat acreage increased by leaps and bounds, and a bumper crop in 1884 produced between fifty and seventy bushels per acre. Grain sold at $40 per ton locally and the Okanagan Valley became known as the 'wheat-field of British Columbia.' The average yield for the area was about twenty-eight bushels per acre, and one milling company shipped sixteen cars (nearly three hundred tons) of flour during July 1891. A heavy Oriental trade developed and more than thirty carloads of flour were shipped in 1895 to Japan (ibid.: 66–8). In 1911 the flour company holding the monopoly in the Vernon area shipped 13,128 tons of flour (*Vernon News*, special edition 1912).

In due course, there were three milling companies in the area – too many for the amount of wheat produced annually in the valley. Ormsby (1931: 73) estimated that the average annual crop was about five thousand tons, which could be ground in these mills in sixty days. Eventually the flour-milling industry in the Okanagan Valley was crippled by the establishment of the very large roller mills on the prairies. Competition drove the local millers out of business as prairie and American mills took over.

Wheat growing did not, however, fade out overnight. Some farmers turned to hog-raising, as did the Okanagan, and made good profits on this supplementary enterprise, especially during the 1890s when the Kootenay Mines provided a good market. Mixed farming was also very popular since good prices could be fetched for eggs, beef, pork, butter, potatoes, vegetables, and oats and wheat at Fairview (*Vernon News* 13 August 1891; Ormsby 1931: 75). But in terms of substantial profits, the demise of cattle raising and wheat farming as capitalist ventures changed the nature of the economy of the Okanagan Valley generally. Wheat farming gave a tremendous boost to a number of Indian farmers at the Head of the Lake, and they suffered in much the same way as white settler farmers when it declined. However, Indians could not subdivide and sell their farms to outsiders for fruit-farming units as the settlers did, and because they lacked capital and irrigation the Indians were not very successful in switching to fruit farming, although some attempts were made.

In addition to wheat, the Okanagan also grew oats, corn, hay, peas, potatoes, and other vegetables. The list below is a crude estimate of what the Head of the Lake reserve produced in 1890 based on the report for the whole agency and prorated according to population ratios:

Wheat	2303	bushels
Oats	462	''
Corn	164	''
Hay	124	tons
Peas	198	bushels
Potatoes	2237	''
Other vegetables	141	''

Wage Labour

In spite of the success of a segment of the Head of the Lake population in the regional economy during the last quarter of the nineteenth century, there were those who had neither cattle nor access to arable land, and owned little but a small cabin and a horse or two. These people constituted a category of wage labourers who are mentioned repeatedly in the literature and occur regularly in the oral tradition. Some worked for white settlers in both skilled and semi-skilled occupations, while some went away as migrant workers for long or short periods of time. And if they did not consciously constitute a proletarian category or class, many of them were eventually to fall into that position by virtue of their relationship with their employers.

It is also important to make a clear distinction between wage labourers and the *activity* of wage labour, in the same way that it is important to distinguish between hunter-gatherers as a societal type and the subsistence activity of hunting and gathering. When the Okanagan first became involved in the wage labour system they often entered into contracts for the sole purpose of obtaining cash for very specific reasons: to purchase trade goods, whether luxury or otherwise, to purchase cattle to begin a ranch, to improve their houses, and so on. And when they had achieved their goals they would terminate their contracts and return to their customary life. Of course, not everyone who entered into wage labour was necessarily incorporated into the system permanently. Once incorporated, however, one was seldom ever able to escape from it, a phenomenon which Marx observed in other contexts.

Some Okanagan, like other native people in the interior of British Columbia, had been involved in the new money economy from at least the 1860s, and cash remuneration for labour was not new to them. But from about 1880 onwards a very definite class of wage labourers emerged, consisting of people who could not make a living on the reserves. Thus, from a very early date the reserves produced a surplus of cheap labour which could conveniently be exploited by the settlers and others when the need arose.

With the development of railways, some Okanagan obtained relatively good jobs as packmen for railroad contractors. As the Indian agent perceptively pointed out in 1883, 'Wages [were] so high in the Okanagan that any man with health [could] earn more in ways other [than farming] unless of course stock farming was their principal means of making a living.' But demand for this kind of work with its high wages was short lived and its palliative effect on land shortages on the reserves soon disappeared.

In the main, wage labourers took whatever work they could find, and by the 1890s they emerged as a class quite separate from the stock farmers and agriculturalists on the reserves. Some got jobs as cowboys and farm labourers with the neighbouring settlers, others worked on the construction of the Canadian Pacific Railway. For British Columbia generally, the department noted that the Indians were engaged in every branch of wage labour: in mining, agriculture, cattle herding, catching and canning fish, deck-hand, railroad work, seal hunting, trapping, manufacturing oil, working at the mills, packing hops.

The demand for Indian labour did not last, as competition from new settlers of every description and nationality increased throughout the province. Thus in 1895 the Indian agent was urging the Okanagan and others to concentrate their energies on the cultivation of their reserves, although he did not recommend that the reserves be increased in size.

Wage labour off the reserve up to this time had consisted largely of men, many of whom now returned to their smallholdings. Household economies suffered from the loss of cash, which had the effect of encouraging Okanagan women to enter the labour market as domestics and in laundry services (see especially Sessional Papers 1902, 1904).

The decline in wage labour as reported by the Indian agents was only temporary and, as the twentieth century got under way, more and more Okanagan became locked into the system, a topic which Knight (1978) has discussed in a wider context for British Columbia as a whole. In 1900 wage labour among the Okanagan accounted for roughly 27 per cent of the income of the reserve, while farming accounted for 68 per cent, and hunting and fishing 5 per cent (NAC, RG 10, vol. 1327). These percentages, it must be noted, refer to the cash value said to be derived from each activity. It is not surprising, therefore, that food gathering is not included, although it was still very common.

Occupational Versatility
It should be unnecessary to have to comment that all reserves, with their multifaceted economies, require that people possess a considerable degree of 'occupational versatility' (Carstens 1966, 1969), but occupational versatility, the idea of a jack-of-all-trades, is as much an indication of the general complexity of regional economic systems as it is of the poverty commonly associated with reserves. Thus, if the Okanagan engaged in ranching, agriculture, market gardening, wage labour, hunting, fishing, and gathering, it was because these were all viable and necessary ways in which they could make a living in the context of reserve society. If the Okanagan hunted, fished, and gathered until the 1890s, they did so either to augment their ranching and agriculture, or because they had no other form of income, or because they had calculated that a combination of economic activities was in their best interest.

Hunting (to a lesser extent fishing) and gathering still take place at the Head of the Lake, but in a very different form and context from traditional days. For example, hunting involves shooting the occasional deer on or off the reserve for the pot; fishing is very occasionally carried out; and gathering is hardly ever carried out on the reserve because people prefer to travel by car to places as far afield as Revelstoke for the outing where there are better supplies of berries.

Returning to the 1880s, we know from the oral tradition and agents' reports that hunting and fishing and gathering were still common, and there were also reports of trapping. Indian women at the Head of the Lake also manufactured buckskin clothing, cedar baskets, and rush mats for tents and carpets, and they picked berries for sale.

When the royal commission was collecting evidence in 1913 the members of the community at the Head of the Lake complained about the restrictions imposed by the game laws and the reformulation of fishing rights. They had been at loggerheads with the game warden, and Chief Pierre Michel lodged complaints on behalf of the fishermen and hunters, especially the effect that the law was having on the numerous people fishing in Salmon River.

To the complex of hunting, fishing, and gathering we must also add logging and collection of firewood. It was not until the 1940s that imported material was used in the construction of houses. Prior to that time local timber was in great demand for the building of houses and barns, as well as for fencing and firewood. Like timber, surplus firewood was also sold to whites from time to time. The demise of Okanagan logging ventures coincided predictably with the issuing of forest management licences to large entrepreneurial logging companies who soon captured the entire market.

CONCLUSIONS

The establishment of permanent reserves in the 1870s placed the Okanagan in a new relationship, not only to the settlers, but also to the region and the rest of Canadian society. In the economic sphere, if this can ever be separated from their political position, the people were obliged to make a living in diverse and multifaceted ways, a situation that required them to be occupationally versatile to survive the vagaries of the regional economy.

The new and complex ingredient in their lives was now wage labour which became a crucial source of income for every family that did not farm; many households made ends meet by combining several sources or income. The 1881 census for the reserve throws some light on the question of occupational variety and the versatility of extended family members, giving the following combination of occupations as being characteristic of a number of large households: farmers, five; farmers and labourers, three; farmers, hunters, and fishermen, one; farmers and fishermen, three; fishermen, two; hunters and farm labourers, two labourers, two (see also Thomson 1986).

Differences in occupation and subsistence involvement did have an important influence on reserve stratification and especially on factionalism in later years. There are many references to conflicts, dissensions, and factions in the agency reports, the causes of which are not always clear, but the hypothesis which comes closest to explaining the major political cleavage among the Okanagan of the late nineteenth century is the discord between what might be called the *peasant-farmer* segment and the *traditionalist* (primitive) segment. The *traditionalists* saw themselves as belonging to a world where producers controlled the means of production (including their own labour) which was geared to kinship and domestic family obligations as well as those of local friendship. The traditionalists' world, moreover, was not involved with producing goods for a market, and the people were even hostile to such production, because much of their world-view was decentralized, local, and largely familial (cf Redfield 1956; Wolf 1966: 2–4). The peasant-farmers, however, held a world-view that aimed at producing a surplus, and some enjoyed entrepreneurial success. The culture of the peasant-farmers resembles a peasant culture in Redfield's sense, but the many families who enjoyed considerable success in their economic ventures should be regarded as farmers in Wolf's sense (Wolf 1955).

On the whole, however, the Okanagan reserve dwellers of that period might be thought of as peasants, or comprising a peasant culture, and in this sense they were not unlike contemporary peasants of Latin America and parts of Africa. Foster (1960–1) has argued that interpersonal relations among peasants always deteriorate when land shortage and its concomitants give rise to jealousies, quarrels, and tensions among local people, a view that makes sense of personal conflicts on native reserves, where land is by legal definition in limited supply (Carstens 1966, 1969).

The social disjunction between the traditionalists and the peasant-farmers is also a function of land distribution, land utilization, and conflicts arising out of local aspirations and expectations. If the Okanagan community has been affected by factionalism, individualism, quarrelsomeness, and excessive consumption of alcohol over the years, these behaviours and tendencies have some of their roots in nineteenth-century subsistence patterns and economic relations within the context of the wider society and the restraining nature of the Indian Act.

Chapter Seven

The Political Incorporation of Chiefs
and the People, 1865–1931

The enforcement of the Indian Act of 1876 effected, at least in theory, the complete political and bureaucratic incorporation of the Okanagan into Canadian society. But the full process of incorporation took a longer time, and from the point of view of many Okanagan the process has never been completed. Nor could it be, given the discriminatory nature of the Indian Act which defined Indians as separate people from other Canadians.

The domination of the Okanagan, moreover, occurred neither in a cultural vacuum nor without intense conflict and serious protest. We have discussed the serious conflicts arising in the region over settler land-grabbing and the creation of reserves. But to understand Okanagan political transformation at this time we need to go back to the question of Chief Nkwala's successor.

At the time of his death in 1859 Nkwala's prestige as an effective double chief was pretty well exhausted – as was the fur trade itself in the area. There was, in addition, no established model for his successor to follow in this new world of acts and agents. To add yet another blow to Okanagan polity, a smallpox epidemic was ravaging the region, leaving people unprepared to look for direction from any political leader. As oral tradition makes clear, there was no immediate recognition of Nkwala's successor. One candidate for the office actually turned it down. Nkwala's sister's son, Chelahitsa, chief in the Douglas Lake area to the west, attempted for a while to usurp the position, but he never gained the support he thought he would get at the Head of the Lake because of his close association with both W.G. Cox and J.C. Haynes, who were recognized as officials who promoted settler interests at the expense of the Indians.

When Nkwala's successor was finally appointed, installed, and recognized in 1865, his position and office reflected three spheres of interest: that of his own people, that of the colonial government, and that of the missionaries. Thomson (1985: 52–61) has argued convincingly that religious conversion and the political transformation of Okanagan went hand in hand, showing that priests often tried to influence the choice of successor to political office. Thus from the colonial period onwards there tended to be an ongoing three-way battle in the appointment of chiefs – the Okanagan's choice, the colonial favourite, and the missionary's man. Sometimes the Okanagan were themselves divided as to whom should succeed to office and these situations gave rise to even more conflict and indecision.

I will now turn to the profiles of the Okanagan chiefs after Nkwala up to 1931, the approximate year which, from an outsider's perspective, marks the full incorporation of chiefs into the Canadian political and ideological system in this reserve community.

CHIEF ISAIAH MOSES (CHILKPOSEMEN), 1865–79

As matters turned out, one of Nkwala's sons was officially recognized as chief by the colonial government in 1865. His mother was of Shuswap stock but she lived at Nkwala's headquarters at the Head of the Lake. His name was Chilkposemen (Five Hearts) which explains why the early Oblates sometimes referred to him as Moise Cinq-Coeur. Generally though, both administrators and priests called him Isaiah Moses, an impressive name which they had bestowed on him. For a while he was a favourite of J.C. Haynes, the same colonial official who dealt with the allocation of lands to settlers and reserves to Indians in the early 1860s.

In spite of his association with colonial officialdom, Chief Moses was the last local Okanagan chief and headman still in a position to negotiate with white officials on traditional Okanagan terms. He was among the first chiefs in the area to receive the Notice from the Indian superintendent in January 1877, which defined their new roles among their people. These new rules provided for the maintenance of order and encouragement for Indians to be more industrious and self-reliant; Indians were to apply for agricultural tools and seed through the chief (or headman) of each tribe personally; and Indians who left their reserves forfeited their rights there, although 'industrious individuals' could leave and move about. Moreover, in terms of these rules, only two persons were allowed to meet with the superintendent at any one time.

Superintendent James Lenihan's Notice marked the enforcement of the Indian Act of 1876 in the interior of British Columbia. It placed an enormous burden on Chief Moses, reinforcing old conflicts and cleavages among the people. Thus, when the Joint Reserve Commission visited the Head of the Lake in 1877 they reported that two rival chiefs were in competition for power without specifying who they were; these were surely Chief Moses and Chief Chelahitsa from Douglas Lake.

When Chief Moses died in January 1879, the agent, F.G. Vernon, MPP, wrote to the Indian superintendent in New Westminster to report that a successor had been selected, namely Chief William (Wohollesicle). Vernon stated that the 'choice [was] an excellent one,' and the superintendent was asked to approve the 'election' in terms of the Indian Act, thereby marking the beginning of interference by the federal government in Okanagan elections.

CHIEF WILLIAM(S) (WOHOLLESICLE), 1879–98

Chief William seems also to have been one of Nkwala's sons at the Head of the Lake, and probably a half-brother of Moses (Thomson 1985: 52). He was the first chief at the Head of the Lake to have his election formally approved by the Department of Indian Affairs. William was also known as Pasile (Basil, Pasil), but he should not be confused with Chelahitsa's son by the same name who became a chief of the Spahamin band. The latter was killed in 1886 by one of his own people in a drunken brawl (*Sessional Papers* 1887: 87; Teit 1930: 274).

Chief William became wealthy by the standards of his time, and was actively involved in ranching and especially in agriculture. In the mid-1880s he and his son worked 150 acres of land and raised large crops of wheat. There are written reports of rivalry between Chief William and an opponent but no indication is given who the rival was or what the nature of the rift was.[1] However, there is strong evidence that the rivalry was between the growing group of Okanagan farmers and those still engaged in more traditional subsistence pursuits. There was also the related question of rapidly developing factionalism in the north Okanagan. By some, though not all, Chief William was regarded as a progressive leader. He worked hard to establish the Head of the Lake as a viable farming community and in 1890, with strong backing from his supporters, opposed the surrender of reserve land for gold-mining purposes, thereby siding with the interest of the local Okanagan farmers (*Sessional Papers* 1891: 85).

---

1 The oral tradition is not very helpful in this matter and there are several versions of local history at this time. It is worth noting, however, that Chelahitsa Sr lived until about 1884 (Teit 1930: 272–3), so the opponent could well have been himself or his son, Alexander Chelahitsa, who seems to have owned some land at the Head of the Lake.

Throughout Chief William's years in office, rival factions vied with each other for power in the community, and towards the end of his term there was chronic dissension as to who should be the next chief. The cleavage at this time was expressed in terms of the old geographical division between the two main villages on the reserve, and in terms of the parallel rivalry between the farmers and those engaged primarily in traditional means of subsistence. In the 1880s when the demand for wage labour increased the new occupational pattern widened the gulf between the two factions even further, transforming the former division into an internal 'class-like' rift (ibid. 1886).

In external affairs Chief William was constantly at loggerheads with white settlers who encroached on Okanagan land. Cornelius O'Keefe was the worst offender, as Chief William made clear in his letter of 11 April 1879 to the Indian commissioner. In addition to settler encroachment, Chief William had also to cope with the problems created by O'Keefe's liquor store on the boundary of the reserve.

Had more land been available there would have been greater scope for farming generally and the farm labourer class would have been much smaller in the community. Yet, although economic development was prevented by the land shortage, improvements were made in other areas. A new church was built (St Benedict) and the 'picturesque covered stand for holding public meetings' was erected close by (ibid.: 92).

In spite of the many problems that plagued the Okanagan during Chief William's time, farming reached its peak, and for some people today, the period represents the golden age in their history, a time when all people are said to have enjoyed a high standard of living; the enormity of settler pre-emption and intrusion has been forgotten and the implications of the Indian Act and bureaucratic control are viewed in their protective roles only. From the vantage point of the farming élite of the day, the golden age of Chief William's time did exist, but over time there also developed a growing gap between rich and poor, and the discord between the two factions was acutely disruptive.

Chief William held office for nearly twenty years, and it is surprising that neither the oral tradition nor the written records tell us more about his life. During this period all chiefs in the Okanagan were supposed to have been elected for life, although by law they could be removed from office by the superintendent for Indian affairs, as did happen many times later on.

CHIEF LOUIS JIM (KEMTIKEN), 1898–1901

Chief William's successor was Louis Jim who was elected to office for a period of three years according to the provisions of the Indian Act. The election was a lively occasion, with his arch-rival Senklip (Edward) running against him. Senklip came from the house of Nkwala, Louis Jim did not. One version of the oral tradition is that Senklip received more votes than Louis Jim, but the Indian agent declared the latter the winner because he disliked Senklip's faction.

Chief Louis Jim was a rich man with a large herd of cattle. Ironically, he had the unique distinction of being the last remaining Okanagan pagan in 1901, when he was reported to have maintained 'a form of worship of his own' (*Sessional Papers* 1902: 260). He did not, however, object to the Roman Catholic presence, and even went out of his way to build a second church on the reserve, St Theresa at Six Mile Creek. His tolerance of reserve Catholicism was nevertheless idiosyncratic because he would not allow any priest to enter the building.

Even today, although priests are encouraged to celebrate mass, the congregation tends to be controlled by lay people, notably women. The church was built on Louis Jim's property, which facilitated his control over the institution. (After his death one of his kinswomen placed her chair in the middle of the church so that she could lead the prayers and the singing – and keep order!)

Louis Jim's position in the political and economic life of the band casts considerable light on Okanagan factionalism as it has developed in the twentieth century. Apart from the allegation that the Indian agent had falsified results of the election, there is another aspect to Louis Jim's election and the tensions it effected at the time and in later years. Chief William had conducted the affairs of the people from the vantage point of the Head of the Lake, as Nkwala and Moses had done before him. His supporters, the old faction, as they came to be called, tended also to be farmers and ranchers and they were better off than the Six Mile Creek people. Chief Louis Jim's election, therefore, upset both the existing power and status structures on the reserve, and his success in cattle farming was regarded as a sort of structural anomaly in the minds of the old faction, who felt they should have the monopoly of large scale ranching and farming on the reserve in addition to political power.

But there is another ingredient that is surely responsible for his success in being elected and appointed to the office of chief. This was his decision to finance the construction of the church at Six Mile Creek. Although the last of the pagans, he calculated that his gesture would give him votes in the election, and ingratiate him with the Indian agent.

Chief Louis Jim established the first political power base among the new faction at Six Mile Creek, but he held the chiefship for only three years when, it is said, he was defeated in the next election by Chwail (Chewilah, Chuoila, Choila). Louis Jim does, however, seem to have acted as a regent for Chwail, who was said to be too junior (whatever that meant) to take office immediately. Louis Jim's new role thus became that of a mediator between the two factions, and during his period as regent for Chwail, Louis Jim is said to have called himself 'Captain' and swaggered around the reserve with his silver-headed cane, giving orders with abandon. The title of captain is an interesting one in colonial history for it so often applies to native leaders whose positions have been legitimated by colonial authority (cf Morantz 1982; Carstens 1966).

CHIEF CHWAIL (CHEWILAH), 1902?–8

Neither the oral tradition nor the written records shed much light on Chief Chwail. I do not know why Louis Jim was his regent, but it is possible that the agent at that time would not accept Chwail's candidature for political reasons. Genealogically Chwail appears to have been descended from one of Nkwala's south Okanagan wives, who came from the same house associated with Captain Tonasket.

After Chief Louis Jim's period in office (which ended in 1901), local politics entered a period of confusion and turmoil while the reserve was encountering an economic depression, and large numbers of people became involved in wage labour as ranching and grain farming declined. The census taken in March 1911 revealed that the reserve population had declined to 207 – 27 per cent lower than it was in September 1877. By 1908 the Department of Indian Affairs was asserting more authority on the reserve than ever, and during the next fifteen years the Okanagan people struggled to maintain their identity while the administration enforced the letter of the law.

ISAAC HARRIS, 1908–9

Isaac Harris was never chief of these Okanagan people, but he was quite certainly placed in office by the Kamloops agent as an interim chief. There is no record of any formal ratification of his appointment by the superintendent of Indian affairs. It is said that he was once a policeman. His mother came from Lillooet country, and he is said to have married one of Cornelius O'Keefe's daughters.

Members of the Harris family owned considerable private property and were greatly admired by various government officials for being 'smart Indians.' A small reserve (No. 3) in the Okanagan is named after the Harris family. Isaac

Harris's appointment as interim chief, however, is best seen in the context of Chief Pierre Michel's first term of office, and I shall turn to that now. Harris was merely an agent's stopgap.

PIERRE MICHEL (PERE NEQUALLA), 1908

In December 1908, Pierre Michel (Michelle, or Machell), who sometimes signed his name 'Pere Nequalla' to attract attention, was chief for a very brief period. He lived up on the reserve flats near the present site of O'Keefe Siding where he owned land. I have not been able to place him genealogically among the Okanagan, but we know that his wife, Susan, was born at Six Mile Creek in 1854, and that he was married in an Enderby church by Father Cooney. Mrs Michel's father, Antoine, came from Penticton but her mother, Elizabeth, was a local woman. It is said that he enjoyed whisky and was convicted for intemperance, and some band members asked that he be deposed. Agent A. Irwin reports that Chief Michel resigned voluntarily late in December. There was certainly more to the Michel case than that. Records show that Isaac Harris, supposedly a band member, was illegally appointed interim chief by the Kamloops agent from the end of December 1908 to February 1909. A good deal must have happened during the few weeks that Chief Michel was in office in 1908, and early in December he wrote to the Indian agent at Kamloops regarding the important local matter concerning the land at Long Lake Reserve but received no reply. Consequently, he wrote directly to the superintendent general of Indian affairs in Ottawa on 7 December 1908. The letter was translated into English by Johnny Alec, a band member, who was fluent in both English and Okanagan.

The issue which Chief Pierre Michel (signing himself Pere Nequalla) was addressing was the 'illegal sale' of land at Long Lake. He pointed out that a public meeting of the band was called at the Head of the Lake to consider the advisability of selling or surrendering this piece of Indian land (nowadays known as Indian Reserve No. 5). A large majority of the people opposed sale or surrender, but the 'Agent and others claim[ed] that the band did sell or surrender their rights.' After the meeting Chief Michel was taken to the magistrate in Vernon where Mr Irwin, the agent, 'demanded of [him] if [he] was going to sell that land or not.' When the chief replied in the negative, Irwin 'told [him] that [he] could no longer be chief, that Isaac Harris would be chief in [his] place.'

Chief Michel continued his letter stating that Isaac Harris was a half-breed Indian whose mother belonged to the Lillooet people, and that he was married to a half-breed daughter of Cornelius O'Keefe. Various allegations regarding

Isaac Harris were made in the letter relating to band monies, property, and his right to be on the reserve, let alone be appointed chief. Michel also asked the superintendent general to send him a band list and a copy of the Indian Act.

Chief Michel's letter created a rumpus in government circles, and Agent Irwin presented his case in a letter to A.W. Vowell, the Indian superintendent in Victoria, dated 8 March 1908. Irwin reported that Chief Michel had been convicted of intemperance several times and that he had resigned voluntarily rather than be deposed. Isaac Harris 'was deputed to act in the interim' until a successor could be elected. Regarding the surrender of Long Lake Reserve, Irwin alleged that Pierre Michel did in fact sign the documents 'prior to his retirement.'

Irwin tried to persuade people to elect Harris as chief at the regular election but a 'preponderance of Indians thought otherwise,' and another candidate, Baptiste Logan, was appointed to succeed Pierre Michel in regular fashion.

The surrender of Long Lake was to become an important issue many years later, but a report dated as early as 6 November 1909 made it quite clear that the surrender was irregular. A majority of those present at the meeting called by Chief Michel did *not* give their consent; irregular votes were cast; no direct vote on surrender was ever taken; and no record of the vote was kept.

Chief Michel, whether he was intemperate or not, was clearly forced out of office because he opposed the authority of Irwin, who was anxious to satisfy white interests to the land at Long Lake. Isaac Harris was Irwin's choice for chief because of the former's close association with settlers and other whites in the area. Having got on the wrong side of both Irwin and some members of an opposing faction at the Head of the Lake, Chief Michel had no choice but to resign. Not only had he objected to the Indian agent in writing, but he had also gone above his head by directing his next letter to the superintendent general of Indian affairs in Ottawa. From the point of view of the white ruling establishment Chief Michel did not stand a chance of winning this important battle, but it is significant that when the same issue was taken up by the Okanagan's legal council three generations later, the courts ruled in favour of the band, thereby reversing the illegal action taken by the administration in 1908 (see also De Pfyffer 1990).

CHIEF BAPTISTE LOGAN, 1909–12

We have seen the extent to which the Department of Indian Affairs now controlled local government, not merely by exercising its power of veto but also by appointing an interim 'chief' to suit its own policy and strategy. Chief Baptiste Logan was installed after his election on 1 March 1909 for an indefinite term. Logan was the grandson of the Kamloops chief TElākā'n ('Male Grizzly Bear') who had succeeded the Shuswap chief Kwolī'la (Teit 1930: 264–5). Kwolī'la, it will be remembered, was Nkwala's Shuswap uncle, the son of his grandfather's Shuswap wife. It is generally said nowadays that Chief Logan came from good stock even if there was a Shuswap connection!

Chief Logan's term of office coincided with the decline in the regional economy and a change from grain to fruit farming in which the Indians could never participate because of the lack of irrigation facilities on the reserve (Surtees 1979). Logan also got on the wrong side of the opposing faction in his community, and crossed swords with the notorious Inspector 'Whiskey' Cummiskey, inspector of Indian agencies for the region.

Some say Logan fell out of favour with one group of people because his conduct was not befitting that of a chief: although 'a married man, he was living with another woman.' But there is more to the situation than that, for it appears that Inspector Cummiskey took it upon himself to interfere illegally in the affairs of the Okanagan reserve, after he had heard rumours of Chief Logan's matrimonial infidelity from an opposing faction. This faction, or part of it, associated itself with the Chelahitsa family of Nicola (Douglas Lake), which had been trying for years to take over the Head of the Lake. Johnny Chelahitsa is alleged to have presented a petition to Cummiskey which apparently contained 'forged names' asking that he be appointed chief. Cummiskey is said to have used this as an opportunity to remove Chief Logan from office and appoint an outsider as chief.

Johnny Chelahitsa's petition has not survived, but one page of a letter written by him to Cummiskey provides some evidence of his interest in taking over the chiefship at the Head of the Lake. His reasons are based on his kinship connection with Nkwala and, of course, his father's status. Cummiskey, for his part, makes it quite clear that he was influenced by Chelahitsa and the Shuswap chief, Loui, in a letter dated 15 May 1912 to J.D. McLean, assistant deputy and secretary of Indian affairs, Ottawa (NAC, RG 10, vol. 3945, file 121698-64). In his letter Cummiskey alleges that the Indians at the Head of the Lake under the rule of Chief Logan and his relatives had made no progress for three years, and that they 'have created a code of immorality which I am determined to no longer permit on the Reserve.'

Cummiskey was not, however, entirely unsympathetic towards the predicament the Indians were in, pointing out that they no longer had any privileges over white men in shooting or taking game, and that he was concerned about Indian logging operations on the reserves because 'in less that ten years this source of existence will be destroyed.' Cummiskey's position was that 'the only preservation for the Indian is to get him to cultivate the land.' He blamed the decline in farming on the bad influence of Chief Logan and three of his councillors, and he referred to an occasion that Logan 'got drunk on bad whiskey and lay out in the snow.' He wrote that the chief has been 'half crazy' ever since and has refused to speak with any government official, or Father Le Jeune, the local priest, or Johnny Chelahitsa. Cummiskey was always prone to exaggeration and inaccuracy.

After completing an 'investigation' with the help of Johnny Chelahitsa from Nicola, Cummiskey 'deposed the Chief Baptiste Logan in the presence of forty Indians. Logan did not attend but as usual ran away down the lake.' Cummiskey's investigation involved a dirty plot to prove that Chief Logan was an adulterer. On the advice of the Douglas Lake chief, he enlisted a man to provide the evidence. The details are quite complex, but the plan worked. Logan appears not to have been living with another woman, although he was in fact infatuated with the estranged wife of Cummiskey's private detective.

An election was held for a new chief and six councillors in consequence of Logan's deposition. Pierre Michel was elected chief by a majority of fourteen votes over Gaston Louie. Twelve councillors were nominated, and the 'following six were elected: Pierre Bissette, Johnny Isaac, Seymour Chewilah, Louis Jacko, San Pierre and Johnny Joseph.' In addition, Cummiskey arranged for the chief and council to appoint their own policemen 'to run down bad Indians and White men who go there with whiskey.'

The irony of this saga is that Cummiskey's four-page letter reached Ottawa on 27 May 1912, six days after the Department of Indian Affairs had received a letter from Chief Logan and twenty-one supporters. The chief's letter, dated 15 May (the same day as Cummiskey's), expressed several grievances:

1 That 'Mr. Cumisky [sic] had caused trouble on the reserve by interfering with their Chief, Batiest [sic] Logan.' They asked that Cummiskey's actions be curbed. They were quite happy working under their agent J.R. Brown.
2 That 'Cumisky is no good being under the influence of Whiskey when he comes here.' There is strong evidence to suggest that Cummiskey was in fact a heavy drinker (see NAC, RG 10, vol. 3580, file 758).
3 That they were 'not willing to leave their lands or in any way have them taken away.' They were referring, of course, to Chief Johnny Chelahitsa's interest in moving back to the Head of the Lake from Nicola and taking over the chiefship.

The letter ends: 'Trusting that you will protect us from further interference in our affairs by Mr. Cumiskey' (NAC, RG 10, vol. 3945, file 121698-64).

When Inspector Cummiskey's letter reached the Department of Indian Affairs in Ottawa, the note from Chief Logan and his supporters had already arrived. Cummiskey received a mild rebuke from the department in a letter dated 10 June 1912 for deposing Chief Baptiste Logan contrary to section 96 of the Indian Act, which states that neither chiefs nor councillors can be deposed without the approval of the governor-general-in-council. However, the following day the assistant deputy minister received a handwritten memorandum from H.C. Ross stating that he was in agreement with Inspector Cummiskey's recommendation to depose Chief Logan for 'intemperance and incompetency.' On 14 June 1912 the acting superintendent general of Indian affairs, J.D. Reid, wrote to the governor-general-in-council recommending that Chief Baptiste Logan of the Okanagan Lake band be deposed for intemperance. Within a week the clerk of the Privy Council had approved Cummiskey's action and formally deposed Chief Logan under the provisions of section 96 of the Indian Act on the grounds of intemperance and incompetence. He also declared that Logan be ineligible to hold office as either chief or councillor for a period of three years. Cummiskey had defended his action in a letter dated 10 June 1912 to the assistant deputy secretary of Indian affairs, and his judgment of the Logan case was eventually accepted without further question, partly because of the support he received from chiefs Chelahitsa and Louie, although neither had any jurisdiction over the Okanagan reserve (ibid.).

CHIEF PIERRE MICHEL (HLAKAY), 1912–17?

On 27 June 1912, after Chief Logan's deposition had been ratified, Cummiskey arranged the official election of a new chief for an indefinite term, an important occasion for the Okanagan and their neighbours. Fifty-three legal voters were present, and many neighbouring Okanagan and Shuswap from Penticton, Douglas Lake, Enderby, and Kamloops attended as interested observers, including Chief Edward from Enderby and Chief Loui, the Shuswap chief from Kamloops. Father Le Jeune, the Oblate missionary, and agent John F. Smith from Kamloops were also there, but Mr Brown, the local agent, did not attend.

The results of this election are of great interest since three voting clusters were reflected in the first ballot: nine voters still remained loyal to deposed Chief Logan, although they knew he could not be elected chief; twenty-one voted for Seymour Chewilah (Chwail); and twenty-three for Pierre Michel. In the second ballot, after Logan had been eliminated, there was a unanimous vote for Pierre Michel. This was the same person who, in 1908, had been deposed after only four weeks in office after getting on the wrong side of the Indian agent. Following his second election as chief he used his Okanagan name, Hlakay, in official contexts, having abandoned his attempt to claim kinship with the Nkwala family. In the first round of the voting for chief, Seymour Chewilah's (Chwail) supporters were old faction voters from the Head of the Lake. Pierre Michel almost certainly drew most of his support from Six Mile Creek, while the nine voters who insisted on remaining loyal to Chief Logan were the forerunners to the reactionaries who were to continue to assert their political ideology through negative abstention in the 1950s and 1960s. The main reason that Baptiste Logan eventually lost personal support was almost certainly because his personal integrity and reputation had been questioned and undermined. Michel and Chewilah similarly received their support from their personal networks. But what swayed the voters in the second and final ballot?

The interpretation offered here is that the occasion was transformed into a highly ritualized drama for the voters by the presence of visiting dignitaries: neighbouring chiefs, the local missionary, and the two government officials. This was no ordinary election because new external factors and influences loomed large, and the electorate closed rank now that they saw themselves as members of an integrated community. The presence of the neighbouring chiefs, notably the Shuswap Chief Loui, discouraged any display of disunity because it would have been unpardonable for the Okanagan to reveal their internal conflicts, local rivalries, and intense factions in full view of their traditional 'enemies.'

The presence of the missionary in this dramatic context gave Father Le Jeune the opportunity to drive home the Catholic preoccupation with sin to the reserve community, and religious and political charters reinforced each other. Thus, after Cummiskey had invested Chief Michel with his honours, Father Le Jeune gave the chief a Christian blessing as part of the official ceremony. Cummiskey had clearly won the contest, having himself symbolically received the King's blessing earlier for deposing Logan, and this ritual occasion near the waters of Lake Okanagan was a celebration of that victory. Cummiskey, moreover, had engineered an atmosphere of revivalism by inviting a priest to attend, and then himself '[attacking] the evil of a number of Indians who had put away their married wives and were living with other women and some living together without being married.'

The power of communal revival at this election should not be underestimated, because the next morning six couples who had been living in sin were married by Father Le Jeune, while a general spirit of piety pervaded the community! In a very special sense, we observe here a revitalization of the community following the Logan witch-hunt by Cummiskey. The disparate groups and factions at the Head of the Lake did close ranks and pull together for a while, and special efforts were made to farm despite poor prospects of success, although the economy did revive to some extent during the First World War. The war also provided jobs for the Indians, and at least twenty men decided to join the armed forces, which in turn helped offset some of the internal conflicts at the Head of the Lake.

Chief Michel's second term as chief at the Head of the Lake turned out to be more successful than his first. But before I turn to that period, let me attempt to put Chief Logan's few years in office in a more general ethnohistorical context. Chief Logan was elected to office at a critical time in Okanagan history. Pierre Michel had been forced to resign in 1908 by public opinion and especially by pressure from the Indian Affairs Department. Logan had also witnessed the illegal appointment of Isaac Harris as interim chief before his own election in March 1909, and he knew a good deal about the power and authority of the department to which he, as chief, was to become answerable according to the terms of the Indian Act.

Logan's period as chief was also marred by the deterioration of the economy in the Okanagan Valley, and the inability of the Indians to compete with white farmers who had access to markets further afield and irrigation schemes necessary for fruit farming. The people on the Okanagan reserve were demoralized and more dependent on the federal government than ever before. Their socio-economic position was fast becoming the antithesis of that of the whites, whose place in the province had now been firmly established.

Although elected for an indefinite term, Logan was chief for less than three years. It was known that he enjoyed alcohol, as many other members of the community did at this time, and it had also been alleged that he had transgressed local standards of Christian morality. He was thus vulnerable to criticism by many band members who interpreted his personal life as being the cause of all the economic and political ills they were experiencing. He also alienated himself from the Roman Catholic church.

Through the efforts of Inspector Cummiskey, Chief Logan (and the people in general) again learned at first hand of the power of the Indian Act and its administrators when Chief Logan was deposed by the King's representative in Ottawa. Some also learned that the British crown, in which they believed so loyally, made the final decision in every important matter relating to Indians on reserves. It must also have been a revelation to the people to discover that their own agent, Mr Brown, was subject to the same federal authority when they learned that Cummiskey had gone over Brown's head to depose Logan.

When the official election was held for Logan's successor, the members of the Head of the Lake band found themselves participating in a drama that reflected their position in their part of the world in 1912. The occasion was transformed into a ceremonial drama in which the actors and audience converged to play their parts on a common stage. The chief actors were the voting members of the Head of the Lake community, while the audience consisted of the government officials, the missionary priest, and neighbouring chiefs. This duality between actors and audience on a common stage is important because it was the first time in their history that the band had been placed in a social situation that revealed to them, in both ritual and symbol, the reality of being reserve Indians. On this occasion internal dissensions were dissipated and the voters completed the ceremonial part of the occasion by voting unanimously for a new chief. They literally turned their backs on Baptiste Logan as they embraced Chief Pierre Michel. Their actions were reinforced by the official acts of Inspector Cummiskey, the ritual blessing of Father Le Jeune, and the public witness of the other outsiders present.

But while insiders (the voters) and outsiders took the stage together, the drama was not carried out for the benefit of the local Indian community per se, but for the federal government in terms of its own charter, the Indian Act. There was, however, some dubious short-term emotional gain for the local community generated through the ceremony, which manifested itself in a minor revitalization movement. But the main function of the whole occasion was to define the parameters of power, especially the omnipotence of external authority and the tenuous status of the chief as a political figure in his own right.

Although these observations are largely derived from the circumstances surrounding the election and installation of Chief Logan's successor, they do reflect the forces involved in the removal of Chief Logan from office and the attempt to erase his influence on the Okanagan reserve. From a somewhat similar vantage point we might also say that the whole ceremony was a reaffirmation of the status quo, the formal rules of the Indian Act as these were being interpreted at that time.

At Chief Michel's installation ceremony he received not only the blessing of the local Catholic priest, but also a medal and a letter from the Canadian government. The medal and the letter were requested for him by Cummiskey as part of his strategy to incorporate the Okanagan reserve more completely into the federal establishment. The letter of 26 July 1912 exemplifies the nature of this incorporation:

> The Department is advised by Inspector Cummiskey that at a meeting of the Okanagan on the 15th. July you were duly elected their Chief in place of Baptiste Logan, deposed.
>
> It has been with regret that the Department has noted the tendency of many

members of your Band to live immoral lives and to indulge in liquor. It is confidently expected that under your chieftainship, and encouraged by your own good example, the Okanagan Band will put away from them all the degrading and demoralizing habits, and the Department looks to you always for support and urge that which is right and good and to co-operate with your Agent and Inspector in their efforts to make your Band one of the best and most progressive in British Columbia.

You will at all times have the encouragement and assistance of both these officers and of the Department itself in your worthy efforts towards this end, and it is hoped that you will try to do all possible both by example and advice to stamp out all such bad conditions as those mentioned, and to elevate your Band to the position it should occupy. (NAC, RG 10, vol. 3945, file 121698-64)

The letter to Chief Michel is essentially a continuation of the ritual process, and instructs the new chief in the values he should espouse now that he is part of the new regime. Moreover, having accepted his medal, albeit in somewhat different circumstances to those of Nkwala and the other Indian chiefs of an earlier era, he now became linked symbolically and politically to Canada and the British crown. Thus, when the members of the Royal Commission on Indian Affairs for the Province of British Columbia arrived in the Okanagan the following year, Chief Michel was able to speak his mind (and his heart) freely, for he too was now part of the royal establishment.

The royal commission was charged with settling the differences between the dominion government and the government of British Columbia respecting Indian lands and Indian affairs generally in the province. The arrival of the commission coincided with the appointment of Chief Michel in the Okanagan, making his tenure an important one, because it marked the final ratification of reserve land for his community, and provided a last chance for the Okanagan and other chiefs in British Columbia to express their grievances over the land that had been reserved for them in the 1870s. It also provided an opportunity to express their displeasure at attempts to reduce the size of their reserves, and to complain about restrictions placed by law on their hunting and fishing rights.

The members of the commission[2] met with the Indians at the Head of the Lake on Saturday 4 October 1913. Isaac Harris (who had been illegally appointed interim chief by Inspector Cummiskey in 1908) was the official

2 A transcript of the local proceedings of the commission was located in the Okanagan band office while I was doing fieldwork.

interpreter. The chairman outlined the powers and scope of the commission to the Indians.

Alexander Chelahitsa, then chief of the Douglas Lake band, spoke first on the grounds that he regarded himself as Nkwala's successor. He welcomed the royal commissioners, drew attention to the English connection, expressed his dissatisfaction about talking to itinerant officials, and then sat down! After this brief statement Chief Pierre Michel addressed the commission:

CHIEF MICHEL: I am glad to see the Royal Indian Commissioners. I feel that if I see the great Government, I don't think that we are to fight over anything or anybody to have any feelings of any sorrow. I am glad to hear all the comments that was to be done here, and I don't think that we are to deal with that at the present time. I know for sure that the Commissioners will not tell me now that those reserves are to be cut off.

CHAIRMAN: How is that?

CHIEF MICHEL: I know myself for sure that the Commissioners with the Commission will not tell me that these reserves are going to be cut off, and I feel all right towards it. This reserve was staked off a good many years ago. Since then I hear lots of times that the Government was going to destroy this Reserve, and I always think I do not know. May be it is so, and may be it is not so, but whoever laid out this Reserve is greater than the Greater Chief and justice, for since I was able to see, and now I see the posts for the Indian Reserve, and I know that these posts are put down to stay and not to be disturbed by anyone. Therefore our Indians say that our Reserves will not be surveyed, and land will not be cut off.

CHAIRMAN: You mean to say that these Reserves are not to be cut up?

CHIEF MICHEL: Yes, that is what I mean. I got one more word to say. I will not take up your time much. All the Indians that have commenced to talk about this big land, about the timber and about other things, and myself I don't feel very strong about that kind of work. I don't feel like if I want to get some money from the whiteman for cutting timber off this Province. I mean that I do not want to claim any money from the whiteman who cuts timber in B.C. I know myself our blood are spilt here first, and we are the right owners of the land, and my heart never gets angry to see any whiteman making money from anything that he is doing in this Province. Just now I hear the Commissioners say that if the Indians want to do anything they like with their land, and I feel glad about that. I want to have one word to say about what the Commissioners said now, and what the Indians say.

About game laws, the Indians they always did kill their games and eat them themselves for their own use – not for sale; and the law is now that we can go to gaol for killing game. We were told by the policemen that we must not use a spear to catch the fish. We cannot catch them by the naked hand, and I don't think that there is one of my people [that] ever went to the river to get any salmon this year. They are all afraid.

THE CHAIRMAN: Where is the river?

CHIEF MICHEL: The Salmon river.

THE CHAIRMAN: What are they afraid of?

CHIEF MICHEL: Going to gaol.

THE CHAIRMAN: How do the other Indians catch fish in their streams – they don't go to gaol, do they?

CHIEF MICHEL: I don't know how it is, but one of the Councillor's boys went down to fish with a spear, and this boy nearly went to gaol. That is all I have to say.

What is most significant about Chief Michel's address is not that he anticipated the possibility that the commissioners would recommend cutting off land, but that he accepted the old boundaries as if they were the traditional boundaries of the Okanagan band. 'I know that these posts are put down to stay and not to be disturbed by anyone,' he says. The belief in these boundaries which were created by the joint commission in 1877 and surveyed in 1881 is really no more than a sort of false consciousness about the past, which Michel had learned to accept over the years. In reality, of course, it was the false view embedded in the Okanagans' unconscious relating to their overt acceptance of the authority of the British monarchy, an idea which they generally associated with Queen Victoria.

But there was a level of rationality in Chief Michel's message to the five royal commissioners, namely, his confident assertion that all the land in the province belongs to the Indians: 'I know myself our blood are spilt here first, and we are the right owners of the land.'

The implication is that agricultural land and ranch land were given to the Indians by the crown, while hunting territory, fishing (water), forests (logging territory), berry fields, and the rest were traditional Okanagan lands, and always had been. This distinction between two kinds of land is a crucial one, because it associates farming with reserves, and hunting and gathering with traditional Okanagan land. Reserves, moreover, were correctly perceived as a sort of second-class real estate acquired by the Okanagan when they were incorporated into the colonial and post-colonial capitalist society. All remaining resources and land were in a very real sense aboriginal land to be used as they had always used it. Chief Michel's complaint about the application of provincial game and fishing laws to Indians should be understood in these terms, since that is the way he and his people perceived them.

Similarly, the Okanagan band member who spoke to the commissioners after Chief Michel stated appropriately: 'This land belongs to my chief, and anything that is on the top of the earth is his, therefore I tell you that this land is mine, therefore I will not sell it and I don't want to have my land cut up.' In supporting his chief's statement he was, in this context, referring specifically to reserve land which was owned by the chief-in-council (i.e., by the people). All other land – the hunting, fishing, and gathering land – was aboriginal land to which all Okanagan had usufructuary rights.

Much of the subtlety of the statements made to the commissioners must regrettably have been lost in translation and transcription, but the meaning is always clear. The Indians were at that time well aware of what was going on in governmental circles. They feared they would lose reserve land, and they simply could not understand why laws were being applied to traditional land over which they assumed they had complete control.

Chief Michel attempted to defend the two kinds of land and the two kinds of rights he and his people believed themselves to have. The evidence he presented to the commission was largely related to reserve lands but, as I have shown, he was also concerned with communicating other grievances shared by his people. What seems to be remarkable about the meeting with the commissioners is that by and large the latter were accepted (and even trusted) by Chief Michel. However, it should not be forgotten that all Okanagan chiefs regarded themselves as falling under the protection of the British crown and the contradictions in this perception are obvious. Chief Michel was not an Okanagan chief in his own right. He had been incorporated into the province and the dominion by the ruling establishment; and he had been ritually blessed (and branded) with the spirit and values of that very establishment at his installation ceremony.

During his period of office, Chief Michel had to cope with the politics of factionalism, as had other chiefs before and after him. He commanded respect from the majority of the band, and it was during his chiefship that allotment of lands to individuals became institutionalized. The practice of individual ownership of certain land had been in effect for generations, but Chief Michel and his six councillors carried out their work in a much more systematic way, although their actions and decisions were always subject to the approval of the Department of Indian Affairs.

Okanagan individualism flourished in this atmosphere, and more and more land owners seem to have been in favour of obtaining title to their land *in the context of the reserve for the purpose of agriculture*. But the pie was already too small for everyone on the reserve to own land and farm as well. The growing Okanagan individualism and the entrepreneurial aspirations of the late nineteenth century were to cause even greater conflicts in the future, now that they had been fired with the spirit, if not the harvest, of twentieth-century Canadian capitalism.

Chief Michel died in 1918. He was a controversial leader, always at logger-heads with someone. His Okanagan name, Hlakay, literally means the person with 'full-grown antlers' after they had hardened with maturity. One of his political rivals was the Douglas Lake chief, Johnny Chelahitsa. It is said that both were fine athletes but Michel was never able to beat Chelahitsa, whether in running or jumping. The athletic metaphor is interesting because it characterizes Michel as a parochial chief who could not deal with outsiders. He did improve his image after his first term of office in 1908 (when he was still a 'soft horn'), but his transformation to Hlakay was for the local system only. Legend has it that when he died he had one withered leg, the result of an athletic injury towards the end of his life. Hlakay, with the withered leg, is a pathetic image to have of a chief, but such was the nature of political life at this time.

Not everyone supported Chief Michel. In 1917 a list of sixteen grievances was presented to the House of Commons in Ottawa by a group of Okanagan Indians. Most of these were directed against the Department of Indian Affairs for its corrupt and inefficient administration, but certain grievances reflected on Pierre Michel, indicating that many people were having second thoughts about his election (*Hansard* 14 June 1917: 2340–4).

Chief Michel was undoubtedly an important figure in Okanagan band politics. Perhaps no other chief (with the possible exception of Nkwala) allowed himself to become embroiled in every facet of local affairs and involved with the world of agents, inspectors, priests, and their superiors. In the local political arena he fitted poorly into either the old or the new factions. He was not related to Nkwala; he lived in the northern part of the reserve and not at the Head of the Lake or Irish Creek; his wife came from Six Mile Creek and seems to have owned one hundred acres of land there, *after* her husband's death; he was opposed to the Canadian government in some situations but not in others; he ingratiated himself with the church when appropriate. In some ways this profile put him in a strong position to mediate between factions and groups, and he was quite successful in this for a while. But once he lost the support of the moderates in the community his influence and credibility waned and he had no base on which to fall back.

GASTON LOUIE, 1915?–18?

There is general uncertainty over the dates when Chief Gaston Louie held office, as there is regarding Michel's second term. Part of the problem stems from the fact that the people often held their own elections which were neither accepted nor acknowledged by the Indian agent, an explanation that solves in part the overlap between Gaston Louie and Pierre Michel during the First World War.

Gaston Louie was the last of the old-guard chiefs to attempt to defy white authority on those occasions when he found an opportunity to assert what he regarded as his rights as leader of the Okanagan reserve. His first wife's name was Helene; his second wife was Martina McDougal from Penticton. He was a well-off farmer who raised pigs very successfully together with wheat and a few cattle and horses. It was a difficult period to be chief, coinciding with the war and all the other uncertainties of the time. In some circles Gaston Louie became a hero for his tough attitude towards government officials, especially after he adopted a policy to keep the agent off the reserve altogether. He defied the authority of the Canadian government by refusing to register births, and was reported 'to have several young children not even baptized,' illustrating his rejection of the church's authority.

Gaston Louie is said to have been voted in by the people. He was not a descendant of Chief Nkwala. His election is erroneously believed by some local historians to have been 'the first time that the Indian agent recorded the votes in his book.'

Shortly after taking office both Gaston Louie and Captain Tonasket were put in gaol by the police because they refused to rent out land under war regulations. Consequently, land was forcibly rented in 1915 or 1916 to Galbraith and Spears (merchants) to grow grain for wartime use. The land was owned by Annie Logan, Alex Simla, and Tonasket. Cummiskey was the chief inspector of Indian affairs at the time, although he died a few months later. Fortunately a Kamloops lawyer named McIntyre, who was an old friend of Captain Tonasket, managed to get both of them out of gaol and that is about all we know of the incident.

The narrative is interesting because it fits the spirit of the time so well, notably the activities of the royal commission in the previous year. Moreover, two of the grievances from the group of Okanagan presented in the Commons in June 1917 indicate that Chief Louie had been accused of incompetence by Inspector Megraw (Cummiskey's successor). Apparently Megraw disagreed with the chief's judgment regarding the criminal and illegal behaviour of one Alexander Henderson on the reserve, and had 'animated his personal spleen against the chief.' Chief Louie represented the old faction, especially the group of 'reactionary' conservatives at the Head of the Lake. He stood in opposition to both the Indian agent and the inspector and also to many of Pierre Michel's supporters (Hansard 14 June 1917: 2340–4).

The wartime period remains unclear, but local historians feel uncomfortable discussing the period as if the topic were taboo. The whole period calls for more research because it contains so many unknown facets, including Captain Tonasket, a descendant of Joseph Tonasket from the south. Just as Nkwala had been unable to control the southern Okanagan in his day, Chief Louie seems to have been unable to control his own people in 1915. In Nkwala's case it was a matter of trying to control too much territory. In Gaston Louie's case it was a question of coping with factionalism and the many other problems of the time. Both Nkwala and Louie tried to solve their dilemmas by creating 'captains' to assist them. It is interesting also that the Tonasket connection lasted so long, illustrating the persistence of some of the old ties between north and south Okanagan.

There is, however, another interpretation of Gaston Louie's place in Okanagan political history. Although an established member of the old faction, he was never part of the cult of Nkwalaism, which surely accounts for his strong reactionary stand. Gaston was not related to Nkwala. Both his parents were from traditional Head of the Lake stock, although neither his father nor mother were baptized. His only connection with Nkwala's descendants was his close friendship with Captain Tonasket. We might characterize him therefore as coming from traditional aristocratic Okanagan pagan background, opposed to the church, and free of the ties that Nkwala and his family had forged with the colonial establishment in the nineteenth century. Gaston Louie was thus an anomalous chief for his time, fitting the qualities of neither faction in that he had no interest in ingratiating himself in any way with either Canadian or British Columbian institutions. He was a true reactionary.

CHIEF BAPTISTE NICHOLAS, 1919–22

After Chief Gaston Louie had been ousted from office (he seems to have been deposed), an election was held on 20 October 1919 and the successful candidate was Baptiste Nicholas. He was a young man of thirty, one of Nkwala's grandsons, and married to a Shuswap woman from Enderby. Chief Nicholas won the election by a single vote and had difficulty holding his office for a variety of reasons, but mainly because he managed to get on the wrong side of both the community and the Indian agent. He was deposed on 30 January 1922. The details of his deposition are not clear, but he left the Okanagan reserve soon afterwards to settle on the neighbouring Enderby reserve, where his wife had inherited half of the family property. Some people argue nowadays that Chief Nicholas was never deposed – simply seduced by his Shuswap wife's inheritance!

CHIEF JOHNNY ISAAC (TCHLOPA), 1924 and 1930–1

After Chief Baptiste Nicholas had been deposed in January 1922 no election was held for two years. The band continued to struggle with the problems of the post-war years, factionalism increased, interpersonal feuds and crises were rampant, and the flagging reserve economy led to more migratory labour.

The election for a new chief held on 18 January 1923 proved a complete anticlimax. Johnny Isaac, son of former Chief Moses and married to Nancy Simla, was elected by the band, but the appointment was never accepted by the department. His election was vetoed by the agent on the grounds that he lacked the virtue of sobriety. Chief Isaac was a direct descendant of Nkwala, and his supporters saw him in that light when they elected him. His election as chief was based on his personal qualities as well as his position in the old faction network as determined by his relationship to Nkwala.

There are enormous gaps in both the written records and the oral tradition for many years around this time. The whole question of chiefship seems to have been temporarily shelved, and there was no election until 1930. Nevertheless, political protest and unrest among the band members continued throughout the 1920s, and when the Indian Act was amended in 1927 all formal political activity was made illegal on the reserve.

At the beginning of the Great Depression, Johnny Isaac's candidacy was eventually accepted by the Department of Indian Affairs, and he was officially proclaimed chief after winning the 1930 election. Chief Isaac remained in office for just over a year until he was again accused of insobriety and deposed by the department at the age of sixty. In actuality, he had been dragged to the agent's office by the arch mischief-maker on the reserve after having had a few drinks.

There were many incredible efforts and interpersonal intrigues to defame this chief. Eventually various individuals (some were friends) were 'hired' to discredit both Johnny Isaac and his wife; and it was on this kind of evidence that he was deposed on both occasions. Insobriety, as should now be clear, was often a euphemism for any act or rumour that could be used against a chief by the agent, and during the depression years bribes were in great demand.

People who still remember Johnny Isaac recall that he was a popular chief who always tried to help the poorer people. After his deposition several people hired a lawyer to write to Ottawa to find out if he had in fact been legally deposed. Chief Isaac, or Tchlopa as he was called, helped people to get permits for logging and he arranged credit for many families at certain stores in Vernon. He is said also to have exposed the corruption of the agent of the day, who is alleged to have pocketed a percentage of wages paid to Okanagan workers by a sawmill company in Armstrong. As one man narrated the incident: 'Agent Coleman was a mean old bugger. He collected people's wages and then paid them the equivalent of welfare while he took the rest. But he had a lot of power and people were frightened of him – not Johnny Isaac though, he stood up for us, and that is why Coleman kicked him out.' It is said that Coleman used to bring an RCMP officer with him for protection whenever he visited the reserve because he was so unpopular. On one occasion, it is recalled, 'H.G. tried to choke old Coleman, but the Mounty did nothing because he knew that H.G. was blind so old Coleman had the advantage over him.'

The attitudes of chiefs towards agents do change, however, in the 1930s after the installation of Pierre Louis. This analysis resumes in chapter 12.

PART TWO

The Contemporary Community

1/ John Chelahitsa, chief of the Douglas Lake band round about 1912. Chelahitsa was Chief Nkwala's sister's son's son. As his grand-uncle had done, he liked to display his medals as an expression of his admiration for the British monarchy. Photo by Marius Barbeau 1912.

2/ Cornelius O'Keefe, pre-empter of Okanagan land. Photo by J.G. Parks, Montreal, ca. 1876.

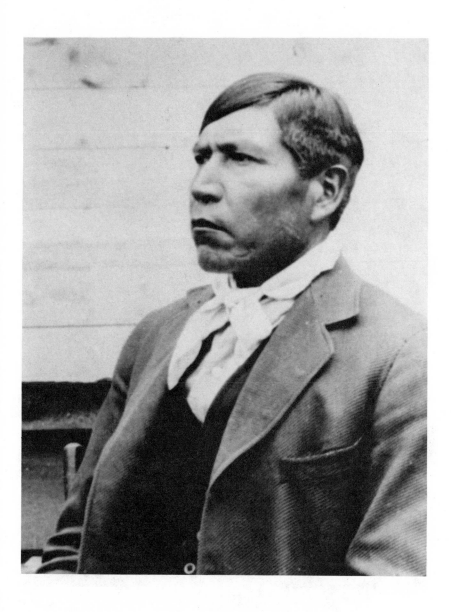

3/ Baptiste Logan (Sta'kan), chief 1909–12. Photo by Marius Barbeau 1912.

4/ Annie Swalwell, a woman of great influence, and a drummer

5/ Mary Abel, 'A woman can do everything'

6/ Mary Powers, full of history and humour

7/ Harriet Lawrence, who loved to dance

8/ Pierre Louis, chief 1932–59. Picture taken at Six Mile Creek against a background of Chief Louis Jim's log house built in the 1880s. Photo by Dr D.A. Ross.

9/ Dan Logan and Louie Marchand, two Okanagan entrepreneurs, taken Easter Sunday, 1963

10/ Jimmy Bonneau, chief 1959–61. Picture taken with Mrs Edwards at Nkwala's grave during his term of office

Chapter Eight

The Okanagan Reserve as
Canadian Community

THE CONSTRUCTION OF 'COMMUNITY'

From many points of view it would have been desirable to have written the whole of this book in chronological sequence. However, using what I have termed a diasynchronic approach calls for conscious breaks in chronology to clarify the merging of space and time – the synchronic and the diachronic. In this chapter I attempt to reflect on the Okanagan community as it emerged through time and analyse it in terms of both the past and those socio-economic and cultural variables that emerged to transform it. The chronological narrative will be resumed later, notably in chapter 12 where I pick up the history and analysis of Okanagan chiefs after the 1930s, and in the other chapters which deal with the sociology of the institutions constituting the contemporary community in the context of the modern world.

A major reason for writing this book has been to present an analysis of the socio-historical and legislative processes whereby one Canadian Indian reserve has been constructed. Of special interest among those complex processes has been the interplay between the conscious reorganization by the federal government of the socio-economic and cultural worlds of the Okanagan people and the latter's *perception of*, and consequent *reaction to*, those often coercive courses of action. The duality implicit in that reaction to conquest is of enormous significance in understanding the perception of community held by the Okanagan, because the way outsiders define them is so different from the way the reserve-dwellers define themselves. This does not mean that the attitudes of white people generally and Indian Affairs officials in particular should be regarded as irrelevant. On the contrary, the understanding of the way the Okanagan as insiders construct their idea of community is greatly influenced by the perceptions those outsiders have of them (see Cohen 1985).

The concept of community is indispensable to all sociological inquiry: 'the community' is the crucial arena in which the intricacies of social life and their cultural expression can be observed and also understood. For its members it is also the stage from which insiders observe outsiders, where the actors observe their audience, so to speak. This is not to imply that the study of community is an end in itself, or that artificial boundaries must limit the nature of the inquiry. Community boundaries vary not only with geography and socio-economic circumstances, but with the way they are constructed by the people themselves. In the interpretative sense, community boundaries may also be said to vary with the whims and theoretical assumptions of the observer and analyst. Thus, to understand the nature of a community fully, it must always be seen as part of wider systems of social relations in both space and time, a perspective that requires that they be analysed as diasynchronic subsystems of society in general. A community is never a static entity (cf Bock 1962). Earlier chapters have provided the context in which to analyse the contemporary community. Now I wish to focus on that community while attempting to contextualize the present within both the past and the wider society.

The romantic myth portraying rural communities as close-knit collections of people enjoying warm personal relations and institutional completeness does not apply for the Okanagan reserve 'community' as it has evolved, any more than it fits the majority of rural reserves throughout Canada and the various other Indian communities in the Yukon Territory (Coates 1988). There is, of course, considerable evidence to suggest that rural farm families generally have never enjoyed idyllic and peaceful lives (e.g. Gordon 1988).

The Okanagan, by and large, tend to live guarded lives and limit their interaction with others to special occasions and manageable situations. Among the many probable causes of this impersonal, and often aloof, behaviour in reserve culture is the important historical reason that the civil servants who created Indian reserves never *intended* them to become properly integrated communities. These reserves were simply pieces of land granted to Indians to enable them to carry out near-subsistence farming; it was largely a coincidence that certain village clusters, now known as the Head of the Lake and Six Mile Creek, were concentrated on what was later to be called Okanagan Indian Reserve No. 1. Obviously, the way reserves were surveyed and defined had a lot to do with the shape and form of contemporary social relations and attitudes.

The Band List

For census purposes, the Okanagan reserve community consists of a specific

TABLE 2

Total population of Indians registered on the Okanagan reserves in British Columbia on 31 December 1985, based on band lists drawn up by the Department of Indian Affairs

Name of band	Population	Percentage living on reserves
Upper Nicola	471	70
Okanagan	899	66
Westbank	246	81
Penticton	400	73
Upper Similkameen	30	77
Lower Similkameen	228	77
Osoyoos	177	84
Total Okanagan band population	2451	72

number of people defined as band members by the Indian Act. At first sight these people would appear to be so bureaucratically and arbitrarily constituted as to rule out any community, but over the years the people have incorporated the crucial bureaucratic rules into their social personalities so that now the band membership list embodies for them the sharing of common community sentiments (McIver and Page 1949: 8ff). This process involved much more than merely transmuting a bureaucratic invention, for it is now generally believed by many people that the names included on the band list were placed there in accordance with unspecified traditional procedures. Some traditional procedures do survive, but the band list per se is essentially a white man's tool to facilitate the administration of the Okanagan. The rules, moreover, have changed over the years, and some people have become Okanagan Indians by marriage, through residence, through guile, or by a combination of these. From time to time serious conflicts have developed over the question of membership in the band of those regarded by some as intruders. Gradually the band list has become the official and generally accepted record of the Okanagan Indians, carrying with it the connotation of club membership or even citizenship (Colson 1953). The list itself is a private census providing the following details: full name, date of birth, marital status, whether resident on or off the reserve, religious affiliation, and a family and individual number for each band member. Very recently the members of the band voted overwhelmingly *against* assuming control of their own membership and the right to establish their own membership rules. Thus on 20 May 1987 the status quo was acknowledged, and people confirmed their faith and belief in the provisions of the Indian Act.

In the narrow sense, the Okanagan reserve as 'community,' as it is perceived by its residents, coincides with the official administrative community established by Ottawa. But in the minds of each of the parties it means very different things. As an administrative community it also has two important population components: those living *off* the reserve and those who spend most of their time *on* the reserve. Further, people live on the reserve in different ways. The family that lives on the reserve surviving on welfare payments is very different from the family whose 'head' works in Vernon as an accountant commuting the fifteen kilometres five or six days a week. Both are different from the entrepreneur who leases property to whites, runs recreational and camping sites for whites, operates a shop, and lives on the reserve permanently. All three are radically different from the large extended family which combines among its members horse breeding, horse racing, farming, and off-reserve employment. Conversely, living off the reserve does not necessarily put at risk or threaten to break ties in the reserve community.

Settlement Patterns

Although there are seven reserves, the main concentration of the population has gradually shifted to the largest of these, Indian Reserve No. 1. A few families still live on two of the other six reserves,[1] but by and large these have become investment properties for the band and certain families who have title to parcels of land.

An important characteristic of contemporary Okanagan settlement patterns, however, lies not in the clustering of households but in their dispersal. Most people try to live at arm's length from both kin and neighbours because they enjoy space and privacy but also because proximity is said to lead to quarrels. The visitor to the Okanagan reserve might well ask: 'Where are the Indian settlements?' Houses are dispersed and often concealed, unlike the gregarious white settlements on the lakeshore. Most households own some form of transport, usually a pick-up truck, and people drive everywhere. You

---

1 See Map 4. In 1987 the main aggregations of the 174 households (houses) on the reserve were found in the Irish Creek–Head of the Lake areas (52 households) and in the Six Mile Creek–Whiteman's Creek areas (77 households). Another cluster of people live in the Salmon River area (22 households) situated in the northern part of the reserve, a good eight-mile drive from the band office. There are also those who live strategically well placed between the Head of the Lake and Six Mile Creek in the Bradley Creek–Newport Creek areas (17 households). The remaining 6 households are located on two other reserves, 2 at Priest's Valley (No. 6) and 4 at Duck Lake (No. 7). Today no band members live on the Harris reserve (No. 3), Otter Lake (No. 2), or on Swan Lake (No. 4), or Long Lake (No. 5) reserves.

drive to visit friends, you drive to the band office, to church, to the rodeo, just as you drive to Vernon to shop. Thus, to speak of the Head of the Lake, or Irish Creek, or Six Mile Creek as if these constituted close-knit local groups is misleading. At best we can say that people tend to cluster quite loosely in different parts of the reserve.

Some of these clusters do have traditional roots, but their nature has been transformed over time with changes in the economy, especially the growth of private property and the emergence of political factions. A predetermining factor in the dispersal of households and homesteads is naturally the private ownership of land which motivates most people to live on their land, but the astute avoidance of residential proximity, even by people who have no farms, is so striking as to call for some comment. Residential patterns are to a large extent related to the system of inheritance, the subdivision of land, and shifting patterns of wealth. Thus, while many people might be said to own the official means of production (land), few people ever become rich from land. Yet people jealously guard their holdings (private property) under the delusion that they may become wealthy one day, even at the expense of a kinsman or a neighbour (see Pearson 1986: 502ff).[2]

Although no tangible core or focus of community may be apparent to untutored outsiders, three such representations do exist. First is the traditional seat of power at the Head of the Lake, the headquarters of Nkwala's empire. Here also is St Benedict's Roman Catholic Church, the community hall (used for elections, general meetings, dances, parties, and other functions), the main cemetery, rodeo grounds, and ball park. Also at the Head of the Lake is the replica of the old open-air council hall and the ruins of the old log jailhouse. Nowadays there is little everyday activity at the Head of the Lake except for special occasions, and most of the day-to-day political action has moved to the second focus, the Irish Creek annex which is the site of the band office. With the closing of the Department of Indian Affairs outpost at Vernon in 1975, the band office rapidly became the administrative centre of the reserve, the 'Little Ottawa,' where all the formal concerns affecting people's lives are transacted. Here is the office of the band manager and his staff, where chief and council meet, where the social worker dispenses social assistance and other services, and where births, deaths, marriages, coming and going from the reserve, estates, and leases are reported and registered. Every possible item linked to

---

2 During the last twenty years, as population has increased and wage labour intensified, the pattern has changed to some extent. But there is little evidence that people are consciously trying to live closer to each other. Some people have become 'rich' through leasing land to outsiders, but there is always a sense of mystery as to who is well off.

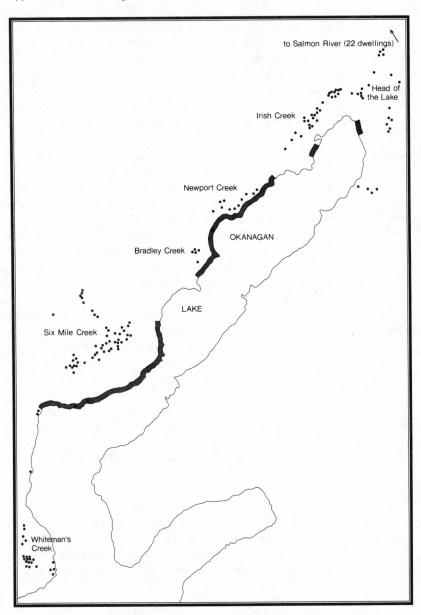

Part of Okanagan Indian Reserve No. 1 showing individual Indian dwellings on the reserve in August 1987 and White cottage and mobile home strip settlement

life as an Indian-status person is dealt with in the band office, and countless facets of people's lives are moulded and consolidated there. As the bureaucracy grows in Ottawa, so does the red tape on the reserve.

The third core in the community is Six Mile Creek, situated as many miles to the south of the Head of the Lake. Despite local attempts to establish an active village core at Six Mile Creek, these had not succeeded until very recently. The old schoolhouse built on the initiative of Chief Pierre Louis in 1922 is now a meeting house for senior citizens, the New Horizons[3] of the reserve. The so-called new school built in 1951 is now used as a nursery school. St Theresa's Church, first constructed by Chief Louis Jim in 1895, was rebuilt in the 1960s, and a ball park was constructed in the 1950s. The band-owned and operated volunteer fire department is also located here. In recent years these facilities have been expanded and improved through council's initiative, and a spendid recreation park with green grass has been created on the site of the Komasket Ranch. The site was used for the pow-wow in August 1987 when all seven Okanagan bands met to sign their Declaration of Aboriginal Rights. A mammoth arbour constructed for future pow-wows and other important occasions was completed in 1988. But in general people continue to focus their activities elsewhere, except perhaps on weekends.

From many viewpoints it is surprising that what is often called the new faction has not succeeded in establishing a strong new seat of power, even in the symbolic sense, at Six Mile Creek. But old labels die hard in the hands of factionalist intrigue, and the tradition that Nkamapeleks (the Head of the Lake) should lead politically has made the majority reluctant to submit to a radical relocation of local government. Irish Creek, after all, is really the annex of the Head of the Lake, and the old seat of power is still visible from the band office windows.

Okanagan villages and settlements have always had a kin base in the sense that they are associated with families who share common localities. This is not to claim that villages have even been coterminous with large kinship groups, but it is possible to say, for example, that the Wilson and the Louis family live by and large at Six Mile Creek, that the Gregoires live at the Head of the Lake, and that the Brewers live at Irish Creek. Although intermarriage has taken place between people from different localities over the years, the extent to

---

3 New Horizons meets several times a month on Wednesdays in the old Six Mile Creek school. Volunteers cook an excellent Sunday dinner, there are plenty of helpers, and the old people have an opportunity to talk to each other and to meet visitors who might drop in. The old women like to drum and sing and dance, and give the impression that they are reliving the golden age of their youth.

which avoidance of affinal ties between certain groups has persisted, for reasons quite unrelated to principles of kinship, is quite remarkable. The key factors of this particular endogamous tendency are clearly associated with status and factionalism and the various ideologies they reflect, which I will discuss in later chapters. The implications of these marital prohibitions and preferences based on status are considerable. They have produced a shortage of eligible spouses over the years, particularly because marriages between cousins were traditionally disallowed, a custom that was reinforced in later years by the Catholic church. As a consequence of this combination of principles of status endogamy and kinship exogamy, there has been considerable recruitment of spouses from outside the reserve community. Some have come from other Okanagan bands, some from Shuswap, Lillooet, Thompson, and other neighbouring ethnic stocks, including the local white population.

As a consequence, it is impossible to speak of the Okanagan at any time in their history as if they constituted a closed population characterized by ethnic homogeneity. Marriage and cohabitation with fur traders, settlers, and other whites have existed for over a century. In theory the old Indian Act only allowed white women who married Indian men to acquire Indian status, but in fact this has not always been the case (see, e.g., Jamieson 1978).

Patronyms

The old system of naming has now almost completely disappeared and few people have an Okanagan name or any interest in having one. The name that is important nowadays is the patronym, however it was originally derived. Some patronyms were acquired during the fur trade and colonial period, for example, Gregoire and McLean. Others were once 'priest names' (given by the priests, or baptismal names which later became patronyms), for example, Joe, Pierre, William(s). Still others are transformations of Okanagan names, for example, Logan (TElāKā'n), Simla (S'imlo'ox).

These patronyms are associated nowadays with the community's two general locales, but in themselves they are not accurate indexes of kinship or social status because they are only the father's patronym. The only reason male patronyms have become 'objective' identifiers in the community is because that was the way people were classified when the Indian Act was enforced and the band list established. Thus in 1877 the nominal census listed people by their individual names, both Okanagan and Christian, but the act eventually changed that by discouraging the use of native names.

The traditional system of naming became extremely confusing after patronyms were first introduced because these used to change every generation. Thus if my name was William Peter, my son might transpose it and call himself Peter Williams. When the people themselves began to take patronyms seriously at the end of the nineteenth century, they also discovered the nominal meanings and found that certain names such as Pierre and Paul had acquired an Indian connotation. As one person said of his grandfather's name change, 'His name sounded too Indian, so my grandpa changed it [to a white sounding name].'

Large families with names such as Marchand, Louis, Bonneau, and Gregoire are fragmented by various rifts, divisions, feuds, and hierarchies, many of which are associated with affinal ties, occupation, 'respectability,' and their various allegiances in the community. Thus, neither the families or the names themselves, nor the divisions within them, should ever be regarded as corporate groups in any sense, although the divisions in large families do often resemble, *by analogy only*, the segments found in large lineages characteristic of some societies.

People do sometimes change their names, but there is no real evidence that this habit is related to patronymic feuds, although it does reflect personal idiosyncracies and conscious efforts to detach themselves from patronymic involvement and commitment. So the patronym is, for quite complex reasons, important to most people in their daily lives. Sometimes a particular patronym is a social asset, sometimes a liability.

Affines

Children born of a married couple are always registered under their father's name. But the mother's patronym is equally important socially. While a woman's status is always modified at marriage by her husband's status, the obverse is also true, and the affinal principle permeates all family networks.

The following discussion of affinal networks is unavoidably patricentred because of the patronymic emphasis to which people have been subjected over the years. Marriage, for example, became patricentred very soon after the entrenchment of the Indian Act, which in some respects was reinforced by the doctrine of the church. Biases relating to the importance of the roles of father and husband also emerged at an early date. So when we come to discuss affinal networks among the Okanagan, we are in fact discussing the networks which originate with one's wife or mother and their respective families (not fathers or husbands). These two sets of affines mediate between families and articulate with all other significant affines of both sexes. While relations of kindred are patricentred and tend to be wide and unevenly structured, linking families in a specific way, affinal networks are not. They are matri- and uxori-centred and tend to ramify out from one focal point.

Because of the legal prominence of the naming system, however, the visibility and the importance of any one particular affinal network tend to be obscured. For example, the political successes of a man may have more to do with the fact that he is the son of woman X and the husband of woman Y whose own father or grandfather was once politically influential than with the fact that he is a member of family Q. Contemporary Okanagan kinship is still technically cognatic but its strong matri-uxori-centredness suggests a strong leaning towards 'mother-right' (Radcliffe-Brown 1952). By analogy, to borrow a principle from matrilineal societies, status, prestige, honour, even authority, are often carried through women while political office is nearly always held by men, not as brothers but as spouses and sometimes as sons.

The illusion that Okanagan women played no part in local politics until recently arose because they did not receive the franchise until the 1950s. Okanagan women have always been aggressively active in every aspect of reserve life; at political meetings they are highly vocal, and at election time they are prominent in the nomination process of candidates for office.

Despite the disadvantages women experience in Canadian society generally and through the Indian Act, Okanagan women have continued to be conspicuous and active in religion (reserve Catholicism), medicine (traditional healing), education, and a successful striving for upward mobility. Women, in addition, inherit property in their own right, and a significant percentage of privately owned land on the reserve is in the hands of women. As wives, women run their households assertively, and a husband who fails to respect 'the woman' might find that his marriage has broken up. Okanagan divorce and separation are common.

Married women might spend a great deal of time in the kitchen, but they are never submissive, and husbands are expected to look after young children both at home and at official functions. I have also observed that daughters receive special attention from fathers. That sons are doted upon and spoiled by their mothers is well known, and there is a strong suggestion of what might be termed cross-sex childhood affection between parents and their children. The high incidence of marriage dissolution may also be related to the dominant mother and the influence she has on her son's inability to develop a compatible relation with his wife. As some say, 'Mothers won't release their sons.' Conversely, some fathers prevent their daughters from marrying by insisting on their obligations to the household.

Family Networks and Family Compacts

Like most rural and semi-rural people, the Okanagan transact the business of everyday living from the material base of their households through the personal configurations of family networks in a manner not unlike those reported by Arensberg for the Irish: 'The sentiments [a person] holds are organized first and foremost round his fellows: the members of his family, household, kindred, and the community. It is towards them that his habit is fashioned and in his relation to them that his social order takes its form' (1937: 203–4).

For many reasons relating to history and tradition, interaction in the broad arena of Okanagan family life is relatively open compared to that of the Irish, and unlike the Irish the Okanagan are perhaps freer of the traditions of the Catholic church. Even the constraints of the Indian Act do not permeate too deeply into this personal arena. Family networks permit people to negotiate convention and articulate ideology relatively freely, giving them room to manoeuvre in an otherwise constrained world. This is not to suggest complete flexibility of action because family networks do reflect a variety of structural patterns.

In general terms there are three kinds of family networks: general patronymic networks, family compacts and 'bunches,' and vacillating family networks.

General patronymic networks refer to those loose categories identified by a shared name, which need to be understood historically in terms of residence and locality and the complex of affinal networks which link families. The influence of general patronymic networks vis-à-vis the community is reflected in local politics and local stratification, but collective action and uniform ideology are not their typical features. Nor are patronyms in themselves good indicators of the phenomena they occasionally reflect.

At the other end of the family network continuum are those closely knit segments which, though often difficult to identify, can be mobilized at short notice for specific purposes of a political nature. I hesitate to characterize these as patronymic cores, because large patronymic families may have several cores which stand in opposition to each other, a trend that is particularly evident at election time when members of families are divided as to the candidates they support. Consider, for example, the case of a father and son who compete against each other for chief, or the husband and wife who run against one other for councillor.

Within each general patronym, then, we can distinguish one or more core segments or *family compacts* which involve both relatively small groups of consanguineal kin and affines, who interact face to face from time to time. These are the segments which promote political action such as the signing of petitions, or pushing for reforms in the water system, or lobbying for candidates at election time. Family compacts resemble the 'bunches' which Lithman (1978: 180–205) analysed for the Fort Alexander Reserve in Manitoba, but my impression is that the Okanagan tend to mobilize themselves more consistently than Lithman reports for Fort Alexander. The reason is that the Okanagan are obsessed with kin networks and carry cognatic principles to their limits to the extent that practically any action set will have a kin base attributed to it. Thus, action sets and other apparently non-family groups among the Okanagan are almost always rationalized in kin terms. If they succeed in promoting a political candidate opponents might say, 'The so-and-so's were successful because there are so many of them,' indicating the belief that success is mobilized at a kinship level. Similarly, failure of a particular band-subsidized project might be attributed to the lack of expertise of the you-know-who's who 'have been known to screw things up for as long as anyone can remember.'

One of the best examples of family compact associations that include close friends is house gatherings which tend to be kin-based in the very general sense but include non-kin on the grounds that they are like family anyway. Such gatherings are never perfectly harmonious occasions and sometimes they reflect rivalries and conflicts between smaller groups and generations. At Christmas and Easter and during the summer, when people visit from afar, these occasions become arenas for keeping people informed of each others' activities and provide opportunities for gossip and endless mulling over of local events and political trends.

A similar kind of association that forges strong ties between individuals is the inter-visiting dyad. These associations are not based on kinship (although they might involve kin), and are properly seen as close-knit friendship networks. They exist among all categories of people. Interaction is exclusive and often quite secret, giving rise to structures very similar to those reported from Ireland and occupying crucial positions in everyday life (cf. Arensberg 1950; Leyton 1975; Ludwig 1984).

In the context of what I have called family networks a distinction has been made between loosely knit general patronymic networks and the more tightly knit family compacts. But there is a third type which is always important in that it represents a sort of synthesis or articulation of these two types. I call these *vacillating family networks*, the constantly changing sets of allegiances and configurations that form, separate, and re-form in different guises almost imperceptibly over the months and years. In a sense these vacillating family networks are central to band life, for the Okanagan think of themselves both very specifically and very generally because community for them is construct-ed that way. When they act, they have, on the one hand, to come to terms with 'the self' as being emotionally involved in primary group ties; on the other hand, there is the much wider context of community loyalty as it applies to each person as a member of the Okanagan Indian band. Hence the principle of vacillation which characterizes inter-family ties may be seen as the result of the dual struggle, conscious and unconscious, to reconcile two very different sets of sentiments and loyalties.

The Reserve Community

The Okanagan reserve community has never been a viable economic unit since its creation in the nineteenth century, and the majority of families have always been obliged to involve themselves, either collectively or through the services of one or more of their members, in wage labour off the reserve for short or long periods of time. The need to be involved in the labour force off the reserve has increased over time, a phenomenon that is related to local population growth, changes in the Canadian economy, changes in the pattern of living on the reserve, and a general striving by the Okanagan themselves towards entry into the Canadian middle class. Another factor has been the acquisition by a small minority of band members of considerable property and wealth on the reserve, without the creation of additional jobs locally for the poorer segment.

Although social assistance rates were originally designed to minimize any of the incentives to move on or off the reserve, significantly recent increases in federal social assistance for band members have not in fact altered the trend.

Reserves have often been characterized as social refuges where people can retire in old age or where they can return when unemployed or sick, or simply when the hazards of living in the outside world become too complicated. Often the more conspicuous off-reserve visitors are people who have made good outside, indicating that membership in the band is attractive to everyone, albeit for different reasons. The major incentive for maintaining band membership has, of course, always been retiring in old age to a pleasing physical environment, especially when kin ties are strong and in good repair. Although some people do leave the reserve to avoid the strain of kin ties, the whims of close-knit friendship networks, and the devastation of factionalism, there is nearly always some incentive to return. For example, many thought that the financial claim of $3,855,072 arising from the Swan Lake and Long Lake cut-off settlement awarded on 12 May 1984 would leave them well off. But the $4030 that each band member received did not go very far, as most people soon discovered. At the present time the prospect of comprehensive land claims has again begun to excite the fantasies of many off-reserve members, providing a fresh incentive to maintain ties with the reserve to ensure *legal* membership in the community by retaining one's name on the band list.

Table 3 shows the trend towards permanent off-reserve residence over the

TABLE 3
Native population of the Okanagan Reserve showing the approximate
number of 'on reserve' residents, 1827–1987. Unless otherwise
stated the figures refer to the end of the calendar year based on the
official estimates submitted to the Department of Indian Affairs

Year membership	Total band	No. on reserve
1827 (November?)	238[1]	–
1877 (September 10)	248[2]	–
1891	165	–
1911	207	–
1921	287	–
1931	310	–
1941	471	–
1954	639	–
1958	653	588 (90%)
1961	711	602 (85%)
1965	621[3]	590 (95%)
1971	709	528 (74%)
1975	743	509 (68%)
1981	810	490 (60%)
1982	859	552 (64%)
1985	953	511 (54%)
1986	976	553 (57%)
1987 (July 24)	1074	Not available

1 HBCA B.97/e/1 (1827); pre-reserve times
2 NAC, RG 10, vol. 10011, census 1877
3 Westbank band separated from the Okanagan band in 1964.
NOTE: Accurate statistics of population movements are not available,
and there is enormous fluctuation during the year (cf Table 2).

years. The marked increase after 1970 reflects the decline in jobs both on the
reserve and in the Vernon area, when more people were forced to move to
other areas if they wished to get regular employment. Many families used to
do seasonal casual labour in Washington State picking apples and other fruit
until the practice was abandoned in the 1970s. Some large families working
full-time together for a few months made enough money to tide them over
until the next season.

The complexities of out-migration, return migration, and 'off-reserve'
residence cannot be dealt with fully here. The chief cause of migration is
largely an economic one and the pattern is always related to the availability of
work. For example, return migration to the Okanagan reserve at the end of the

Depression and the beginning of the First World War was influenced by the growth of the lumber industry and the development of the fruit-canning and other related industries in the area. Demographic observations, however, indicate quite clearly that the reserve cannot contain a population much above five hundred people given current economic trends in the region.

Although the size of the band as reflected in the official list prepared annually by the Department of Indian Affairs continues to increase, the number of permanent residents has begun to decline both relatively and absolutely. Band members come and go as they always have done and the pattern of fluctuations in the size of the community is difficult to determine. Those who remain on the reserve permanently nowadays are generally the old people, those employed in the band office, those few involved in entrepreneurial and other profitable enterprises (including farming) on the reserve, those who find employment within commuting distance, many young children, and the majority of the students unless they live off the reserve with their parents.

There are several factors acting in concert which affect community size at any one time. The passing of Bill C31 and the subsequent amendments to the Indian Act on 17 April 1985 influenced the composition of band membership because the legislation made it possible for people on the 'periphery' of the band to reapply for membership. These include women who lost status by marrying men who were not registered Indians (that is, white men); children whose registration as status Indians was rejected because only their mothers were status Indians; children in the 'Double Mother Rule' whose mothers and fathers' mothers were not status Indians before their marriage.

The full effects of anticipating great wealth from land claims and all the ramifications of the 'New' Indian Act following Bill C31 have not yet manifested themselves, but in June 1985 fifty-three women were reinstated on the band list, accounting for the significant increase in the number of females in the 1985 census (see Appendix 2). In addition, by July 1987 eighty children had been reinstated (see Table 3). A number of men are also in the process of trying to document their right to become band members, a status which redefines them as Indians.

The Okanagan reserve community is, however, not limited to its legal members and a handful of non-status Indians. A few white people live in the community and are accepted as if they were band members without any political rights.

There is another group of white people with whom many band members are involved in intense interaction. These include the social worker who, among other things, is responsible for approving social assistance and other grants to band members; those white men and women who enter into business relations and partnerships with individual band members; the Catholic priests who have been involved with the Okanagan over the years; the now defunct Indian agents, inspectors, and superintendent; the teachers and others who used to be involved with Okanagan education on the reserve and in the old residential schools; and nowadays we would want to include the teachers and white students with whom the Okanagan interact in the schools they attend in Vernon. There are also the physicians with whom individual Okanagan have forged close ties over the years. The late Dr Hugh Campbell-Brown, for example, was closely involved with the people at Six Mile Creek for many years before his death. Today people are able to choose their own physicians and dentists from a large group of practitioners in the Vernon area.

But are these people really part of the community? From the point of view of an academic outsider, the answer might be definitely yes. To the Okanagan, no matter how intimate, warm, affectionate, and intense the bonds with these people might have been, the answer in every case is no. The beer-drinking guitar-playing priest, when it comes to community, is just as much an outsider as a treacherous autocratic Indian agent, as is the close friend from a neighbouring reserve.

There are two exceptions to Okanagan clannishness when it comes to the admission of outsiders to their community. The marriage of a woman of any origin to a band member and the marriage of a man from a neighbouring band to an Okanagan woman nearly always guarantee acceptance into the community. But there is an inequality here with regards to status after marriage, with a strong bias in favour of women entering as wives of band members, illustrated by the disproportionate number of alien wives who become both leaders and pillars of the community.

ACTUAL RESERVE POPULATION

The reserve community, as I have characterized it, derived its membership over the years from different sources. And while its core was rooted in traditional and post–fur trade culture, the first band list was not drawn up until 1877, a year after the passing of the Indian Act. As people internalized the new law, further modifications in their culture occurred. One of its many manifestations was the acceptance of the band list as a bona fide record of community members, an acceptance that has continued to the present day. Yet another significant demographic entity consisted of all the people who actually live on reserve land. I will refer to this as the *reserve population*, a territorial aggregation of people consisting of both Indians and whites, without the hallmarks of community. There is often no interaction between them and sometimes no acknowledgment of each other's existence.

A pilot survey of the seven pieces of land (reserves) that make up the land officially granted to the Okanagan band reveals that more white people live on them than Indians. The white population in summer is probably as high as two thousand, and roughly one-third of these live permanently in dwellings on Indian land. This surprising fact results from the leases and rentals of property by the Okanagan to whites, which represents a major source of revenue to a few Okanagan landlords. It is important to highlight the extent of the white presence on reserve land for two reasons. First, it points to the decline in the agricultural value of band land and the increase in its value for recreational and residential purposes. Lakeshore property is thus a prized possession for the Okanagan and jealously sought after by whites from as far afield as Calgary and Vancouver for low-rental summer cottages. Other areas of band land are permanently occupied by whites who live in large mobile homes and comfortable houses in trailer parks created by Indians on their own land. Priest's Valley reserve has a large mobile home park, as does Duck Lake reserve, and at least three mobile home parks have grown up quite recently on the main reserve. For a minority of band members, the increase in the white presence on the reserve is an economic asset. For the majority of the band, however, these whites are treated either with indifference or their presence is barely acknowledged. Underneath the indifference is a deep-seated hostility which emerges on occasions at political meetings, and in casual conversation. People without such profitable land often become bitter and angry when they learn about the relatively large incomes earned by a minority of families.

The second reason why the white presence should not be overlooked is because it reflects the 'exploitation' of Indians by whites. Rents and leases are low and many white people enjoy living in the beauty of the Okanagan Valley for nominal rent, which some have begun to regard as their legal right. Land is also rented to campers, while a few people have been allowed to build houses on reserve land and enjoy the advantages of registered twenty-one-year leases. Other leases are made of agricultural land to market gardeners. Part of Hiram Walker Distillery is located at Duck Lake and several other commercial and industrial projects are housed on reserve land. The band also leases communal land to increase its own revenue.

Many white residents on the reserve play down the fact that they live on Indian land, and some visitors are unaware that they are on a reserve. Over the years band council has tended not to flaunt signs which draw attention to the existence of the Okanagan Indian Reserve, possibly out of deference to landlords, and as an attempt to inflate the value of non-saleable, rentable lakeshore land.

RESERVE AS CANADIAN COMMUNITY

If communities are always parts of wider socio-cultural systems in both space and time, any attempt to isolate a specific community for sociological analysis must surely fail. Similarly, communities are not mere symbolic constructs in the minds of insiders (Cohen 1985). Yet from a native point of view, culturally legitimate members of a community pay attention to a range of boundaries in their characterization of the differences between 'us' and 'them' and the relations between them; while the view that the outside world has of them also influences the view they have of themselves.

In this chapter I have attempted to delineate the parameters of the Okanagan reserve community by drawing attention to some of the boundaries between insiders and outsiders in anticipation of the structural issues central to the subsequent chapters. Generally, the issues are obvious, but I would like to emphasize that the members of the Okanagan reserve community continue to live in an asymmetrical world in so far as most other communities that impinge on their lives are concerned. Twenty years ago, for example, whites living on the reserve, or sharecropping with Indians, could have their contracts terminated quite simply, although some persistent tenants were difficult to evict. Today, as more and more white tenants insist on longer leases for rental property and as the white population on the reserve has increased, this last little bastion of superordination over the outside world has begun to decline. Reserves, like the smallest Russian doll in a sequence of relationships, are at the end of the line, the innermost formation of a little world within a wider world. But the analogy breaks down when one looks at the quality of the reserve. Unlike the smallest doll within larger dolls, the reserve is not a replica of the larger systems of concentric formations that enclose it. In the final chapter I will examine this asymmetrical world in some detail.

Chapter Nine

Okanagan Factions

Much of the character of community life on the Okanagan reserve has been shaped over the years by rampant factionalism, a phenomenon that has been alluded to in several of the preceding chapters. While carrying out research I was constantly plagued by various manifestations of this factionalism, often to the point of wanting to abandon my field project altogether. Some people refused to look at me, not because I was a *samma* (white man), but because they felt I spent too much time with the 'wrong' faction. One very close friend pretended to be out of town for a week because he was upset that I had been talking, more than he felt I should be, to the people down near Whiteman's Creek. Another person delighted in getting me to phone him from the public phone at Six Mile Creek so that I would be seen in the 'right' faction's area.[1]

The English word faction has been used for a long time by the Okanagan to refer to a variety of divisions and cleavages in their reserve community. There is a word in the vernacular, *nkw'tswixtn,* which is sometimes used for faction,

---

1 Fieldwork is never easy. One wakes up in the morning having carefully planned the day's work only to find that everything has changed. The woman who promised to tell you about children's games and adult bingo has gone to Revelstoke to pick berries, and the family that was going to introduce you to the chief's mother in the afternoon has gone to town to buy groceries. These kinds of experiences are well-known sources of irritation and frustration to anthropologists. But there are more serious problems which tax every fieldworker's guile. These are related to questions of social differentiation of one sort or another, such as attempts at understanding conflicting ideologies and values between partisan groups on Canadian and American Indian reserves and the ubiquitous phenomenon of factions. Nagata (1970: xiv) reports in the preface to his Moenkopi study that one of the reasons he found fieldwork difficult was the 'recurrent factionalism among the Indians.'

but the word itself simply means 'a different village,' suggesting that factions are often identified with a village or locality. But clearly there is more to it than that. Silverman and Salisbury (1977: 1) are not too keen on defining factions for some very good reasons, notably their fear that analysis will become static and classificatory or look for equilibrium states or some other transgression of the spirit of modern anthropology. Thus, they emphasize 'factionalism' instead, and manage to convince their readers that all social situations involve processual dimensions, formulation of new ideologies, social restructuring, and so on – all the kinds of phenomena which can be illustrated by the Okanagan material. Factionalism is indeed an ongoing phenomenon.

Despite warnings to the contrary, there is some virtue in trying to define a faction for the sole purpose of clarifying a sociological concept. Unlike cliques which are small exclusive groups, factions consist of quite large aggregations whose members insist that they share certain specific common ideological commitments and interests. These ideologies and interests are always shaped and maintained by opposition to the principles of other factions or to the status quo. The Oxford English Dictionary implies that there is always an imputation of selfish or mischievous ends or the use of unscrupulous methods in factionalism, but we should qualify this assumption by pointing out that the members of a faction at any one time see themselves as holding the proper and desirable ideals against which the ideas of others stand in opposition.

Clearly, factions are not corporate groups; in fact, they are not groups at all since interaction between members tends to be sporadic, situational, and often casual. And it is an exaggeration to stress recruitment by a leader as Nicholas (1968: 28–9) and others do because recruitment is usually quite informal. Thus I prefer to see faction membership being mobilized by strong cliques (Beals 1959) or family compacts, or what Lithman has termed 'bunches.' And while disagreeing with Gulliver (1977: 63–4) on the specifics of leadership in factions, I like his characterization of factionalism in terms of conflicts of interest, competition over scarce resources, the competition for power and influence, the significance of ideological factors, and the importance of recognizing fluid and flexible networks of social relationships rather than well-defined groups.

If we are to study factionalism in any society we need to identify the factions, which admittedly is not easy. Factions are important because they constitute the informal and unstructured associations for channelling conflict, for reinforcing particular ideologies, for drumming up support for action surreptitiously and even mischievously. Factions are theoretically open categories and can be infiltrated by fifth column operations of opposing factions. But they can also close ranks in order to prepare for some kind of concerted action, as in the case of a faction transforming itself into a political party.

The role of ideology in factions has been played down in some of the literature, but here I want to emphasize the opposite – namely, its over-whelming importance especially with respect to reserves and other closed communities. In a recent study of the Rehoboth reserve community in Namibia, Pearson has demonstrated how important ideology is in local level politics as expressed through factions. He also argues that 'factions are very likely to arise in situations in which the electorate believes that the choice which is made at the polls will make very little difference to the material circumstances of the voter. It is in precisely such situations, too, that ideological rhetoric is likely to be most extreme. It can be, I would suggest, a case of a great deal of ideology, rather than too little' (1986: 442 et passim). Of course, factions are always active in political movements and the election of political leaders, but Pearson's observation for a Namibian reserve rings true for the Okanagan. I suspect, moreover, that the more general function of factions might be to achieve immediate emotional gratification for members and hangers-on, rather than the solution of more practical problems or immediate material gain.

Recognizable Okanagan factions have been in existence for a long time. In both the written record and the oral tradition mention is made from time to time of 'the chief's faction,' 'the opposition faction,' 'the Church (i.e., priest's) faction,' 'the Head of the Lake [and Irish Creek] faction,' 'the Six Mile Creek faction,' 'the old faction,' and 'the new faction.' From the 1890s to the 1950s adherents of factions were preoccupied with the question of chiefship and related matters. As we have seen, factions were involved in the unscrupulous process of deposing chiefs by certain Indian agents, and in mischievous attempts to oust a particular chief and other prominent band members by questioning their origins and by vicious character assassination (see also chapter 12).

Although new factions seem to emerge, transform, disappear, or regroup, I would argue that all factions on the Okanagan reserve up to the early 1980s have persisted over the years and owe their origin to locality and people's perception of their past. Thus the physical division between the Head of the Lake and Six Mile Creek has factionalist overtones even today. But there is more to this division than the existence of two villages or neighbourhoods; the view that the Head of the Lake has of Six Mile Creek is coloured by Okanagan history in which the former saw themselves as traditionally superior, having originated as horsemen, ranchers, and agriculturalists – people who lived their lives up on the bare hills hunting game and feasting on meat. The 'others' they regarded as 'Lakers,' people still housed in kick-willie dwellings by the lake, living largely on a diet of berries, roots, and fish. Thus, the earliest division among the Okanagan was partly geographical and partly based on status differences measured by criteria, real or imagined, associated with specific modes of subsistence.

Some of the basic principles by which Okanagan factionalism can be best understood are expressed in a series of oppositions represented as follows:

Head of the Lake (Nkamapeleks)	Six Mile Creek (Sntlemuxten)
meat-eaters	fish-eaters
ranchers	lakers
the seat of power	absence of power
Nkwala's people	others
'old faction'	'new faction'

For years after the establishment of the Indian Act, the Head of the Lake people dominated the rest of the community politically and economically. This pattern goes back to the eighteenth century but the structure crystallized during the fur trade as Chief Nkwala strengthened his 'seat of power.' I don't think one could speak of a true faction during Nkwala's lifetime since there seems to have been general acceptance of his position and authority. But some years after his death, during the colonial period and after the smallpox epidemic of the early 1860s when Okanagan autonomy had been questioned, a new process of factionalization began to emerge. By the mid-1870s when the Shuswap and Okanagan were attempting to forget their differences and unite in a liberation movement against the settlers, it was the rampant factionalism within each group that destroyed their chances of asserting their rights over land. After the members of the Joint Reserve Commission had finished their job of pacifying the natives, the Okanagan presented their internal conflicts to the rest of their world in the form of a basic division which was often spoken of as the old faction and the new faction, respectively. Significantly, at this time a number of Six Mile Creek people were beginning to challenge the authority of the Head of the Lake by questioning the ideological basis of its continued supremacy. I would suggest that this uniting of a number of families against the Head of the Lake gave rise to the two core factions, the new and the old, as they began to be called. Thus the new faction in this context became the first faction, and the old faction emerged in reaction to it as the hegemony of Nkwalaism was challenged.

All the early factional intrigues stemmed from new tensions emerging between what had originally been two Okanagan villages in the Head of the Lake confederacy. And in a very special sense, factions and factionalism have followed that pattern. The initial reaction to the questioning of their authority by the Six Mile Creek people outraged the Head of the Lake core and the abusive reaction is still expressed on occasions by people born before 1930. But the lines of cleavage between factions are constantly changing as they have done over the years, and at best we can speak of factional cores grounded in powerful family compacts, similar to Lithman's bunches, which keep fuelling the fires of perpetual conflict and discontent. Analysis of interpersonal conflicts and gossip in Okanagan reserve culture could lead one to near libellous conclusions about the character of the people. But that behavioural profile takes on quite a new meaning when it is seen in the context of factionalism as I have defined it. Let me suggest that one of the functions of factionalism is to provide a certain degree of control over personal anger and ideological disjunction. Thus much of the emotional component of factionalism in the Okanagan would be handled quite differently in many African cultures, where witchcraft accusations would predominate in comparable situations.

To illustrate the fickleness of behaviour within the context of Okanagan factionalism, let me give an example drawn from the 1930s when the members of the chief's faction (nominally the old faction) secured the services of a legal firm to express their grievances in a letter to the superintendent general of Indian affairs, giving details of Chief Isaac's arrest in 1931 before he was deposed by the agent. Many personal details were openly stated, the role of the agent in factional behaviour was revealed, and the fluidity of factionalism uncovered the fickleness of behaviour. One paragraph of the letter states:

One day shortly before [Chief] Isaac was deposed, he had been to Vernon. Following his return to his home in the evening and while he was engaged in lighting the fire, a car stopped at his house and [A] stood in the doorway. The latter looked at Isaac and said nothing, but went to the car in which [B], the Indian policeman, was sitting and told [B] that Isaac was drunk. [B] then came into the house and attempted to arrest Isaac. The latter refused to go because he was not drunk, so [B] called for help and [A] came and assisted him and the arrest was made. Isaac was taken to Vernon, also his wife. He was charged with being drunk, but the magistate dismissed the case. This was the chief reason when the Indian Agent deposed him. (See Chiefs File, Department of Indian Affairs 982/3-5-1 March 1879–Dec. 1947)

The extent to which Indian agents used factional affiliations to their own ends is clearly illustrated once again. We might also observe that person A belonged to the new faction and incidentally became chief himself for a short while in the late 1950s. The Indian policeman at that time was a well-known mischief-maker on the reserve normally associated with the old faction, but who changed his affiliation on this occasion while under the protection of the law. The agent, moreover, sided with the new faction because he was interested in getting their representative appointed in place of Chief Johnny Isaac.

Some people changed factional affiliations in the 1920s and 1930s because of the tremendous uncertainty over entitlement to band membership that grew up after the visit of the royal commission in 1916. The commission had not simply been interested in 'cutting off' reserve land but also in reducing the size of band populations. Consequently, some band members took it upon themselves to 'smell out' people whom they considered intruders into the Okanagan band. Thus, belonging to an Indian band has many parallels with being a citizen of a country, especially when people's origins are called into question. Criteria based on origin are particularly susceptible to malicious scrutiny because they can be interpreted in so many different ways and from different perspectives. It is not surprising, therefore, that members of the two factions revelled in the process of scrutinizing each other's pedigrees with a view to getting rid of some band members altogether.

In 1917 there was an intriguing debate on Okanagan affairs in the federal House of Commons following a petition containing nineteen grievances drawn up on behalf of one faction. One of the grievances addressed the question of 'illegal' membership in the band and requested the removal of twenty-eight men from the Okanagan reserve on the grounds that they were either Indians from the United States or local British Columbian half-breeds and Indians with no right to be on the reserve. The list of names included two future chiefs and one man whose family later claimed ties with the house of Nkwala through one of his American Okanagan wives (Hansard, 14 June 1917: 2340–4; Christie n.d.).

The same petition was followed up seventeen years later in 1934 when an official Board of Investigation for the Department of Indian Affairs looked into the pedigrees of every household on the reserve, then comprising some 346 people. The purpose of the investigation was purportedly to settle some of the disputes and reduce the bickering that had been going on for more than two decades between the old and the new factions. Inevitably the investigation created so many conflicting opinions about people's origins that neither faction was satisfied with the results and no conclusions were ever drawn. The only achievement was to stoke the fires of factionalism on both sides with more material for derogatory character assassination. In due course, the process of smelling out aliens seemed to subside for a while, as members of both factions took stock of their origins and their roots. It did not take long for members of the old faction to resume their attack on the new chief and his kin, an assault which continued for another twenty years (see pp. 208–15).

CONTEMPORARY FACTIONS

Okanagan factionalism in its traditional form comprised the struggle for recognition and power between the old faction and the new faction. These two factions reflected a variety of spatial, economic, and cultural cleavages in the community, some going back to near traditional times. Generally, though, factionalism in its most virulent form is a product of reserve culture in concert with adaptations to colonial frontier society.

In 1954 when Hirabayashi was carrying out his research on the reserve, he identified four different political factions which he labelled the reactionaries, the conservatives, the liberals, and the progessives. These were his own analytical categories and they have had a considerable influence on my own interpretations. I do not regard them as true political factions in the sense that I have used the terms because his scheme detracts from the old faction–new faction dichotomy which is so crucial to understanding the Okanagan community through time. His typology is useful in that it enables one to see factions as comprising families and individuals with different attitudes towards their cloistered world as each perceived it.

The *reactionaries* were said to be anti-government, suspicious, and anti-change, and wished to return to the 'old days.' Some were so extreme that they refused to accept old age pension and family allowance cheques, and were even opposed to sending their children to school.

The *conservatives* still spoke of the Queen's promise: 'As long as the sun shines and the river flows, Queen Victoria gave us these promises.' They were described as being essentially conservative as opposed to reactionary, and believed that their children should go to school in order to compete with the whites.

The *liberals* realized that the old ways had gone and there was no point in trying to recapture them. They were, moreover, willing to accept the laws that had been imposed on them.

The *progressives* were characterized as those who 'know nothing of the old days and care less.' They regarded the conservatives as holding the reserve back by obstructing improvements. They encouraged their children to get as much education as possible, and even went so far as to suggest that the reserve system should be abolished in time.

Converting this typology into old faction–new faction terms we can see that the former was made up of conservatives (with its reactionary wing) whose ranks tended to articulate the view of a golden age in the past – not the distant past of traditional times but the heyday of farming and ranching in the nineteenth century, a period still under the halo of the post-Nkwala era.

Hirabayashi's liberals were those who made up the main body of the new faction as he would have encountered them in 1954. His progressives, judging from the names he mentions, were the few entrepreneurs who stood outside factional issues, although, paradoxically, both of Hirabayashi's progressive informants always regarded themselves as having emerged from the core of the old faction.

The cleavage between the two factions still exists albeit in a muted and often obscure form, a transformation that can be attributed, first, to the fading of the vision of a golden age in the past as more people understood the negative dimension of the early days of the reserve system. The second factor that has undermined the ideological base of old-new factional cleavage stems from a growing trend to look to a dubious golden age in the future when the reserve will become a little utopian enclave financed by the billions of dollars the people will receive as part of a comprehensive land claim deal with Ottawa, as an alternative to getting back all their traditional lands.

The decline in the hostility between the two factions has in fact centred on the weakening of Head of the Lake old faction power and credibility. As the new faction, with its Six Mile Creek base, acquired more political and economic power, so also its members have achieved higher status in the community and become the vanguard of a middle-class movement. The decline in the intensity of the rift between the old and new factions is also related to the levelling-out of regional differences, now that most people own motor vehicles and many have telephones to provide efficient transportation and communication. Equal opportunity in education has also facilitated interaction between people throughout the reserve.

The number of adherents of the new faction increased enormously during the 1950s, and especially in the 1960s. By the 1970s its liberal ideology had transformed the faction into an aggregation of liberals bearing some resemblance to a political party (but not to the Liberal party of Canada). By the early 1980s this new faction party split along conservative-progressive lines. One of these I will call the *new conservative faction* with a strong Six Mile Creek base representing rural respectability, made up of older people who think the world is going to the dogs: 'too much freedom for the kids,' 'no respect for the elders,' 'wild ways,' 'all that music and dancing – these are no good, why can't they dance the way we used to dance, square-dancing was nice and old Jimmy

Bonneau used to wear a red handkerchief round his neck and do the calling.'
The new conservatives spend much of their time grumbling about the present,
and they object to the presence of whites on the reserve, especially those
leasing Indian land. Some of the new conservatives have good lakefront
property which they refuse to lease or develop for ideological reasons. The
members of the *progressive modern faction*, in contrast, are irritated by this
new conservatism but there is not much they can do about it. When property
and inheritance matters are involved, people feel they have to toe the
conservative line because they fear their mothers and fathers might will the
property to someone else. There are thus strong sanctions against factional
disputes which might divide families. In this regard it is significant to note
that at election time some families deliberately nominate candidates to run
against each other because of internal disputes among family members related
to property matters.

Many people question the view that the intensity of traditional factionalism
has declined and that there has been a levelling out of regional differences.
From the perspective of the ideological component of factionalism they are
probably correct, for there is still room on occasions for the expression of
surreptitious emotionally laden attitudes reminiscent of the traditional
cleavage. But I believe it is true to say that the sociological component of that
cleavage as expressed through family networks and compacts has lost much of
its strength, an observation that applies particularly to the old faction with its
depleted ranks, kept alive only through the determination of a small élite and
their preoccupation with regaining their lost power in a world long past.

Having experienced the side-effects of Okanagan factionalism myself, I
could never pretend that it no longer exists. However, what I observed in
others and experienced myself was muted by comparison with reconstructed
accounts of factionalism in the 1920s and 1930s when conflict was exacerbated
by the political contingencies of the times.

Chapter Ten

Making Ends Meet
in the 1950s

It has long been established and even measured[1] that Indians are, on average, poorer than other Canadians. Here my immediate concern is not so much with comparisons of that order, but rather with aspects of the domestic economy of the Okanagan Indian Reserve, especially the sources from which families actually living on the reserve obtained their income. I will also attempt to assess the degree to which families on the Okanagan reserve are dependent on the wider economy in order to make ends meet.

The total population of the Okanagan Indian Reserve in 1954 was 639. This was made up of 108 households having an average size of six people. At that time not more than 10 per cent of the band population seems to have been actually living off the reserve, and the members of most domestic families were involved in a variety of occupations, including farming and ranching (on

---

1 Hawthorn et al. (1958: 209–29) demonstrated how unenviable British Columbian reserves in general are as productive economic units. The general survey of band households in the province in 1954 revealed that the net business income from fishing, farming, ranching, logging, trapping, handicrafts, guiding, commerce, etc., constituted only 18.6 per cent of the average household's income, and social security allowances 16.8 per cent. The average household income for reserve Indians in British Columbia in 1954 was $3304 for a family of five or six persons, the equivalent of about $14,000 in 1986.

The authors offer various interpretations of these crude figures, and they are quick to point out that the average figure of $3004 per annum is essentially a crude mean and inflated by the 'numbers of Indians in British Columbia with high incomes.' They also point out that when comparisons are made between Indian household wage-earners and British Columbia household head wage-earners in general the former earned $1853 per annum and the latter $3208 per annum in 1951.

their own farms), logging, and migratory farm labour and casual labour.

Hirabayashi[2] portrayed the subsistence activities of the reserve in 1954 as if they were centred in farming, which he thought could be developed if the people would only apply their energies properly. He writes in his notes: 'There is land to be cleared and a young man with enough ambition and energy can acquire bush land for the asking and clear that land for his farm.' He provides two examples. A band member, who had ten dollars in his pocket, obtained fifty acres of bush land from the band and cleared twenty acres for the cost of $1300 by renting a bulldozer and using an army grant, a provincial government grant, and selling posts from his bush land. He was allowed four years to pay back the provincial grant. His new land eventually permitted him to raise twenty acres of hay a year, but this was a job he did in his spare time. He had a full-time job with a logging company which was his main source of income.

The second example was of an established conservative farmer who claimed that there was plenty of uncleared land on the reserve. The farmer also asserted, 'if any of my boys want to go into farming, I'll give them some [of my] land so that they can start.' It was not mentioned that the boys (sons) had full-time jobs in logging off the reserve, and that the farmer had spent years off the reserve himself working as a migrant labourer to obtain the cash to start his horse-breeding business and to develop his agricultural land.

Both of these cases illustrate how crucial it was for each farmer to support his enterprise with revenue derived from wage labour. Indeed, they confirm that the emphasis placed on agriculture in the reserve economy essentially reflects the cultural aspirations of people wishing to be farmers in spite of the limitations of land shortage.

I have already shown that for almost as long as the reserve has existed the Okanagan have been involved in wage labour in the wider society, a practice that has not changed over the years, although the sources of income on and off the reserve have altered quite radically. Thus, even when people appear to be developing their farming enterprises, their operations are always subsidized by outside employment, most generally by wage labour. The same can be said of the few highly successful entrepreneurial endeavours.

Let me now turn to the Okanagan reserve economy as it was in 1954. This account is based largely on Hirabayashi's field notes, but my own research has influenced the interpretation of the data.

---

2 In 1954 James Hirabayashi carried out fieldwork on the reserve (see acknowledgments) and I have been able to reconstruct the domestic economy at that time with the help of his excellent field notes.

RANCHING, AGRICULTURE, AND HORSE BREEDING

In the 1950s there was a greater emphasis on, and involvement in, agriculture (including gardening) and ranching than there had been in 1987 but considerably less than there had been in 1887. Farms varied in size and type but most were a combination of ranching with grain farming, although at that time farmers strove towards cattle ranching alone because it was more profitable. Any household that kept cattle – whether one milch cow or a herd of 250 animals – aimed at growing its own hay and feed. It was reckoned that fifty acres of hay was sufficient to raise a hundred head of cattle. Ambitious farmers estimated that if they could grow all their own feed (enough to get them through the winter months) they could build up their herds and still have an income by keeping all the heifers and selling the bull calves for veal. Some calculated that each head of cattle consumed about a ton and a half of feed each winter. The goal at that time was to build up a sizeable herd so that one 'would not have to go down to the States in summer and fall with the family' as wage labourers. However, the assumption was always that cattle ranching involved sporadic work 'well suited to filling in slack times with casual work.' In other word, farmers always expected to earn a supplementary income from wage labour.

Grain farming on the reserve had begun its decline at the turn of the century, as it did in the Okanagan Valley generally, so that by the 1950s those few farmers still trying to rely on grain farming for their principal income were wishing they could be free of the hazards of agriculture. The biggest grain grower on the reserve in 1954 said: 'I bought equipment and went behind in my payments because of poor prices and the finance company wanted their pay so I sold the cattle to pay it off. I haven't got a start [on extensive cattle ranch] since then.' Grain farmers needed sizeable land holdings, and some used to rent additional land from other members of the band. Grain farming, like ranching, fitted in well with casual wage labour.

When truck gardening became profitable in the valley some Okanagan tried their hand at it, but they were never very successful. Generally the fertile bottom land with rich black soil near the lake was leased out to Chinese and Japanese market gardeners. The Indians attributed their own lack of success as truck gardeners to the fact that they 'don't have the know-how for growing crops,' although they worked hard, or that 'vegetable gardening is just not my class,' or that they simply didn't have any luck at it. One farmer said he lacked education and business knowledge. There are really no reasons to accept these negative self-evaluations as the real cause of failure because there were several gardeners who did quite well for a time. The principal reason for their failure was simply that, like many market gardeners, they ran into difficulties when they were short of capital. In cattle ranching and grain growing, people could do part-time wage labour (as the majority did anyway), but market gardening requires constant attention. One Okanagan gardener did do well for a while and employed sixty workers from spring to fall, but his operation failed in 1953–4 when the price of vegetables dropped; and he was never able to recoup his $14,000 loss.

I showed earlier that the Okanagan on the reserve were in a poor position to compete with non-Indians as fruit farming developed in the valley because they lacked capital and irrigation facilities. Several people did attempt to establish orchards on the reserve as a part-time endeavour, but never produced a surplus above their own domestic needs. In 1954 the chief still had his apple orchard, but most people had given up their efforts at fruit farming, especially after the severe frost which killed the peach and apricot trees (and some apple trees) in the early 1950s.

After his bankruptcy, the market gardener mentioned above turned his hand to fruit farming in his spare time. He had been forced into wage labour (truck driver for a logging company based on the reserve) but after his shifts and on weekends he established a forty-five-acre orchard with over twelve apple trees, four hundred plum trees, a few cherry trees, and some grapevines despite poor irrigation. On paper the scheme was a good one, but he never made a profit, only just covering his expenses. He would not have been able to support his family without his regular job as a truck driver which paid $3500 a year. In addition to the cash from his job, the family also made $1200 leasing land to non-Indians and $672 family allowance, giving the household of ten people an annual income of $5372.

What income did the average Okanagan family derive from all forms of farming, including ranching, in 1954? My estimate, based largely on Hirabayashi's data which are clearly biased towards the fourteen better-off farming domestic families on the reserve, is that the mean average household income derived from farming was $1205 for the whole year (see Appendix 3). Most reserve families did not farm because they had no land, and some families made no profit out of their farming endeavours. I have estimated, moreover, that for the reserve as a whole about 30 per cent of the incomes of domestic families came from farming, but again this figure is weighted in favour of farming families. This clearly demonstrates that for the majority of domestic units on the reserve farming accounted for much less than one-third of their annual incomes.

Although the Okanagan were once renowned for their horses, they traditionally valued these animals more for the prestige associated with owning them. Thus in the 1880s when horses and cattle were competing for fodder and it became clear that the stock had to be reduced, many people had to choose between prestige and capital. By 1954 the improvement of roads and the increase in the number of automobiles had made the horse less important as a form of transportation, so in general it was the horse that lost out to cattle. A few families continued to breed horses for rodeos, riding stables, racing, and use on the cattle ranges. Nevertheless, the horse is still part of the local culture and most men dress as if they had horses and were about to ride up on the range. In the absence of appropriate numerical data, I have not attempted to quantify the value of horses in terms of the income generated by them for domestic families in 1954.

LAND LEASING

The practice of leasing out land has changed enormously during the past thirty years. In 1954 most leases were related to some form of farming; agricultural land was leased at rates varying from $25 to $35 per acre per season. The largest land lessees were the cannery companies who in turn sublet to Chinese or Japanese truck gardeners. Additional labour for these operations came from the reserve, but in the 1950s Ukrainian immigrant workers were trucked in from Vernon each day. Nowadays Okanagan landlords look back to that period with some amusement as a time when they did not have to give their children pocket money because 'the kids were able to go down to the lands after school to work for the "Chinamen" [and others] we rented our own land to.'

The land leased to these truck gardeners was the very rich bottom land near the lake. Some Chinese farmers were able to raise onions on the beach land in spite of its gravelly texture. Other areas were leased out for wheat, oats, and alfalfa. Some of these leases were made on a sharecropping basis – usually a quarter-share of the crop or profit to the landlord. In a few cases the landlord received one-third of the crop.

Other kinds of deals were also made, such as partnerships and alternating harvests: 'I went into partnership with another fellow [Indian] on 80 acres ... going to have grain ... I [had] to go into partnership because I [didn't] have any equipment to farm.' Another band member told of his deal with a white entrepreneur in Vernon: 'This year [1954] I made a deal with Beck. He summer fallows my land and in the spring I give him alfalfa seeds and he planted it along with oats. In the fall he harvests the oats off and I have an alfalfa field good for about 5 years.'

All leases were supposed to be registered in the agent's office, after which they were recorded in the regional office and eventually in Ottawa. Payments were made through the agent's office 'to protect the Indians.' Another type of lease which never passed through the agent's office was the 'secret leases' between band members who 'did not trust the agent or the government,' and between Indians and whites who said they 'were in a partnership.' The whites favoured these partnerships because they avoided the payment of property tax on rented land. Secret leases were highly prized by the Okanagan because they created contracts which they themselves controlled, giving them the assurance that they were in charge of their land. The Okanagan have always valued personal relationships and these secret leases epitomized that ideal.

In the 1950s, however, many Okanagan thought leasing land was dangerous. Some said that leasing out spoilt the land, and there was a general ideological commitment to keeping land away from non-Indians because Okanagan land was sacred. There was also the idea that if you leased land it would be in the records and would be sent to Ottawa, and count 'agin' you. This fear of getting your name on the official landlord's (leaser's) list had complex roots. In part it related to the concern that you might never get your land back if it got registered by the bureaucrats in the federal government; but it also reflects a general apprehension of violating the Indian Act. And then there was the belief that leasing might involve you in some kind of cut-off scandal reminiscent of the Swan Lake–Long Lake sagas. But there was a more subtle psychological factor which created anxiety over leasing. Many Okanagan would get advance payments on their leases, having earmarked the money for a project in the summer. Meanwhile they would run short of cash, spend their false surplus, and get themselves in a financial mess which they promptly regretted.

In this connection, I use the term 'landlord' somewhat guardedly to refer to band members who leased land out to anyone, Indian or white. Landlords anywhere must feel a little anxious about leasing, sharecropping, or partnership arrangements, but the fears of reserve Indians are of a different order because of the enormity of the bureaucracy which controls them. From many perspectives, the Okanagan (and other Indians in Canada) are involved in a type of enfiefment. Their land is held in trust for them and is controlled by the federal government. If they lease land to another party, their landlordship can only be legitimated by the system itself. Thus a canning company which leases land from an Indian and then subleases to a Chinese truck farmer also involves itself in the system of enfiefment for that particular segment of its operation, while the rest of its business is part of the capitalist system.

From another viewpoint, one might argue that the Okanagan do become powerful landlords when they lease reserve land to industrial companies and to whites for residential purposes. This practice had not been fully developed in 1954 and I shall postpone discussion of it to a later chapter. In these cases the Department of Indian Affairs does in fact protect the landlord through the process of registration, and for these particular kinds of leases government recognition and support are actively sought by band members.

The leasing of land under its jurisdiction by band council must also be considered. This corporate leasing involved a few sites for industrial use, and commonage for institutional use (for example, military manoeuvres and rifle-range practice by the Canadian army). Another form of revenue for the band has been the leasing of commonage to white farmers and speculators for stock grazing. The grazing fee for a specified number of stock over an agreed period was formally established and the money paid into the general fund of the band. Other concessions granted to whites included logging permits and permits to cut specified numbers of Christmas trees.

How much money did leasing generate in 1954? Estimates reflected in Appendix 3 suggest that the average household obtained $248 a year from leasing and sharecropping, representing 6.25 per cent of their total annual income. But this figure is based on a sample weighted in favour of families with leasable property. A larger sample would have produced a much lower percentage, since over 80 per cent of band members own no land at all. It must also be noted that landlords on the reserve, in spite of their belief to the contrary, were in fact receiving only about one-third or one-half of the market value of the land they leased to outsiders.

WAGE LABOUR

By the early 1950s even the more successful farmers in the community had had some experience of wage labour. Some found it necessary to subsidize their farming enterprises, others had worked in wage labour of some sort or other before they farmed. For those who did not farm, wage labour off the reserve was doubly important. In 1954 there were a few families who prided themselves on having self-supporting farms, but it would be extremely difficult to prove that no member of those families had ever been a wage labourer.

Any discussion of wage labour has inevitably to face the complexity of this heterogenous activity. Here I have found it useful to distinguish between four kinds of wage labour: seasonal migratory wage labour; casual wage labour; regular wage labour; and regular migrant wage labour.

Seasonal migratory wage labour refers almost entirely to involvement in the three- or four-month berry and apple-picking (and apple-thinning) season south of the border in Washington State in which individuals, and sometimes whole families, became migrant workers. They were housed for the season in cabins on these American farms and were paid well above the Canadian rate for the same activity. Families with older children worked as teams and were highly sought after for their productive labour. Some farmers sent buses to the Okanagan to collect their workers.

In 1953 one family went down to Washington State to pick apples. Between them they made $1700 and brought $1400 back. Living quarters were provided for the whole family and an additional $400 to $500 pocket money was made thinning the apple trees before the picking season. Two brothers went down to the United States for the same reason, worked long hours, and returned with $2000 between them, putting the money towards the domestic family budget. Families were paid on a commission basis which, as can be inferred, was far in excess of the Canadian rate at that time, which was 45 cents per hour.

Casual wage labour did not involve migration, nor was it necessarily seasonal. Casual wage labourers were those who obtained jobs from time to time on and off the reserve and were able to live at home. These included those who worked for local white farmers or for other band members, and those who did odd jobs for employers in Vernon. I would also be inclined to regard seasonal labour in the district as casual wage labour because workers were able to maintain ties with their domestic groups and with their core community.

Closely resembling causal wage labour was *regular wage labour* involving people in permanent jobs either on the reserve or within commuting distance from the reserve. In 1954 there were very few people in white-collar jobs and no one had professional qualifications, but a high percentage of band members did hold steady jobs as farm labourers, as workers in local sawmills, as truck drivers, and in local factories. A few men owned logging teams and did log skidding for local enterprises, but this was often seasonal and many of the loggers were also farmers.

Regular migrant wage labour involved full-time work away from the reserve for long periods of time. In theory, regular migrant wage workers were expected to contribute to the domestic economy by sending remittances to boost household budgets and/or to improve farms and houses. Money or commodities (for example, an automobile) brought back after a stint away were also acceptable, but some people spent all their earnings and brought nothing home. There seems to have been very little ideological commitment to regular migrant labour in the early 1950s, although people did describe it to me, and I know that some were absent from the community for long periods of time. I was, therefore, surprised to find no identifiable case of regular migrant wage labour recorded in Hirabayashi's rich data. It is an illusive category among the Okanagan and very different from forms found in other parts of the world. There is, for instance, no ideology among the Okanagan regarding remittances (cf Philpott 1968; Mayer 1961; Schapera 1947; Rubenstein 1987), and no evidence that strong sanctions were imposed on people to maintain family ties when they left home for any length of time.

At best we might say that an incipient form of regular migrant labour was to be found both in seasonal wage labour and in other forms of wage labour. Individual Okanagans often left the community to work on the big white-owned cattle ranches that had grown up in the area, but these people were always able to remain in close contact with kin and friends on the reserve, and seldom went too far away. Even the seasonal migrant labourers who went south to Washington State saw themselves as close by because they were generally near American Okanagan reservations and former Okanagan territory.

In Hirabayashi's notes on wage labour he records that 15 per cent were casual wage labourers and 65 per cent regular wage labourers. After I had analysed the data on which these percentages are based I was surprised to discover that *regular* wage labour was the main activity, having hypothesized that *casual* wage labour would have predominated. Subsequently I found that most people prefer regular wage labour provided they do not have to leave home, which explains also why regular migrant wage labour is so unpopular. There are many cultural reasons for avoiding it. In the first place there is no glamour attached to going away from home base, no ideology proclaiming the excitement of the bright lights of Vancouver and Seattle, and no urgency to see the world. Apple-picking in the United States had its appeal mainly for the money, although some did say that a change of scenery was a good thing. There is absolutely no evidence that life in downtown Vancouver was actively sought after or even thought attractive. Even today 'other places' too far from the valley – especially cities – are suspect.[3]

In all periods in Okanagan history it is important to make a clear distinction between band members who leave the reserve every so often to work elsewhere and those who live and work more or less permanently off the reserve. The latter may maintain kinship and friendship ties on the reserve but their only connection with the band may be the fact that they still keep their titular legal rights to remain on the band list. There were such people in 1954 but their numbers have increased during the past thirty years. Other

3 For an excellent, if tragic, biographical novel about a young Okanagan man corrupted by the city see Jeannette C. Armstrong, *Slash* (1985).

Okanagan who may otherwise have left the reserve permanently have renewed their ties because they say that they 'do no want to miss out' on possible multi-million dollar land claims. Today there are a few band members who are essentially absentee landlords and have been for some time. They are relatively well off and augment their off-reserve income by leasing out their property on the reserve. Theoretically a dozen band members could control all the valuable property on the reserve in this way, lease it out to whites and enjoy absentee landlord status off the reserve, provided they kept certain minimal prescribed ties with the band. Such people would be neither wage labourers nor migrants.

For the majority of people living on the reserve in 1954 some form of wage labour was crucial, and nearly every household needed this kind of income to make ends meet. The estimate that 42 per cent of the average domestic family's annual income came from wage labour illustrates that while farming might have been the desired way of life at that time, it was not the most profitable financially or the most feasible.

SOCIAL ASSISTANCE AND INCOME FROM OTHER SOURCES

In 1954 a significant source of household income on the reserve came from family allowances, old age pensions, veteran's, war widow's, and war orphan's allowances, and public assistance such as rations and cash payments. The data show quite conclusively that the most important of these were the family allowances (baby bonus) granted to children up to the age of sixteen years. Social assistance, as it operates at the present time, did not exist in 1954, and the baby bonus had enormous appeal to households as a source of regular income. The rate varies according to the age of the child, the range in 1954 being between $5 per month for children under six and $8 for children between thirteen and sixteen, after which it was discontinued. Thus, a fourteen-year-old 'brought in' $96 per year, and a family with twelve children would receive about $1000 per year.

I have estimated (see Appendix 3) that approximately 19 per cent of household income came from family allowances, pensions, etc. for 1954, family allowances accounting for about two-thirds of all social assistance. Several households would not have been able to make ends meet without family allowances, while for others the extra income enabled them to enjoy a few luxuries. In short the baby bonus was always seen as a household allowance by the Okanagan to top up income derived from other sources.

The Okanagan community has always been a source of revenue to the commercial world outside the reserve. There was no store on the reserve in the

1950s, and most shopping was done in Vernon, as it is today. Many families used to obtain credit from Vernon merchants, paying accounts at the end of the month or after the harvest, or after the apple-picking season in the United States. The baby bonus provided a regular form of income and a convenient way of paying off credit. Indians have always had great difficulty in obtaining loans to develop their farming and other enterprises, but local merchants who appreciated their value as consumers facilitated a process by which money earned by Indians always found its way back into the commercial world. For the Indians, buying on credit was often a necessity and even today there are a few people who still patronize a corner store for their groceries instead of paying cheaper prices in supermarkets to keep their options open for obtaining credit.

In 1954 there were two additional sources from which people on the reserve could obtain financial aid in the form of loans. First, the band controlled loan funds of about $3500 a year. This fund was administered by the agent (after a vote by band council) and loans at 5 per cent interest per year were granted for a variety of purposes, including clearing land, buying land, building houses. The second was a revolving fund set up through money acquired from the British Columbia Special Vote. Only $100,000 was available to be shared by all the Indians of British Columbia, and loans were difficult to obtain because most Indians lacked security. The loans were almost exclusively for irrigation and agricultural improvements. One of the greatest sources of irritation and puzzlement to the Okanagan has always been how difficult it is to obtain a loan to start a new operation or to improve an existing enterprise, while whites are perceived to encounter little trouble in obtaining loans without any moveable security.

SOME CONCLUSIONS ON THE DOMESTIC ECONOMY (1954)

In 1954 the local Indian agent said: 'L.M., E.B. & J.B. [were] the richest men on the reserve. He [figured] their income must be around $3000 to $4000 a year.' What the agent did not figure out was that there were other quite prosperous households on the reserve at that time, and that income also came from sources other than farming for most people. There was an element of truth in his claim (despite the fact that he understimated their incomes), because when one looks at the sources of household income for the top six families, success in farming, in all but one instance, was an important index of high economic status. In other words, a family that did well in farming was most likely to be at the top. However, this presupposes that the family had a significant amount of land to begin with. In fact, the two best-off domestic families in 1954 derived 83 and 61 per cent of their gross income respectively from farming and *nothing* from wage labour. It did not take much detective work to discover that both these families had been involved extensively in wage labour in the past. Other good examples of this process can be found in those families which, in 1954, were building up capital from wage labour to acquire more land to expand their smallish farms. As time went on they were able to phase out wage labour and devote their energy to new enterprises on the reserve, especially when leasing cabin sites to whites became profitable.

Land has always been a scarce commodity on the reserve and there is room for only a few ranches and grain farms by modern standards. For the majority, therefore, wage labour of some sort as a permanent career was becoming the order of the day.

The mean average amount of cash generated for a household in 1954 by leasing land and sharecropping was quite small – about 6 per cent of a total annual budget. It should be noted though that the majority of the population had no access to land, and even the landowners in 1954 benefited only to the tune of about 13 per cent of their total household incomes from leases and sharecropping.

An extremely important source of income in 1954 for every family, rich or poor, young or old, was the various kinds of financial aid available to them. Families regarded all kinds of institutionalized assistance as regular income in much the same way as they would regard income from regular wage labour, but with greater veneration because it could be relied upon to arrive regularly and the cheques could be easily cashed in any shop or grocery store. These payments were often said to be better than wages which could get lost, used to pay debts, spent on liquor, or terminated with the job. Similarly, in farming crops often failed, animals died, and market prices were usually fickle or did not come up to expectation. Leases also had their disadvantages when people defaulted on payments and when advance payments got spent too quickly leaving nothing for the lean winter months.

The importance of social assistance (19 per cent of all income for domestic families) cannot be underestimated and many families still build their lives around them (pensions included), since they bring with them a feeling of security in an unstable economic world. Thus, in a family with children sixteen years old and under in 1954, there was a focus on the baby bonus. In the case of families with old people, the pension became the centre of the budget. Often several forms of assistance were combined, as in the case of the war widow with three children who combined war widow's and orphan's allowance with the baby bonus. By reserve standards they were considered to be quite well off at the time.

There was another aspect to all these forms of financial assistance, namely, the symbolism of the benefits. Over time these government payments were interpreted as being part of the general reserve system in which they were involved and its method of administration as dictated by the Indian Act. Thus, there is an enormous qualitative and ideological difference between non-Indians in Canada and reserve Indians receiving assistance; for Indians, there is an identification of the source of assistance with many other things in their lives. This does not mean that the Okanagan, or any other reserve Indians, are somehow better integrated than other people in their local communities. On the contrary, the institutionalization of the community within which the Okanagan live produces more conflicts and more contradictions than it does in people living in the 'open' society. Some perceptive Okanagan families in the past used to refuse any form of welfare (*auperah'*)[4] because they said they were too proud to get help from the Indian agent.

By 1954 the Okanagan reserve community, formerly dominated by the ranchers and agriculturalists, had been in gradual decline for more than half a century. This decline was related to many factors including population increase, subdivision of farms, fluctuations in the price of beef and grain, and the greater involvement and control of the community by the federal government through more effective enforcement of the Indian Act which had been significantly amended in 1951.

Another very different change was taking place at this time, which in turn influenced the motivation and aspirations of many people. This was the acceptance and cultivation of current Canadian bourgeois values. It is true that the Okanagan had enjoyed the material culture of fur traders and the settlers, and the many photographs taken early in the twentieth century illustrate the degree to which they followed the fashions and styles of the time. But by the 1950s people began to pursue middle-class values more aggressively in an attempt to catch up, as it were, with people outside the reserve. So while the provisions of the Indian Act involved them increasingly with reserve life, there was more than ever before a concerted effort to follow the conventions of the non-farming outside world and to incorporate those values into reserve culture. People began to ask for better schools, and some students were enrolled in white schools; women especially became more interested in better housing with cultivated interior styles that reflected the middle-class ideas of the times; a lively interest in expanding sporting activities developed through the establishment of local clubs; an interest in homemakers' clubs was

4 *Auperah'*, as I understand it, is probably derived from the word 'pauper.' Sometimes the word is spoken with a soft 'p' as pauper.

emerging; English became the language of the aspirant 'middle class' while Okanagan continued to be associated with the conservative farming tradition; some women acquired secretarial skills and became office workers. But it was not simply the adoption of a general middle-class culture, but the spirit in which this was done. People had been involved with bourgeois culture for decades, but in the 1950s it was cultivated with definite ends in mind, in particular the improvement of status. This is not to say that status differentia-tion did not exist in the past but concern with one's status and for other people's statuses now preoccupied people, especially women, as they sought to remould their local cultural arena after the fashion of post–Second World War Canada.

The net effect of this assertion of Canadian middle-class values was to downplay the farming tradition and speed up the transition to a new kind of community. By the early 1960s when I first did my preliminary fieldwork on the Okanagan reserve this movement had permeated many facets of the community and was one of the main influences in changing the status of women in the political arena. Women started being nominated for council positions at elections in the 1960s for the first time since they had received the vote in 1951, although they had to wait twenty years before the first woman was elected as a councillor in 1981.

By the 1950s it was clear to the Okanagan that, although they owned their traditional means of production, land, they did not now own it equally, nor were they all benefiting from this right. Theoretically there was supposed to be the semblance of equality in their reserve world, but this was no longer the case and the assumed primary means of production (farming) was found not necessarily the most fruitful – a contradiction that both stimulated and fostered the exploration of alternative lifestyles, the cultivation of which required ready cash.

Wage labour had long been known and actively engaged in, not simply to make ends meet but to make possible the enjoyment of a few luxuries. But by 1954 every family on the reserve was, peripherally at least, preoccupied with wage labour *for its own sake*, figuring out its complexity, and investigating new ways of maximizing its energy so as to increase its income.

Nevertheless, in spite of the fact that wage labour had become the major source of income in the household economy by 1954, the prevalence of farming should not be played down. Although fewer than 20 per cent of households could properly be called farmers, most people had vegetable gardens and many non-farmers had milch cows. There was, moreover, an elaborate system of sharing and exchange of locally produced food and services among kin. Thus even the combined average sources of income from rural wage labour (42 per cent) and farming (30 per cent) still gave a definite agricultural character to the reserve in 1954. I must concede, therefore, that Hirabayashi was justified in focusing his research on farming at that time, when the cultural values were strongly constructed around ranching, horses, and agriculture, a local view of the world that permeated every other aspect of life.

Chapter Eleven

Household Economy and
the Wider Society in 1980s

Many Okanagan would say they are materially better off today than they were in 1954. People now have more cash in their pockets, housing has improved enormously, most people now have electricity, running water, and telephones, and there are more automobiles, refrigerators, and television sets than before. However, the same could be said of the changes in the material lifestyles of all Canadians, making the notion of 'being better off' worthless unless it is examined in a more comprehensive context. Thus, in order to answer the question 'Are the Okanagan band members better off than they were in past,' we need to examine a variety of factors, including the occupational structure, differences in family incomes, and a variety of issues relating to the band's economy in general.[1]

OCCUPATIONAL STRUCTURE

By the mid-1970s it was unrealistic to pretend that the Okanagan Indian band

1 The statistical data analysed in this chapter were not all collected at the same time, and there are time differences of up to twelve years, which make for both discrepancy and some incomparability. But the same could also be said of the non-quantifiable material analysed in this work and in ethnographic analysis generally. There does not seem, therefore, to be any reason for rejecting temporally diverse statistical data altogether.

However, more serious than those objections is the questionable quality of the data on household budgets. As is apparent, I did not attempt to collect data myself because it was too time consuming and not the sort of exercise people would have wanted to co-operate in. Consequently, I made use of official census material which I interpreted myself in the light of knowledge based on my fieldwork.

was a community of farmers or even a farming community. This reality is clearly reflected in the occupational profile of that time. I have constructed this profile (Table 4) using aspects of a report by William Kerr and Associates (1975) and material from my own field research.

I did not study *housework* in any great detail during my Okanagan research; nor have I dealt directly with the gender division of labour. Only part of the blame for this sin of omission can be attributed to lack of time or the limitations of being a male anthropologist; the Okanagan themselves must shoulder some of the responsibility. In the first place, neither women nor men were particularly interested in the topics of gender relations or the status of women, at least not overtly. One summer, a young woman from a neighbouring reserve did a survey of attitudes of band members towards Indian women losing their band status by marrying white men, but to my knowledge the results were never made public. I was embarrassed by the conservative utterances and answers of some of my male chauvinist friends to my questions. I was also surprised that not all the women gave me much support.

In general, Okanagan women do most of the housework, but husbands help with the children and the shopping. Women never complained to me about doing housework any more than anyone else did about doing other kinds of work. Although women do a lot of work in the home, especially married women, they do not feel themselves downtrodden by men. 'You can always split the blanket if things don't work out.' In short, women are quite independent and usually get what they want. One wife even got her bingo[2] allowance with her housekeeping money, but that could also be interpreted as husband domination rather than equality.

Neither divorce nor separation is frowned upon too heavily as a way of solving domestic unhappiness, hence the practice of serial monogamy is common. If husbands do not like the idea of their wives leaving home to upgrade themselves to get better jobs, their objections fall mainly upon deaf ears.

I have put housework at the top of the occupation table, because housework always has to be done, but I have not attempted to quantify the men's contributions to it because some of my Okanagan male friends would question its relevance! Apart from housework, which includes 'minding the kids,' fewer women worked than men in 1975, and more women were unemployed. But

---

2 The new leisure activity which attracts men and women, old and young alike, is bingo, which many regard as as costly as drinking. In recent years when it has become fashionable to 'go on the wagon,' many of the ex-drinkers have turned to bingo, and at least two reformed alcoholics are so involved with the game that they find it impossible to quit.

TABLE 4

Occupational profile of 'on reserve' Okanagan band members in 1975: total band population, 743; 'off reserve' population, 234

No. of females	Occupation	No. of males
100++	Housework, etc.	?
0	Ranchers	2
0	Ranchers also doing part-time wage labour	5
0	Ranchers-cum-farmers-cum wage labourers	4
0	Manager	1
3	Teachers	0
3	Nurses, etc.	0
4	Skilled artisans and semi-skilled workers	11
11	Clerical workers and government employees	4
2	Bus and taxi drivers and car sales workers	4
0	Loggers (16) and sawmill workers (15)	31
0	Labourers regular (23), casual/irregular workers (31)	54
0	Handicapped, largely unemployed	10
20	Unemployed	11
15	Upgrading	4
29	Retired	30
17	High school and university students	21
40+	Other students (10–15 years old)	40+

NOTES

1 This table does not include forty women reported as 'not in market' because all of these were doing housework and are included in that category.
2 The categories used are my adaptations of those used in William Kerr and Associates, *Okanagan Band Economic Development Officer Study* (1975).
3 Landlords leasing property are not included in this table.

fifteen women were upgrading their education at college and/or university at that time, a trend which has continued. By 1985 many more women were employed and more women were holding jobs in skilled, semi-skilled, and clerical occupations than in the previous decade. Women have led the middle-class movement in recent years, both by enhancing their status through cultivating bourgeois attitudes and by acquiring professional and white-collar skills. Becoming middle class is not simply a question of being drawn into a consumer society, as one of my critics seems to think I am suggesting. It is significant that women were employed in higher-status (often higher-paying) jobs than men in 1975. The majority of employed men were loggers and labourers, while women, apart from housework, enjoyed occupations such as teaching, nursing, and secretarial and clerical work.

In 1975 only eleven people (all men) thought of themselves as *ranchers*, and only two of these saw themselves as having ranching as their only profession. Five also did part-time wage labour themselves, and four combined farming (agriculture) with wage labour. Nevertheless, many families do occupy a good deal of their spare time with some kind of farming – haying, gardening, attending to a horse or a milch cow, and so on – creating the illusion that the reserve is economically still a farming community when in point of fact it is nowadays closer to a quasi-peasant culture.

Although some men living on the reserve are involved in *skilled* and *semi-skilled* work with some managerial and white-collar work in addition to ranching and farming in 1975, the majority were *loggers, sawmill workers,* and *general labourers.* The number of loggers and sawmill workers declined enormously after Hoover's sawmill,[3] which had operated on the reserve for about thirty years, closed down in 1975, and in 1981 when the band sawmill shut.

Unemployment rates are difficult to measure. There would appear to have been 30 per cent of the local labour force unemployed in 1975. In 1980 there were about the same number, judging from the number of people drawing social assistance at that time and from my observations during fieldwork.

An alternative to unemployment during the past fifteen years has been to *upgrade* one's education, especially by getting involved in practical programs offered by local community colleges (for example, forestry, wildlife preservation, counselling programs for drug and alcohol addiction). These programs are normally subsidized by the Department of Indian Affairs. One important source of local employment is the Round Lake Treatment Centre for alcoholism and drug addiction. Although not strictly a band project, the centre is located on reserve land and receives special support and encouragement from council, providing also a wide range of jobs for band members.

As one looks at the interests, abilities, and qualifications of band members at the present time, we can observe a growing *under-employment* of people as they become better educated yet remain on the reserve in anticipation of finding local employment in some of the few skilled and semi-skilled jobs that become available from time to time, or getting a good job in Vernon or in one of the other neighbouring towns. But the outlook for the future is not

---

3 Hoover's sawmill operated on land leased from the band. Logs were trucked in from crown land and processed at the mill. At least 50 per cent of Hoover's sawmill workers were supposed to be band members in terms of an agreement with council. But the company seldom fulfilled its obligation, and generally employed no more than fifteen to twenty band members, which was considerably less than the quota agreed upon.

encouraging because there is little suggestion that Vernon will develop industrially as quickly as Kelowna or Kamloops have done, and there will simply not be enough jobs to go around.

HOUSEHOLD INCOMES IN 1980

In 1980 the average household income on the Okanagan reserve was estimated to be $13,716 per year, with a range of from about $1500 to nearly $40,000 a year. In Figure 2 I have ordered the data on income (see Appendix 4) to reflect five categories of households according to their annual reported incomes. The discussion below attempts to estimate the relative value of each source of income vis-à-vis total income in each category.

Very Low Income Households (15 per cent of All Households)
These households report incomes of less than $5000 per annum, having an average income of $1697. They are very poor by any standard, and fieldwork shows that they consist of younger people setting up households for the first time. The census data suggest that these include some residual households with absentee members, which explains both the small family size and the low mean income. These households derive 72 per cent of their income from government assistance (social assistance, unemployment insurance), 28 per cent from wage labour, and nothing from farming. They own no land and are not likely to, unless they eventually inherit it.

Low-Income Households (30 per cent of All Households)
These households report incomes between $5000 and $9999, with an average income of $7529. They are also poor, and in that respect differ only in degree from the previous category. But there is an important characteristic which distinguishes them from all other households. They are the *contemporary farmers*, the householders who try to make a go of ranching and agriculture in the modern world. Typically they fail, making only 27 per cent of their total annual incomes from farming, and have consequently to augment their incomes with wage labour (32 per cent) and government assistance (41 per cent).

Middle-Income Households (20 per cent of All Households)
These households report annual incomes of between $10,000 and $14,999, with an average income of $13,432, which justifies our categorizing them as 'middle' since this figure is roughly equal to the mean average household income for the whole reserve. Middle-income households derive about two-

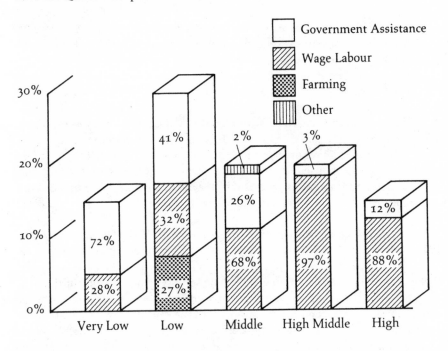

Income

Very Low = Less than $5000 (mean $1697)
Low = $5000 to $9999 (mean $7529)
Middle = $10000 to $14999 (mean $13432)
High Middle = $15000 to $24999 (mean $20509)
High = Over $25000 (mean $33875)

Note Mean average household income for all categories is $13716

Figure 2

Estimated distribution of Okanagan household incomes in 1980 based on 1981 Canada Census (see also Appendix 4)

thirds of their income (68 per cent) from wage labour and salaries, more than twice as much as the lower-income households. Most of the remaining balance of their income is derived from government sources, notably from unemployment insurance and retirement pensions.

As a category these middle-income households might be characterized as the group of families who have recently abandoned farming altogether in favour of wage (and salaried) labour.

The High Middle-Income Households (20 per cent of All Households)
These households stand apart from the middle income category in a number of ways. First, they earn much more – between $15,000 and $24,000 – an average of $20,509 per annum. Second, they report that their income comes almost entirely from wage and salaried labour (97 per cent). Third, they receive no income from government sources other than family allowances (2.4 per cent). They even report some investment income (0.68 per cent), and no one appears old enough to draw an old age pension.

From field experience I can identify most of these households as having members with regular jobs off the reserve. Others may work on the reserve in the few positions available at the band office. They tend to be upwardly mobile, live in good houses, own good transport, and represent mainly the group of people I have characterized as aspiring to Canadian middle-class values.

The High-Income Households (15 per cent of All Households)
These households stand apart from all others by virtue of their incomes – over $30,000 with a mean annual income of $33,875. Some of these households, together with households in the previous category, include even better-off people who, out of irrational fear of having their money taxed,[4] do not declare their full income from their land leases. Some report that most of their income is derived from wages and salaries, and regard their lease incomes as if they were salaries and/or wages, which in a sense they are. High-income households also have a number of older members who draw the old age pension. Their household size is large, sometimes containing three generations. Some of them have involved themselves in entrepreneurial ventures which have failed, as reflected in the income loss they report.

THE DEMISE OF FARMING?

Whatever the limitations of this analysis of 1980 household budgets, it is clear

4 Status Indians residing on reserves are not liable to federal or provincial income tax.

that farming as a source of income has practically disappeared, and wage labour and salaried employment have become the major sources of cash. This does not mean that all forms of farming have been abandoned. There were four quite successful ranchers and a number of less successful farmers in 1980; during the summer roughly twenty families carried out extensive haying operations; during the year about three-quarters of families had gardens; and a few had their cows, while some had horses. But most farming operations run at a loss nowadays, and to make ends meet you have to have a job or join the ranks of people on social assistance.

PATRONAGE

The study of the domestic economy and its place in the community and the outside world is more complex than the interpretation of household budgets and their sources of income. One complex dimension of these issues is reflected in the pattern of patron-client relationships on the reserve which pervades the arenas of factionalism, local politics at election time, the administration of the reserve, the allocation of resources such as land and housing, the distribution of band money, the allocation of social assistance, and particularly kinship and friendship. Lithman (1978: 145–232) tends to underestimate the importance of patronage in his Fort Alexander study, despite the strong indications in his own material that a subtle form of patronage permeates social relations generally. Here I wish to analyse the systems of patronage found in certain economic relationships in some households and in the domestic economy generally in the Okanagan reserve community.

Apart from building sites and band-owned commonage, there are two kinds of land that have value nowadays for the Okanagan: commercial land and agricultural land. Both are in demand, especially commercial land which may also be good agricultural land that can be leased out as industrial sites (for a sawmill, for example), or as lakefront recreation property for summer cottages or mobile homes on long- or short-term leases, or leased out to white entrepreneurs who will develop the land and then sublease it at considerable profit to themselves.

Patron-client relationships occur to a large extent in the context of land ownership on the reserve. Some involve kin, some involve other band members or Indians living on the reserve, and in some instances non-Indians occupy positions of clientage. Let me give three examples in the form of generalized cases:

1. P owned a large house. When his sons married, he gave them land and

helped them with the construction of separate houses in return for financial assistance at a later date, after they had established themselves on their land and in good jobs off the reserve. P was consequently able to expand his own farming operations and some related business. When his wife died, he still had two sons living at home, one of whom had just got married. The young couple stayed on in the household and raised a family. In later years one of the grandchildren had children of her own and also remained in the home as a single parent. In return for being allowed to stay on in the family home, and for the use of farm equipment and land, the younger generations kept house and fed the widower and helped him farm. In this case the members of the younger generation found themselves locked into a system which gave them very little freedom, particularly because they were interested in inheriting both the land and the substantial family home.

2. Z was short of labour and anxious not to lay out too much cash for wage labour, so he offered X and his wife a place to live. X was a newcomer from another band who had not yet established himself on the reserve, and he welcomed the chance of getting free accommodation and a few dollars in return for his labour. Within a few years, after he had fulfilled his obligation to Z, X was able to move to a lot of his own where he built his own house and established himself with his family on the Okanagan reserve.

3. D was a white man who had several Okanagan friends and was well known on the reserve. He was a qualified engineer but could never hold down a job. G was a comfortably well-off band member from a large respected family. He needed some help in his orchard and vegetable garden so he approached D, who welcomed the opportunity to live down on the lakeshore in G's cabin and tend to the garden during summer and fall in return for free accommodation, an ample supply of fresh fruit and vegetables, a good supply of rum and beer, and a little pocket money to augment unemployment insurance income. This is not an isolated case of Indian patronage and white clientage. In fact, many white and 'half-breed' men began their careers on the reserve as clients of Indians and later married into the band and became members. A well-known white man, J.H. Christie, although never admitted to band membership, received various privileges from the Okanagan for the petitions and letters of protest he wrote for the members of the band, notably for his loyal support around about 1916.

Patron-client relationships vary from one situation to another in human societies and Pitt-Rivers's 'lop-sided friendship' is as much a patron-client relationship as are those involving economic exploitation and political domination (see Pitt-Rivers 1954: 140; Eisenstadt and Roniger 1984; Pearson

1986). Patron-client relationships are always lopsided in some way but the level of exploitation varies, as does its context. Bodemann's (1982) fear of anthropologists getting caught up in people's 'own ideological perception of the social order' needs to be borne in mind, but this could be said of just about everything else. Whatever one's view of the nature of patron-client relations might be, they always involve some degree of unequal status as well as a certain amount of reciprocity.

Case 1 above provides an example of lopsided kinship relations involving access to the home and other usufructuary privileges by the clients in return for labour. And while the married son worked for over twenty years for a logging company and enjoyed his income without rent, the whole relationship was filled with resentment and anger because he and his wife felt they could not free themselves from the obligations in which they had become involved. Their main resentment was that they had no control over the situation, particularly the inheritance of property when the father died. They also resented the fact that they were totally ignorant of what his intentions were after 'working for him for thirty years,' and what 'choked them with anger' was the fact that they had absolutely no power to do anything about it.

A variation of this type of kin patronage, which is seldom recognized although it is quite widespread, involves granting close kin, especially married sons and daughters, part of leasing profits in return for a variety of favours – ranging from running errands in town, writing letters, collecting rent from tenants, to other services. In many cases these appear to be simple examples of distributing wealth among kin, but there is always an element of lopsided patronage present. We should also note that many low-income families are subsidized by well-off kin, although this is not reflected in household budgets. For example, the so-and-so's have about forty summer lakeside lots which they lease out, bringing them in about $40,000 a year tax free. About half of that money goes to a married daughter and a married son who are struggling to make a living. Perhaps we could call this potlatch patronage. Although this practice takes place in very different social situations, Smith's (1984) principle of economic co-operation among 'federations of households' in Peru seems to apply here in a very real sense.

The second case is of a different order, for here is a newcomer to the reserve entering into a patron-client relationship with full knowledge of its asymmetrical nature and of the degree of exploitation involved. This particular relationship (and others like it) is open-ended in that it can be entered into freely, terminated relatively easily, and used as a stepping stone to a better economic position. These kinds of patron-client relationships do much the same for newcomers and other marginal people on the reserve as voluntary associations do for migrant workers and newcomers to cities (cf. Meillassoux 1968) in third world countries. It is important, therefore, to point to the voluntary nature of some patron-client relations. An individual enters into them voluntarily and leaves them when he or she wishes and it is only during the actual period of involvement that 'exploitation' and asymmetry of interaction exists.

The third case resembles the previous example in that it is also open-ended and voluntary. But in other respects it is very different since it is closer to lopsided-friendship than the patron-client dyads. These Indian-white relationships afford Indians the opportunity to interact with relatively high-status white people in situations of patronage. While giving the impression of balanced reciprocity (Sahlins 1965: 147–8), in fact they involve the Indians in positions of tremendous power and influence over their clients for as long as the relationship is maintained. Any white man who enters into such a relationship on the reserve has to submit entirely to the whims, if not the full authority, of his patron. In two other similar cases the white men were full of resentment after what they had imagined were partnerships turned out to be nothing of the sort. In many of these relationships the white men believed that they were the patrons in the sense that it was they who were patronizing their prospective patrons, only to be disillusioned later by their misjudgment. These white-Indian relationships are important in the analysis of the Okanagan community in the context of the outside world in that they exemplify the fine dividing line between high-status middle-class Okanagan and their white counterparts in the wider society. They also reveal how many Okanagan feel about their white peers outside the reserve. Given the present system, the only way they can join that 'society' is by incorporating individual whites into the reserve and exploiting them. For the whites it may well reflect their own feeling of inadequacy in their own society, and their belief that they might not only enhance their understanding of the world but also benefit materially from association with the Okanagan. But whatever else they reflect, these particular relationships between whites and Indians bring home the cultural similarities between the two peoples while exemplifying simultaneously the structural differences between living on a reserve and living in Canada. In the case of whites becoming clients of Indians, we see a process of inversion occurring whereby the members of each estate change category in the false belief that a dramatic transformation is taking place. Thus, the Indian patron feels that he has become like a white man ('90 per cent white,' as one man told me), while the white man soon realizes that he has to become like an Indian if the relationship is to continue for any length of time. Patrons and clients are here the inverse of each other.

These few examples of patronage on the reserve do no more than skim the surface of an extremely complex system which still needs to be fully explored. However, I would like to indicate here that the main area of institutionalized patronage is a collective one involving what we might call 'Ottawa' and the members of the Okanagan band. By virtue of the reserve system every band member, both as an individual and as part of the social formation, stands in a position of clientage involving extreme dependency on the federal government, which in turn is the arch patron of the reserve community. In earlier publications (Carstens 1971a, 1971b), I presented this relationship as part of the more general question of class (and in some respect status) relations. I will discuss this problem again in the final chapter. Here I only wish to make it clear that although patron-client relations are not class relations, the socio-economic dimensions of patronage articulate to a considerable degree with those of societal stratification in the broad sense.

ENTREPRENEURIAL VENTURES

In spite of the early success by some people in ranching and farming, the Okanagan community has a poor record of entrepreneurial success or even endeavour. The most profitable enterprises on the reserve have tended to be 'multiplex' in the sense that a well-thought-out balance between several ventures generates higher incomes than single occupations, although there is considerable evidence that wage or salaried labour alone is now, on average, the most profitable.

Private business enterprises on the reserve, separate from farming and ranching, resulted in a low level of success if not complete failure. For example, the Six Mile Creek grocery store which opened in 1954 lasted for only a few years and probably ran at a loss. The Irish Creek store which opened in 1978 with pool tables in the basement closed in 1986 having never displayed much evidence of success. A gas station has opened recently at Six Mile Creek; as the only gas station on the reserve, it should make an enormous profit, but this has still to be demonstrated. There have been attempts to open a lady's hairdressing shop, a leather shop, and a bakery, but that is about all, apart from some success in transport and trucking ventures. A laundromat has been established very recently at Six Mile Creek, but the prognosis for its success is minimal unless it is used extensively by whites in the summer months. In general there is no great demand for any of these enterprises by the people on the reserve. Most people shop and do their business in Vernon, providing white merchants with a monetary benefit of at least $2 million per annum.

Although the majority of entrepreneurial ventures on the reserve have failed for a variety of reasons, one has not. Motorists travelling through the reserve south on Westside Road will be alerted by prominent signs directing them to Newport Beach Recreational Park. This is no ordinary recreational playground. It is the fifty-five-acre estate of band member Daniel Matthew Logan which houses forty white families in 'permanent' homes, provides fourteen cabin sites for summer residences, a campground with thirty full hook-ups and forty partial hook-ups for trailers, and some thirty campsites. There is also a well-stocked year-round grocery store and a 'Burger Cabin' open in summer, and much more. The estate is attractively laid out, the roads are in good repair, the water system is excellent by any standard. The campground has two shower-toilet buildings with hot water and flush toilets, a swimming beach, boat-launching facilities, a wharf, boat rentals, and firewood. There is regular garbage removal, a dump station, and everything on the estate is regulated by the management, in accordance with the rules laid down by Dan Logan. Dogs and young children are forbidden on the upper levels where most of the permanent residents (all white) live in a suburban setting with their well-kept gardens and lawns.

Every part of the estate is well kept, from the superior cattle guard at the main gate to the trees, gardens, and fences. The owner prizes the elegant ponderosa pines: 'They are like people and [I] hate to see one harmed in any way.' He encourages bird life, although the recent infestation of crows and magpies anger him with their early morning cries and chatter in summer. 'They are negative birds,' he says.

But infrastructure, cleanliness, and order are not everything at Newport Beach. There is also the philosophy and the spiritual aspect of the place which loom large, as customers soon learn if they don't like what they find and complain unreasonably. Newcomers, whether they plan to stay for a night or a lifetime, are told that this place is governed by 'The Thing' (Spiritual Reality), and 'if you don't [unmentionable] well like it, you can [unmentionable] go right through that [unmentionable] gate where you came from and go negative which is what you are.' In other words, it is the tenants' moral responsibility to accept the place and 'The Thing,' because that is what Newport Beach is all about. Thus, the ideology and moral philosophy of the place *are* also the rules and this is an absolute matter. These are not mere *Cider House Rules* after the world of John Irving, for Newport Beach is a utopia created by its owner. Max Weber would see it as a Heaven on Earth, which is exactly the way Dan Logan sees it. 'It is a little bit of the Kingdom of Heaven.' But what was its origin?

In 1949 Dan Logan sold the ninety-acre family estate he had inherited from his mother to a friend for $9000. This included the house, the farm equipment, barns, animals, harnesses, and the rest. Five or six years later he bought ninety acres of land from another band member for $3500 and built a house and a barn, installed a water system, put in fences. A few years later he bought roughly thirteen acres of bush land at Newport from another band member. Then in 1962 he traded the ninety-acre land for the balance of the Newport property, paying a few hundred dollars in cash as well for the forty-two acres. This gave him fifty-five acres of good land between Westside Road and Lake Okanagan. There were a few summer cottages on the lakeshore then occupied by whites, but the rest was bush and forest.

Logan also acquired other property in the 1960s. He bought a sizeable piece of land at Priest's Valley (Indian Reserve No. 6) and established a campground with toilets, septic tanks, and water. Later he turned the property over to his wife after they separated. She leases it out to a white man on a twenty-one-year lease and receives about $40,000 a year for it.

In 1967 Dan bought thirty-seven acres of land at Winfield (Indian Reserve No. 7), 'cleaned up a bit of the land, put in some power, and a well with a pump; then leased it out in 1969 and got $6000 to $7000 for it.' This lease was renegotiated in 1981 for twenty-five years and he now receives $32,000 for that property. Moving closer to home, he bought ten acres of lakeshore property almost adjacent to the Newport property. There were six cabins on that property which brought him in $3000 a year. In 1982 he leased out this land to a white man for twenty-five years for $7000 a year, because it was 'too much bother to develop it [himself].'

How was Logan able to buy all these properties, which cost considerably more than the $9000 he received from the sale of the family estate in 1949? There are two factors. First, he worked extremely hard for B.C. Hydro as a driver for fifteen years. Much of the time was spent away from home base, and he was able to save a good deal of money. Second, he received a handsome cash entitlement in the late 1950s from the United States through his mother, who was an American Okanagan before her marriage to a band member in the north. Logan incidentally is also a qualified baker, having served a five-year apprenticeship in Washington State. The purpose of these details is not to present a personal history of Dan Logan, but to demonstrate that any form of expansion or development of one's economic status on the reserve can be achieved *only* by augmenting one's income from external sources, particularly wage labour of one sort or another. The cash entitlement was also important, but some of that money went towards ensuring his wife a private income through the property made over to her.

But do these material and financial factors alone explain Dan Logan's success? I think not, because there are a number of band members who have acquired cash through wage labour and other means but have never been able to succeed in their various ventures.

Before I attempt further analysis of the success of the Newport enterprise let me elaborate on the extent of the business and the plans for expansion. At present there are forty families in permanent mobile homes. The tenants (all white) are carefully selected by Dan Logan and have been encouraged to plant lawns, fruit trees, and attractive gardens, to construct verandahs and sheds, and to obey his rules. He provides good water through a modern pump system, a sewage system, and garbage removal, for a total rent of $115 per month (1987). His tenants pay for their phones and electricity. Logan says he still has room for twenty-five more units, but at the moment he is satisfied with the $55,200 rent he receives anually. He has fourteen lakeshore sites and is in the process of transforming these from summer cabin sites for which he now receives a total of $11,200 a year to government-approved leases valued at $2400 a year each, which would increase his total annual income from rent to $33,600. The campground offers a potential gross annual income based on full occupancy for a forty-day summer of $44,000 but in practice this is much lower owing to such factors as weather and chance. A grocery store which opened in 1985 yielded an annual profit of roughly $14,000 but the Burger Cabin ran at a loss during its first summer.

Newport Beach and Recreational Park as it stands today was begun in 1978, virtually from scratch apart from the summer cottages which had been there for some time. An enormous amount of money was required to create the enterprise. Most of this came from the rent paid by residents as they moved in, from the campers, and from the Winfield property which was leased out. In 1979 Dan Logan got two substantial grants from the Department of Indian Affairs on a 'pay back half basis if you can show half to begin with.' But there was so much red tape attached that he returned most of the loan before he used it, after he had the pleasure of shouting obscenities over the phone (which I cannot record here) at the official in charge. Eventually he took a departmental loan of $40,000 at 13.25 per cent. There have been enormous profits from the operation by the usual standards of reserve operations, but most of this money has been reinvested in the property in preparation for further expansion, and for maintenance.

Dan Logan employs only a skeleton staff on a casual basis. During the initial period of development he employed a white man full-time and several labourers. When a skilled job needed to be done (for example, the pumps for the water system) he employed the best worker he could find. His bookkeeping has always been done by trained white women. It is probably incorrect to speak of his staff because that is not the way things work. He has his one client associate, a white person, and then he farms out work as it needs to be done. To the uninitiated it is amazing how the work gets done at all, and some people gain the impression that Logan does it all himself. This is not entirely untrue because he refuses to delegate authority except to his client associate, and the rest is accomplished on the basis of his remarkable ability to exploit and manipulate his extensive network of Indian and non-Indian personal relationships.

What goes on at Newport Beach, however, is not perceived by its owner-director as a pure business enterprise, but rather as the fulfilment of his spiritual and religious beliefs. He rejected Roman Catholicism as a young man, and now as a fundamentalist free-thinking Christian he sees his mission in life as the fulfilment of 'the good Lord's plan' as he calls it, 'right here on my property.' Logan tried to retire in the early 1970s and live off the money he received from his leases. Financially he was very well off by any standard, but he was too much of an Okanagan to live in town by himself or contemplate living on the reserve doing nothing. That is how he explains the genesis of the fine profitable business venture he has built in less than a decade.

But Dan Logan had surely planned Newport Beach or something similar to it a generation ago. In 1962 I took a photograph of him standing on the wooden dock of his newly acquired lakeshore property looking across the clear waters of Lake Okanagan. I do not think there was any doubt in his mind then that he was a superb businessman. The only question was how this should be realized in the context of the reserve. He eventually solved his dilemma by creating a reserve within a reserve – a reserve for white people in a reserve for Indians, involving a reversal of roles whereby the Indian administers the whites according to his own idiosyncratic rules.

When Hirabayashi classified Dan Logan as a leading member of the progressive faction on the Okanagan reserve in 1954, he was only partly correct because he did not appreciate the complexity of the personality he met during fieldwork. In this case the progressive element was also grounded in old faction conservatism and Canadian liberal conservatism, epitomizing the struggle between being an Okanagan Indian on the reserve and a Canadian citizen. His success as an entrepreneur on the reserve reflects his genius at coming to terms with that reality.

As an Okanagan he is associated with good old faction stock from Irish Creek at the Head of the Lake. From his mother he claims relationship with Nkwala through the house of Tonasket. He speaks Okanagan fluently, has an excellent knowledge of Okanagan history and culture, identifies himself with the local countryside, and possesses remarkable knowledge of the genealogies of practically every family on the reserve. As a boy he learned numerous practical skills on his parent's ranch and attended school on the reserve before going off to Residential School in Kamloops with other Indians.

As a Canadian he has cultivated an enormous range of personal networks with whites, partly through his B.C. Hydro connection but also through his own effort over the years. Throughout his adult life he has tended always to have one close white friend, 'a buddy,' whose role is always subordinate to him in the relationship. He is also a member of the Canadian Legion, an association which stands him in good stead in gaining admission to other clubs in Vernon. During the past thirty years he has probably spent as much time with whites as he has with Indians and has lived off the reserve for long periods of time. To shop with Dan Logan in Vernon or even to walk down the main street with him is to gain the impression that he knows everyone, and that everyone knows him.

The success of the Newport Beach project was based on the creation of his own private reserve on the Okanagan reserve. The experiment was essentially to build a utopia. The estate is fenced in (reserved), and has begun to take on the form of a separate village with its own water supply, sewage system, garbage disposal, grocery store, burger cabin, private beach, and some sense of community. No Indians live there, and apart from the few that drop by the grocery store for pop, ice cream, bread, and cigarettes, very few come in through the gate. Occasionally during the summer some Okanagan children go down to the beach for a swim after they have paid at the office for the privilege of using the facilities of the campground. The point that I wish to make is that Newport Beach is an independent enterprise, subject to the rules of the owner-landlord and the provisions of the Indian Act, although in this case the latter does no more than register the leases to protect the landlord and his tenants in terms of their agreements.

If every venture and enterprise on the reserve is subject, by and large, to the same principles, what is unique about Newport Beach? The answer is unequivocally the personal commitment of the owner to his own personal property, his tenants, his utopian ideology, and the Okanagan reserve itself. He lives on his property and is as much involved with the welfare of his tenants as he is with the superstructure, and he sees these inextricably bound up with each other. If the enterprise does in fact have the religious and spiritual ingredients the owner claims it to have, then these must be seen as a local expression of a puritan ethic committed to the creation of a little heaven on a small part of the earth. At the same time it provides a social situation where he can express his religious ideas to a manageable number of people on his own terms.

No other entrepreneur on the reserve has ever shown similar commitment to a business enterprise. Other entrepreneurs have continued to manage their projects from the reserve base, on reserve terms, and have never attempted to incorporate the outside world into their own world on the reserve. Reserves in themselves are inefficient as economic units, and local businesses require more direct links to the wider society to make them successful. This is not to say that Newport Beach is as economically productive as it would be if it operated on the open market. The rents are very low for what people receive, but from Logan's point of view 'you must give people a fair deal and then they will treat you good too.' I believe there is something of the concept of 'just price' in that sentiment, and there is also an implicit element of taboo attached to going overboard and charging too much and becoming too rich so that you might be tempted to flaunt your wealth. Thus often needless reinvestment in one's property, together with unostentatious generosity, has a sort of potlatching effect for people who earn too much above the average on the reserve. The feelings of 'Indianness' prevent one from becoming too successful. In the case of Newport Beach a balance has been struck between things of the reserve and things of the outside world – a balance few people have been able to discover.

If it is in fact taboo to become a millionaire *on* the Okanagan reserve, one might also ask why so few people have invested their money in property or business enterprises *off* the reserve in Vernon, Kelowna, Kamloops, or even as far afield as Vancouver. There are a number of families earning $20,000 to $40,000 tax free dollars a year from property leases who could establish themselves in business or investment off the reserve. The explanation is surely complex, but I would like to suggest that going outside the reserve to invest money also carries with it a taboo element, as well as a negative stigma. The people are always preoccupied with their personal and financial security from their reserve base where, even if you own nothing or have no job, you receive protection in a social refuge. There is also the fear of losing one's legal rights, having to pay income tax, or finding the world outside more difficult than it can appear on certain shopping days in Vernon. In a real sense there is a strong belief that one should stay put on the reserve and do one's business there. The taboo against buying property off the reserve is a very strong one for people socialized in a system where everything is theoretically owned by the state, even though one can claim individual entitlement within the context of the Indian Act.

I do not wish to give the impression that no other property-leasing enterprise exists on the reserve, or that Newport Beach is some sort of anomalous fluke. Property leases are very common and property owners take advantage of their potential income. These, too, are reserves within the reserve. What sets Newport Beach apart from all others is the personal commitment of the landlord to his tenants, and his constant presence on the property, not just for their welfare but because the landlord has been able to rationalize his status as the real owner of his personal property.[5]

THE BAND IN THE ECONOMY

As the political and administrative kernel of the reserve, the Okanagan Indian band office, to use its full title, also handles the revenue of the band. The band office is no longer a one-horse outpost of the Department of Indian Affairs, but an important bureau in the Okanagan Valley involved, *inter alia*, in the regional economy.

In the mid-1960s the Department of Indian Affairs began to increase its financial assistance to bands as part of the general grants-to-bands program which facilitated the process whereby band councils were encouraged to do much of the work that used to be done by the Indian agent and his staff. The Okanagan band budget has grown enormously over the years. In 1961 it was reported as $6468, and by the 1970–1 fiscal year it had grown to $16,475. By the late 1970s the budget had increased phenomenally because by this time the band office had taken on so many additional duties. Thus, the budget projection (target figure) for 1977–8 was $257,689, of which only 10 per cent was core funding for running the office; the major part of the budget was to finance social assistance and welfare, educational programs, and so on. A recent analysis of the sources of actual revenue for the band from 1979 to 1989 illustrates the extent of the budget for the Okanagan reserve (see Appendix 5).

During the past twenty-five years the band through its council and staff has become more and more involved in a number of special projects of a general 'municipal' nature. These include the construction and repair of houses, improvement of the water supply, the development of recreation and community services, negotiating land claims, improving the garbage dump, giving special attention to all forms of education, and attending to the needs of the old and infirm.

The band derives its income from various sources: its land leases to outsiders, grazing fees obtained from neighbouring farmers who run cattle on

5 Dan Logan died suddenly in May 1988 at the age of sixty-seven, and Newport Beach is now managed by his two sons and two daughters. He was buried on his property, and his funeral was attended by equal numbers of Indians and whites. Eulogies were delivered in the Okanagan language and in English.

reserve commonage, fishing and hunting permits, money received for rights of way, and so on. It has also attempted entrepreneurial projects to increase its revenue and provide jobs for its members, but these seldom produced a profit. Round Lake campsite, for example, was established in the 1970s for overnight visitors and day fishermen, but the enterprise never generated any revenue for the band.

The best-known enterprise in recent years was the sawmill project. In January 1972, band council discussed the project and planned to establish the Okanagan Indian Band Sawmill to 'supply enough lumber for the reserve and provide jobs for six or seven working men.' In March 1973 the band membership voted in favour of using capital funds to begin the sawmill operation. The mill continued to be supported by the band throughout the ups and downs of its eight-year life, until it closed down in the middle of 1981. If it ran at a loss by business standards at times, this does not mean that the experiment failed because it employed twenty people at its peak – a significant achievement for the many people who worked hard to make it a success.

Many factors contributed to the difficulties the sawmill experienced. Most significant was the general shortage of timber on the reserve as a result of years of exploitation by large capitalist enterprises. There is also a suggestion that some of the equipment purchased proved to be defective, and in general the enterprise was always in competition with more financially secure companies. On the positive side it should be recorded that, for the first time in its history, council found itself responsible for a project involving a large sum of money that gave it some experience of deficit financing and shifting monies from one account to another. The project also gave council the opportunity to find alternatives to the local market by dealing directly with a lumber broker in Vancouver. It also afforded people the opportunity to view the complexities of processing their own resources from raw material to a finished product.

The Okanagan band, like many other bands across the country, has been preoccupied since the early 1970s with what is called economic development, an idea which has been part of Indian Affairs policy since at least the 1950s, particularly after the publication in 1958 of the Hawthorn et al. study of the Indians of British Columbia. Lithman (1983) has discussed many of the theoretical implications of economic development (underdevelopment) based on his excellent work on a reserve in Manitoba. And Hansen (1985) has written on strategies for development on Nipissing Indian reserve in Ontario. Both these studies demonstrate what many know already: that many band projects 'fail' only in the sense that they seldom generate capital. Economic development on Indian reserves has in fact become part of the administrative package and is largely funded by the Department of Indian Affairs whether projects succeed or not.

THE RESERVE AS AN ECONOMIC COMMUNITY

The study of reserves and other so-called closed communities raises questions about their economic viability – as if one expected them to be as self-sufficient as experimental utopias are in the minds of their founders. Nothing could be further from the truth, and my analysis of the Okanagan reserve over time has revealed growing involvement in the economy of the valley, British Columbia, and Canada in general. Thus the peak of ranching and stock farming in the valley was paralleled in the reserve, as was that of agriculture and market gardening. A notable exception to these was the rise of fruit farming, which could never be established successfully on the reserve. Not only were irrigation schemes never provided for the Okanagan, but reserve land could not be subdivided and sold to individual fruit farmers on the open market, which is how many white farmers had coped with the decline in beef prices and the collapse of grain farming. What distinguishes the Okanagan economically from their white neighbours has therefore very little to do with their 'Indianness' or their traditional culture, but the special socio-economic position bestowed on them by the reserve system.

Over the years the Okanagan have engaged in hunting, fishing, berry picking, root digging, horse breeding, cattle ranching, agriculture, gardening, logging, firewood cutting, wage labour, migratory wage labour, and land leasing. This occupational versatility, their ability to turn their hands to a wide variety of work whether for subsistence or for cash accumulation, is quite remarkable and has taken many different forms and combinations over the years.

During the past thirty or forty years, however, considerable changes in these patterns have occurred as people have become involved in a simpler, more structured occupational system. Various household studies demonstrate that the main source of provisioning has moved steadily in the direction of wage labour and away from farming; that for many people government sources of income (such as social assistance and family allowances) are necessary to make ends meet; and that more and more people are obliged to leave the reserve temporarily or more or less permanently because there are insufficient jobs in the immediate environs.

In 1954 roughly 42 per cent of household income was derived from wage labour and 30 per cent from farming. In 1980 the average household derived nearly 80 per cent of its income from wage and salaried labour and only 4 per

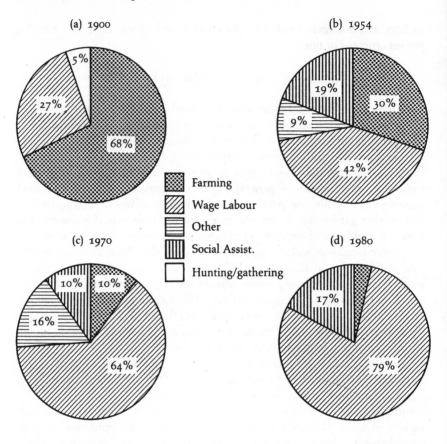

Figure 3

Main sources of household income on the Okanagan Indian Reserve (1900–1980)
a) *PAC* R.G. 10 Vol. 1327
b) Hirabayashi's field notes
c) Canada Census 1971. "Other" probably reflects income from property leases.
d) Canada Census 1981. Income from property leases is included with wage labour.

cent from farming, the latter representing a small handful of people. In 1954 the average household derived about 19 per cent of its income from government sources; in 1980 it was roughly the same (about 17 per cent). Thus we see that the two main variables over the years have been wage labour and farming, and that the most important of these has been wage labour.

Without this enormous increase in wage labour over the years, the drastic decline in farming would have resulted in unprecedented unemployment and the need for enormous social assistance payments. Unemployment among the Okanagan is still high by Canadian standards. In 1975 about 30 per cent of the labour force was without work; in the 1980s unemployment rates have not changed.

It is not simply in terms of household income that the Okanagan reserve's dependence on the outside world is reflected; we have only to consider the sources of actual revenue administered by the band. In 1980–1 over $1 million was transferred to the band by the federal government alone (see Appendix 5).

It is difficult to answer the question: 'Are the members of the Okanagan band better off in 1980 than they were in 1954 and 1970?' Using the simple price-index method based on average household incomes we might conclude that incomes have changed very little over the years, although the relatively high average incomes reported for 1970 do suggest a decline in household incomes during the next ten-year period, which parallels the wage trend in Canada generally. But when we look at income distribution for each of these periods and consider this in relation to housing programs, improvement in the water system, and the tremendous advance in education, one is forced to conclude that, on the whole, people are materially better off than they were in 1954. But they work harder, and travel farther to work, and have higher standards of living to satisfy (see Gonzalez 1987: 227). There are most certainly more poorer people and more richer people than there used to be. Yet there does seem to be more in formal distribution of wealth in the context of kinship networks. There are no ostentatiously rich people on the Okanagan reserve as there are on the Westbank reserve to the south, largely because they do not have the same land-leasing resources. But the Okanagan, in spite of their persistent individualism and laissez-faire attitudes, mistrust uncontrolled use of property and resources by others. While close kin seem to be able to exercise some sort of prerogative over the property of their relatives, the flaunting of wealth is taboo.

Chapter Twelve

The Assimilation of Chiefs, 1932–1987

In chapter 7 I presented a brief analysis of the processes involved and the techniques used by the Department of Indian Affairs to incorporate chiefs into the reserve system during the last thirty-five years of the nineteenth century and the first thirty years of the twentieth. Here I will continue that political history, using again the profiles of later chiefs to illustrate the transition of Okanagan political representation in the modern world.

Formal band politics after the First World War until the early 1930s were at a low ebb, a trend that worsened after an amendment to the Indian Act in 1927 disallowed overt political activism on the reserve. Consequently everything went underground, factionalism reached angry proportions, and internal conflicts were so extreme that the Okanagan came to be regarded by the Department of Indian Affairs as an ungovernable people. Yet in spite of long periods without an elected chief there were always one or two councillors who carried on some of the duties of chief and worked with the Indian agent, an arrangement that provided a link of sorts with minority opinion in the community.

When Chief Johnny Isaac was finally voted back into office in 1930 he faced, as we have seen, the onerous tasks of attempting to reintegrate an impossibly divided community and also confronting the officials of the Department of Indian Affairs who had deposed him in 1924 and banned political gatherings in 1927. His response to the challenge was, we learned, to confront the administration directly by exposing corrupt officials, especially agent James Coleman's aberrant behaviour relating to Indian wages and his abuse of power as an administrator (see pp. 135–6). Predictably, Chief Isaac's action cost him his chiefship and he was deposed for the second time towards the middle of 1931, while Coleman remained as powerful as ever.

CHIEF PIERRE LOUIS, 1932–59

On 14 May 1932 a new chief was elected. Pierre Louis was to weather the storms of Okanagan politics for the next twenty-seven years. As a chief, he stood in the opposite camp to Johnny Isaac. He was prepared to co-operate with the Department of Indian Affairs, and in the context of the reserve community he represented the new order of liberals who were exploring ways of coming to terms with the reserve system.

Okanagan chiefs, as we have seen, have performed very different roles at different times in history. Even those chiefs appointed under the Indian Act have not all been cast in the same mould but have reflected the changing needs and aspirations of the people, some more effectively than others. Chief Pierre Louis was chief for more than a generation. During this period he looked beyond the confines of the reserve in some respects, but he also wanted to preserve some of the past. On the one hand, he called for better formal Canadian education of the Okanagan and cultivated middle-class values; on the other, he attempted to re-create something of 'traditional' Okanagan culture, thereby insisting that people should be fully conscious of their Indianness, however that was interpreted.

Throughout his life and his chiefship Pierre Louis forged links with white people, cultivating their friendship, respect, and loyalty. He was a keen churchman, a champion of education for young and old. He took a middle-of-the-road view in local politics, got on well with the Indian agent and other officials of the government. It would be untrue to say that he ingratiated himself with the white establishment in the same manner that Nkwala had done, but he did identify himself with the white hegemony of the time, for which he, too, was rewarded. In 1936 he received a special award from King George V for outstanding service to his country and his people. Only eight other chiefs in Canada received similar awards. In 1953 he received another award from the British monarchy, when he and his wife were presented to Queen Elizabeth II. In 1967 he received a Canada centennial medallion. A fine sculpted bust of Pierre Louis now stands in the Vernon museum.

It would be an error to attribute all this recognition from the outside world merely to Chief Louis's association with the white establishment, for he was also admired for his Indianness both on and off the reserve. This took two forms. First he tried to instil traditional culture into young people: he was a keen story-teller and extremely knowledgeable in the old lore. He even familiarized himself with the anthropological work on the Okanagan, including the contributions of James Teit. Second, he looked back to what he believed to be the golden age of the Okanagan, a perception which he shared with many other people, conservative and liberal alike. The ingredients of this golden age included horse breeding and training, bronc riding and attending rodeos across the country. He was also accomplished in leathercraft, lacing, and braiding. He farmed a little and kept cattle. Thus the golden age which he cherished was based on a cultural synthesis of old Okanagan equestrian culture and the agricultural nineteenth century which developed on the reserve, together with overtones of colonial Christianity and education. We might even describe it as the Indian cowboy culture (and society) of the Okanagan Valley, and many of its qualities were shared also with the settlers.

The influence that Chief Pierre Louis and his descendants had on the Okanagan reserve is reflected in his genealogical background. He came from Okanagan stock and spent some of his years in the United States. His father, Louis Paul, was an Okanagan from Osoyoos. His mother, Mary Lawrence, was a native of the Okanagan reserve. He was born in Oroville, Washington, while his mother was visiting kin there. They returned to the Okanagan reserve in 1900. He was received into the band by Chief Louis Jim, and was able to purchase sixty-three acres of his own land on the reserve in 1911. In 1917 his membership in the band was objected to on the grounds of his American birthplace.

In 1905 he married Catherine Haynes, an Okanagan from Penticton, well known for her connections with respected settler families. Louis's younger brother, Alec Paul, later took his father's second wife's name and became a Marchand, a family that was to become extremely important patronymically and socially on the reserve, and very complex in terms of origins. Alec Marchand had strong ties with the United States and owned an allotment south of the border in 1934. Louis and his wife had four sons and five daughters, the majority of whom (and their children) were to play an important part, directly and indirectly, in the political life of the reserve.

Pierre Louis was not necessarily a charismatic leader, but he did command a great deal of admiration among the members of the so-called new faction for his liberal decency. He had been a councillor for six years before his election as chief, at a time when no chief was allowed to hold office because of departmental objections. There was, however, considerable bitterness in some quarters over his election. One version of public opinion indicates that he was an 'agent's appointment' which was not accepted by Ottawa. One local historian says he remembers 'a letter coming from Ottawa saying that Johnny Isaac was chief *not* Pierre Louis.' Thus his appointment intensified the rift between the two major factions on the reserve, and some of his opponents never accepted the legitimacy of his accession to office. So great was the bitterness when he was first nominated for chief that some of his opponents, mainly from the Head of the Lake and Irish Creek, walked out in protest, leaving his supporters to return him virtually unopposed.

From the point of view of factionalist politics, certain old faction adherents were quite justified in wishing to declare Pierre Louis's first election invalid because they had never accepted Pierre Louis as a band member, regarding him among other things as an American intruder. But not all those identified with the old faction were so extreme in their views and records show that there was not a complete boycott of the election by the old faction on 14 May 1932, as is sometimes insisted upon by some local Okanagan historians. The election details are as follows. There were five candidates for chief and Pierre Louis only narrowly defeated the old faction candidate, Joe Nicholas, by two votes. The other three candidates represented marginal positions in both the new and the old factions. The four councillors elected were Joe Nicholas, Jimmy Bonneau, Ernest Brewer, and Jimmy Joseph. On 26 May 1932 these results were confirmed by the Department of Indian Affairs in Ottawa.

But this was no tidy election, in spite of the fact that a system of secret balloting was introduced for the first time by agent James Coleman. No sooner had the results been confirmed than Joe Nicholas, Jimmy Joseph, Pierre Jack, Mrs [Pierre] Logan, and one other band member consulted their lawyer in Kamloops to protest the election. Letters passed back and forth between various parties, and the agent tried to dismiss Joe Nicholas and suspend Jimmy Joseph from council in a series of illegal moves which cannot be dealt with here. It needs to be noted, however, that Coleman eventually succeeded in getting Joe Nicholas removed from council, although he lost out on Jimmy Joseph, who was reinstated by the department.

The election was, therefore, quite irregular in a number of ways. Of particular interest is the way in which Coleman was himself involved in new faction ideology, and how he actively opposed the old faction. Thus Pierre Louis was recommended to the department by Coleman, not only because he obtained the most votes but because Coleman (and his predecessor, Ball) felt Louis was the 'one man ... who would make a good chief.' He was said to be 'thoroughly honest,' 'well educated,' a 'hard worker,' and a 'loyal Indian.'

Jimmy Bonneau, William Ashton, and Alex Marchand were recommended by Coleman as councillors without much attention to votes: Jimmy Bonneau because he was 'industrious and progressive,' 'without a police record and addiction to liquor;' William Ashton on the grounds that he was 'a clean-out [clean-cut?] type of man of much more than the average Indian intelligence and held in great respect by the white residents of the Valley;' Alex Marchand for no particular reason other than his close kinship link with Pierre Louis; Joe Nicholas, in spite of receiving a large number of votes, was *not* recommended by Coleman on the grounds that he 'was supported by the old, non-progressive faction and [was] a truculent type of Indian not averse to assuming a threatening attitude towards officials, and it has been necessary for me [the agent] to discourage this attitude.' Joe Nicholas was also alleged by the agent to have been in trouble with the Vernon city police, to have distilled liquor, and to have 'caused bodily harm to his wife.'

In a sense the 1932 election was a new faction election because it was tied so closely to an ideology which they shared with their agent. Coleman even went so far as to write to Colonel G.S. Pragnell, inspector of Indian agencies, that acceptance of the election results as he had presented them to the department 'would bring the Reserve under full control and put a finish to all the nonsense that has been going on out there ... There will of course be a tremendous howl from the old bunch and the Council will not have an easy time' (Chiefs File 982/3-5-1).

Not only did the agent appreciate the reality of the factional schism, but he was determined to get rid of the old faction so that he could get his way without any further opposition, and administer the fine print of the Indian Act. He thought this could be achieved by changing the power base, thereby eliminating the old faction. But he did not understand that both Pierre Louis and Alex Marchand had, in the minds of the reactionaries in the old faction, never been recognized as band members since their arrival on the reserve round about the turn of the century.

In 1947, after fifteen years of new faction power and political involvement, the old guard of the old faction tried a new tactic to unseat Pierre Louis, who was still chief. A petition, dated 27 January 1947 and signed by twenty-five men, was submitted to the department in Ottawa. It read as follows: 'We, the Indians of Okanagan Indian Reserve No. 1, wish to depose Chief Pierre Louis, as we consider him incompetent.' The details of the allegation were quite unfounded, but it is of interest to us here to see factionalism writ large operating in an apolitical medium.

In November 1947 three old faction members followed up the petition with a visit to the regional office in Vancouver, this time asking that a new election be called for chief and council, thereby using a different strategy to unseat the chief and his supporters. In 1943 the same group had visited Nespelem, Washington, to review the status of Pierre Louis and others at the Colville Indian Agency.

The politicians in the old faction did not let up on their attack for over thirty years and then only after a formal hearing by Commissioner C.W. Morrow, QC, in Vernon in 1954 (see PABC, GR 725, 1954). After years of factional intrigue the protesters eventually resorted to the law in an attempt to get their way. They employed the services of a barrister to represent them, and the hearings were held in the community hall on the reserve. In addition to the commissioner, two officials of the Department of Indian Affairs, an RCMP constable, and a reporter attended. There was also an interpreter and two barristers representing the protesters and those being protested. The hearings took several months to complete and the occasion was taken very seriously by all parties.

The reason for the protest was against the inclusion of Chief Pierre Louis and others among the registered members of the Okanagan band on the grounds that they had accepted allotments of land or were in receipt of a compensation from the United States and were registered as American citizens. I will not discuss either the evidence or the legal arguments here, except to point out that the whole case rested very much on the interpretation of the law in terms of the Indian Act as amended. The commissioner found that all the Indians protested against were in fact Indians and members of a band for whose use and benefits lands had been set apart within the meaning of the Indian Act. He therefore recommended that the protests against them be disallowed and their names confirmed on the band list.

The details of the hearing are of considerable interest because they reflect the tremendous interest in factionalism, especially the rift between the old and new factions. Two hundred Okanagan turned out, which at that time would have constituted the overwhelming majority of the male and female voting members living on the reserve. The occasion gave witnesses the opportunity to drag in their favourite attacks on personal character and discuss pedigrees, among other things. But the hearings also brought people in contact with the law, notably the Indian Act, and this large section of the band community was afforded the opportunity of flaunting their internal dissensions on the political stage. In that sense it did have an integrating effect on the reserve community within the parameters of their structured position in Canadian society. It also demonstrated the tremendous faith the Okanagan had in *their* Indian Act. Both parties were represented by legal council, whose main interest was the interpretation of the act for their clients.

The outcome of the case was generally accepted, although several old faction agitators continued to look for ways of removing these 'American intruders,' as they continued to call them. Even today, long after Pierre Louis's death, a few people believe that their letters to the Queen will be answered and 'the cause of all the trouble on the reserve' will be solved. However, the general acceptance of the commissioner's ruling supports the general thesis regarding the sacred power of the Indian Act. The commissioner, it should be noted, also journeyed to Nespelem, Washington State, to inquire into the position of those American Okanagan who had moved to the Canadian side of their traditional territory. The evidence did, of course, demonstrate quite conclusively that the 'Americans' had as many, if not more, kin ties in Canada as they did in the United States.

The complexity of Okanagan factional structures and some of the contradictions inherent in these legal hearings figured prominently throughout the case. For example, one of the principal objectors to the American Okanagan being registered with the Canadian band could, from another viewpoint, be regarded as an intruder himself on the grounds that his mother was the daughter of a settler who had pre-empted vast tracts of Okanagan land in the nineteenth century. It is situations like this that shed light on the opposition to Pierre Louis by the old faction. The opposition had many facets and at the risk of over-simplification I will list them here:

- He was not related to any of Nkwala's households and was said, therefore, to have no right to chiefship or any involvement with the 'seat of power.'
- He was not considered to have affinal ties to redeem him, although he claimed kin ties with a former chief, namely, Louis Jim.
- He was also identified with Six Mile Creek where he lived and owned land.
- He was alleged to be in league with the agents, which explained why 'he was so weak' – 'not like the old chiefs who used to tell the agent to go to hell.'
- He was said to spend too much time with white people.
- Most of the old faction was illiterate at that time, and they resented Pierre Louis's ability to read and write, particularly letters. How the old guard of the old faction would have liked to have been able to write their own legal letters!
- Finally, he was an American Okanagan. This was always brought out and the fact that a special formal hearing was devoted to it in 1954 suggests that all the other reasons above are trivial and irrelevant. But are they?

The key to understanding the old faction–new faction cleavage and especially Pierre Louis's position as chief lies not so much in the established fact of his American association, but rather in the Head of the Lake's ideological interpretation of that association. It does not take much probing into Okanagan history to discover that association with American Okanagan was believed by the old faction to belong exclusively to them. In other words, to have an American connection was not regarded as a Six Mile Creek right, turning Pierre Louis and certain others into structural misfits. I base this conclusion partly on Okanagan reasoning but also on the fact that many Head of the Lake families had members who were constantly flaunting their American Okanagan connections. Nkwala himself had strong American roots and, as we have seen, some of the assumed superiority of Head of the Lake people is derived from these southern connections. I do not believe the new faction ever pointed this out or ever used that argument against their opponents.

But the matter is even more complex, and we must look again at the social personality, the career, and the achievements of Pierre Louis. In the minds of the old faction (and some marginal new faction people also) he was too successful too soon and in too many ways. He had received schooling, he read books, he wrote letters, kept a notebook, got on well with white people, and even used the Coldstream Ranch library in the years he was employed there. He owned horses and was a champion bronc rider. He planted fruit trees, kept cattle, grew all his own vegetables. He had lots of children and they married well and had large families. He was a staunch member of the church, and he encouraged education, and so on and on. Remarking on his success, someone pointed out to me that 'he was always so calm that people did not notice that he was going up the ladder; so nobody had a chance ever to pull him down' (meaning he avoided competition).

The point about Pierre Louis's success was that nobody understood how he did it. He looked like an Indian but he did not behave like an Indian who had been socialized on the reserve. He was an anomaly to many people, and the old faction took it upon themselves to try to destroy him; they never succeeded and that is what infuriated them most. He moved along with the new faction but somehow kept himself out of the intrigues in which he was a central figure.

What stands out so strikingly about Chief Pierre Louis is that from the vantage point of the Indian agent, the Department of Indian Affairs, and the new faction's perspective, he was a 'model Indian.' By this I mean he made the most of the options open to him within the context of the system of which he was part, and he encouraged others to do likewise. If the new faction has forged ahead in the sense that its ranks have increased beyond the boundaries of Six Mile Creek, this is because it opted for an ideology that would maximize people's chances of material advancement in the reserve through education and any other support the Department of Indian Affairs would give them. In this sense Pierre Louis proved a successful, if not a charismatic, leader while he was chief from 1932 to 1959. From the standpoint of factional politics, however, it must also be remembered that it was the collective ideology of Six Mile Creek that was challenging the traditional hegemony of the Head of the Lake.

The old faction–new faction cleavage was thus analogous to a sort of Sadducees-Pharisees relationship. (The comparison is not intended to be in any way judgmental of either faction in Okanagan history and is used here merely as an analytic device.) The core members of the old faction had preached the doctrine of their aristocratic origin among the south Okanagan in what is now Washington State. Like the Sadducees they represented the 'Tory' or 'Conservative' party among the north Okanagan. For a long time they were the wealthiest group of people and resented any economic or cultural success among anyone else, leaving no place for new faction members in the upper echelon of reserve society. To begin with, members of the new faction were seen as separatists (Pharisees) by the old faction because they refused to toe the political line and submit to their jurisdiction. Later their Pharisaic inclinations were read into their striving towards literacy and better education, and especially in the pious way in which they insisted on following the letter of the law of the Indian Act. The struggle in which Chief Pierre Louis was involved was thus essentially an ideological one, in which the new faction emerged triumphant after a long battle.

Over the years the Pierre Louis family compact came to dominate elections for chiefs and councillors. Louis himself once stated his position on reserve policy and the opposition of others to it:

> Some people are against me for several reasons. I am in favour of education and also because I say that we have to comply with the law. Some on the council say that the government has no right to tell us what to do – just so long as the majority of the council approves it, it is O.K. But I tell them, it is no use if it is against the law. I [had once] thought I could make by-laws and we drew some up and sent them in (e.g., fence lines etc.) but they said we couldn't have any by-laws that would conflict with the Provincial Act. (Hirabayashi's notes, 7.14.54)

If Chief Nkwala's people dominated reserve politics through the nineteenth century, it was Pierre Louis's people who began to develop a new order from the 1930s onwards. Pierre Louis was able to combine the values of more traditional Okanagan society with nineteenth-century cowboy culture and integrate these, in theory at least, with what was permitted or available to Indians from contemporary Canadian society. In short, he 'modernized' the conservative world of both the peasants and farmers, and built the base on which the Okanagan would be transformed in the future. Every estate in the community tended to look up towards the British monarchy, but the Pierre Louis compact looked further than ritual symbolism and cultivated the more practical things they found in the establishment. Formal school education was one of these.

But Louis's economic status in the community also required that he work hard outside the reserve. Prior to the First World War he was employed on the Coldstream Ranch for seven years before quitting in 1912, and it was here that he formed new close associations with settlers. He then did contract logging sporadically for thirty-five years, and when he was not cutting and hauling logs he worked on his own ranch on the reserve. While he was logging he got paid $7 per thousand. He had a crew of eight or nine, of which four were his own sons. For a time he worked on road construction in British Columbia, and when he was younger he worked on various jobs down south across the line.

How are we to characterize Chief Pierre Louis's twenty-seven years of titular leadership in the Okanagan reserve? He was the first chief to have had any formal education (though he did not claim more than grade four achievement, he had in fact attended the Old Tonasket School, St Mary's Mission, and a school in Oroville). Having himself enjoyed the advantages of education, he advocated the same for all people on the reserve. He encouraged people to be self-sufficient during the Depression, and by inspiration and example he helped many families survive those lean years. Some people even recall that Okanagan on the reserve were often better off than many whites off the reserve at that time. He aspired to join the ranks of the Canadian middle class, and largely succeeded, although he always recognized the fact that he was a reserve Indian. Lastly, he broke the general acceptance of the political dominance of the Head of the Lake and its exclusive claim to be the seat of power, thereby granting political legitimacy to Six Mile Creek. But his influence, and the changes for which he appears to have been solely responsible while he was chief, were part of a general trend on the reserve. He was perhaps the person who led into action a stream of wills that had been influenced by two world wars and the general trend towards 'modernization' and 'self improvement.' As the Okanagan themselves say nowadays, 'We have come along and up quite a bit lately.' Chief Louis had a 'gift of grace' which he put to good effect in the context of the practical affairs of band life, a life that derived so much of its form from the Indian Act.

In spite of his tremendous influence in the community and his considerable following, Pierre Louis had bitter enemies at the Head of the Lake. His progressive liberalism had to contend with the obduracy of the old conservative faction, whose influence frequently cut surreptitiously across geographical regions and political clusters in the community. Consequently, every three years Pierre Louis had to face the ordeal of election, including even more intense character assassination by his enemies. And when the Indian Act was amended in 1951 to order elections for chief every two years, that change considerably increased the challenges by his opponents.

CHIEF JIMMY BONNEAU, 1959–61

In 1953, when the first election under the amended act was held, Pierre Louis was unsuccessfully opposed by Ernest Brewer, an old faction conservative from Irish Creek with some progressive leanings. Two years later Pierre Jack, another old faction spokesman, ran unsuccessfully against Pierre Louis, losing by thirty-seven to fifty-one votes. In 1957 Jack tried again, but the voters turned out in record numbers and Pierre Louis won by eighty-nine to sixty-two votes. But the opposition persevered and finally in 1959 Jimmy Bonneau, an arch-conservative old faction personality, won the election by the narrow margin of seventy-nine to seventy-one votes. Chief Pierre Louis, now getting on in years, was finally voted out of office.

Chief Jimmy Bonneau represented a very different ideology on the reserve. He was largely illiterate, having never attended school. He had made an attempt to enter the entrepreneurial world by opening a small shop at Six Mile Creek in the 1950s, but the enterprise did not succeed, and for the most part his life centred on farming and ranching and occasional wage labour. Politically he was unsophisticated and unable to reunite the enormous variations of opinion among the members of the old faction. Some were for the church, others against it; some were anti-white and anti-Canadian but great champions of the British queen; some were always opposing western medicine and seeking out 'Indian' doctors; some were so reactionary that they would not accept family allowances, and one couple were so proud of their Indian ancestry that they even refused their old age pensions!

Chief Jimmy Bonneau was essentially the last of the genuine old-time conservatives. If he failed to unite the old faction, it was partly because by the late 1950s and 1960s many of its members had become disillusioned, anarchical, and reactionary because they could make no sense of the bloated bureaucracy that was now administering the Indian Act. Commenting on Jimmy Bonneau's lack of success in uniting his supporters, an astute apolitical friend remarked: 'Jimmy was really for the old faction at Irish Creek, but pressure on him through his children and others made him go Six Mile Creek-wise, because they live out there.' But the pukka old guard dismiss such comments as irrelevant; for them old faction unity and power can be achieved only through leadership from the house of Nkwala, a genealogical position that Chief Bonneau did not enjoy.

Thus Jimmy Bonneau can best be considered as a grass-roots conservative who wished to maintain the political status quo. He wanted to see improvements on the reserve but he was not prepared to accept modernization as a view of the future; he simply wanted everyone to be a better farmer. He was not a politician and as people look back to the late 1950s, they see him as the chief who only distinguished himself by defeating Pierre Louis.

PRESENT-DAY CHIEFS

The relatively weak support base surrounding the chief at the end of the 1950s came abruptly to an end in 1961 when Murray Alexis, after serving two terms as a councillor, defeated Jimmy Bonneau for chief in an overwhelming victory of one hundred votes to forty-two, a majority unknown in the reserve's history. Chief Alexis was a young progressive liberal with strong support from Six Mile Creek. He was well educated, having graduated from Kamloops Residential School in 1952 – the Vernon school system did not accept him because he was an Indian. He had strong and extensive networks throughout the community. He was well connected through both marriage and descent, being married to Chief Pierre Louis's granddaughter and connected through his mother's sister to an influential old faction family at the Head of the Lake.

At the time of his first election most people saw him as the ideal chief, although nowadays many may not admit it. He had a good head for reserve business matters which suited the progressives, who were interested in leasing land to market gardeners and lakeside cottage sites to whites. He encouraged education, and he survived attacks from the reactionaries and arch-conservatives, who opposed the move to bus all children to better and integrated schools in Vernon. He was a talented musician, a keen and able sportsman, and a pillar of the Catholic church. He had connections with people off the reserve and he was anxious to involve the Okanagan in both federal and provincial politics. One of his uncles was active in the Liberal party of Canada.

The main complaint of the old faction about Murray Alexis was that he was not 'tough enough with the Government, like them old chiefs used to be' – that is, before Pierre Louis. For the progressives, however, he was ideal, because they 'were not interested in old style chiefs anymore. What [they] wanted was management.' Not that Alexis was cut out to be a good manager, nor paradoxically did they necessarily want him *to manage*. But they expected him to be the central figurehead as the community modernized (and managed) itself, which is what happened over the years.

During his first term in office (1961–3), Chief Murray Alexis was clearly the young 'modernized' successor to Pierre Louis. However, his home was geographically well placed on the reserve, situated roughly halfway between Six Mile Creek and the Head of the Lake, a vantage point which created an aura of neutrality that to some extent dissipated his involvement in factional issues.

After two years as chief, Alexis decided not to let his name go forward for re-election because 'he wanted to spend more time with the family,' devote his energy to building up his farm, complete his house, and attend to his lakeshore properties leased to whites. He and his family had spent the whole of the 1962 apple-picking season in the State of Washington in order to build up some capital. So he stepped out of politics for the next eight years.

There were two candidates for chief in the 1963 election, Ernest Brewer and Jimmy Antoine. Ernest Brewer was a conservative from Irish Creek whose first wife, Amy Chacko, was a woman from good Thompson Indian stock. He had never received any regular formal school education but he was not illiterate. In his younger days he had been very well off, owning prime agricultural land, a car, a threshing machine, and other farm equipment. He also had a logging outfit and the concession to cut timber off the reserve on crown land in the 1940s and 1950s. Born in 1893, he was getting on in years when he entered the contest for chief in 1963. He had tried unsuccessfully to oust Pierre Louis in the 1953 elections, and this second attempt at the chiefship was supported by the old faction and some of the progressives who were determined to prevent Jimmy Antoine, an educated, reactionary eccentric in the old faction, from getting into office. In fact, Brewer owes his success in the election partly to the bad reputation Antoine had acquired over the years relating to land disputes, court cases and other circumstances.

Chief Brewer's fence-sitting conservatism attracted many liberal supporters over the years and he won subsequent elections in 1965 and 1967. But in 1969 Murray Alexis returned to band politics fully prepared to cope with questions of native rights, self-determination, brotherhoods, demonstrations, occupation of the agent's office in Vernon, and the setting up of an independent office on the reserve.

Although the conservatives and what was left of the old faction closed ranks, they were not strong enough to return Brewer to office, and Murray Alexis won the election by sixty-eight votes to fifty-eight. At the next election in 1971 Alexis won again, defeating three candidates: an inexperienced ambitious progressive, a wealthy conservative progessive, and a young reactionary. At the following election in 1973, Alexis again scored a victory over three opponents, including Brewer.

The 1970s proved difficult for Alexis, who had to cope with the enormous changes that were taking place in the formal structure of the band. Most important of these was the creation of the office of the band manager which would eventually take over the work of the superintendent in Vernon. When the first election for Okanagan band manager took place in October 1971, Alexis entered the competition himself while still chief, and won. With this dual appointment, he attempted 'to run his own show on the reserve,' as one person put it. Inevitably his popularity soon declined 'because chiefs and band managers don't match,' even though he still had enough supporters to win the 1973 election. But by July of that year fierce battles were raging in council and an attempt was made to remove Alexis from both the office of chief and that of band manager. While the conflict lasted a chairman had to be appointed to run the band meetings.

Despite the tumult in the community surrounding Alexis's double role, he won the 1975 election against enormous odds with the support of his loyal followers in the large Louis family. In August he was deposed from office in accordance with the provisions of section 78 of the Indian Act for being absent from three consecutive meetings of the band council. The politics of his deposition on a technical matter is particularly interesting because three councillors (all close kin) were also ousted from council at the same time. He was also dismissed from the office of band manager.

In the September by-election to fill the vacancy for chief, Alexis ran again. Also nominated were Wilfred Bonneau, a grass-roots new faction liberal conservative from Six Mile Creek, Tommy Gregoire, an old faction conservative from the Head of the Lake claiming kinship with the house of Nkwala through his mother; and Emery Louis, youngest son of Pierre Louis. Predictably, Alexis lost the election against the conservatives from two regions and Wilfred Bonneau won.

Chief Wilfred Bonneau, the eldest son of old Chief Jimmy Bonneau, had virtually no formal schooling. His wife was a member of the traditional Simla family. He was a hard-working farmer and rancher who lived a life somewhat removed from the rest of the community, spending his summers across the lake on the east arm of the reserve. Although the family has a strong conservative side, it also has strong progressive aspirations linked to education and commerce. One of his daughters, for example, read law at the University of British Columbia and received a law degree in 1982. It is important to note that Wilfred Bonneau's victory was part of a compaign by the Bonneau family compact to unseat Murray Alexis, a campaign that has continued for fifteen years.

In 1979, after Wilfred Bonneau had withdrawn from politics on the grounds that he found the bureaucratic nature of council meetings too taxing, his son Reynolds entered the campaign for chief. At that time Reynolds Bonneau was a young man of thirty, and had been band manager for a while. The 1979 elections were poorly attended and there were only two nominations for chief, Reynolds Bonneau who obtained forty-three votes, and Murray Alexis who received forty-eight votes. This narrow victory for Alexis was reversed in the

1981 election when Reynolds Bonneau gained a small majority and held office for two years.

In 1983, however, Alexis was returned to office by just one vote. Bonneau challenged the result on various technical grounds but the electoral officer declared Alexis the winner. In the same election the rump of the old faction once again nominated Tommy Gregoire who, running under the banner of 'hereditary chief' through his Nkwala connection, obtained roughly one-quarter of the votes.

The Bonneau compact has continued to nominate Reynolds for chief but he has not been able to defeat Murray Alexis since 1981. This contest for chief since the mid-1970s demonstrates the extent to which the former factional dichotomy has become blurred in recent years, having less and less importance in band politics. In addition, the Six Mile Creek versus the Head of the Lake division has begun to lose its original meaning as the seat of power has moved in the direction of Six Mile Creek. Old struggles over chiefship have been transformed into a contest between a liberal progressive movement (Murray Alexis's 'party') and a grass-roots conservative progressive movement (the Bonneau family). Thus, as the differences between political *factions* have diminished, we might want to speak of the emergence of two quite similar political *parties* on the reserve.

CONTINUITY OR DISJUNCTION?

It would be intellectually presumptuous to attempt a detailed sociological analysis of the political significance of all the Okanagan chiefs whose names have been recorded in this book. If one started with Nkwala's father, Pelkamolux III, and ended with Murray Alexis, one would have covered a period of nearly two hundred years of unevenly documented history. Modern chiefs obviously perform very different roles from traditional chiefs, and neither resembles a fur trade chief such as Nkwala. Even after the duties and powers of chiefs were defined by the Indian Act, there has been tremendous variation in the way individual chiefs have responded to their mandates to serve their reserve communities and negotiate with the wider society. The Indian Act, for all its authority in the local government, can only lay down the parameters within which chiefs must or should operate. Individual chiefs have to articulate with the local system as it has been constructed at particular periods of time. The election and appointment of chiefs has always been dependent on who they are and who backs them. Thus continuity in the chain of chiefs as far as their roles are concerned exists for quite short periods only, giving rise to a general pattern of considerable disjunction through time. This means that political dimensions consist of a series of interlocking subsystems rather than consecutive sequences in history.

There are, therefore, some observations that can be made about the nature of local political formations and their headmen and chiefs over the years. In traditional Okanagan society headmen figured prominently in their bands, which were small recognizable groups. During the fur trade many bands began to amalgamate and chiefs such as Nkwala tried to claim jurisdiction over much larger units. After the fur trade declined and reserves were defined in terms of the Indian Act, out of necessity chiefs began once again to involve themselves with smaller social units. Thus, as the influence of the Indian Act has intensified, so contemporary chiefs and their councils have tended to focus more and more on their own reserves and their own local needs. For example, in the Okanagan Valley there may be a nominal brotherhood between the Okanagan, Penticton, and Westbank bands, but each band, as a political community, is primarily concerned with its own material and moral interests and identity. This course has nothing to do with traditional patterns, but is determined almost entirely by the Indian Act and the nature of reserves, notably their relation to the wider political economy. This centripetal trend might be seen as a reaction to the external milieux, which creates mini-political and ethnic units. These are the antithesis of pan-Indianism, which is the ideal of the conference table, but not of the band office.

Another trend that runs through the history of headmen and chiefs among the Okanagan is the primacy of status over descent in the acquisition of rank and political position. Although sons quite often take over the political office of their fathers, this does not constitute a rule of descent or a principle of succession among the Okanagan. Rather one should see this pseudo-lineality in terms of personal status emanating from family esteem and often bolstered by the status of the wives to whom chiefs and their agnates are married. It is important to have the right mother and the right wife to become a chief. Thus, the fact that Isaiah Moses, William, Chwail, Logan, Gaston Louie, Baptiste Nicholas, and Johnny Isaac were old faction chiefs representing Nkwalaism and neo-Nkwalaism is not always a matter of kinship. Nkwalaism is largely a question of status snobbery, adding somewhat to the obtuse quality of old factionalism. Louis Jim, Pierre Michel, and Pierre Louis were new faction chiefs for reasons that were also unrelated to kinship.

It would be misleading then to give the impression that Indian Act chiefs reflect a smooth unbroken chain of political leaders over a period of 110 years. At times there was no chief in office, at others there seem to have been two chiefs, an Ottawa chief and an Okanagan chief, and on at least one occasion the agent simply appointed an individual to represent him as if the appointee were a chief. But whatever the aberrations, the role of chief in relation to the agent was always clearly defined. It is not surprising, therefore, that new conflicts and stresses overwhelmed the institution of chiefship between 1971 and 1975 when the chief himself also tried to hold the new position of band manager. This incongruous situation would have been like allowing the chief in earlier times to become the agent as well, and it created a situation of intolerable discord for most people. Thus the political campaign to back a grass-roots chief in 1975 can be interpreted as an unconscious attempt to reaffirm the nature of chiefship as people understood it.

The creation of the office of band manager marked an important change in reserve affairs. In some ways, it appears to have been a move in the direction of self-government, independence, and liberation from the grip of Canadian bureaucratic control. But in fact the structural changes concomitant with the creation of a band manager resulted in even greater federal involvement and more permanent dependence on Canadian polity and its economic resources.

Okanagan chiefs under the Indian Act have occupied unenviable positions in their community, and they have received very few rewards (and often little praise from those who elected them) for the work they have been expected to do. But certain chiefs have been able, against tremendous odds, to contribute to community welfare. The most harrowing period in Okanagan history was between 1908 and 1932, not simply because of world warfare and economic depression, but because of the autocratic arrogance of Indian agents and their conscious efforts to break the spirit of the chiefs and other key people so that the moral and alien will of the administration could direct the future of the reserve.

The history of Okanagan chiefs over a considerable period of time shows the extent to which political conflict has always been associated with factionalism on the one hand, and rivalry between villages and other territorial groupings on the other. In distant traditional times, village rivalry more than any other factor seems to have sparked off political conflict, while after the establishment of reserves disjunction between rival political leaders has tended to be expressed through factionalism. Yet if one now looks closely at the ramifications of local politics, it is impossible to separate ideas about factionalism from ideas associated with residence, and in many people's minds rivalry between the Head of the Lake village cluster and the Six Mile Creek cluster is still at the heart of any matter of factionalism. To facilitate the understanding of present-day chiefship I need, at the risk of over-simplification and repetition, to recapitulate some details that have already been analysed.

The two main settlements or village clusters approximate the two 'reserves' allotted to the Okanagan in the colonial period by Haynes in 1865. Most old faction people identify themselves with the Head of the Lake, but not entirely. Most new faction people identify themselves with Six Mile Creek, although this is an over-simplification. There are conservatives at both the Head of the Lake and at Six Mile Creek, but the real reactionaries are oriented towards the Head of the Lake. People sharing progressive ideologies are found everywhere, but in many respects it is Six Mile Creek that fosters the progressive ideology in the context of present-day politics.[1]

If we ignore the factor of locality, the old faction can be characterized as conservative, providing an ideological umbrella for the reactionaries. The new faction, in contrast, is essentially liberal and progressive, although it does have a conservative wing consisting largely of older people. It is in this way that the two factions tend to overlap, thereby preventing an implacable schism in the community. The old faction–new faction cleavage resembles in many ways the rift betwen the 'red blanket' traditionalists and the 'school' people among the Xhosa of South Africa, but the dichotomy never seems to have been as dramatic as that portrayed by Philip Mayer (1961, 1980).

---

1 On 6 February 1991 Albert Saddleman was elected chief by a significant majority. Saddleman, a former councillor, has been involved, amongst other things, with crucial environmental issues in the region.

Chapter Thirteen

Band Government, Administration, and Politics

The Okanagan, like other Indian bands in contemporary Canada, are subject to the exclusive legislative authority of the federal government by virtue of section 91(24) of the British North America Act. As we have seen, the charter which made this condition possible was the Indian Act, section 18(1) of which states: 'Subject to this Act, reserves are held by Her Majesty for the use and benefit of the respective bands for which they have been set apart; and subject to this Act and to the terms of any surrender, the Governor in Council may determine whether any purpose for which lands in a reserve are used or are to be used is for the use and benefit of the band.' This is an enormous and sweeping mandate and its implementation is made possible by the Indian Act itself. More specifically, the act 'grants government officials power to control virtually everything that is done on the reserves' (Cumming and Mickenberg 1972: 236ff). It is the administration of the Okanagan band and its ramifications at the *local* level to which I will now turn.

The headquarters of the Department of Indian Affairs and Northern Development carries an Ottawa label, although the physical location of the department with its enormous bureaucracy is across the river in Hull in the province of Quebec. The regional office for the Okanagan band is in Vancouver, but band members tend to visualize a direct link between themselves and Ottawa. Now that a permanent band office has been established on the reserve it is viewed as a Little Ottawa by the cynics: 'I don't even need to step inside that place [the band office] to see how many people work there earning big money. I just count the coffee cups in the window as I drive by.' The Little Ottawa homologue is quite appropriate and accurate because the band office has become the local centre whence the Indian Act and all that it represents permeates the community. The atmosphere there is very different from that of the old Indian Affairs office in Vernon where the operation was dominated by the personality of the agent himself as if it were still a nineteenth-century colonial outpost.

Before the demise of the Indian agent (or superintendent as he came to be called in later years) in the 1970s, local government and administration was centred both in the agent's office and in the person of the agent himself. Consequently, time in the band's political history tends to be remembered in terms of who the agent was when an event occurred, and from every point of view we might characterize the agent as the person who embodied the community's ambivalence towards the administration in general. On occasions he is portrayed as autocratic, corrupt, insensitive to Okanagan feelings, not doing his job properly, and so on. At other times he is seen as carrying out his job as the Queen's agent, respecting the chief's opinion, and in general giving people what they want. The agent never seems to have been thought of as an impersonal bureaucrat, and his actions were always interpreted in very personal terms. I recall one agent in the 1960s whose occasional insensitive and moody behaviour was explained by the whims of 'his old woman who was mad at him for something or other.' In a neighbouring reserve the agent's abrupt manner and bureaucratic officiousness were attributed to an incurable illness from which he was said to be suffering.

Agents were very powerful people, not merely because they wielded federal authority, but because they provided a personal link with that authority. People might say they hated all agents, but they admitted that some were worse than others. They also protected their agent because they knew that he was the essential person, the key nurturer, a symbolic mother's brother in their dealings with Ottawa. If any aid, assistance, or advice was to come their way, the agent was the person who would dispense it. The personality, qualifications, and disposition of the agent seem, contrary to Dunning's view (1962), to have had little to do with the manner in which the act was administered. Rather the social position of the agent was a reflection of the administrative system which he served and the response and attitude of the people towards that system as they grew to understand it over the years. From 1914 onwards his paternalistic permission had to be obtained for 'Indian Dancing' and individuals could not tog up in aboriginal costume without his approval. The gradual pre-emption of the people's right to make their own decisions can be seen again in 1918 when the Indian Act was changed so that reserve land could not be leased to white farmers without the consent of chief and council and the agent's approval (Lithman 1978: 54). From the 1920s onwards the agent became, so to speak, the official patron of the people on the reserve, after some significant changes in his duties in the early years of the century had been made. And in 1927 local political meetings were virtually banned.

THE AMENDED INDIAN ACT OF 1951

The 1951 amendments to the Indian Act introduced significant structural changes at both the local and national levels. The 1951 Indian Act marked the beginning of the greater involvement of the Canadian establishment in Indian affairs, a trend towards modernizing the status quo. Some white people saw themselves as champions of the Indian cause while others were quite hostile to the Indian presence. In the early 1960s, for example, quite amicable relations existed between the Okanagan and whites at the north end of the Lake, while in Penticton to the south there were serious conflicts and many restaurants were still refusing to serve Indians. White interest in Okanagan land was much greater in Penticton at that time than it was in Vernon, and one of the causes of the conflict was closely related to white jealousy over reserve land and their inability to usurp it. But whatever might be said about negative attitudes to Indians by whites in the Okanagan Valley or elsewhere in Canada, the federal government remained as closely involved with reserves from an administrative point of view as it had been since 1876.

For the Okanagan the main changes in the 1951 Indian Act were as follows:
- People were permitted to drink in beer parlours and other licensed premises after years of being deprived of this right, although they still could not purchase liquor in liquor stores at that time (sections 95, 96, 96A).
- Women band members were given the vote. This meant that everyone on the band list over twenty-one years of age could vote in local elections, and be nominated for the positions of chief and councillor (sections 73, 79).
- The term of office for both chief and councillors was reduced from three years to two, thereby increasing the turnover of local elected leaders (section 77).
- The band council could now, if it so chose, make by-laws for a wide range of purposes, from law and order and health to the surveying and allotment of reserve lands among band members, and raising money to support band projects and pay chiefs, councillors, and officials to carry out their duties (sections 80, 82). All by-laws made by council were subject to ministerial approval and veto at any time.
- Provisions were also made for granting bands the right to exercise control and management of their reserve land (section 60), while section 69 laid the foundation for band councils to manage their own revenue money. It also

provided the basis on which large grants of money could be made available to bands for local projects and development schemes.

The advent of the 1951 act did not produce many immediate changes, but it did (admittedly in hindsight) anticipate most of the trends that were to emerge in the 1970s both in the community and outside in government circles. One change that had an important immediate effect was the opening of beer parlours to Indians because it got people out of the reserves and fostered interaction with the wider society. Not everyone drank or wished to drink, but at least the opening of bars to Indians removed one of the racialist clauses from the Indian Act and further entrenched the Indian presence in Canadian society. It took just over a decade for the Okanagan to establish a place for themselves in the bars of Vernon, providing one of the few arenas where band members and whites could face the realities of daily life together. It is true that the two groups more often than not kept to themselves, but at least a common arena had been established.

By granting them the vote, women were brought out of their political purdah on the reserve, thus encouraging their assertiveness in the world outside. I remember very clearly discussing race relations with two Okanagan women in a beer parlour in 1962. One had recently returned to the reserve to play an active political role, and both had run in recent elections for councillor.

There were few other immediate effects of the new act. Some old political conflicts seemed to intensify as people began arguing over the changes in the act, because they felt that Ottawa was tampering with Queen Victoria's text. One group, I should add, felt that the pre-1951 version of the Indian Act was a codification of traditional Okanagan law and custom.

The main effect of the 1951 Indian Act was also its cause in the sense that it was the inevitable evolution of the 1876 Indian Act and its various amendments, all of which were created to fulfil the mandate of the British North America Act. If Indian bands were to remain subject to the exclusive authority of the federal government, then the existing legal and bureaucratic procedures needed to be updated from time to time to maintain that authority. From a macro-sociological point of view, the 1951 Indian Act and all its subsequent amendments were merely steps in the process of modernizing the total reserve system while retaining the control over the Indians whom the legislation itself defined. The fact that the provinces have become more and more involved in the administration of Indian reserves over the years does not mean that the federal government has relinquished its authority. On the contrary, it implies that the whole operation of Indian Affairs has become so complex as to require that some of its facets now be handled by the provincial government (for such services as child welfare, education, medical services, roads).

These generalizations are based on the assumption that the full operation of Indian affairs in Canada is a function of the latter's relationship with the wider political, economic, and religious systems which permeate Canadian polity. Indian affairs are, moreover, maintained by the hegemonic effects of the ideology which informs that polity.

The above hypothesis is sufficient to explain the direction of Indian affairs in Canada and its reflection in the 1951 act. We do not have to find other reasons for the refinement of Indian affairs from the 1970s onwards or the lack of change in the 1950s and 1960s. It is probably true that there was limited public knowledge of Indian issues and few effective lobbying groups among both Indians and whites in the 1960s, and that all this miraculously changed when 'a collective sense of guilt about the historical treatment of Indians emerged and the federal government came under heavy criticism' (Weaver 1981: 15). It is probably also true to say that the American civil rights movement, Pierre Trudeau's new liberalism, and the 1969 white paper faux pas (cf Ponting and Gibbins 1980: 25–30) all contributed to the expansion of the Department of Indian Affairs and Northern Development in the 1970s and the deep involvement of the Indians in their affairs from that time onwards. But I would suggest that the vast expansion of bureaucratic (and fiscal) enterprises would have taken place anyway. At the local level, such extreme social determinism may not ring true, but from a macro-sociological point of view it makes good sense, especially when one realizes that two influential surveys of Canadian Indians were requested by the Ministry of Citizenship and Immigration before Indian Affairs was recognized as a separate department.[1]

Ponting and Gibbins, in their excellent socio-political introduction to Indian affairs, draw attention to the assimilationist philosophy inherent in Canadian society. While not denying that assimilationism and segregationalism exist side by side in Canada as ideologies, my judgment is that as far as the 'development' of reserves is concerned, segregationalism is the stronger. In the Okanagan Valley many whites want a stake in Indian land, but when the

---

1 The first, published as *The Indians of British Columbia* by H.B. Hawthorn, C.S. Belshaw, and S.M. Jamieson (1958), had been commissioned in 1954. The second was released to the public as *A Survey of the Contemporary Indians of Canada* in two volumes under the direction of H.B. Hawthorn (1966, 1967). Both these reports had an enormous influence on the custodians of Indian life, and they helped stimulate the growth of a bigger bureaucracy and the extension of Indian development *in the context of the reserves*. Both reports mirrored many of the expectations of the government, and Hawthorn himself was a liberal scholar and a staunch believer in applied anthropology.

Okanagan start to buy residential property in Vernon, for example, there will be a public outcry. At the same time the Indian presence on the Okanagan reserve near Vernon is an enormous asset to commerce, to the medical profession, and to some extent to industry, in that small interior British Columbia city. Similarly, the institution of Indian affairs is big business in Canadian society generally, providing well-paid jobs for many people, the majority of whom are not Indians; and most of the revenue generated flows back into white society.

FORMAL STRUCTURE OF OKANAGAN BAND GOVERNMENT

The Indian Affairs office in Vernon closed down in 1975 and the work shifted to the local band-run administration which was already operating on the reserve. This was a lively period for the people, characterized by ambivalent feelings towards the white man in general and Indian Affairs in particular. Local factionalism took on a new character at this time and many people were confused by the invasion of the American Indian Movement and what were referred to as 'hippie-type people' who had invited themselves to the reserve.

Prior to the closing of the Indian Affairs office, a quasi-dual system of local government had grown up over the years, having its roots in the three stormy decades that surrounded chiefship at the turn of the twentieth century. On the one side was the Indian Affairs operation which administered the Indian Act under the authority of the agent, his staff, and most of the councillors. On the other side was the reserve-based council, elected according to the dictates of the act, which tended to oppose formal bureaucratic control and tolerated the agent and his staff on sufferance only. Although the personnel constituting the 'councils' overlapped, the Okanagan used to make a clear distinction between the two bodies: the one was department-oriented, the other reserve-based. Prior to the 1920s there appears at times to have been two distinct councils, one elected under the supervision of the agent, the other elected according to the same rules, but without him.

Given this background, it is not surprising that it took almost a decade to routinize the new system of local administration while the agent was being phased out and the reins of power were being transformed. A new functionary in the system of local government was the band manager, who was eventually to become a key person in the Okanagan community. The expectations of him were superhuman, and the office carried with it no security of tenure. As the new post has evolved, so its encumbent has begun to resemble a civil servant, which he is not. He is at everyone's beck and call; he is a client of council, but receives little patronage; he is expected to have ideas, but only those which council will accept; he must tread delicately at all times, which means he must be well informed, but not give the impression that he knows too much.

At the council meeting on 10 March 1971 the chief and six councillors discussed what the duties of the new post of band manager should be, and how the new office should be run, in anticipation of the time when it would be directly answerable to an administrator in the regional office of Indian Affairs in Vancouver. For some the new system seemed to be a move towards self-government, but the only significant change was that the administrative powers of the superintendent moved to the regional office, while his duties shifted to the band to be shared by the chief, councillors, and the band manager. The introduction of administration grants to finance the appointment of a band manager, increase the stipends for chief and councillors, and provide a surplus to pay for various additional services did give band council more responsibility in addition to more work.

Hawthorn et al. (1958: 454–7) reports on the wide gap between superintendent and council in the 1950s, indicating how much time was taken up in meetings bridging the gap between the two groups. As the chief local administrator for the Department of Indian Affairs, the superintendent was largely interested in obtaining council's support to implement policy and obtaining information about band members to enable him to make administrative decisions. Council, on the other hand, was interested in getting the superintendent to act on the matters in which it was interested so that it could 'get what [it could] out of the government.' What is of special interest to this analysis is the fact that the agendas at meetings were basically the same as they are today now that the superintendent has disappeared and band managership has been created.

When the specific duties of the office of band manager were being defined by council they must have recalled their expectations of the superintendent in the past. The new position carried with it enormous responsibility, with far more demanding expectations of competence in both planning and administration than had been required of superintendents. The band manager was to be responsible for the whole field of economic development, the domestic water supply and land irrigation, housing, lakeshore development, recreational needs, and parks.

It took several months to appoint the first band manager, a position for which there was considerable competition. The successful candidate was elected by secret ballot of the councillors at the 13 October meeting in 1971, and turned out to be Chief Alexis himself. He was to receive a tax-free salary of $7200 per year. The conservatives and reactionary old-timers were outraged. 'How can a chief also be the agent?' asked a number of people. As matters turned out, it took two years for the chief to be deposed and his job as band manager to be terminated, and it would be another four years before the community established a niche to sustain a permanent band manager. Council made at least six appointments in that period, and all failed.

We pick up the saga in August 1977 when the post was openly advertised with a starting salary of $1000 per month plus a travel allowance. There were five applicants and the successful candidate was appointed on 3 September 1977, only to provoke another ruckus. Now the whole question of council electing people to office was challenged and there were allegations of favouritism and corruption on the part of council; everyone seems to have been fed up with council in some way or other, as the minutes of the November band meeting show. The social services co-ordinator said, 'I'd like council to decide right now whether you feel that I'm incompetent at my work.' One of the band sawmill workers blamed council for the sawmill's failure and asked about cheque forgery. Another band member complained that council would not give her a house on the grounds that she was not yet legally married, and so on.

The band meeting brought out all kinds of tensions, conflicts, complaints, jealousies, and resentments, in addition to the allegations of favouritism. The reason is obvious: people could not get used to council taking over responsibilities on behalf of the band and were uneasy about its control of the new resources. In addition to the band manager there were also secretaries and other office staff plus the various semi-professionals – social worker, educational officer, economic development officer, among others – all of whom receive salaries. These attacks on council and councillors stemmed, therefore, from a general feeling among band members that they were missing out on something new, as if it were something of the order of a land claims settlement. Some people even got the idea that the prize had already arrived but that its distribution was in the hands of a few people who had been elected to do something quite different. That council did have money at its disposal was proved to one band member by the fact that it made a donation of $1000 to Vernon Jubilee Hospital in 1977.

Attitudes towards the band managership formed part of this general feeling, especially when the incumbent was a chief or councillor. A chief who did an agent's work simply did not fit Okanagan views of being an Indian, living on a reserve, and being under Ottawa and the Indian Act.

Family alliances, cliques, and factions also seemed to disrupt the band manager's chances of filling the office without conflict. When one band manager resigned his job on 15 May 1978 two other members of his kin group resigned their jobs in the band office. It took nearly a decade for the Okanagan community to sort out the roles which members of the new administration needed to play if the Little Ottawa was going to work on reserve soil, and the incumbents of these positions, whether chiefs, councillors, band manager, office workers, and so on, had to learn the cultural code that best fitted the jobs they had to do from the 1970s onwards. The specific strategies needed to be a successful band manager, chief, or councillor will be discussed later.

As the band's (or more accurately, the council's) emissary, the band manager's duties are defined for him by local convention, and not by the Indian Act. It is ironical, therefore, that modern Okanagan chiefs and councillors, whose titles transmit a feeling that they ought at least to have token 'traditional' roles, have in point of fact none, because their duties and authority are defined for them by the Indian Act. This formal charter defines the parameters in which their political actions and ideas operate as it has evolved over the years, but it has not changed very much since 1876.

The Indian Act of 1876, however, regarded all political leaders as chiefs, although a distinction was made between the 'head chief' and ordinary chiefs, the latter being the equivalent of councillors today. This must have made some sense to the Okanagan at the time because they themselves differentiated head 'chiefs' (for example, Nkwala) from all other headmen. However, after the amendment of the Indian Act in 1880 they began to use the term councillor, and later a clear distinction between chiefs and councillors emerged, although it was not codified until 1951.

What is important in this discussion is that the idea of traditional leadership among the Okanagan as it was in 1876 disappeared very quickly after the Indian Act was first applied; chiefs and councillors nowadays bear virtually no relation to any form of traditional leadership. In the nineteenth century formal elections with some sort of voting procedures were soon established, although at that time Okanagan councillors were first voted in as a back-up team to reinforce the assumed authority of the chief. Perhaps this arrangement could be interpreted as a traditional system, in the sense that it reflects a reaction to Canadian rule and a transformation in the structuralist sense of the pre-colonial system. The role of missionaries in this whole process of transformation has already been alluded to. Thomson (1985) shows quite convincingly in his history that local political leadership was severely tampered with by the Oblates during the 1860s. And even today the chief reflects some of that influence in his elected status as the senior political leader.

The contemporary Indian Act does make provision for choosing chiefs and councillors according to the custom of the band, but the Okanagan have never attempted to revive that tradition. Following the text of the Indian Act of 1970 (as amended) the Okanagan now elect their chief by a majority of votes of the electors. All nominations must be moved and seconded by persons who are themselves eligible to be nominated. This means that any man or woman who is twenty-one years of age (eighteen from 1987), a member of the band, and ordinarily resident on the reserve is qualified to vote for the chief on election day.

Similar rules apply in the election of councillors, who are elected at the same time but voted for separately. In some Indian bands across Canada the chief is elected from among the elected councillors, a practice totally unacceptable to the Okanagan, who view their chiefs in a very different light to councillors. A few Canadian Indian bands retained the idea of hereditary chiefs, but I am unable to sense whether they see their chiefs as being 'more traditional' than other bands do. Okanagan chiefs are regarded nowadays by the voting community as the band's negotiators with the outside world, the outside world being defined as the Department of Indian Affairs, the federal government, the British Columbia government, the white man, and the Queen. It is true that this view of their chiefs is derived from past experience, but this past belongs to the last quarter of the nineteenth century when chiefs under the Indian Act did negotiate actively with the agents, inspectors, and other government officials who represented the crown.

Both chiefs and councillors hold office for two years only. Some are re-elected time after time, others get re-elected on an alternating basis, in for two years, out for two years, reflecting the whims of people not committed to the two major factions. Both chiefs and councillors can be deposed from office if they are convicted of indictable offences, if they do not attend three consecutive council meetings, or if they are found guilty of bribery, dishonesty, or malfeasance in connection with an election. These rules for deposing chiefs and councillors are of long standing and we have seen the extent to which they were used and abused by the agents and inspectors in the past. Nowadays it is the community itself, through council, that initiates the removal of leaders from office. Earlier I showed how Murray Alexis and several councillors were deposed in the 1970s, allegedly for not attending meetings, and how the affair was related to the tensions surrounding local government and administration. In this connection it is interesting to observe how the people themselves have begun to use the Indian Act to conduct their affairs now that the office of local government has shifted to the reserve. But this does not mean that they are any less controlled by the act than they were when they were under the tutelage of an agent.

The Okanagan band council is made up of the chief and nine councillors. The number of nominations for councillor before election day seems endless, but at polling time, with the secret ballot, only the serious nominees figure significantly in the results. Nomination time is more than a simple political occasion; many people are proposed out of a sense of obligation or simply 'because it is a nice thing to do,' illustrating the importance of kinship and friendship links in election results.

Nomination procedures for chief are more controlled, and in the absence of formal political parties there are informal campaigns involving kin and friendship networks. For example, the Alexis and Bonneau campaigns over the past fifteen years have a variety of personal strategies based on close-knit networks. Murray Alexis is an old hand at informal campaigning through his meticulous use of his kin ties (notably through affines) and his ability to mobilize appropriate networks – networks which enabled him to ride out the band manager storm in the 1970s. The Bonneaus, in contrast, might have been more successful in their grass-roots campaigns had they been able to overcome the rifts in their kinship and friendship networks. Three generations of Bonneaus have been chiefs during the past twenty-eight years, but they have never been able to build a broad enough base to cultivate and maintain their chiefship in the community generally.

Although the 1951 Indian Act did give more powers to the band council, the nature of these changes was essentially one of degree. Similarly, the Indian Act of 1970 as amended and administered in the 1980s was a modernized version of the earlier legislation. In addition to these 'powers,' council is now responsible for a good deal more, and with the assistance of the band manager and his staff they administer the Indian Act for the minister although this is not laid down clearly in the text of the act. Nevertheless, the powers given to council are in fact clearly designed to parallel the minister's. The clause 'The council of a band may make by-laws not inconsistent with this Act or any regulation made by the Governor in Council or the Minister' reinforces that idea. Even matters concerning wills, transmission of property, loans to band members, and the general control of revenue are handled by council.

The chief and councillors are neither civil servants nor federal government officials, but they owe their existence to the federal government by virtue of the act. They receive stipends from the administration grant paid to the band, and with the assistance of the band manager and his staff (also paid by that grant) the administration of the Indian Act is made possible. Nowadays chief and councillors receive $90 for every meeting they attend, and comfortable expense allowances when they have occasion to travel. Each member of council might receive up to $4000 per year for his or her services to the band. Band by-laws, however, have no effect outside the Okanagan reserve, nor do the rules, regulations, and other procedures created by the minister, since each

Canadian Indian reserve is considered a territorial and administrative unit. Chiefs do not appear to have received stipends in the nineteenth century, but they certainly had hand-outs and special concessions from agents in return for the assistance they gave in the administration of the act (Thomson 1985).

The formal structure of local government on the reserve today centres on the band manager, who has become the key bureaucrat in the community. He is appointed by council to work for them, and it is in that role that he represents the kernel of the administration. In many ways he is the official secretary to council, and this position places him in direct contact not only with the regional office and with Ottawa but, in the general position of special negotiator, with the outside world. He keeps the minutes of meetings, arranges meetings, ensures that council's decisions are carried out, and creates the order and the red tape without which council would be unable to operate. The band manager is assisted in his work by an office staff, some of whom are experts in their special fields (for instance, the social worker, the education co-ordinator, the recreation co-ordinator). As the duties, powers and obligations of council have increased over the years, so committees have been created to divide the work. But the band manager must always be close to the hub of each unit so created.

POLITICAL LEADERSHIP

Any discussion of the formal political arena of the chief, the councillors, and their band manager must also be concerned with what is sometimes called leadership (see also Carstens 1987). The term 'leadership' is both confusing and complex and has been used for many different situations as though it can be evenly applied. In studies of Canadian native peoples there is enormous confusion. Some writers (for example, Boldt 1980, 1981) use the term as though it can be applied to any native person in Canada who holds high office in some organization and expresses his or her views on general political issues. Lithman (1978) and Sieciechowicz (1985), however, focus on one band community and see leadership in terms of interest groups and factions. Like them, I am concerned here with some very general aspects of contemporary Okanagan chiefs, councillors, and band managers as leaders within the context of one local band and the social system in which they operate.

The Okanagan have very different perceptions and expectations of their chiefs vis-à-vis councillors. Chiefs are expected to express the wishes of all band members from the point of view of their traditional 'Indianness,' however that might be defined (cf Tanner 1983) – an expectation which could in fact never be realized. Councillors are viewed more as practical people who should get things done at the local level, a quality also expected of chiefs to some extent. Chiefs must have some charisma to be elected, but any chief who tries to be a bureaucrat is immediately accused of violating the people's wishes.

The dichotomy between chiefs and councillors is clearly exemplified in nomination patterns over the years. Candidates for chief tend to be pre-selected before nomination day. Councillors are elected in deceptively casual fashion and those who get re-elected time and time again remain almost without exception as councillor and are seldom nominated by their followers and supporters for the position of chief. In terms of electoral sentiments of the band, chiefs may be said to represent the collective unconsciousnesses of the members, the winner in any one election representing the largest faction or clusters of factions in the community as these are aligned at any one time.

It is difficult to arrive at a theoretical conclusion regarding the nature of Okanagan chiefs as leaders because these modern chiefs cannot be said to lead into action a stream of wills; rather, a stream of wills determines who the chief will be. In de Jouvenel's sense, a chief under the Indian Act is not a *rex*, not merely because he does not regularize and rule, but because he is always at the mercy of an electorate and has no control over the electorate in the absence of formal political parties. It is true that in the Weberian sense his authority is legitimated by a formal election, but he stands apart from the councillors, many of whom may not even regard him as their leader in committee. Under the Indian Act the chief is a person who represents public opinion at one period of time but can never *articulate* that opinion, since the act does not confer upon him any real executive or bureaucratic powers. Moreover, as a representative of public opinion, the modern Okanagan chief stands in structural opposition to the band manager, who is a paid bureaucrat (or responsible officer) of the band with an ambiguous and contradictory status because the band manager is appointed by the chief's council.

Throughout their more recent history Okanagan chiefs have occupied unenviable positions in their community. It might well be asked why anyone even bothers, or wants, to run for chief given his actual political impotence and the ambivalence with which he is regarded. The answer is complex, but there appear to be three crucial factors. First, candidates for the office of chief are pre-selected by the main interest groups and factions who support them. Second, there is an income involved and the office carries with it a stipend from the band based on the chief's attendance at numerous committee meetings. Third – and this is a crucial factor – chiefship enables an individual to increase his personal esteem in the community by forging informal (sometimes formal) ties with the wider society. Thus, it is often felt by band members that the social perquisites of office come to chiefs from outside the community. Candidates for chiefship may feel this too, but chiefs never get rich on the Okanagan reserve, as one or two have on neighbouring reserves. We might say, then, that Okanagan chiefs run for office largely because their supporters expect them to, and also for the personal esteem it brings them inside and outside the community. Over and above these factors, all five elected chiefs I have known have been interested in the two general and specific welfare of band members, and the two most recent chiefs have been particularly concerned with matters of economic and social reform.

Band managers may be no more than secretaries to chiefs-in-council, but in practice they occupy strategic positions from which they can manipulate the wishes and actions of the band council by compulsively following the letter of the law. A band manager does not have the power and authority of the former Indian agents, but he is better able to administer the Indian Act because of his dual ties to both Ottawa and the Okanagan Indian community. A band manager may incur the wrath of the band members by becoming the scapegoat for personal grievances directed against the federal government, but he is generally trusted because he is expected to know the rules of the Indian Act which have now been internalized as part of Okanagan tradition. Band managership, unlike chiefship, is a purely bureaucratic vocation, but it carries no security of tenure.

In theory, the chief stands at the apex of the band. But such a position is impossible to maintain, and he has to face constant criticism for his inevitable failure to create a little utopia in the white man's space. Band members, moreover, are constantly involved in a process of re-evaluating their positions within the context of their factions and family networks, and in coming to terms with their attitudes towards local government, pan-Indianism, the Department of Indian Affairs, land claims, the Canadian constitution, and other matters of current concern. Thus, if chiefs often fail to be re-elected, the answer lies not in personal inadequacies, but rather in the sociological and ideological positions they occupy in the community. The office of chief is predictably hazardous.

Contemporary political leaders, chiefs, and councillors, in spite of their very different roles, are all involved in a general game of strategy within the context of the Indian Act. Every successful and astute political leader, even if his or her period of office is short-lived, seems, once elected, to conduct affairs according to procedures which may be categorized by three principles:

1 Promote the Indian Act but do so in such a manner that your supporters and followers will gain the impression that you have no love for the white man.
2 Never rely on any group, faction, opinion, or persuasion in your communi-

ty for support, even if you think you know who your supporters are. This is the T.S. Eliot principle.[2]

3 Manipulate the local status hierarchy in the community for your own ends. This is the traditional Okanagan headman principle.

The reason so many aspirant and potential local leaders fail seems always to relate to at least one of these three principles. The councillor who condemns the Indian Act out of hand may be suspected of plotting to sell land to whites. The chief who sides openly with one faction is often accused of failing in his duty to promote band harmony and welfare. The councillor who does not know how to boost his social position by acquiring personal esteem and by outmanoeuvring his rivals renders himself impotent in the next round. Women were unsuccessful in their attempts to be elected to council for more than thirty years until one woman candidate learned the importance of principle 3, and was immediately elected to office. In the following election two women were elected. It is significant to record that all three women councillors have been outsiders – that is to say, they married into the band from other bands, providing a very good example of the Frankenberg principle (Frankenberg 1957; Carstens 1966: 227ff) which postulates that outsiders or aliens in certain communities often get elected or appointed to office. But the under-representation of women on council is not necessarily a reflection of their low status in the community. Some say, 'women lost their power [in the community] when they got the vote.' In other words, as long as wives and mothers control their husbands and sons in politics their interests will be adequately represented.

I have not attempted to develop a typology of Okanagan leadership in terms of the kinds of authority and influence held by people in positions of political superordination, but I have tried to place the offices of chief and councillor in both sociological and ideological contexts. We saw that these offices were not necessarily tied to stable groups with clearly defined memberships, giving the individual incumbents of these positions at least some leeway to negotiate with their followers and supporters. Thus a chief and his band members do not constitute a tidy social organizational scheme of leaders and followers with a static structure, and it is quite erroneous to assume that chiefs reflect the aspirations of every member of the community.

Local political leadership in the Okanagan at the present time articulates

2 In his *Notes towards a Definition of Culture*, T.S. Eliot wrote: 'an indefinite number of conflicts and jealousies ... would be profitable to society. Indeed the more the better: so that everyone should be an ally of everyone else in some respects, and an opponent in several others, and no one conflict, envy or fear will dominate' (1962: 59).

local attitudes and culture with the Indian Act, and with perceptions people have of their past and the wider society generally. There is, however, a strong suggestion that the idea of followship is disappearing and that leaders have to maintain their positions through supporters who share common values at a particular period of time. In the Okanagan reserve community there has long ceased to be a feeling of pure *gemeinschaft*. By the turn of the century *gesellschaft* had begun to dominate most social relations in the same sense that Tönnies (1955) saw this transformation of his society taking place. In the arena of government, it is probably more accurate to see the transformation as a change from status to contract (Maine 1861). Tönnies, it will be remembered, derived his basic societal dichotomy from Henry Maine's work, particularly *Village Communities in the East and West* (1871), and his distinction between *gemeinschaft* and *gesellschaft* was not absolute but allowed both forms to exist together.

The organization, intrigues, and games of local politics tend nowadays to be based in kin and friendship networks, as major associations on the reserve, such as the church, have ceased to influence political attitudes and behaviour. But there is one associational sphere which deserves some mention because it impinges in quite significant ways on politics and political behaviour. This is the loosely organized institution of sport, comprising such activities as baseball, rodeos, boxing, and hockey (see Appendix 6). Chiefs, councillors (even band managers), and special project officers have often had some affiliation with sporting ventures and sporting clubs. This does not mean that every chief and councillor has been a champion (although some have been), but rather that the sporting arena, as an area of interest, provides a platform where people can be seen in action. The significance of the sporting stage is that candidates for political and/or administrative office can be 'tested' for their general acumen in local politics and administration. This means, of course, that depending on one's performance one could be proved unsatisfactory for those positions – a sort of divination system through sport.

The process, I think, involves the analogy between the games and strategies that occur in sport and politics. Both enterprises involve parallel social personalities at the local level, and many of the conflicts and ambiguities that emerge in sport and leisure also come out in local politics. Similar observations could be made in most communities, but the argument here is that, because of their unusual social conditioning, the Okanagan tend to use similar idioms and metaphors in all aspects of their lives. In other words, formal government and politics, through the Indian Act, permeate all institutions, even sport which, at first glance, may appear to be quite remote from the Ottawa syndrome and its concomitants. The trend in sport over the years has tended also to rotate from time to time. A baseball craze would wane after a few seasons to give way to the appeal of the Head of the Lake rodeo. This might be followed by hockey mania before further obsession with baseball. At first glance these trends seemed to be no more than fluctuations in fashions (Kroeber 1919), but on careful examination they are much closer to Sorokin's forgotten work on fluctuations in forms of art, music, philosophy (Sorokin 1937–41). Here it is maintained that politics and sport display similar propensities for fluctuation which are not mere random changes in fashion, any more than fluctuations in voting patterns for chiefs and councillors reflect random meaningless attitudes of band members eighteen years of age and over.

Chapter Fourteen

Band Council Affairs

The powers and duties of council are defined by the Indian Act but the manner in which they are executed is not clearly fixed, and band members are able to negotiate with council over a variety of issues. Similarly, council members have a certain degree of choice in deciding how they will present themselves to the public, especially those who elected them to office. In order to bring the operation of band council to life, and to reflect on some of the changes that have occurred over the past twenty-five years, I will examine some of the trends in band meetings as reflected in the minutes kept since 1961, dividing the discussion into four periods (cf Inglis 1968).

From certain perspectives the matters that come before council are tediously uniform, but over time we can observe the increasing bureaucratization of local government and administration, and the change in the relations between councillors and band members. It is also interesting to reflect on changes in attitudes towards the outside world, particularly since greater involvement with 'the world' has not necessarily given rise to greater tolerance of external associations.

THE BAND COUNCIL, 1961

The early 1960s constitute an important period in the affairs of local government because they highlight council's concern with individuals, both on the reserve and in their dealing with the wider society. At this time council acted as a personal broker between parties in some matters, and as the authority which dealt with routine requests from individuals as they came in. The same issues still concern council today, but as the duties and functions of council have been elaborated, so the manner of administrating duties has changed.

In 1961 there were a number of requests by whites to graze cattle on the reserve. All these were granted ($2 per animal per month), as was a request to graze horses ($3 per month). But the application of a speculator from Kelowna to graze 320 sheep at the Head of the Lake was turned down.

Numerous band members requested personal loans for specific reasons – to build houses, make repairs to roofs, buy cattle, and so on. Some people simply asked for cash. Most requests, however, were for loans to build, repair, or improve houses and these were nearly all granted. Interest payment was generally expected, although two old people seemed to have been exempted provided they returned the money quickly. Written promissory notes were always required and these were signed by five councillors. Most of the money for this fund came from a large sale of timber on the reserve for about $7000 in the mid-1950s. The money was kept in a special account, and the fund was run entirely by the councillors without assistance from the local superintendent. When people did not pay their loans, council tended to table the matter out of embarrassment, hoping the debtor would pay up soon.

There were also several requests by individual band members to lease their land to outsiders, and one complaint from a white man that a band member had not kept his agreement regarding a lease. Council was not sympathetic to the complaint and the white man was ordered off the reserve.

Disputes related to property loomed large at this time and council devoted a lot of energy to sorting them out. Quarrels over property had been familiar enough to the Okanagan for years, but the 1960s marked the beginning of new kinds of tension as more and more people acquired surplus cash and with it the incentive to buy and sell property. I learned the severity of those tensions in 1963 on my second fieldwork excursion. I was visiting Okanagan friends for dinner on Easter Sunday and we had run out of beer, so I decided to drive into Vernon to ask an acquaintance to lend me a case since the beer store was closed. Two Okanagan friends accompanied me. Near the centre of the reserve we saw old so-and-so with a bloody nose and a swollen eye standing near two cars on the side of the road. Thinking there had been an accident I slowed down. My friends shouted at me to keep on going. But being a 'stupid samma' I pulled up quickly. The car had barely stopped when one of my friends jumped out and there was a fight, the details of which I will not go into. However, when the fracas was over and I had been miraculously spared a 'punch-up' myself for stopping the car, I learned that both my friends and the two people on the side of the road had been involved in buying and selling a piece of land which had changed hands three times in a few days. The anger and hostility I had witnessed was related to jealousy over the price of the land and who ended up owning it. Not more than twelve hours earlier I had been at midnight mass, which had been delayed for more than an hour waiting for old so-and-so to go to confession. In short, the property dispute had spilled over into the arena of reserve Catholicism and an earlier altercation presumably had to be expiated before the communal ritual could begin. At the core of everything was the fluctuating value of a piece of land that was being jealously sought after.

In 1961 some councillors were beginning to take a more serious interest in 'discrimination against Indians and Okanagan rights' on the reserve. Thus, J.M. made a motion of protest at one September meeting over the fact that Indians receive only half of the value of social assistance given to whites, declaring that because of the disparity all hunting and fishing rights would be closed to whites: 'This is definite.' In October there was more talk about hunting permits and it was decided to discuss the 'welfare rate' with the Indian Affairs Department.

Earlier in the year council had sent a letter to the minister of agriculture complaining about the new pound system in the Ewing Landing district, and a 'strong letter' to the postmaster general about the poor mail delivery on the reserve. At another meeting the chief and councillors decided to go and talk to Hoover and tell him that he should be employing more band members in his sawmill on the reserve: at least 50 per cent of the workers were supposed to be Okanagan according to a previous agreement.

In November the problem of increased unemployment in the winter months was discussed by two councillors who also felt that more doctors should be available to treat sick people. The chief said he was worried about the whole welfare system and placing children in foster homes outside the reserve. The improvement of reserve housing for individual families was also a major concern.

One councillor who was concerned with the question of job opportunities for band members suggested 'opening up of the [gold] mine on the East side of the Okanagan Lake [to] create Indian employment.' He also suggested a vegetable cannery for the reserve. Another councillor suggested a 'sawmill for employment and also to put more revenue into the band revenue account.' These suggestions are significant because they signal the encouragement of 'aid' from Indian Affairs to create jobs for the band, rather than a concern with the regional economy. Among other matters considered in 1961 was a request in September by a band member to become the press agent for the council, together with a request by the same person (representing a white firm) to cut sixty thousand Christmas trees. Both requests were granted. In November there was concern over adequate fencing at Whiteman's Creek and Siwash Creek, and the state of the water at Irish Creek. There was an invitation from the Rotary Club to the chief and council to have lunch on 29 November but council 'decided not to go.' Meanwhile, the chief, who had been very busy looking into the affairs of the band, asked for a 'salary' for travelling around and for the work done. Council agreed to pay him at least $100 per month. There was also an inquiry about irrigation water at Six Mile Creek. And wills and estates were major preoccupations.

THE BAND COUNCIL 1962–7

For the next six years the minutes continue to reflect concern for property and property-related matters – land, leasing, loans, houses, cattle, and boundaries – although during the winters council became preoccupied with the realities of unemployment and wage labour. The whites continued to be interested in grazing cattle on the reserve, and in cutting trees and logging. But there were some important changes. For example, personal disputes were not brought before council as they used to be. In the local economy there was more circulation of cash, goods and services, and labour, largely because there was more money on the reserve and more buying and selling, and much more leasing of band property. Moreover, fewer people were going to the United States to work for extra cash, as the community enjoyed some of the benefits of the booming regional economy. The band's budget more than doubled, increasing from $4840 in 1962 to $9720 in 1963, and remained at that level for some time.

Women's clubs flourished, notably homemakers' groups. Women showed more interest in band politics than hitherto. They also brought pressure on the local priest to insist that there be no drinking at parties held in the church hall at the Head of the Lake. Later the women asked for a policeman to be appointed to curb drinking on these occasions. Eventually council passed a resolution asking the RCMP to patrol the reserve.

Apart from the pressure from women, the 'get tough' campaign seems also to have been related to the election of a progressive conservative chief, an older man, well established, well off, and full of what some people called 'Irish Creek superiority (arrogance).' Thus, when the army asked council why it had raised its rental of reserve property for their training manoeuvres, the chief replied that it was originally leased as a rifle range 'and now you are using tanks.'

Many other events and trends occurred during this period both in and outside the community, all of which characterize the 'modernization' of the reserve and the growing preoccupation with the broader aspects of local issues. Three issues do, however, stand out from the others both in the way these affected the community as a whole, and how council had to deal with them. Westbank's secession, the closing down of both the schools on the reserve, and the management of revenue funds by council under section 68 of the Indian Act.

In January 1963 the Westbank community presented a petition containing thirty-one signatures to the chief and council indicating their wish to break away from the Okanagan reserve and become an independent band with a chief and two councillors. The many problems relating to land ownership were noted, and the petition was eventually sent to Ottawa. The Westbank issue had been in the air for some time and certain Westbankers, realizing the value of their land near Kelowna, were now impatient to gain their autonomy and reap the benefits alone. However, as they were part of the Okanagan band, the minister was reluctant to act until the wishes of the whole band had been carefully considered. The chief then selected a committee to look into the matter and eventually Westbank presented a new resolution requesting Indian Reserves No. 9 and No. 10 as their own, together with the major control over No. 8. They requested a per capita share of capital and Revenue Trust Accounts. Provision was also made for 'Okanagan Indian Band people now living on Indian Reserve[s] No.9 and No.10 [to be] eligible for membership in our new Band, and [for] all Indian people from our Reserves No. 9 and No. 10 now living away from our Reserves [to be] eligible for membership in our new Band.'

It took a long time to settle these issues fully, and some matters dragged on for more than twenty years. A separate reserve was created eventually on 18 October 1963 when a letter was received from the department stating that Reserves No. 9 and No. 10 at Westbank were allowed to break away. The contentious issues were the concerns over the division of lands and other assets between the members of the mother band and the Westbankers.

By 1962 most of the school-going children were being bussed to Vernon where they attended 'white' public and separate schools. A few younger children stayed on in the two primary schools at Irish Creek and Six Mile Creek, but on 24 January 1964 the chief Indian commissioner informed council that both schools were being closed for teaching and the buildings would now be available for the community's use, with three provisos: council must be responsible for light, heat, and water; it must keep the buildings in good repair; and should the Education Division ever require the use of the buildings again for further education, council must vacate them upon receiving reasonable notice.

It is clear that the closing down of Indian schools on the reserve and the transfer of all children to 'regular' schools in Vernon provided students with an important centrifugal social link. But it also coincided with the centripetality of the administration, the creation of 'Little Ottawa' on the reserve itself. The school at Irish Creek could now become the band office, the centre of local administration. The symbolism, as well as the reality, of this rearrangement was significant; it revitalized the status of council and gave it a new respectability, especially in the eyes of the growing middle-class movement in the community. Education and council became closely connected, particularly from the 1970s onwards with the establishment of the Okanagan Curriculum Programme, the appointment of a local education co-ordinator, the creation of a library, the building up of the photo-files (a sort of band family snap album), which were all located in the same building with the local administration.

Having its own building, in the physical sense, was crucial to the bureaucratization of council, especially as the school building had been entrusted to it by the regional director. But what added to this legitimation was the third important development on the reserve at this time, namely, council's handling of its own budget.

At the April 1963 meeting the white superintendent suggested that council consider handling its own budget under section 68 of the Indian Act. The suggestion was enthusiastically received and a resolution drawn up immediately requesting that 'the Management of our Revenue Funds be transferred to the Band.' There were to be five conditions: that funds be approved in a normal manner for specific purposes; that funds not be used for other purposes without the authority of the minister or his representative; that funds be transferred to a 'bank account either in whole or as required throughout the [fiscal] year'; that two band members be given authority to issue cheques; and that an auditor be hired and band members given access to the auditor's report.

It could be argued that the Okanagan Indian band had moved a little closer to achieving autonomy over their affairs now that council virtually controlled all revenue funds. But it could equally be argued that the community had in fact been further incorporated into Canada's federal bureaucracy. But during this period band members did become increasingly preoccupied with their own affairs. For example, in August 1964, B.C. Hydro was granted the authority to provide power to at least fifteen homes at no cost to the owners. There was talk of building a new church at Six Mile Creek. The councillors announced quite complacently that 'they would like to see films about Indians from other countries.' When the Mormon church asked permission to form a boy scout group, council replied that it had no objection to boy scouts but that it was not in favour of Mormons preaching their religion.

When the subject of the 'Okanagan Tribe as it was years ago' was raised in council, the chief was asked to find out who the chiefs on the other Okanagan reserves were, and to arrange a meeting to discuss what land the Okanagan tribe claimed 'before the reserves were set up by the Government of Canada.' At the time subjects such as these had little more than superficial interest to council, as was borne out by their attitude to national and provincial organizations of Indians. For example, when the North American Indian Brotherhood (NAIB) was discussed at a meeting, the chief and a member of council said they would go to the next meeting to be held in Lytton in December 1964, and to another meeting in April 1965. However, by the following April council refused to support the brotherhood's request for a dollar-a-head donation from the band because the organization could not show concrete grounds for wanting money. And by March 1967 council was so negatively disposed to the NAIB that it passed the following angry motion: 'That we the members of the Okanagan Reserve are not interested in the North American Indian Brotherhood from now on. If we have any business we will look after it ourselves.'

This illustration brings home the parochial sentiments of the community at that time. When the seeds of Red Power were supposed to have been germinating across the country, the Okanagan simply intensified their preoccupation with local affairs and local issues. The very idea of brotherhoods put most people off, as I had learned as early as 1963 after I had been guest speaker at the North American Indian Brotherhood Convention at Chilliwack. My Okanagan friends nearly disowned me at that time for 'messing about with all that Shuswap rubbish.'

Instead of involving themselves with external affairs, council members worked hard to keep the peace at home. They looked after the needs of their supporters with sufficient confidence to be able to vote themselves small honoraria from the funds which they now controlled. At the February meeting in 1963 it was agreed to pay the chief and all the councillors $125 each for work done during the past two years; the money came from the Band's Farmers' Assistance Account. The new budget for that year made provision for 'a salary' of $15 a month to be paid to the chief and his councillors.

It was during this period from 1962 to 1967 that chief and councillors became more legalistic in the sense that they started to take an interest in the letter of the law for its own sake rather than for its practical value. As council became more bureaucratic so the budget for the fiscal year 1967–8 allocated a third of its $10,790 revenue to general government ($1680 for the chief and his councillors and $1950 for band administration).

THE BAND COUNCIL, 1968–May 1978

Although council's actions are largely determined by the administrative system built around the Indian Act, local government on the reserve also reflects the changing issues that concern people generally. These concerns become the special issues which mark a particular period rather than mere isolated events.

The central preoccupation of council during the ten-year period from January 1968 to May 1978 was to iron out the conflicts that plagued the 'Little Ottawa' as it set about strengthening its position and improving its bureaucratic efficiency. It was a complex period for everyone, as people wrestled with the controversial ideas of hippies and Red Power, the transformation of the Indian agent to a band manager, and handling a band budget that suddenly seemed to make everything possible, from unlimited education to the employment of people with grand titles like Economic Development Officer.

When Murray Alexis defeated Ernest Brewer in the 1969 election on a split vote he thought he could transform local politics by making the administration more efficient overnight. He informed council that he would be introducing a committee system which would divide the task of administration among the councillors and staff. He promised to look after finances more effectively than had been done in the past. He invited the RCMP to discuss the possibility of once again having an Indian constable on the reserve. He proposed transforming the reserve into a municipality. He wanted to set the speed limit at 65 kilometres an hour on the reserve, and to rename all the creeks by their Indian names. And in these and many other proposals he even consulted the local Catholic priest for moral support and spiritual guidance.

Most of these proposals were acceptable to the majority of the band - in theory at least – and within two years the chief had established a power base on the reserve which he hoped would eventually be free of the growing bureaucracy of the Department of Indian Affairs.

In addition to the band manager there was an economic development officer, an education co-ordinator, a recreation officer, a land and estates officer, and a growing secretarial staff. Although there were job descriptions for each of these, everyone was inexperienced and there was no model on which the band office could base its operation. Hence council had its hands full adapting to a system it was in the process of creating, not to mention doing all the things people had been promised.

As the number of personnel in the band office increased so did the office work and projects for which the staff was to be responsible. Thus we find council concerning itself with adult education in addition to the many problems being experienced by the students who now attended schools in Vernon. There were also questions relating to improving the housing for band members, improving the water supply, negotiating leases, debating the possibility of taxation on the reserve, and trying to encourage people to have both their land and building lots surveyed.

In 1971 a letter was received from Ottawa asking council if it wanted to take a percentage from all leases made with whites. Council replied in the negative, stating quite specifically that 'It is the Okanagan Band's policy at this time that all lease revenues are to be paid to the landowner' (Minutes, 13 September 1971). The resolution is important because it reaffirms the autonomy of property owners and the Okanagan's ideology of individualism which they insist is quite unlike their neighbours to the north of them.

There was more money in the community at this time, partly because people were earning more but also because government grants were easier to get for band projects. The best example of the availability of funds for development was the establishment by council of the sawmill. At roughly the same time the band received a library grant of $2625 based on per capita reserve residents. With time the project was discontinued and many books found their way into private homes because there were no facilities to house them.

The budget for the 1977–8 fiscal year was $254,189 made up as follows:

Core funding	$ 25,000
Recreation	2,650
Library	435
Social assistance	108,000
Welfare aid	10,600
Care of adults	3,500
Other welfare	950
Community improvements	16,457
Education committees	1,405
Other education	77,115
Program administration	11,577

All projects ultimately fell under council's jurisdiction and there was simply neither the time nor the expertise to keep track of everything that was going on. Nevertheless, if certain projects did not turn out as planned, the members of the band were introduced to the idea of projects and the cultivation of local initiative. From this point of view, council played an important part in reinforcing the direction of the change taking place in the community generally. Council was particularly adept in involving band members in the new political trend. More general meetings of the band were held, and the details were dutifully recorded in the official minutes of council and circulated.

In February 1968 fifty band members met to discuss what items should go into the brief being prepared for Ottawa regarding the future of Indian reserves. Delegates were selected to represent the band at the North American Indian Brotherhood meetings in Chilliwack, and the possibility and difficulties of getting into the House of Commons were debated. In April another meeting was held to discuss aspects of the Indian Act, and most voted in favour of retaining the status quo on a number of issues, including support for the convention that the children of unmarried Indian mothers should continue to take their mother's status. In short, people reaffirmed their attitudes towards the department in much the same way as they had done in the past in spite of the fashionable dictate that 'Indian Affairs' was a dirty phrase. In November another band meeting addressed aspects of the Indian Act and once again the majority expressed the conservative point of view along with council. And a year later members of the band discussed the white paper policy: 'The Act should stay the same,' they said. 'We should not let the Province take over.' 'Stay with the old Act [and] challenge the Government [otherwise] the Provincial Government will do anything they want.' At this important meeting eight resolutions were accepted:

- The Okanagan No. 1 band rejects the white paper.
- The Indian reservations [sic] must remain Indian land indefinitely.
- Indian land must not be taxed by any government - federal – provincial, or otherwise.
- The surrender clause in leasing Indian land should be eliminated.
- Land purchased by a band should be taken into the said band's lands and be recognized as Indian reserves and be exempt from taxes.
- Education, health, and welfare benefits to Indian people should be spelled out in no uncertain terms.
- The fishing and hunting rights of all members of all bands of Indians should be held and retained.
- The band shall be in support of any further land claims in British Columbia.

I list these resolutions in full because they show the lines along which both council and members of the community were thinking at the time. If there were internal squabbles and conflicts, these were related to matters other than the paradoxical ideology which people shared, namely – a general confidence in the Indian Act and their unquestioning dependence on Ottawa as the source of material welfare.

Community concerns extended to elections and eligibility for voting, particularly the question of the legality of off-reserve residents taking part in elections. People were also concerned about the consumption of alcohol on the reserve in public places, such as the rodeo grounds and the recreation hall at the Head of the Lake. Consequently guidelines for beer gardens were drawn up by council and most people seem to have been satisfied with them. Other concerns and actions involved research into the two reserves that had been cut off by the royal commission in 1916. A good deal of the initiative came from people other than council members, and their actions must be seen as crucial in solving the cut-off issue in the future.

In February 1969 the Okanagan Telephone Company informed the band that it was prepared to install telephones on the reserve if the chief and council were willing to deposit $200 before the work began. The initiative for this arrangement originated from the council. Its realization changed the character of local communication and facilitated better interaction with the wider society. The telephone preceded *Senklip*, the local newsletter, which was started nearly six years later and distributed from the band office to disseminate information formally to members of the community.

The question of maintaining law and order with assistance from the RCMP was raised many times in the 1970s. Council was particularly concerned with the negative influence of political intruders and vandalism on the reserve on certain occasions. Thus they invited the RCMP to come and 'interrogate any and all suspicious or undesirable Non-Indian people on the Okanagan Indian Reserve' and arrest and remove them if necessary. The pressure to request this action came largely from the conservative factions, who saw the presence of political agitators, notably the American white activists, as a threat to the status quo. They also feared that these interlopers would acquire land. Vandalism does not seem to have been directly related to the interlopers, but problems had arisen on occasions such as Hallowe'en and in remote parts of the reserve where teenagers often got out of hand. We should, however, interpret council's interest in policing the reserve more in the light of a conservative trend rather than signalling the existence of serious social problems.

In spite of its preoccupation with internal matters and with maintaining the status quo, council started to become more tolerant of the influence of some alien institutions. For example, the Mormon church had been trying for years to get a foot in the door of reserve Christianity, only to be told: 'Keep out! We are Catholics.' It met with no objections in June 1975 when a request was made to hold meetings in the Head of the Lake hall; a decade later a member of the Mormons was elected to council. In 1976 the Okanagan Tribal Council held a meeting at The Head of the Lake and all band members were invited to attend to discuss the creation of a new federation of Okanagan bands sponsored by the Department of Indian Affairs. By 1978 council was sending band members on trips to Colville in the United States and to other British Columbia reserves to attend meetings with the NAIB and the Union of B.C. Indian Chiefs.

Council even celebrated good relations with a neighbouring Shuswap band with an engraving, subsequently mislaid, thus inscribed:

1877 1977
In Recognition of 100 years of peaceful co-existence
of the Spallumcheen and Inkamaplux (Head of Lake)

This new interest in actively establishing links with the outside world was short-lived and seems merely to have served the purpose of testing council's new confidence in itself and its ability to operate in wider contexts. No sooner had it proved its new skill at satisfactorily negotiating and managing external issues than it began to disengage itself from such action. This apparent about-face should not be surprising because reserves, as closed micro-political units, are by nature inner directed and parochial, and over time they have generated feelings of exclusiveness which discourages outside involvement, especially formal collaboration with other reserves. The idea of pan-Indianism is generally alien to the Okanagan although people will sometimes argue that 'We Indian people in Canada must unite against the white man if we are going to get anywhere.' In practice, though, band councils always tend to favour their independence, particularly when negotiation can be effective without having to share the rewards with others.

The decade from 1968 to 1978 was an important period of experimentation for council as the office of band manager was being accommodated to the local political arena. The proliferation of local projects was enormous: just looking after the complex sawmill was in itself a full-time job. But there were also constant requests from band members for new and better housing, the allocation of building sites, sorting out the rules and complexities of leasing cottages to whites, not to mention the routine tasks of general administration. Council started to handle the now vastly expanded workload that had previously been done by the Indian agent and his staff.

Council and staff resolved the problems of the decade without much guidance from the Department of Indian Affairs. However, in 1975 after the crisis arising from the deposition of one chief and the election of another, council hired a white accountant to sort things out. Performing the role of office manager, he helped put in order the budget, the bank accounts, and the general running of the office. Other white experts were also brought in from time to time, largely because they had expertise which no band member seemed to have at that time.

Just as the conflicts among the personnel constituting council and office staff seemed to have been ironed out and the system appeared to be running smoothly on the surface, a major upheaval flared up. On 7 March 1978 a special council meeting was called to meet with three bureaucrats from the regional office for an 'open question and discussion session' about local administration. Everyone was given a chance to express their opinions and many of the tensions between council and office staff were exposed. At the next meeting on 4 April two members of the staff, the recreation co-ordinator and the home and school co-ordinator, decided to prove to those present that they, at least, were efficient in their work. Their action was calculated to take the wind out of the sails of one councillor, who at the previous meeting had alleged that 'only 50% of what staff is doing is [ever] made known.' At this same meeting it was revealed that certain staff members had not received their 9.5 per cent cost-of-living increases, and there were rumblings about the disposition of the payroll sheet.

On 1 May the band manager phoned in to say that he was not feeling well and would not be attending the meeting. On 15 May council accepted his resignation, and one of his close kin, a councillor, also resigned his position. Both men were signing authorities for the band and a Band Council Recommendation (BCR) was prepared forthwith to revoke this authority. On 23 May the secretary-receptionist, who was also related to them, also resigned her position. The purpose of giving these details is not to allege corruption but to provide another example of the process whereby actors in the drama of band politics get shifted around to accommodate other changes in personnel. In this case the three resignations were closely connected with the chief at the time, who was then losing his support in the community. The complexities of the situation cannot be dealt with here, except to point out that the three resignations prepared the way in a roundabout manner for the election of the new chief in February the following year.

THE CONTEMPORARY PERIOD, JUNE 1978–85

What I have called the contemporary period began on 19 June 1978 with the appointment of a new band manager, which also quite fortuitously coincided with the month I returned to do fieldwork in the community after an absence of fifteen years. Lyle Brewer was very much in charge of the band office and continued to remain in charge, as the minutes so accurately reflect.

The new band manager matriculated in the Vernon school system. He had received some college education in Vancouver, was a keen and able sportsman, and he possessed not only the rudiments of office administration but also the ability and interest in perfecting them. He had a stolid personality, few close friends and no enemies. He had no apparent interest in politics, despite the fact that his father was a popular councillor and his late grandfather had once been chief. It was almost as if he was the man of everyone's choice, and he had the perfect disposition for a bureaucrat. On assuming office his first request was to become a 'Commissioner for taking Affidavits for the Okanagan Indian Band', which is the way the minutes phrased it. This request gave him immediate authority, but no power in that he became the arch 'civil servant' of the band on the band's terms. However, the authority of commissioner of oaths gave him an aura which many people liked – that of a little officer of the Queen for the benefit of the Okanagan band.

The office administration changed overnight. Everything seemed to have been reorganized without anyone noticing it. The minutes of meetings soon lost their personal flavour and, as someone remarked, 'The band office is now like a real office.' Everything started running according to the book, and even the debates in council operated according to 'the rules.' Things started to get accomplished at meetings despite numerous questions being asked about financing and financial matters, such as projects, housing, the purchase of estates. Office efficiency and committee rules now predominated over informal strategies and procedures.

It would be an error to attribute these changes entirely to the work of the new band manager. Rather we should see the new order as a 'development' over the years, and the new band manager as a product of that development, who now promoted the bureaucratization of council's work. An example of that process was the unprecedented formal request by a band member for a twenty-five year lease to operate his own recreational park on his own property. Such a request confirmed the acceptance of the old principle of the right to private property in land, but it did make a concession to government supervision, if not to government control. It demonstrated, moreover, the value of land, notably lake frontage, to individual owners for leasing, and even its potential real estate value.

No controversial decision involving any individual matter was now ever made without the formalities of a Band Council Recommendation. From the beginning of 1979, more and more items were being tabled by council, or merely recorded for information with the hope that the issue would not be raised again. In part, this apparent evasion of items for immediate discussion was a strategy for coping with the increased volume of business. But from another perspective, this type of action was now considered to be the appropriate way to conduct business.

Murray Alexis was re-elected chief in February 1979. At the second meeting of council after the election it was announced that the new chief would be representing the Okanagan Indian band in England for talks concerning the new Canadian constitution, and many people thought he was going to London to visit the Queen. As a liberal conservative he was the obvious choice for this role, and he accepted the honour as a chief recently re-elected by the people.

A major preoccupation of council and staff during the contemporary period has been solving the cut-off land issue (relating to Swan Lake and Long Lake reserves) and working out how the money would be used. After considerable discussion and after polling the members of the band, the $3,855,072 award (less legal fees and expenses) was divided on a per capita basis. Each band member received $4030, but minors (i.e. under nineteen) had their share held in trust until they came of age.

No sooner had this issue been resolved than the whole question of more comprehensive land claims and aboriginal rights loomed large. Council began to make plans to co-operate with other Okanagan bands through the Okanagan Tribal Council.

The most important structural change, reflecting also an ideological change, was the election of the first woman to council in 1983, and two in the 1985 elections; women had finally reached the inner sanctuary of band political affairs. Earlier I commented that these women were successful, in part at least, because they had learned basic strategies of winning support from the electorate. They are all outsiders who had married into the band, which suggests that the band elected women to office who were marginal to the community, thus placing them in a symbolic category that made them different from local Okanagan women. Another factor which accounted for their success were their affinal ties: they were all connected with good families through their husbands, although the latter as individuals were not of councillor calibre. It is interesting that the conservative trend in the 1987 election returned only one woman to office, and then only by the luck of the draw on a tied vote.

Council also took a firm stand at this time, as might be expected, on Indian rights and the patriation of the Canadian constitution. They voted a $100 per day honorarium for two representatives to join the Constitutional Express to Ottawa and later on to Europe. For the Okanagan band, the patriation of the constitution signalled the possible termination of the Indian Act and particularly the privileges it provides, notably free education, free medical and dental services, and tax immunity. It was for these reasons (which council specified) that they were so concerned about patriation. Another reason was that some older people still believed that the Indian Act, as part of the constitution, belonged in Buckingham Palace with the Queen. It is ironic that in November 1980, during the constitutional talks, council turned down a request from the Union of B.C. Indian Chiefs to add their band's name to a collective protest to be sent to Ottawa, on the grounds that they needed to find out first what the cost of such a protest might be 'to our band.' Once again there was very real and deep reluctance by council to dilute or weaken their autonomy by joining in this pan-Indian movement in Canada.

It is not surprising, therefore, to find council still paying great attention to individual concerns and projects in much the same way as it had done in the past. For example, enormous attention is given to rental housing, and there is a preoccupation with solving personal boundary and property disputes. Applications from individual band members for grants from such associations as the First Citizens' Fund and special ARDA grants to start new enterprises are enthusiastically supported by council. Council even spent time looking into a claim by the widow of a former chief asserting that the band office building and property still belonged to her because her late husband had never made it over to the band.

In 1986 council overspent its budget on the needs of individuals involved in getting higher education and had to make a special appeal for more funds so that the programs could be continued. There is extreme reluctance on the part of council, in spite of its heavy workload and bureaucratic involvement, to abandon its concern with the needs of individual band members living on the reserve. In a very special sense the idea of development is a central one to Okanagan reserve-dwellers, and council is very concerned with making improvements to reserve superstructure in a wide range of areas, including housing, water supply, hydro. In order to protect the system of individual entitlement to land, land transfers have recently been made both difficult and expensive. They now require either legal surveys or metes and bounds descriptions of property to be fully recognized. In addition to education, council pays special attention to the needs of youth by encouraging sport, recreation, and hobbies, and by obtaining special financing to make these possible.

Thus, in the contemporary period council has assumed the enormous responsibility of looking after the local interest of band members, while reinforcing at the same time a laissez-faire ideology. Paradoxically, the result is more red tape to maintain and protect individual interests. As a consequence, a more recent community response to council's actions has been to nominate a wide spectrum of candidates for positions on council every two years. In 1981, the same year that the Constitution Express went to London, there were six nominations for chief alone, illustrating the proliferation of interest groups (rather than factions), and the belief that the right chief would be able to represent one's case on council.

The recent move towards so-called self-government has imposed enormous strain on chiefs and councillors, economic and educational development officers, and band managers in reserves across Canada as demands on their time, energy, and talents have increased. Many whites may attribute the failure of Indians to construct instant utopias to lack of experience and expertise. But such explanations are totally unfounded; the answer lies almost entirely in the structural positions into which reserve communities have been cast over the years.

TOWARDS AN IMPERSONAL POLITICAL WORLD?

Over the years, the actions of council have become an extremely important index of the major conflicts and contradictions in the community. On the one hand, council is supposed to look after individual interests and tries to do so. On the other hand, it has grown into a highly formal and institutionalized body. Council, it might be argued, has two parts, a soft and a hard part. The soft part consists of the individuals that make up its ranks, the various persons elected by their supporters and patrons. The hard part is council as an institution, an ingredient of the Indian Act. Hardness is thus the bureaucratic element directed by the band manager who is employed to do that work, and whose persona is protected by his office. It is paradoxical, therefore, that all the complaints and criticisms of the system tend to be levelled at the soft part – the councillors and particularly the chief – rather than at the system itself. One of the many effects of the reserve system is to divert people's anger and resentment away from the real source of power in Ottawa, a process which perpetuates the reserve system through the culture which has grown up parallel to it, if not as a result of it.

Implicit in these reflections on the direction of council's actions since 1961 is the observation that increased bureaucratization has not destroyed council's obligation to pay attention to individual grievances, requests, and expectations. It is true that bureaucracy with its formal rules has increased over the years, but so also has the intensity of involvement with issues in the lives of individual band members. Even the appointment of two RCMP officers on the reserve should not be interpreted as a function of bureaucratic impersonality, as is borne out by the monthly police reports which do much more than present criminal statistics. Moreover, the recourse from time to time to legal opinion and action by band council in connection with such matters as land and conflicts with outsiders, and legal consultations by individual band members concerning local problems, does not necessarily imply that social relations are less personal than they used to be. In the first place, recourse to lawyers to solve institutional as well as interpersonal conflicts in terms of

Canadian law has been taking place for at least a hundred years. In the second place, the Okanagan have never regarded the law (that is, institutionalized legal sanctions) as an impersonal phenomenon, and even the process of coping with red tape is dealt with at a highly personal level.

To understand these attitudes it must be remembered that the Okanagan, as Indian-status persons living on reserves, were so defined by the Indian Act, a piece of impersonal formal legislation that people had no choice but to accept. Over the years, though, many Okanagan have inverted or reversed this impersonal labelling, thereby transforming their perception of themselves, and preventing devastating loss of personal identity.

At the risk of further psychologizing, I would suggest that many of the political conflicts in the community during the transition to a reserve-based local government in the late 1970s had roots in the differences in people's perceptions of and attitudes towards the Department of Indian Affairs. Some thought the growth of a 'Little Ottawa' on the reserve marked the coming of a new golden age, others detested it.

Chapter Fifteen

Why Education?

As in many other parts of the world, literacy and education in the western sense were introduced to the Okanagan by missionaries. Here I am concerned only with education in the schools on the reserve as these were established by the Department of Indian Affairs after the turn of the century, and with subsequent trends in local education, especially the personal advantages associated with school achievement.[1]

The first proper school was built in 1922–3 at Six Mile Creek. Students were admitted in February 1923, fourteen in all, coming mainly from two prominent Six Mile Creek families (Louis and Marchand). An additional school was built there in 1951, the same year that the Irish Creek school opened for the first time. The three schools admitted students from grades one to seven or eight, although not everyone remained for the full program. A few went beyond grade eight by boarding in private homes in Vernon so that they could attend the local high school. Otherwise they went to the Kamloops Residential School.

There were always difficulties in staffing these reserve schools and teachers (all non-Indian) did not stay for more than a year or two. A notable exception was Peggy Brewer (Greene), a qualified teacher from Prince Edward Island who taught for eight years, married into the band, and remained as one of the pillars of the community.

1 Since the publication of *The Indians of British Columbia* (Hawthorn et al. 1958) and *A Survey of the Contemporary Indians of Canada* (Hawthorn 1966, 1967), a body of literature on many aspects of Indian education has grown. See especially Barman, Hébert, and McCaskill (1986, 1987).

By 1962 all students, with the exception of kindergarten, were bussed to Vernon where they attended school with whites for the first time. The first matriculants, who were largely products of the Indian system, included Harry Harris (1915), Murray Alexis and Dorothy Bonneau (1952), Leonard Marchand (1954), Vera Marchand and Raymond Williams (1955), Bertha Williams (1956), Rita Louis, Margaret Marchand and Geoffrey Lawrence (1957), Rose Marie Louis, Walter Matthew Louis and Joan Marchand (1958), Victor Antoine, Marjorie Gregoire, Barbara Marchand, and Rhoda Louis (1963). These seventeen people constituted the vanguard of the movement towards higher education in the reserve community. All did extremely well in later life. Leonard Marchand stands out among them, having gone on to complete a bachelor of science degree at the University of British Columbia and a master's degree in forestry at the University of Idaho. In 1968 he became a Liberal member of Parliament and more recently a senator.

According to my estimates, nineteen band members were awarded university degrees between 1958 and 1986, seventeen of these after 1972. In addition there have been 98 awards of various university and college diplomas, and at least 148 band members have received grade twelve diplomas since 1952, the majority of these being awarded from 1966 onwards.

The extension of Canadian education to the Okanagan in 1962 increasingly involved both students and the whole community with white society and culture. Students from the reserve then went to the following schools in Vernon: Alexis Park Elementary, W.L. Seaton Senior Secondary, Vernon Senior Secondary, and St James Catholic School (up to grade seven). In recent years Vernon Christian and Valley Christian Academic Schools have opened their doors to Indians. At the post-secondary level, several students have gone on to the University of British Columbia and the University of Victoria for degrees and diplomas, but the majority attend Okanagan College and other British Columbia colleges, while a few go outside the province.

Almost all the extra cost (for example, travel and books) involved in attending Vernon schools is subsidized, and needs to be, by the Department of Indian Affairs, the local school board, the province, and the Okanagan band. Let me explain the Vernon school arrangement first. The transport to and from Vernon is paid for by the school board. The drivers come from the reserve. All students up to grade seven receive $20 a year for books, those in grades eight to twelve receive $25 a year and an additional $25 on request if they need it. Then there is an attendance allowance for students in the higher grades: for full attendance at school eight- to tenth-graders receive $10 per month while eleven to twelve graders receive $20 per month. Thus during the school year a student in grade eleven might receive $230 from the Department of Indian Affairs as a reward for attending school. In the majority of cases school attendance would be impossible without these subsidies.

Those students who wish to go on to a university or a college must first satisfy the entrance requirements before negotiating with the education co-ordinator in the band office for financial subsidization. In most of the cases known to me all fees, books, and living costs are paid for under the Master Tuition Agreement which is financed by the province. However, families do have to make enormous sacrifices to pay the additional costs. Without financial assistance higher education would be outside people's reach.

I have outlined what might be called the statistical achievements of the youth in formal education over the years, showing that within the last generation there have been enormous opportunities for good formal school education as well as encouragement to attend university or college for more education and professional training. Much of this achievement has been made possible by funding, although incentives, encouragement, and material sacrifices have come from kin and the community in general. Good education probably ranks at the top of most people's list of priorities, together with desire for good housing. What do housing and education have in common for the Okanagan? The answer, I think, is that both are seen as symbols of status in the community. A good job with a good salary is important but not in the same way as education and a good house, although proper housing is also sought after as a basic right and a primary need. Education is very special and sacred, a complex sentiment to which people do not necessarily admit but act out on certain occasions, particularly at the annual graduation dinners held on the reserve.

I have attended two of these graduation dinners at which the students were honoured by the community, one in 1982 and another in 1983. The ceremonies are held at the end of June each year at the hall at the Head of the Lake. The occasion is very formal. Women wear their best dresses and perfume and have their hair done for the event, men wear newly pressed white shirts. The tables are tastefully set out with little bowls of fresh flowers and programs at each place. Everyone is welcomed by the master of ceremonies, grace is said by an elder in the Okanagan language and most people cross themselves in good Catholic fashion. The menu is excellent – ham with pineapple, turkey with stuffing, mashed potatoes and gravy, green salads and jellied salads, devilled eggs, celery and cheese, carrot sticks, tomato and cucumber slices, home-baked buns and butter. For desert there is fruit salad, jello, apple pie, cherry pie, lemon pie, and huckleberry cake. There is also a graduation cake, fruit punch, tea and coffee, but no alcohol. The meal is prepared by the organizers, and the families of the graduates donate pies and cakes.

In 1982 the chief was the master of ceremonies. After dinner there were prepared speeches on behalf of the parents, the high school graduates, and the university and professional graduates. When these were over, several people each said a few words, while others were invited to speak. Some stood up and smiled, being too shy or emotionally too moved to say more than two words. The anthropologist was asked to speak one year, but people didn't want to hear such nonsense that in traditional times education was just as important as it is today, so he sat down politely when people started getting restless.

What people wanted to hear was something quite different. They wanted to hear about the sacrifices families had made for their children to enable them to go away to college and university. They loved the speech in 1983 by one of the parents who congratulated everyone: you have all done your bit, some more than others; the graduates will be important in the years to come because they will direct the band and lead it to higher things in the future. He spoke at length of how hard they had worked, how many sacrifices their families had made for them, how many sacrifices some of the older graduates had made themselves (referring to the fact that many had children and husbands). He then said he wished he had gone further in school, and that he had done more for his children. The emphasis was, of course, on the overwhelming importance of education. All members should and must strive for more and more of it. After the speeches, each graduate was presented with a scroll plus a cheque for $50 from the band council and each had his/her photograph taken. One year the Arrow Lake Drummers drummed and sang the honour song.

Who attends the graduation dinners? Apart from the graduates, there are the organizers and other 'officials' of the band, and the guests who are mainly family and close friends of the graduates. There were a few grandparents, but this was not an occasion for the elders; rather it was for the parents' generation and those younger. Women outnumbered men by about three to one, and the largest category present were mothers. Most of the speeches were given by men, but the occasion was dominated by women who prepared the food, printed the programs, and organized the ceremonial, all with a sense of great fervour and duty.

These occasions are both sacred and solemn affairs. There is absolutely no unseemly behaviour, no rowdiness, no horseplay, no joking, no teasing, no swearing. But if they typify what is sacred in the community in some respects, we must also see these occasions in the context of the contradictions they present. Each graduation dinner I attended was an overwhelming success and a great community occasion, but graduation dinners do not necessarily reflect the community, and should be interpreted to some extent as part of the main movement towards 'middle classness,' which I have dealt with elsewhere. There were absolutely no symbols relating to farming, agriculture, or ranching (with the possible exception of the chief's new cowboy hat), and no protests or outcries against the iniquities of the past or the present.

Higher education creates in some people extraordinary confusion about the future because of the duality it represents. The possibility of a job is always considered and obviously everyone wants a good job, but very few can ever be certain of getting the job they want, where they want, and when they want it. My argument is that the glamour of education as a means to upward social mobility and to Canadian middle classness tends paradoxically to cloud temporarily, at least, the difficulty of getting a job and the emotional problems it creates.

This is not to suggest that the young are lazy or unwilling to work, or even unmotivated to work, but rather that it is immensely difficult for a person conditioned by the reserve system to take on a new kind of occupation, and nobody wants to leave the reserve community now that housing has improved. To give two examples: the graduate in business administration does not want to take a job in Winnipeg, and the photographer does not want to work in the forensic department of the Halifax police force. The fact that the reserve is a social refuge area for everyone is not erased by higher education, and people understandably like to stay close to home.

An important aspiration is to move up in the world, and the cluster of people who promote this philosophy is highly visible in the community. They were all educated at a time when schooling was difficult to obtain, and the majority of them have experienced upward mobility themselves. Some came from quite lowly stock and know what education can achieve, and they work very hard to make the young like them, sharing their values and ambitions.

The old reserve schools that were phased out in the late 1950s and early 1960s, and even the residential schools, were also prized and admired because they taught basic skills and some general knowledge. But people saw this type of education as teaching their children to become better *Indians* in the context of their culture, the reserve system. Never for one minute did the old system make people feel that they were becoming better-educated *Canadians*. The modern system is not only different, it has reinforced the new middle class ideology in those still living more or less permanently on the reserve. It has also created new conflicts.

In the nineteenth century and on into the early part of the present century, schooling was closely associated with the work of the Catholic church. At the higher levels the residential schools provided a somewhat gloomy reminder of continued Indian segregation in secondary schools, and the part that the church played in that process. Modern education is very different; it enables people to participate equally with other Canadians for the first time in a major institution. Secular education is, therefore, valued for the prestige and esteem it generates locally and for the potential it offers for admission to the wider society. The demand for better education does, moreover, correlate with the decline in the authority of the Catholic church on the reserve and people's lack of commitment to it.

Chapter Sixteen

Reserve Catholicism

I provided a very brief account of the work of early Jesuit and Oblate missionaries in chapter 2. Here I want to touch equally briefly on the structural nature of the Catholic church itself at the present time. There are two churches on the reserve, St Benedict's at the Head of the Lake and St Theresa's at Six Mile Creek. There is no resident priest and no local formal organization which can be identified with the churches. Church attendance has declined so dramatically over the past twenty-five years that one is scarcely aware that every Sunday at noon (and occasionally at other times) a priest is saying mass to a handful of faithful Okanagan and to a larger number of whites who live on the reserve. These observations are very different from my South African research experience on reserves where mission stations were always at the core of social and economic life, and where I was conditioned to believe that a similar situation would exist in every Canadian reserve.

In 1962–3 people still went to church in the sense that the churches were always packed at Easter and Christmas. In 1963, for example, Easter midnight mass at St Benedict's was a lively occasion and one got the impression that everyone on the reserve had shown up, because among other things the priest was still hearing confessions long after the mass was supposed to have begun. In the 1940s and 1950s large Corpus Christi feasts and processions were still being held. Okanagan from other bands as far away as Penticton used to come up to the Head of the Lake to St Benedict's. Things are very different today; many have abandoned the church altogether, and some have joined other denominations. But the majority are still nominal Catholics in the sense that they are listed as such on the band list. Actually everyone is still listed as 'RC' except one rebellious family which for years has insisted it was 'UC'. In a sense, being listed as RC on the Okanagan reserve nowadays is a little like many English in England claiming to be Church of England when they have never entered a church except perhaps when they were baptized or married.

There are a variety of factors involved in the loss of interest in the Catholic church on the reserve, a trend probably no different from the pattern observed among Canadians in general. Okanagan scepticism is, however, quite specific and is directed at the rules of the church, the authority of the priest, and the question of sin. Many people, including several old conservatives, take the view that the priests deliberately deceived people in their teaching, forcing them in their ignorance to accept 'a lot of lies about God and the world.' The whole question of sin and the obligation to go to confession is viewed as professional humbug. One of my informants put it this way: 'Well you see, Pete, them old priests deceived the people ... "If you don't confess you go to hell", they said, "or have bad luck." Later we see that is all crazy.' What was especially revealing in my discussions with people about the questions of priests, power, sin, and confession was the rather obvious discovery that sin was said to be common knowledge in the community. 'Sin is what everyone 'round here knows [about everyone] already.' In other words, everyone in the moral community, as Durkheim would have argued, has access to the information about people's sins and transgressions. It is rather like saying that sin is communal property. Thus, the objection by members of the community to priests hearing confession is based on a principle of secrecy (Simmel 1950). 'Them priests did not know what was going on 'round here. So the way they found this out was through confession.' Confession, therefore, was seen as a mechanism whereby the priest, through his religious power, was able to find things out: steal the secrets of the community using a technique of spiritual divination, and sometimes pass the information on to the agents. Over the years the Okanagan have gradually eased the priest out of their lives as part of the process of becoming more isolated and encapsulated in the reserve system. The blame for these doctrinal matters is always placed on individual priests and never on the institution of the church.

If the Okanagan have rationalized their scepticism of Catholicism from their vantage point on the reserve, over the years the priests have justified their withholding of certain sacraments from the people, a move which simply reinforces people's opposition to, and withdrawal from, the church. It is now almost impossible to get a child baptized unless the parents make the effort to go to mass. Attending three masses seems to guarantee a baptism, but most parents are not prepared to subject themselves to these requirements, which would also normally include at least one confession. In a few cases the parents themselves, if young, have never been baptized.

What is so striking about the attitude of modern priests (some more than others) is their stricter enforcement of church rules for Indians than for whites. It is almost as though there has been a return to the old missionary position of the 1860s when admission to full membership in the church was extremely difficult, demanding exemplary behaviour, frequent confessions, and regular church attendance. That early missionary period was very different from the period beginning in the 1880s and lasting for about ninety years when characteristic Catholic leniency and tolerance seems to have prevailed. Today most people enjoy the final ritual, a Catholic burial, but as one cynic remarked; 'that's only because most people die in hospital anyway, and that's where they get you back into this confession business!' Okanagan funerals are always well attended, the number of people present being determined by the status of the deceased and the size of his or her kin and friendship networks. Wakes are so important that they qualify for both material and moral support from band council.

Marriages used always to be blessed by the Catholic church, in theory at least. But now, more and more people are avoiding their old church by getting married in the magistrate's office, in non-Catholic churches, having 'traditional' marriages, or simply enjoying the freedom of a common-law arrangement.

Over the years people have joined, or become associated with, other denominations, including the Mormons, the Vernon Alliance Church, the United Church, and other more fundamentalist groups. The Baha'i faith has been around the reserve for over a generation, and the Christian Indian Fellowship is now active in some parts of the reserve.

Unlike reserve dwellers in southern Africa, active church membership does not seem to add to status or prestige among the Okanagan (cf. Marais 1939; Carstens 1966; Wilson 1966; Pearson 1986). It is true that certain women are looked up to because 'they know how to pray' for the sick and the souls of the dead. Although he was a pagan, Chief Louis Jim built St Theresa's church on his property at Six Mile Creek, presumably because he saw that another church would have some moral value for the community south of the Head of the Lake and for himself. But these idiosyncracies fall outside the domain of the Catholic church.

It would be difficult to defend the view that the Catholic church on the reserve in recent years has created an atmosphere whereby individuals or groups could achieve upward mobility through their involvement with the church or priest or through participation in mass. Thomson (1985) implies that during the nineteenth century certain members of the Okanagan community often achieved high office because they worked with the priests, but there is no real evidence that Christians were ever considered superior to pagans, or that today church affiliation is correlated with political position. The Catholic church, however, did play a part indirectly in reinforcing the division between the Head of the Lake and Six Mile Creek, but this could hardly be said to have been consciously created by church policy. At best it can be shown that St Benedict's and St Theresa's, notably the latter, came to be regarded as monuments to each division or faction, and to a large extent they remain so today.

The church among the Okanagan – reserve Catholicism as I have call it – has always occupied an anomalous position throughout its history. It did have the effect of integrating the members of the community up to the modern period, but only because the priests as missionaries worked closely with government officials by recognizing the legitimacy of reserves as places where Indians lived, farmed, acquired some rudimentary schooling, became Christians, and so on. But the church never became a fully integrated part of the community, in part because the priests did not live on the reserve for more than a few weeks at a time each year. For many years now priests have only occasionally stayed overnight on the reserve, although one priest used to have his summer cottage at Newport Beach for his own recreational purposes. The Okanagan for their part have tended to keep the Catholic church at bay because of its involvement in moulding reserve economy society and culture, not only in the colonial period, but also later when priests and agents played complementary roles. This surely explains the fear expressed by my informant of letting priests find out too much through the sacrament of confession.

There is one other perspective. I asked a woman and her husband, both pillars of the church who attend mass regularly every Sunday, why they thought membership in the church had declined. Both volunteered that the personalities of the priests they had in recent years, together with their unnecessary enforcing of church rules, were the main factors responsible for the near demise of the church. But while we were discussing this rather unsatisfactory 'explanation' the husband started talking about his cousins and the people he knew who had joined other churches because they were allowed much greater freedom to do things on their own. 'You can even stand up [in those other churches] at any time and say a few words of your own, even talk about your work and how you are getting on with that.'

It is not my intention to test or dwell on the 'Protestant ethic hypothesis' here, but when I probed the religious affiliations of the most successful entrepreneurs and others in the community I was very struck by the significant numbers who had left the Catholic church to involve themselves in free-thinking religious movements while adopting the same kind of values that

Max Weber and others identified with entrepreneurial success. Of course, Catholicism itself has not inhibited free enterprise or hard work, but the attraction of alternative systems of belief and practice seems to have provided some people with an ideology that is consistent with building up treasures for themselves on the reserve. One highly successful entrepreneur, a very religious non-Catholic man albeit in a somewhat unorthodox way, told me just that, adding that he prayed every night for guidance and strength to be even more successful. I also observed that a change in religious affiliation towards free-thinking denominations was related to upward mobility. A marriage, for example, held off the reserve in a Protestant church with a good Hammond organ, no altar, and plenty of room for a large entourage, followed by a reception in a community hall in a neighbouring town, lends itself to the cultivation of bourgeois ideas and symbols. And while such occasions would not necessarily ease movement into middle-class Canadian society, they do certainly help to free people from the limitations of old reserve ideologies and add to the growth of middle classness in very general terms.

PART THREE

The Wider Framework

11/ Ernest Brewer, chief 1963–9

12/ Wilfred Bonneau, chief 1977–9. Photo by R. Bonneau.

13/ Chief and councillors, 1987. *Standing*: Murray Alexis (Chief), Grayden Alexis, Herby Simpson, Tim Alexis. *Sitting*: Matthew Bonneau, Cecil Louis, Albert Saddleman. *Absent*: Molly Bonneau, Raymond Gregoire

14/ Reynolds Bonneau, chief 1981–3

15/ Murray Alexis, chief 1961–3, 1969–77, 1978–81, 1983–91

16/ Office staff, 1987. *Standing*: Molly Penning, Richard Payne, Beatrice Bonneau, Patricia Wilson, Thelma Marchand, Judy Marchand, Mary Gregoire. *Sitting*: Lyle Brewer (band manager), Ken Hewitt, Walter Louis.

17/ Josephine Saddleman, receptionist-secretary for many years in the band office

18/ Senator Len Marchand, addressing the Okanagan 'nation' at the pow-wow in August 1987 after the signing of the Declaration

19/ Tommy Gregoire, political historian at the Head of the Lake

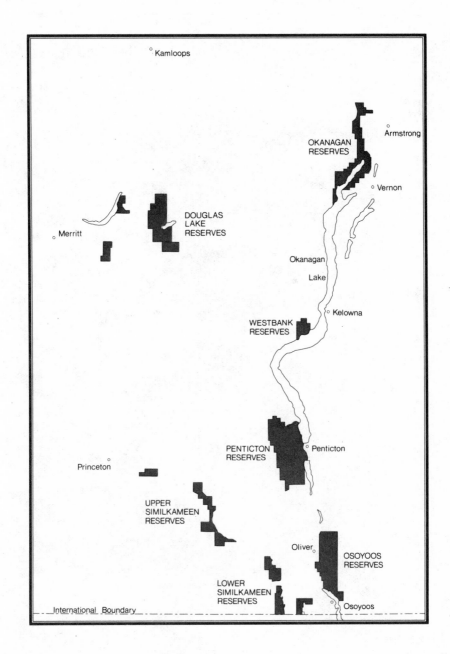

Okanagan reserves today (1990)

The Queen's People:
An Anthropologist's View

When the fur trade got under way early in the nineteenth century the Okanagan were well established in what is now the interior of British Columbia. While the 'partners in furs' scenario has romantic appeal for liberal academics, the Okanagan could hardly be said to have benefited in the long run from their association with fur trade companies. Most people were seriously inconvenienced by the Hudson's Bay Company presence although a few political leaders made a good personal investment and obtained considerable material rewards by ingratiating themselves with company officials and representatives of the British crown. For example, Nkwala became a sort of 'double' broker chief, and in his later years straddled two establishments and two cultures. The advent of missionaries and gold miners entrenched the colonial presence further and they, in concert with the fur traders, placed the Okanagan people under the hegemony of Canadian institutions. This marked the beginning of the loss of the Okanagan control of their own identity and destiny.

Traditional Okanagan society was neither static nor inflexible and slow-changing, but as interaction with white culture agents intensified, the unrealistic demands and stresses placed on the institution of chiefship and the political system in general had unfortunate results. Traditional chiefship was inherently weak, and its disintegration during the colonial period made the Okanagan vulnerable to settler intrusion in the 1860s and 1870s, a process that was accelerated by a smallpox epidemic in 1862–3.

The colonial period (1858–71) marked the creation of the first reserves to protect Indians yet satisfy settler demands for large parcels of land. Native land and political policies were, therefore, part of a process of 'clearing the land' for immigrants and settlers, policies that were part of Canadian and British Columbian collective action towards their native peoples.

By 1875, as they became involved in ranching and agriculture like the settlers, the Okanagan seriously considered taking back their land by force. The plan never got off the ground, largely because of their weakened political organization, concomitant factionalism, and the support for the whites and Queen Victoria by an Okanagan chief aided by a priest's secular intervention.

The Okanagan, therefore, lost their traditional territory through two processes: by having to 'agree' to have their *own* land 'set apart' (reserved) for them, and by uncontrolled settler encroachment. The latter involved legal pre-emption of land under colonial law, military land grants to ex–British officers, purchase of crown land, and theft. From an early date, then, the Okanagan were discriminated against, especially since under colonial law they were prevented from pre-empting land themselves because they were Indians.

Thus, before the Indian Act of 1876 was enforced, the Okanagan were already disadvantaged by physical, cultural, and economic encapsulation. The Indian Act transformed Okanagan status to one of complete political dependence, rendering them powerless in the modern world. The process whereby they had been pacified was gradual and subtle, beginning with mild hegemonic influence and ending with complete institutionalized legal control. The role of missionaries in this process of accommodation was probably more significant than the data suggest.

The Indian Act created a new class of white officials, and over the years a complex system of relationships developed between the Okanagan and their new administrators. It provided, among other things, the primary set of institutionalized principles and rules by which the destiny of the Okanagan and other status Indians in Canada was to be determined. It defined the limits of social expression on reserves and fashioned many facets of reserve culture. In short, the lives of the Okanagan were to be administratively determined and their social personalities correspondingly influenced.

As the Okanagan were contained in reserves so they also became involved in economic relations with the wider society. An increasing number aspired to become successful ranchers and/or agriculturalists, while others entered wage labour. By the end of the nineteenth century an almost complete transformation of Okanagan mode of subsistence had taken place. But reserve status did not facilitate Okanagan integration into mainstream Canadian society, and as the local population grew, the ability to make a viable living from the land became increasingly difficult.

By the dawn of the twentieth century the Okanagan were involved more and more in wage labour and less in farming, while hunting and gathering, in so far as they still took place, were no more than 'after hours' activities. Dependence on the dominant economy and society continued to increase for many Okanagan, while their new peasant status began to resemble that of a rural proletariat as the process of economic incorporation extended to political, religious, medical, and educational institutions. There was an intensification of conflict which resulted in extreme factionalism, quarrelsomeness, and excessive consumption of alcohol in the first two decades of the twentieth century.

The study of the role of Okanagan chiefs throws considerable light on the nature of change in Okanagan society from early pre-contact days to the present. Chiefship has taken many forms over the past seven or eight generations, and we examined the institution in traditional times, during the fur trade, during the first fifty-five years after the promulgation of the Indian Act when chiefs fought losing battles with the Indian agents and Ottawa's bureaucracy, during the period of bureaucratic domination, when chiefs submitted to the system, and finally, during the contemporary period of negotiation with the bloated bureaucracy. Although there have been enormous changes in the Indian Act since 1876, this legislation continues to dominate people's lives; the community is overwhelmed by federal involvement, and dependent on the Canadian polity and its economic resources. For well over a hundred years individual chiefs have been in the unenviable position of playing the roles of mediator and go-between, but for the majority of those years they have found themselves in a subordinate position vis-à-vis administrators and legislators.

When we turned to analyse the socio-cultural processes in the contemporary Okanagan reserve community we found them inextricably interlinked with the similar processes in the wider society: household economy, patronage, entrepreneurial ventures, local government, political leadership, factionalism, status, class relations, education, religion, leisure, are all as interrelated with the wider system as they are with the past. Of particular concern in my analysis were the variations in individual and collective behaviour, despite the parameters of socio-economic and cultural life on the reserve defined externally by the Indian Act. It is thus erroneous to assume that increasing complexity of social relations, bureaucratization, and loss of control of the means of production always involve loss of *gemeinschaft* in the face of mounting *gesellschaft*. *Gemeinschaft* and *gesellschaft* are not mutually exclusive conditions in changing human conditions, as Tönnies himself pointed out; the Okanagan are no exception in spite of tremendous constraints inhibiting social expression.

Although my concern in this study is never with the psychology of individuals, implicit in this book is a very conscious awareness of the effect reserve life has had on the individuals (and groups) who have been confined for nearly five generations in an artificially created physical and cultural environment. Okanagan (and other reserve-dwellers) have reacted not only to conquest, but also to their social and cultural isolation. Thus, if the contemporary Okanagan do reflect different behaviour patterns, values, and ideologies from those of other British Columbians in their daily lives, many of these seem to be unrelated to their 'Indianness' per se – a view that may not be acceptable to everyone. This conclusion does not seem too different from that held by Kathleen Mooney (1979), although she may not want to accept the idea that 'Indian ethics' in the household ideologies of the Indians of British Columbia are in fact reserve ethics.

RESERVE-DWELLERS AS PEASANTS

It has been important for social anthropologists to formulate an appropriate paradigm in their researches among peasants for a number of reasons. In the first place it encouraged and taught social anthropologists to have a better sense of history. It also forced them to think seriously about the implications of such issues as class, status, power, and inequality in a way they had not done before. It made them consider the socio-economic and cultural relations rural communities of all kinds have with the modern world in a different context from that of culture contact. It also prepared anthropologists to comprehend the problems of the third world in a manner they had never done before, and it forced them to modify some of their romantic middle-class notions about the noble savage. As a result the peasant model enabled social anthropologists to continue to use the idea of a community while broadening the context in both space and time.

The peasant model came into social anthropology largely from American scholars who had worked in Latin America (for example, Redfield 1934, 1941, 1956; Foster 1953; Wolf 1955). But there were other pioneering writers whose work influenced the direction of social anthropology. Perhaps the more important of these were John Embree (1939), Horace Miner (1939), and Raymond Firth (1946). However, it was Robert Redfield's characterization of peasant groups as part-societies and part-cultures (following Kroeber 1948), together with the idea of 'intermediate societies' (see Casagrande 1959), which stimulated many social anthropologists to understand the dynamics of small communities in relation to wider socio-ecomonic systems, and also to introduce ideas of stratification and class in their work.

Why does the peasant model lend itself to the analysis of reserves? It is because of the nature of their socio-economic and cultural dependence on the wider society. Reserve-dwellers and peasants are dependent on the wealthier and more powerful dimensions of their world networks to survive and to maintain and reproduce the various requirements dictated by that dominant external system. Similarly, both peasant and reserve culture require continual communication of ideas originating outside their arenas to maintain themselves (see Redfield 1956: 40–1). In my analysis of the Okanagan I have shown how they became not only politically and economically involved with and dependent upon dominant Canadian institutions, but also how their education, their religion, even their leisure, have become part of, and dependent upon, those institutions. Some would argue that so broad a definition of peasantry is useless, because it places nearly everyone in the category of peasant, rural and urban dwellers alike (for example, Vidich and Bensman 1960; Gans 1962).

Another objection to extending the peasant morphology to reserve-dwellers is that the necessity of producing surpluses simply does not apply to the latter. Peasants must produce two kinds of surpluses: a surplus to maintain and reproduce their own households,[1] and a surplus to pay rent to their landlords or the ruling class which controls their land.

When we examine the history of the Okanagan reserve community we see that its members, too, have been placed in a structural position which obliges them to produce a surplus, not only to maintain their households and keep kinship and friendship networks active, but also to pay a hidden rent to the larger society on which they depend. This 'rent' is paid in a variety of ways. First, the salaries of councillors, band managers, education officers, secretaries, stenographers, and others who administer the community for the Department of Indian Affairs are considerably lower than those paid for equivalent work in the wider society. Second, band members who lease agricultural and residential property to outsiders do so below the value on the open market. And, most important of all, the Okanagan are able to reinvest little, if anything, in their own community, while the existence of the reserve is of enormous value to the merchants, physicians, and dentists in the neighbouring communities, notably the city of Vernon. The structural relations of dependence between reserve-dwellers and the outside world are, therefore,

---

1 Households must produce a surplus for: *subsistence*, providing enough food for household members; *replacement* of their minimum equipment for both production and consumption; and their *ceremonial fund*, to maintain social relationships in terms of local custom, such as marriages, wakes, religious rituals, and parties to keep kinship and friendship networks active (see Wolf 1966).

extremely complex and, although asymmetrical, never operate only one way. Thus from some points of view it would be extremely difficult to decide which group was more dependent on the other to reproduce the existing order.

The Okanagan reserve is, therefore, very like peasant communities in many parts of the world in terms of the *structure* of its economic relations with the wider society. And, like peasants, the majority of householders sail very close to the wind economically. This is especially true at the present time when the increase of 'middle-class' status and values makes people more susceptible to the pressure of consumerism. Wage labour, especially migrant wage labour, is on the increase and it is only by this means that the reserve community can sustain itself even at the peasant level.

The Okanagan, also like peasants, can make few choices in their daily rounds as to how they should run their lives. The choices that are made, notably among poorer people, tend to be Hobson's choices (cf Carstens 1969; Gonzalez 1987). Moreover, while all members theoretically have access to the means of production (land), they do not control it. While the few 'successful' affluent reserve-dwellers might reinvest in their local enterprises, they do so for very little profit by comparison with the open market outside the reserve.

Thus rather than reject the general applicability of the peasant concept in social anthropology, we should be embracing it for its value in analysing and understanding such social formations as Indian reserves. In a very real sense, reserve communities can be characterized as peasants *par excellence* because they fit the model even better than the communities on which Redfield, Foster, Wolf, and others based their pioneering work (Carstens 1961, 1966, 1970, 1971a, 1971b). Another difficulty some people have with extending the peasant model to other social formations is their primary commitment to a mode of subsistence/mode of production definition, rather than relations of production definition of peasantry. Even Eric Wolf (1955) helped sow the seeds of that misconception in his paper on types of Latin American peasantry by assuming that all peasants ought to be agriculturalists. This misses the crucial point because the peasant model's usefulness results from its emphasis on the structural relations among peasants, between peasants and landlords, and between the community (however defined) and the outside world, rather than the narrow focus on mode of subsistence.

RESERVES AS SOCIAL CLASS

If peasant communities and reserves are both dependent on the wealthier and more powerful dimensions of their world networks for the survival and the reproduction of their socio-cultural positions, might they not also constitute social classes, since these relations of dependence are also imbued with a strong element of conflict? Both Marx's and especially Max Weber's view of social classes permit the inclusion of reserves and peasantry as they have been defined here. Marx was quite specific about the conflict inherent in class systems between the dominating and the dominated, the entrepreneur and the worker, the rulers and the ruled. More recent writers on class relations, such as Ossowski (1956, 1963), provide more sophisticated paradigms on class and stratification, which can accommodate reserve systems in their schemes. Shanin's 1971 essay on peasantry as a political factor is particularly valuable for extending the class definition to peasantry in the very general sense. Elsewhere I have discussed the question of reserves, peasantry, and class in more detail with regard to Canada using in addition to my own work (Carstens 1971a, 1971b), some of the important pioneering work of Dunning (1958, 1959a, 1959b, 1962, 1964) and Hirabayashi and French (1961) to formulate my ideas. For more recent analyses of Canadian reserves in class terms, see Elias (1975), Mortimore (1974, 1975), and Lithman (1978, 1983).

One proposition I have put forward is that 'Peasants, the working class, and people who live in reserves belong to the same social genus in terms of the relationship in which they stand to the dominant segment of the social milieux' (Carstens 1971a: 139). The existence of migrant wage labour among both reserve-dwellers and modern peasants is often taken for granted, but it is an extremely important feature that brings out the proletarian structural dimension involved, as I have illustrated for the Okanagan. Thus, even those who aspire to Canadian middle classness do so in structural terms from a proletarian base. More and more the Okanagan reserve is being transformed into a reservoir of cheap labour and also a location for the unemployed. In *A Survey of the Contemporary Indians of Canada* it was pointed out that the Canadian Indians 'are growing faster than any sectional rate of increase in Canada, and many of them are accustomed to living in regions and latitudes that are seeing vital new industrial development' (Hawthorn 1966: 10). The Okanagan Valley may not be undergoing agricultural and industrial expansion at this time, but there is considerable demand for labour. In addition, local commerce in Vernon benefits enormously from the wages generated by that labour, together with revenue derived from various forms of social assistance and transfer payments made to the reserve.

Although the Okanagan do not necessarily speak of themselves as belonging to a social class of reserve-dwellers – a vantage point from which they would experience class consciousness – they do express a collective view of themselves as members of an underprivileged community. This view contains at least some of the ingredients of class awareness, particularly their cognizance of occupying a subordinate position in an asymmetrical world. But no class system ever constitutes a pure form of social stratification, and we need also examine any systems that might support class relations and co-vary with them. So it would be misleading to leave the impression that all members of the Okanagan reserve belonged to one general category of social stratification – viz. a class of reserve peasants and proletarians – when in point of fact there is considerable internal stratification.

Weber saw this relationship between class and status very clearly when he wrote: 'Status *may* rest on class position of a distinct or an ambiguous kind. However, it is not solely determined by it: Money and an entrepreneurial position are not in themselves status qualifications, although they may lead to them; and the lack of property is not in itself a status disqualification, although this may be a reason for it. Conversely, status may influence, if not completely determine, a class position without being identical with it.' (1968: 306).

Social Status and Stratification
I have from time to time throughout this book drawn attention to various aspects of internal stratification among the Okanagan, depending on who has control of the means of subsistence and production. With the decline of farming more and more people have become involved in wage labour off the reserve. With the increase in the circulation of cash more and more people, notably women, have cultivated Canadian middle-class values, all of which have in turn complicated earlier forms of local stratification. To say that the Okanagan of today can be characterized in terms of poor, middle, rich status or by some other simple scheme is analytically useless (see Galeski 1972: 110–11) because social status at the sociological level of analysis is always related to the expression of individual feelings, ideas, and a preoccupation with personal esteem (Weber 1968; Ossowski 1963; Stavenhagen 1966; Carstens 1971b).

For Max Weber, status (*ständische Lage*) was the effective claim to social esteem in terms of positive and negative privileges, based on lifestyle, formal education, hereditary or occupational prestige, criteria which expressed themselves in everyday life in a variety of ways such as connubium, commensality, tradition, and sometimes monopolistic appropriation of political power. Thus, status 'groups' consist of a plurality of persons who successfully claim special social esteem and often status monopolies as well (Weber 1968: 302–7, et passim).

Weber, of course, was writing about very different kinds of social situations, but his ideal typical view of status groups does facilitate the interpretation of social differentiation among the Okanagan as they live today in a Canadian reserve. Which of these variables are prized by the Okanagan today as they vie for places in their scheme of status gradations? (See Ossowski 1963; Warner and Lunt 1941.) Unfortunately the Okanagan do not have many words or phrases that might assist us in classifying people in a gradated system. There are some derogatory stereotypes for low-status people, but there is no term for people at the top except perhaps 'the elders,' although that is essentially a term of respect for seniority by age. Some people occasionally speak about 'Okanagan aristocracy' when they refer to Chief Nkwala and his relatives (real and assumed). On the surface people seem quite unpreoccupied about status in their daily rounds, a delusion that is also reflected in everyday speech. By and large adults, irrespective of age, call each other by a first name or a nickname, although young adults and children may refer to old people by the classificatory kin term *tat'o'pa* (great-grandparent), but even that is uncommon nowadays. The same apparent lack of concern with etiquette is equally misleading; and in general there are very few overt status markers even in dress, with the important exception of upwardly mobile women (and women at the 'top' of the hierarchy), who are noticeably fastidious about dress as an index of their status positions.

However, as I analysed the community from the inside during the course of my fieldwork, Okanagan preoccupation with esteem, prestige, and status emerged as a cultural reality that had to be reckoned with because of its pervasiveness. Connubium, political power and influence, lifestyle, education, are all connected with status.

Political power among the Okanagan has always been difficult to define because of its tremendous variability and particularly its elaborate mutability during the past seventy-five years. But people's political affiliations, both historical and contemporary, can stand them in good stead in their struggle to maintain or increase their esteem or to avoid 'losing caste' when other variables in their lives count against them. Take, for example, the man who is on welfare, addicted to bingo and occasional all-night binges at 'the Kal' (the Kalamalka Hotel) and Polson Park, but pulls himself together from time to time and reminds everyone that he himself has a little bit of Okanagan virtue through his family connections, including possible chiefship in the 1920s. Such a person will never retrieve lost prestige by flaunting his pedigree because his status position is influenced by both positive and negative factors through time.

Any person who gets elected to council will previously have been in good standing in the community. Thus, becoming a councillor does carry with it considerable personal esteem, partly because of the political power associated with the office, but also because of the visible status position associated with it. But if you are on permanent welfare you simply do not stand a chance of being elected even if your friends nominate you.

It is very difficult to separate political power from other variables, such as occupation, education, and lifestyle, at the present time when political roles have become so formal and controlled by bureaucratic protocol. In the 1920s and 1930s and earlier there were people who were recognized for their political skills alone, independent of other variables; local political activity in the 'pre-bureaucratic' days provided more scope for personal expression, and the community was more tolerant of personal idiosyncrasies. The explanation lies, I think, in the extent to which political power was controlled by the Indian agents at that time, thereby preventing the chief and his council from realizing their power as community representatives. In other words, the alienation of local politicians from local government placed them on the periphery of the local power nexus in marginal positions in which eccentricities were tolerated because they had virtually no clout anyway. Being in a marginal position did, moreover, produce a certain amount of personal arrogance and aggression towards the Indian agent by way of protest against his authority.

There is a correlation between certain occupations in the band office and educational training and achievement – for example, social worker, typist, bookkeeper, band manager, educational officer. And over the years there has been some evidence that better-educated people get semi-skilled jobs in Vernon before those with little schooling. But for most people with higher education the reserve is not the place where one expects to be employed, and it is the recognition of that reality which has devalued occupation by itself as an indicator of high or low status. This is not to say that the Okanagan have no interest in what people do for a living. Quite the contrary; families living entirely on social assistance are afforded low status and negative esteem especially when, as people say, it is combined with heavy drinking and 'unwillingness to work,' as some call it. Hence being on welfare as an 'occupation' is not difficult to rank, although some individuals are able to conceal it quite successfully.

But how do farmers and landlords compare in a system of prestige ranking? There is no clear answer to this because there are so many factors that impinge on their status. However, a successful rancher (there are perhaps only three left) who works hard, has an acceptable lifestyle, comes from good stock, and has strong affinal connections will be ranked above the landlord who does little more than collect rent from his tenants, even though he makes more money. Farming continues to carry with it a certain degree of traditional admiration, illustrating the extent to which the modern community in this respect still has its roots in the nineteenth century. This apparent anachronism is reflected also in most people's everyday dress (leaving out those women in smart dresses who lead the middle-class movement) which one might characterize as displaying the accoutrements of 'cowboy' culture. One is particularly struck by this image at large funerals when four or five hundred people are milling around the church and cemetery. Very often farmers are also landlords, in that they lease out part of their land to maximize their chances of increasing their income, as the data on household economy demonstrate. But being a landlord and making good money out of lakeshore properties does not in itself carry with it personal prestige and esteem because people who 'have it easy,' as some argue, are often suspected of having got the advantage over others during their lives by cheating someone else out of property, by deceit, or by obtaining money from illegitimate sources (for instance, membership in an American Indian band). Many of the attitudes and emotions found in factionalism occur also in these status and prestige relations as coping behaviours that are related to the inequalities that exist in gaining access to resources, as well as to differences entrenched in plural ideologies.

The material symbols most sought after are the automobile and a good house. For example, although every household may have several automobiles, even if only one is in working order, people do aspire to have a good pick-up truck if they can afford it, and it is quite easy to identify the well-off people by their vehicles. More and more women drive and own cars today, and new cars have become important status symbols for professionals and secretaries. Even the older conservative landladies (landlords) with good incomes from land leasing regard a nice new car as an emblem of their position. One could extend the value of material symbols into other practical items such as ranges, refrigerators, television sets, satellite dishes, but it is the *house* itself that stands out as a key indicator of status. Housing has improved enormously over the past thirty years, and a spacious suburban-style house is highly prized. It has been instructive to observe how much upwardly mobile people have improved their houses over the years as their economic positions have changed. However, members of the old guard from the old faction who had good houses a generation ago have done little to improve them or to enhance their status according to the standards of the times.

There is an interesting contradiction between political status and material symbols with regards to holding elected office or chief or councillor. A councillor whose housing shows outward improvement shortly after his or her election runs the risk of losing support at the polls the next time round. Thus, it is important if you want to be successful in politics that you or your family not be seen to benefit materially from holding office. However, it was quite acceptable (even expected) for the RCMP officer, who is also a band member, to build a fine, conspicuous white-painted home on the main road that runs through the reserve.

Lifestyle is also reflected in the way people run their lives, where they shop, what they eat, with whom they eat, and the extent to which they aspire to achieve middle-class Canadian values.

Closely linked with lifestyle on the reserve are male-centred sports ranging from bronc riding to baseball and hockey. Bronc riding had enormous appeal twenty or thirty years ago and skill at riding was often associated with high-status people: some chiefs have been bronc riders. But over the years the positive value of equestrian culture has been weakened by the cultivation of modern Canadian organized sports. This shift is partly due to the exposure young men get to these sports in the school setting in Vernon, and through the media. Thus the value of playing hockey and baseball – even boxing – for acquiring status among the new generation is best seen as part of the contemporary middle-class lifestyle, while bronc riding and horse racing tend to stand apart in this scheme, being firmly grounded in nineteenth-century values. There are some notable exceptions, however, among people with enough money to afford the cost of thoroughbred horses and the means to transport them around the rodeo circuit.

Education, in the sense of formal schooling comparable to that expected in mainstream Canadian society, has been available to children and young adults of the Okanagan reserve (through bussing) for about a generation only. But in that relatively brief period education has become a sacred institution which is highly regarded in all circles. It is valued not necessarily because it might lead to a good job, but because education in itself involves acquiring knowledge, and brings with it association with whites from different social strata, providing new paradigms for understanding differentiation and discrimination as well as new strategies for the achievement of bourgeois virtues. Of course, education has been a great equalizer on the reserve, and it certainly contributed to the transformation of the old-new faction cleavage. But it has created divisions of its own, such as the hierarchical difference between university and college graduates, and others. These are nuances which are also marked in the wider society but within the confines of reserve life are made all the more obvious. Education is perceived today as providing people with effective material to claim social esteem, despite the fact that education does not in itself guarantee a person a job.

One of the better indexes of the way the Okanagan perceive themselves in the local status hierarchy lies in their intervisiting patterns and general commensality. Visiting people in their homes is a very private and personal matter, and in many ways a secret activity. People seldom talk openly about visits with or from others largely because the occasions are reserved for close friends and kin considered to have equal social status. For example, two upwardly mobile families with secretarial and white-collar jobs revel in weekend entertainment in each other's homes because the occasions provide an opportunity to parade in new dresses, show off the children, and eat a specially prepared dish. But while such visiting is designed to boost confidence in having middle-class lifestyles and values, such occasions can be ruined by a visit from a distance cousin and his friends aggressively looking for a drink and food on a Sunday afternoon. Consequently, there is always anxiety surrounding commensality and intervisiting because of the fear of having one's esteem polluted by people whose lifestyle is unbecoming to the position one believes oneself to occupy in the local hierarchy. A friend once said to me: 'Let's go and visit old so-and-so now that we are out at Six Mile, he is there now I can see the chimney smoke. No, we had better keep away, he might be drunk and those goddamn people across the road might see us going in.'

The attitude is very similar to that found in factionalism, where identification is partly dependent upon holding the appropriate ideological view and providing others with the necessary symbols to be able to place one in the right camp.

In theory, all members of the Okanagan band should from a materialist point of view have equal access to the means of production, namely land, which is held communally in the context of the reserve system. In practice, however, relatively few people ever own significant amounts of land, a reality that is reflected in the status hierarchy. But people who own no land at all, apart from a building lot and a garden, might have high status because they have good jobs in the band office or in a neighbouring town to which they commute every day. In the Okanagan reserve community there are enormous differences in status. Many of these differences are related to the scarcity of resources (there is simply too little land) and the fact that too many people have access to the means of production while too few control it at any one time. But status is also related to personal esteem and the way in which the variables that constitute it blend into the whole.

However tempting it is to deduce what a synthesis of all the variables involved might be, and produce a Warnerian characterization of the Okanagan community, I have not attempted this task here largely because the Okanagan cognitive scheme is essentially subjective and does not lend itself to 'objective' analysis (cf Warner and Lunt 1941; Warner et al. 1949). But it does seem worthwhile to attempt an answer to the deceptively simple question: What combination of characteristics attributed to an individual give him or her high status in the contemporary Okanagan reserve community? This is the same question that I asked many years ago in the Steinkopf reserve in South Africa (Carstens 1966: 132–3). He or she must be a band member because this gives access to the rights available to Indian status people according to the provisions of the Indian Act. A person should come from good stock in terms of both descent and connubium. He should be a successful farmer/rancher and/or a landlord, both of which occupations imply ownership of good land: there is no point in owning five hundred acres of rock and infertile land or a kilometre of lakefront without drinking water or road access. In addition to land ownership, other acceptable occupations would include the professions, skilled artisans, managerial positions off the reserve, or senior administrative positions with the band. He or she should display a 'desirable' and 'respectable' lifestyle – meaning a nice up-to-date house, a large expensive pick-up truck, good clothing (mainly applicable to women), and so on. He or she should have received a sound education and be fully literate *and/or* express progressive attitudes towards education for young people generally. Knowing the Okanagan language does not in itself carry any special merit, but it is necessary to give support to any plan to teach Okanagan in the local schools. Similarly, knowledge of traditional Okanagan culture (medicine, story-telling, history, drumming, dancing) might have no particular value in itself as an index of status, but upwardly mobile bourgeois parents will often speak about encouraging their daughters to do 'traditional Indian dancing' in much the same way that members of other Canadian ethnic groups do, and for exactly the same reason. A minority of middle-class Okanagan reject their heritage outright and instead of Indian dancing choose ice-skating and ballet for their daughters. Finally, he or she should choose his or her friends carefully with particular regard to commensality and intervisiting. Some people go so far as to avoid intimate association with others in the community, and attempt to find their friends off the reserve because they say it is safer!

There are also behaviours that should be avoided. Most important of these is drinking in public. Beer parlours are not the places to be seen if you are looking for approval, whether you get drunk or not. There are a number of high-status people who like to drink, but they always take careful precautions not to be seen. If you *do* drink in public you choose the 'high-class' bars or the dark cocktail lounges. I stress the question of drinking because of the many unpleasant stigmas attached to it which are so unlike any associated with pre–beer parlour days. Drawing social assistance must also be singled out as having very negative connotations, and to be seen picking up a welfare cheque every Friday counts against you because it lowers your personal esteem in much the same way as being seen going into a beer parlour.

I was surprised to discover that church membership and participation was not necessarily positively rewarded in the status hierarchy, although some of my friends often said, giving a few examples, that going to mass might get you a couple of votes at an election.

The Okanagan, therefore, like other rural peoples, have a complex con-figuration of variables pertaining to status, which seems to suggest the existence of as many systems as there are identifiers of them. My analysis of certain reserves in South Africa provided a similar conclusion, as did that of Pitt-Rivers (1960) for a rural village in France. In other words, we cannot speak of one system of stratification but rather the articulation of several such systems based on different criteria. What is peculiar to this modern Okanagan system, though, is its fluidity and lack of commitment to any one set of factors.

I never clarified the relation between status group and faction in analysing my South African material more than twenty years ago. Ignoring the differences between social class and social status (see Carstens 1966, 1971b), I tended to place factionalism entirely within the context of stratification, a view that was only partly correct. In retrospect, what I called the cleavage between the conservatives and the 'new people' was in fact quite similar to that existing between the old faction and the new faction in the Okanagan.

In analysing the Okanagan material I have separated the processes of factionalism from those of social status, although each is bound up with the other. In the Okanagan we have seen a form of circulation of élites whereby a new ethic has superseded the old conservative one (Pareto 1963; Inglis 1968). However, this change was achieved not merely through the dynamics of factionalism with all its intrigues and manoeuvres, but in concert with the manipulation of rank and social status, demonstrating the commonality of factions and status group in Weber's sense. Factionalism has long been related to matters of status and power in the community. This trend has been intensified in recent years as individuals have become more preoccupied with their feelings of personal esteem as part of the pervasive movement directed at values on the reserve.

RESERVE CULTURE

The Okanagan and other Indians in Canada who fall under the Indian Act and live within the economic, territorial and political confines of reserves are not wards of the federal government, as is sometimes said, but members of little colonies within the borders of the controlling nation. Peter Worsley (1964) made a similar observation of the peoples of northern Saskatchewan in a lecture delivered in 1961. Parallels have also been drawn with South African reserves at that time (Carstens 1966: 134–5). Robert K. Thomas (1966–7) draws illuminating parallels working from the context of an American Indian reservation which he compares with colonial Africa. What is especially interesting is that Thomas also regards reserve-dwellers as rural proletarians in the classical sense of the word (see also Watkins 1977; Coates 1985).

It might well be asked: What use was the creation of Canadian Indian reserves was to their architects? Initially, it could be argued, the establishment of treaties and the creation of the reserves took care of native peoples by getting them out of the way for settler expansion. But Indians have also played an important part in the labour force in spite of their small numbers (see Knight 1978) and their contributions to the Canadian economy over the years have been very significant. Yet today most Canadian reserves are probably regarded as liabilities and political embarrassments (or simply nuisances) by the establishment. The same could also have been said of other colonies in different parts of the world in the 1950s, 1960s and 1970s when many imperial powers granted political independence. The other perspective which we have discussed is that reserves like the Okanagan provide an important source of revenue for the commercial sectors of neighbouring regions.

Another theme implicit in this book has been the effect of reserve life on the individuals and groups of people who have been confined for four or five generations in these artificially created communities. The one factor that has remained constant over time is the Indian Act of 1876. After its promulgation in a particular reserve, it determined many of the behaviours and attitudes among the people within and outside the reserve. Some Okanagan even regard the Indian Act as a custumal of traditional law prepared especially for them by Queen Victoria and her men. The Indian Act, therefore, defines most of the parameters of reserve behaviour, producing what I have called a system positively shaped by a process of *administrative determinism*. As a band member on an Indian reserve one is almost completely dependent on the dictates of the act and its local interpretation in whatever one does. This is not to say that the administration is coterminous with everything that goes on in the community but that the administration overwhelmingly permeates the other institutions. For discussions of the way different institutions dominate community life in other societies see Godelier (1975) and Schapera (1956: 1–66).

Since dependence is so important a concomitant of reserve systems and so closely interrelated with the process of administrative design, let me state very briefly some of the psycho-social consequences of both reserves and their political and legal institutionalization. The enormity of this process of political conditioning that has taken place for the Okanagan over the years is shared by other reserve communities in Canada and the United States (e.g., Nagata 1971).

Interpersonal relations on reserves are generally characterized by far greater degrees of conflict than in other Canadian communities because of the marginal or dual life that people on reserves lead. The question of land shortage and shrinking of reserves with population increase is well known. Foster (1960–1: 174–8) has discussed the comparable implications for peasant communities. I shall, therefore, deal only with the question of dual life situation here.

My work both in the Okanagan and in 'Coloured' reserves in South Africa documents the conflicting situations people face as they try to come to terms with their marginal positions in their respective societies (see Stonequist 1937; Dickie-Clark 1966; Wakeam 1977). People's reactions to these marginal situations are complex, involving both avoidance and acceptance, and these reactions are often tinged with aggression which stems from frustration. It has been suggested by several earlier writers that this behaviour is reminiscent of 'lower-class behavioural patterns,' a characterization which partly supports my earlier argument relating to reserves as lower social classes. From another perspective we might want to apply the 'marginal man' thesis to these situations. Thus, if Indians accept 'disease and other unpleasant life situations' and display 'poor self-images, feelings of unworthiness and apathy towards the environment' (Hirabayashi and French 1961), we can probably understand these better from a more psycho-cultural perspective.

Indians sometimes give the impression of their acceptance of feelings of aggression, but so often these express themselves later in joking relationships with each other and with whites; whites often report Indian irresponsibility, inefficiency, and apathy at work without realizing that these are manifestations of aggression and ambivalence arising from what we might call reserve culture (see also Inglis 1968; Braroe 1975; Lithman 1978).

Overt aggression by Indians against whites occurs very seldom, perhaps because the hidden taboos produced by the system tend to internalize and displace aggression. Therefore, many kinds of personal violence are resolved locally on a personal level. Among the Okanagan there are many kinds of personal feuds that are resolved by shouting insults at each other or in fist fights; often drinking is involved, which reduces inhibitions (Hawthorn et al. 1958). So-called Indian drinking is always related to the psycho-social situation, and is in itself an example of aggressive behaviour. Vandalism is another form of displaced aggression, often directed at public property as a rejection of white institutions, although I found very few occurrences of it among the Okanagan. The Okanagan display much of their anti-white aggressive behaviour in subtle speech, tonality, and especially their gestures when they parade in white territory. Even on their own reserves they express aggression towards whites through avoiding them, and often in rhetoric. Elsewhere I have discussed some of these issues for an earlier period in the history of British Columbia with some appropriate comparisons with South Africa, based on observations on the Okanagan reserve as well as the Lytton and Kamloops reserves (Carstens 1971a).

Although some contemporary writers will surely disagree (for example, Miller 1989), there is an urgent need to study the psycho-social effects of the Indian Act and the concomitant existence of reserves in greater detail than I have been able to do for a variety of reasons. Most important is to understand more fully the processes whereby social and psychological reproduction occurs and how these relate to certain behaviours which are so often erroneously attributed to traditional Indianness, when in point of fact they relate to an administratively created reserve culture. For example, over the years I have observed enormous changes in drinking patterns, dependence upon alcohol, and the incidence of alcoholism. These observations show quite conclusively how important socio-economic and cultural factors are in understanding the problem of Indian drinking. My argument, therefore, is that most of the so-called differences between Indians living in reserves and other Canadians need always to be explained by factors that stand external to them as individuals, that is, as part of reserve culture and those other phenomena which are and have been administratively determined (see also Robertson 1970; Zenter 1972). In the summer of 1987 there were two suicides on the reserve and two victims of suicidal accidents. All four of these people were young men who were just beginning to look at the wider world for the first time. These deaths, I suggest, were the flags of sinister distress in the comunity in general, notably among young people. The Okanagan do, of course, share most of the problems experienced by other people in the region, but as reserve-dwellers they also have to cope with the local stresses inherent in their dependent and encapsulated lives.

The term paternalism is often used to characterize government policies which limit the freedom of subject peoples by well-meant and benevolent regulations. Indian policy in Canada qualifies for the paternalistic label, as has often been asserted. However, rather than simply label Indian policy as a static category I would like to place that policy on a paternalistic-maternalistic continuum. By maternalism I mean policies which encourage some innovation and some local political expression while still maintaining the status quo. Among the Okanagan and other Canadian Indian groups paternalism has been greatest during periods of colonial expansion of territory and consolidation of coercive control. Maternalism has been strongest during periods when the status quo is maintained by permissiveness and fiscal generosity. For example, the contemporary period (1966 to the present) constitutes one of the maternalistic variety, while 1876 to 1880 leaned strongly to paternalism, and the period 1880 to 1902 was a combination of both.

Throughout this book I have been concerned with an analysis of the Okanagan over time, paying detailed attention to the relations between the community and the outside world. But what images do outsiders have of the Okanagan and other groups of Indians living in reserves? There are, I think, two basic models in the minds of outsiders when they reflect on native peoples in Canada, and very often these models are paradoxically and confusedly combined, or people vacillate from one to the other.[2] First is the view that most Indians are irresponsible and lazy, poorly educated, dirty and criminal, and prone to alcoholism and tuberculosis. This state is believed to be genetic by the racists – 'it's in the blood,' they assert – while the liberals say it is because traditional Indian culture was destroyed by the white man and the Indians were incapable of adapting to western civilization. The second image held by outsiders is a romantic, semi-academic, natural history view derived from museums, films, books, and 'mother's knee' history. In their original state, they say, Indians lived rich and statisfying lives as noble savages differing only slightly from bears, seals, and white whales; they were a happy blend of the best qualities of animals and the spiritual domain. In this pristine state they are admired for their many qualities, especially their knowledge of naturopathic medicine and their mystical familiarity with nature.

Readers will be familiar with these two ideal type models and the way non-native opinion vacillates between them: when Indians are out of sight white people opt for the romantic natural history view; when they are too close they opt for the racist, inability-to-adapt model which also explains the 'published facts' view of Indians. It is not surprising, therefore, that non-Indians are confused in what they think and feel, given the extent to which Indian reserves and settlements are separated from society. Situated both physically and socially outside the 'normal' scheme of the Canadian vertical mosaic, they occupy marginal structural positions, but not by choice, as my analysis has endeavoured to show.

2 For a detailed and scholarly historic study of white images of North American Indians see Berkhofer (1978). Both Braroe (1975) and Lithman (1978) have made important contributions to the perceptions reserve Indians have of themselves together with white attitudes towards Indians. It is interesting that both Braroe and Lithman are Scandinavians who carried out research in Canada round about the same time.

The final words of this book are those an Okanagan spoke in 1962. Tommy Gregoire was reflecting on the quality of life in the contemporary material, social, cultural and spiritual worlds of his own people now that the white man has made his mark.

I will tell you some things about the Okanagan people and the White people here in these parts.

The first thing is that the ways of the Whiteman have corrupted us just as they have upset the balance of nature. Now that the balance of nature has been upset we Indian people cannot go back because the old ways don't work any more. You see the magic has gone. Let me explain what this all means. Take a thing like *electricity*. If there is a complete power failure today we have had it because we need the electrical power. But this [modern electricity] has destroyed something very important to the Indians. The use of electricity is taking the electricity out of the earth. We can't even make fire according to the old custom because we have no electricity left in us. We used to make fire by rubbing dry pine needles together in one's hand: we got the electricity in our bodies by sleeping on the ground.

Then there is *water*. All life used to come from rain. The rain brought down certain properties from the sky coming from the sun and the moon. (The idea of a flight to the moon is therefore bad. White man will never achieve this - that may be the end of the world.) These properties went into the earth and made the crops grow. Now irrigation washes all the goodness out of the soil which is being even more spoiled by these fertilizers. Here in the Okanagan [Reserve] fertilizers are put in by the Chinamen who lease land from us.

There is not so much rain there used to be, and it is much colder now. The cold stops you from sleeping on the ground and the body doesn't get any electricity.

Then there are the diesel trains. These are also killing off things by their fumes – things in the soil and the insects, that's why the [game] birds have gone away. Spraying the crops is also bad for the same reason [as the diesel fumes].

But there is nothing we can do to change all these things. The best we can do is to think about the old times, and tell our children about them. We can't go back to the old times because all the [old] magic has gone. So we have to make the children go to school. Education of children is a good thing.

Now that the Whiteman has come to stay and has changed everything we have to go along with him, even though the Whiteman [with his technology] is always taking things out of the earth. Cars, trucks, tractors, and engines all need petrol and oil. Lights and television and radio need electricity. Even the houses are not as good as they were because the rain has gone, and now the sun takes the strength out of the wood.

OTTER LAKE INDIAN RESERVE NO. 2 (62 ACRES)

This reserve is situated at the south end of Otter Lake adjacent to Deep Creek (Meadow Creek). It consists of roughly 40 acres of arable land and 22 acres of marsh land. Otter Lake reserve is surrounded by extremely productive land. In 1913, when the royal commission visited the band, Chief Michel reported that Otter Lake was used for hay only and farmed by one person, Isaac Harris, a band member. This little reserve is of particular interest in the present context because it illustrates so well the way in which reserves were created in 1877, setting aside a piece of land for Indian use without interfering with settler pre-emptions and aspirations for fertile land.

HARRIS INDIAN RESERVE NO. 3 (160 ACRES)

The Harris Reserve corners present-day Highway 97A approximately two kilometres southeast of Otter Lake and about seventeen kilometres north of Vernon. At the time it was created by the commission in 1877 it was inhabited by several families. The royal commission of 1913 was informed by Chief Michel that the Harris reserve was still being used for agricultural purposes and that less than half was under heavy timber. According to the royal commission one big family lived there at the time – the Isaac Harris family – who cultivated it as well 'as any white man could.' The family also had twenty-five head of cattle, eight horses, and a number of pigs. At the present time four adult members of the one family control the reserve. They have leased out 113 acres of agricultural land, and there is still 35 acres of uncleared land. A large impressive house in poor repair stands on the reserve, but this too is rented out to non-band members.

SWAN LAKE INDIAN RESERVE NO. 4 (68 ACRES)

Swan Lake Reserve is situated at the north end of Swan Lake about ten kilometres north of Vernon and is crossed today by Highway 97. In 1910 Baptiste Logan, Kimas Kite, James Logan, and Thomas Lindley were regarded as the rightful owners of the Swan Lake Indian Reserve. When the royal commission visited the area in 1913, Chief Michel informed the members of the commission that Swan Lake Reserve was fenced and that half of it was cultivated, while the other half was used for hay. One family lived on the reserve. On 18 November 1913 the royal commission illegally ordered that Swan Lake (Indian Reserve No. 4) be 'cut off' and revert to the crown, and the band was deprived of the land until the question was resolved in the 1980s.

LONG LAKE INDIAN RESERVE NO. 5 (128 ACRES)

Long Lake Reserve is located at the north end of Long (Kalamalka) Lake, roughly seven kilometres to the south of Vernon. The area was in active use in 1877 when the joint reserve commission declared it an Indian reserve. The Okanagan used the area as a campground and fishing site among other things. There is also an Indian burial site near the eastern boundary.

When the royal commission enquired about Long Lake Reserve in 1913 they were informed by Chief Michel that it consisted both of hay land and of cultivable land, but that half of it was mountain. Cropping had, however, declined over the years and only hay was put in. One family was living there at the time (Jimmy Antoine, his wife and child). In addition, it was reported that about a dozen white people occupied land on this reserve in their summer houses and tents, for which they paid rent to the Antoines. The reserve has a splendid beach. On 18 November 1913 the royal commission illegally ordered that Long Lake Indian Reserve No. 5 of the Okanagan tribe be cut off together with the Swan Lake Reserve.

PRIEST'S VALLEY INDIAN RESERVE NO. 6 (83 ACRES)

Priest's Valley Reserve lies some six and one-half kilometres west of Vernon and part of it flanks the east shore of Lake Okanagan. It consisted of good bottom land except the swamp on the lake side. The land did not require irrigation, being naturally irrigated by the creek which flowed through it.

During the visit of the royal commission in 1913 it was reported that three families resided there and cultivated the land, the chief agriculturalists being Mr Jack, his son Pierre, and Mrs MacDougall, all members of the Okanagan band at the Head of the Lake. At this time both 'Ten-dollar Jack' and his son Pierre, and Mrs MacDougall, needed interests in other reserves to make an adequate living. I point this out to emphasize that 83 acres was insufficient agricultural land for two or three families. In this connection it should be remembered that settlers in the 1860s were able to pre-empt 160 acres and most of them expected and did get more.

There is no agriculture on this reserve nowadays, and its main value is commercial. There is a large Okanagan-owned mobile home park on it, and part of Vernon Municipal Airport overlaps the reserve.

DUCK LAKE INDIAN RESERVE NO. 7 (457 ACRES)

Duck Lake Reserve is the most southern Okanagan reserve. It is located north of Kelowna airport at Winfield contiguous with Duck Lake. About half the land is very poor and rocky while the rest is fair arable land suitable for ploughing and raising crops. But the arable land is not up to the standard of equivalent land on the main reserve. When the royal commission met in 1913 it was noted that a limited acreage was under irrigation and that four families lived there. In 1901 twenty-four band members lived there. There was a small church but today only the graveyard remains.

In recent times agriculture has been completely abandoned to be replaced by a residential trailer park, a branch of the Hiram Walker Distillery (leased land), and a packaging and pallet plant. The importance of this reserve lies in its commercial lease value, which also applies to Priest's Valley.

It should be noted that in 1963 a segment of the Okanagan band residing in the Kelowna area separated from the band to form the now independent Westbank band. The Westbank people always regarded themselves as a separate community from the Head of the Lake within the context of the Okanagan nation, so the break in 1963 was inevitable. Mission Creek (I.R. No. 8) 5 acres, Tsinstikeptum (I.R. No. 9) 154.59 acres, and Tsinstikeptum (I.R. No. 10) 768.34 acres were all transferred to Westbank at this time. We will not be concerned with them here, except to point out that their land is ideally situated to benefit from its proximity to the city of Kelowna.

APPENDIX 2

Okanagan Indian reserve population by sex and age, 1982 and 1985

	Males				Females			
Age	1982		1985		1982		1985	
0–4	39	(4.54)	47	(4.93)	44	(5.12)	47	(4.93)
5–9	41	(4.77)	43	(4.51)	39	(4.54)	38	(3.98)
10–14	36	(4.19)	36	(3.77)	38	(4.42)	48	(5.03)
15–19	58	(6.75)	33	(3.46)	52	(6.05)	41	(4.30)
20–24	48	(5.58)	60	(6.29)	53	(6.16)	64	(6.71)
25–34	77	(8.96)	89	(9.33)	81	(9.42)	99	(10.38)
35–44	54	(6.28)	60	(6.29)	56	(6.51)	89	(9.33)
45–54	30	(3.49)	35	(3.67)	26	(3.02)	40	(4.19)
55–64	25	(2.91)	23	(2.41)	23	(2.67)	26	(2.72)
65–69	5	(0.58)	7	(0.73)	4	(0.46)	8	(0.83)
70+	14	(1.62)	10	(1.04	16	(1.86)	10	(1.04)
	427	(49.67)	443	(46.43)	432	(50.23)	510	(53.44)

Total 1982 = 859; 1985 = 953

Note: Percentages in parentheses

APPENDIX 3

Annual sources of income of domestic families (households) in the Okanagan Indian Reserve in 1954 based on 27 households; average household size = 7.5 persons

	Dollars	Per cent
Wage labour	45,166	42.07
Farming, ranching, etc.	32,550	30.32
Family allowances, pensions, etc.	20,408	19.01
Leasing out property and sharecropping	6,696	6.23
Other	2,516	2.34
Total	107,336	99.97

The average individual household income in 1954 was $3975 made up as follows: wage labour $1673; farming, ranching, etc. $1205; family allowances, pensions, etc. $756; leasing out property and sharecropping $248; all other sources $93.

NOTE: This table is based on data collected by James Hirabayashi in 1954. Two observations must be made. First, the households 'sampled' tended to be the most visible families on the reserve, and include the most wealthy families, leaning heavily towards an élite segment in the community. Second, the families tend also to be large because the heads of households are older. The average household size for the whole community was 5.9 in 1954. The average for this 'sample' is 7.5.

Okanagan Indian household income by household income groups, giving sources of income for 1980* (adapted from 1981 census)

Income	No. of households	Average household income ($)	Average household size	Average wages & salaries ($)
$1–$4,999	15	1,697	1.8	476 (28.00)
$5,000–$9,999	30	7,529	3.4	2,426 (32.22)
$10,000–$14,999	20	13,432	4.7	9,132 (67.99)
$15,000–$19,999	5	19,392	4.0	18,869 (97.30)
$20,000–$24,999	15	21,627	4.1	21,024 (97.21)
$30,000–$39,999	15	33,875	6.3	31,487 (92.95)
Total	100	13,716	3.9	10,834 (78.9)

Note: Percentages in parentheses

Average farm employment income ($)	Average employment income ($)	Average income ($) government	Average retirement pensions ($)	Average investment income ($)
–	476 (28.00)	1,221 (72.00)	–	–
2,036 (27.04)	4,462 (59.26)	3,067 (40.73)	–	–
–	9,132 (67.99)	3,502 (26.10)	797 (5.93)	–
–	18,869 (97.30)	523 (2.70)	–	–
–	21,024 (97.21)	456 (2.10)	–	146 (0.68)
–	29.905 (88.28)	3,922 (11.58)	47 (0.14)	–
538 (3.92)	11,145 (81.25)	2,376 (17.32)	174 (1.27)	20 (0.14)

APPENDIX 5

Sources of actual revenue administered by Okanagan band council (1979–89)

Funding source	1979/80	1980/81	1981/82	1982/83
Federal government	$	$	$	$
Dept. of Indian Affairs	808,210	1,104,243	1,268,237	1,509,023
National Health & Welfare	32,304	31,577	39,006	47,317
Employment Development				
Branch	27,528	5,821[1]	136,386	41,970
Canada Mortgage & Housing	–	2,843	25,567	87,057
Canadian Forest Service	–	–	–	34,403
Provincial government				
First Citizens' Fund	27,138	3,167	–	–
Ministry of Labour/				
BC Forest Service	6,198	–	–	22,282
Band revenue	41,359	(28,968)	98,667	112,244
Other	2,431	2,348	6,352	24,309
Long-term debt financing	–	–	–	836,000
Total	945,168	1,121,031	1,574,215	2,714,605

1 The funding contributions of the Employment Development Branch, the CMHC, and the First
Citizens' Fund have been combined and shown together for 1980/81 because of the
small funding amounts and scale of the chart.

1983/84	1984/85	1985/86	1986/87	1987/88	1988/89
$	$	$	$	$	$
1,857,617	2,174,418	2,321,774	2,271,072	2,333,971	2,142,773
54,723	54,723	59,475	62,321	61,853	61,703
76,696	150,461	38,360	8,146	72,316	52,255
163,973	14,655	250,750	323,920	289,758	302,535
59,661	–	–	–	19,394	71,293
–	–	5,150	–	–	–
–	–	–	–	–	–
2,631,583[2]	176,229	173,545	195,005	138,038	132,285
80,123	1,756,614	679,322	880,129	545,546	539,705
–	–	–	–	–	–
4,924,376	4,327,100	3,528,376	3,740,593	3,460,876	3,302,549

2 Of this amount, $2,435,270 represents a one-year-only land claims settlement. (An additional amount of $1,419,802 plus interest was paid to the band for the Swan Lake–Long Lake claim the following year. Author.)

3 The full details for this table have been taken from the Okanagan Indian Band records.

APPENDIX 6

A Note on Sport
(With Tim Isaac)

There were many different games and pastimes in traditional Okanagan society about which there is little memory today, as modern sport and activities have begun to preoccupy people's leisure time. The oral tradition does, however, inform us of games designed, among other things, to sharpen one's skill. The hoop game, for example, involved rolling a wooden hoop or a ring of grass while the contestants attempted to throw their spears or shoot their arrows through the moving target; and the entertainment which delighted and preoccupied large numbers of people was the game of *sla hal* or *tsillallacome* (see Ross 1849: 331–6).

Sla hal, which is still played on occasions, is essentially a game of chance involving players and gamblers. It might attract up to a hundred people and continue for a week. The game involved two teams who competed against each other in an elaborate process of juggling two small oblong polished bones, one of which was marked and held in a fist of one of the players while the pointer of the opposing side had to guess which fist it was in. The game was not only based on the simple principle of guessing, but involved highly ritualized procedures and sleight-of-hand. Each team had always to have the same number of players who knelt down facing each other at a distance of about three feet. Each team started with ten 9-inch sticks and every successful guess required that one stick be transferred to the winner's side, after which another round began. The winning team of the whole contest was announced when all the sticks were held by one team, which then claimed the stakes that had been set out before the game.

As important as the game itself was the drumming and singing which accompanied the action. Each player was furnished with a small drumstick which was used to beat time on the log or the piece of wood that separated the teams. Drumming was always accompanied by a song, the idea being to rivet full attention on the game. *Sla hal* songs had an almost hypnotic quality especially when performed by large teams and witnessed by a crowd of non-playing gamblers. It was a highly complex game which could involve large numbers of people in intense interaction. As a sport it was a great leveller of differences in rank, although the players often acquired prestige for their skills, drumming, songs, and sleight-of-hand.

Teit (1930: 260–1) says he did not learn much about traditional Okanagan games, but he does refer to *Sla hal* and the dice game played by women, together with the contest games requiring special skills which were often related to hunting. To these I would also add the numerous dances and songs relating to many aspects of life, sacred and secular, all of which fostered interaction between people. Story-telling was a highly developed dramatic institution among the Okanagan, occupying an important place in their leisure hours and providing a system of communication which transcended some of the formal divisions in the society.

The horse was as much part of traditional Okanagan culture as it still is among certain people and it figured prominently in sport and leisure. Horse racing, with its gambling component, remained popular for a long time. Both Penticton and the Head of the Lake were famous meeting places for horse racing, and heavy betting was usual. At the turn of the century the 'money pots' (*hutchum*) reached amounts up to $1500 and people would travel great distances to attend these meets, which sometimes lasted for a week.

Foot races were also common until well into the twentieth century. Even political rivals such as Johnny Chelahitsa and Pierre Michel used to compete with each other in these events and the results were taken seriously. There is no evidence that foot racing was rendered redundant by horse racing, and while the horse races were generally associated with gambling, foot races were essentially individual contests and measures of personal attributes. In more recent times, Easter Sunday was set aside for sport of various kinds – horse racing, foot racing, horseshoe pitching, penny pitching, and so on – and the Okanagan were joined on these occasions by their Shuswap neighbours and more distant people such as the Kutenai. The Okanagan at the Head of the Lake were so involved with their horses that they were sometimes referred to as 'horse Indians' because they had abandoned canoes as a means of transport by the third quarter of the nineteenth century (Holliday 1948: 150).

Bronc riding fascinated many people as the forerunner of the rodeo which evolved later. The rodeo was very much an institution of the 1920s although its origin goes back to the 1870s in the United States. Okanagan participation in rodeos is relatively recent, but before All Indian rodeos were established in the 1950s, the Okanagan took part in so-called 'white' rodeos in the United

States and Canada. Some people from the reserve still travel a great deal in both countries and many are obsessed with the sport to the point where at least one marriage has broken up after the wife grew tired of being a rodeo widow. Later, the Head of the Lake became an important rodeo centre and people travelled less.

Organized sport on the reserve derived from the Canadian tradition begun late in the nineteenth century. Teams tended to be selected from the local community alone, and some were even based on allegiances to locality and factional divisions within the reserve.

Soccer was introduced by the settlers in the 1880s and various reserve teams were organized. Some of these are reported to have played against the settlers themselves, (Holliday 1948: 147–8). Cricket never caught on because the tremendous enthusiasm for the game by the English settlers and remittance men enabled them to do without the Indians.

It was baseball that attracted Okanagan interest most and the game has been played on the reserve since the early 1900s, possibly before. But the first official team, known as the O.K. Okanagans, was not founded until 1924. They played against other reserve teams from Shuswap reserves such as Chase, Enderby, and Salmon Arm. These were all trophy matches and attracted considerable attention and interest among the Indians. A new team, the Bluebirds, grew out of the old one and won its first tournament trophy in 1937. Some years later they played their first game against a non-Indian team called the Vernon Blues. It was a Japanese team whose members used to come out to the reserve to practise and play.

What is especially significant about these early baseball teams is that their centre was essentially at the Head of the Lake. Some team members belonged to other areas, but the decisions were nearly always those of the old faction contingent. In the 1940s the Six Mile Creek people began to form their own team, and practised on the piece of land just below St Theresa's church. They called themselves the Six Mile Royals and most of their best players were young men who had learned baseball at the Kamloops residential school. The creation of the Six Mile Royals was closely related to the friction that existed between Six Mile Creek and the Head of the Lake/Irish Creek area, a situation that created an appropriate atmosphere for competitive matches, and further expansion of baseball on the reserve.

In 1920 a hockey team, the Stampeders, was formed. The history of hockey on the reserve paralleled quite closely that of baseball, with local teams growing up to compete with rival groups, but these never enjoyed the same degree of fervour found in baseball.

The status of organized sport on the reserve changed enormously from the

1950s onwards. Boxing was introduced, a softball team emerged, and as the community was drawn closer to the Indian Affairs Department through the paradox of taking more responsibility for development and management of its own affairs, so sport was also incorporated into the process. Teams were transformed into clubs and their former diversity and corresponding disjunction was incorporated under new organizational umbrellas. By the 1970s hockey, boxing, baseball, homemakers clubs, softball, and band administration were so interconnected that each arena tended to lose its focus and identity. Even the old sporting rivalries began to disappear.

In anticipation of this new trend on the reserve a community organization for everyone in the band was started in 1947. This new club had a Six Mile Creek base and during the four years of its existence the people helped clear the land for the ball ground in the area, but achieved little else. Then in 1953 the Department of Indian Affairs was instrumental in forming the Homemakers Club with the explicit intention of encouraging people – mainly the women – to become more involved in the community. This they did with a vengeance. The homemakers involved themselves in activities ranging from cooking food for wakes and giving wedding showers to helping clubs like the Bluebirds and Royals raise funds. They seemed to be aspiring to take over the whole reserve in their attempt to bureaucratize sport and leisure with resources provided by the Department of Indian Affairs, but the harder they tried the more the umbrella structure weakened before it finally collapsed.

By 1968 the Bluebirds dropped out of league play and the Homemakers Club fizzled out in the early 1970s. Other teams were racked by dissent, and new personal and factional issues permeated the sporting arena generally. The world of organized sport began to resemble the new political arena in that both seemed now to have merged and taken their places under the roof of the band office.

The argument advanced here is not that all Canadian sport on the reserve declined from the 1950s and 1960s onwards or that the advent of homemakers clubs caused all the conflicts and the decline in sports clubs. Rather the issue centres in the question of the diversification of sport and direction towards planned centralization. With the growth of professionalism and the expanding bureaucracy, Okanagan sport and leisure did lose much of its spontaneity in reflecting personal feelings. The same might also be said of sport generally in Canada, but its meaning in the context of reserve encapsulation is somewhat different.

Looking at Okanagan sport and leisure in the context of history suggests a very strong decrease in spontaneity over the years as the various arenas have become institutionalized and as new values have changed the cultural fabric of the community. The delights and inventiveness of *sla hal* have given way to bingo at considerable material and emotional cost. The factional intrigues of old style baseball now find expression in formal band politics, although voters still look to the sporting arena for their leaders, hoping to find tangible evidence to support one candidate and reject another.

Bibliography

Arensberg, Conrad M. 1937. *The Irish Countryman: An Anthropological Study.*
New York: Macmillan

Arensberg, Conrad M., and S.T. Kimball. 1940. *Family and Community in Ireland.*
Cambridge, Mass: Harvard University Press

Armstrong, Jeannette C. 1985. *Slash.* Penticton: Theytus Books

Aron, Raymond. 1985. *History, Truth, Liberty. Selected Writings of Raymond
Aron,* edited by Franciszek Draus. Chicago: University of Chicago Press

Balf, Mary. 1978. *The Dispossessed: Interior Indians in the 1800s.* Kamloops:
Kamloops Museum

– 1985. 'Hwistesmetxē'qEn.' *Dictionary of Canadian Biography* 8: 421–2.
Toronto: University of Toronto Press

– n.d. *Nicola: A Very Great Chieftain.* Kamloops: Kamloops Museum (mimeo)

Bancroft, H.H. 1887. *History of British Columbia, 1791–1887.* San Francisco:
History Company

Bank(s), Judith J. 1970. 'Comparative Biographies of Two British Columbia Anthropologists: Charles Hill-Tout and James A. Teit.' Vancouver: University of British
Columbia, MA thesis

Barman, Jean, Yvonne, Hébert, and Don McCaskill, eds. 1986, 1987. *Indian
Education in Canada.* 2 vols. Vancouver: University of British Columbia Press

Beals, Alan. 1959. 'Leadership in a Mysore Village.' In *Leadership and Political
Institutions in India,* edited by Richard L. Park and Irene Tinker. Princeton:
Princeton University Press

Begg, Alexander. 1894. *History of British Columbia from Its Earliest Discovery to
the Present Time.* Toronto: W.W. Briggs.

Berkhofer, Robert F., Jr. 1978. *The White Man's Indian: Images of the American
Indian from Columbus to the Present.* New York: Knopf

Boas, Franz. 1890–1. 'Report on North West Tribes of Canada.' *British Association for the Advancement of Science, Proceedings*

– 1928. 'Territorial Distribution of Salish Tribes.' *41st Annual Report of the Bureau of American Ethnology (1919–1924)*. Washington, DC

Bock, Philip. 1962. 'The Social Structure of a Canadian Indian Reserve.' Harvard University, PhD Thesis

Bodemann, Y.M. 1982. 'Class Rule as Patronage: Kinship, Local Ruling Cliques and the State in Rural Sardinia.' *Journal of Peasant Studies* 9 (2): 147–5

Boissevain, J. 1968. 'The Place of Non-groups in the Social Sciences.' *Man* 3 (4): 542–6

Boldt, Menno. 1980. 'Canadian Native Indian Leadership: Context and Composition.' *Canadian Ethnic Studies* 12 (1): 15–33

– 1981. 'Enlightenment Values, Romanticism, and Attitudes towards Political Status: A Study of Native Leaders in Canada.' *Canadian Review of Sociology and Anthropology* 18 (4): 545–65

Bonneau, Phyllis. n.d. 'The Okanagan Sawmill.' Unpublished ms

Bouchard, R., and L. Pierre. n.d. 'How to Write the Okanagan Language.' British Columbia Indian Language Project, Victoria, unpublished ms (mimeo)

Bourdieu, Pierre. 1977. *Outline of a Theory of Practice*, translated by Richard Nice. Cambridge: Cambridge University Press

Braroe, Niels W. 1975. *Indians and White: Self-Image and Interaction in a Canadian Plains Community*. Stanford: Stanford University Press

Braudel, Fernand. 1980. *On History*, translated by Sarah Matthews. Chicago: University of Chicago Press

Brent, Marie Houghton (Mrs. William Brent). 1935. 'The Indians of the Okanagan Valley.' *Okanagan Historical Society Report* 6: 122–30

– 1966. 'Indian Lore.' *Okanagan Historical Society Report* 30: 105–14

– n.d. *The Memories of Marie Houghton Brent*. Victoria: Provincial Archives of British Columbia

British Columbia. 1866. *Columbia River Exploration, 1865*. New Westminster: Government Printing Office

British Columbia. 1875. *Papers Connected with the Indian Land Question, 1850–1875*. Victoria: R. Wolfenden, 'Report of the Government of British Columbia on the Subject of Indian Reserves'

British Columbia, Legislative Council. 1864. *Journals*

Brown, W.C. 1914. 'Old Fort Okanogan and the Okanogan Trail.' *Oregon Historical Quarterly* 15: 30–34

Buckland, F.M. 1926. Settlement at L'Anse au Sable. *Okanagan Historical and Natural History Society Report* 1: 9–12

– 1935. 'The Hudson's Bay Brigade Trail.' *Okanagan Historical Society Report* 6: 11–22

Bundy, Colin. 1972. 'The Emergence and Decline of a South African Peasantry.' *African Affairs* 71: 369–388

– 1979. *The Rise and Fall of the South African Peasantry.* London: Heinemann

Cail, Robert E. 1974. *Land, Man, and the Law: The Disposal of Crown Lands in British Columbia, 1871–1913.* Vancouver: University of British Columbia Press

Caldwell, Warren W. 1953. 'An Archaeological Survey of the Okanagan and Similkameen Valleys of B.C.' *Anthropology in B.C.* 4: 10–25

Calvin, Martin, ed. 1987. *The American Indian and the Problem of History.* New York: Oxford University Press

Campbell, Maria. 1973. *Halfbreed.* Toronto: McClelland and Stewart

Canada. *Census of Canada.* Various dates

– 1871–1912. *Sessional Papers*

– 1916. *Report of the Royal Commission on Indian Affairs for the Province of British Columbia.* 4 vols. Victoria: Acme Press

– 1977. *Canada Year Book.* Ottawa

– 1984. *The Historical Development of the Indian Act,* edited by John Leslie and Ron Maguire. Ottawa

Carr, E.H. 1961. *What Is History?* Harmondsworth: Penguin

Carstens, Peter. 1961. 'The Community of Steinkopf: An Ethnographic study and an Analysis of Social Change in Namaqualand.' University of Cape Town, PhD thesis

– 1966. *The Social Structure of a Cape Coloured Reserve: A Study of Racial Integration and Segregation in South Africa.* Cape Town: Oxford University Press

– 1969. 'Hobson's Choice and Poverty with Particular Reference to a South African Reserve.' *Canadian Journal of African Studies* 3 (2): 367–76

– 1970. 'Problems of Peasantry and Social Class in Southern Africa.' Paper presented at 7th World Congress of Sociology, Varna (Bulgaria), 14–19 Sept.

– 1971a. 'Coercion and Change.' In *Canadian Society: Pluralism, Change, and Conflict,* edited by Richard J. Ossenberg. Scarborough: Prentice-Hall of Canada

– 1971b. 'Problèmes de la paysannerie et des classes sociales en Afrique du Sud.' In *Sociologie de l'impérialisme,* edited by A. Abdel-Malek. Paris: Editions Anthropos

– 1975. 'Some Implications of Change in Khoikhoi Supernatural Beliefs.' In *Religion and Social Change in Southern Africa,* edited by Michael G. Whisson and Martin West. Cape Town: David Philip

– 1987. 'Leaders, Followers, and Supporters: The Okanagan Experience.' *Anthropologica* 29 (1): 7–19

Casagrande, Joseph B. 1959. 'Some Observations on the Study of Intermediate Societies.' In *Intermediate Societies Social Mobility, and Communication*, edited by Verne F. Ray. Seattle: University of Washington Press

Census of Indians of Okanagan Band according to Classification made by Board of Investigation. July 1934 (detailed document located in Okanagan Band Office)

Chiefs' File. 982/3-5-1. March 1879 – December 1947. Department of Indian Affairs Archives, Vancouver

Christie, J.H. n.d. Correspondence between J.H. Christie, B.C. Armstrong and Department of Indian Affairs 1916–1917. Victoria: Public Archives of British Columbia

Cline, Walter, et al. 1938. *The Sinkaietk or Southern Okanogan of Washington*. Menasha: General Series in Anthropology. No. 6

Coates, Ken. 1985. *Canada's Colonies: A History of the Yukon and Northwest Territories*. Toronto: James Lorimer

– 1988. 'Upsetting the Rhythms: The Federal Government and Native Communities in the Yukon Territory, 1945 to 1973.' In *Northern Communities: The Prospects for Empowerment*, edited by Gurston Dacks and Ken Coates. Edmonton: Boreal Institute for Northern Studies

Cohen, Anthony P. 1985. *The Symbolic Construction of Community*. London and New York: Tavistock

Cohn, Bernard S. 1980.' History and Anthropology: The State of Play.' *Comparative Studies in Society and History* 22 (2): 198–221

Cole, Jean Murray. 1979. *Exile in the Wilderness: The Biography of Chief Factor Archibald McDonald, 1790–1853*. Don Mills: Burns and MacEachern

Comaroff, John L. 1978. 'Rules and Rulers: Political Process in a Tswana Chiefdom.' *Man* (n.s.) 13: 1–20

Colson, Elizabeth. 1953. *The Makah Indians: A Study of an Indian Tribe in Modern American Society*. Manchester: Manchester University Press

Cox, Ross. 1831. *Adventures on the Columbia, Including a Narrative of a Residence of Six Years on the Western Side of the Rockies*. London: Henry Colburn and Richard Bentley

Cumming, Peter A., and Neil H. Mickenberg, eds. 1972. *Native Rights in Canada*. 2nd ed. Toronto: General Publishing Company

Curtis, Edward S. 1970 (orig. 1911). *The North American Indian*. Vol. 7. New York: Johnson Reprint Corporation

Dacks, Gurston, and Ken Coates, eds. 1988. *Northern Communities: The Prospects for Empowerment*. Edmonton: Boreal Institute for Northern Studies

Dawson, G.M. 1891. 'Notes on the Shuswap People of British Columbia.' *Transactions of the Royal Society of Canada* 2: 3–44

De Jouvenel, Bertrand. 1957. *Sovereignty: An Inquiry into the Political Good.* Cambridge: Cambridge University Press

De Pfyffer, Robert L. 1976. 'Okanagan Indian Band Cut-off Lands.' Vernon: Consultant's Report

– 1982. 'The West-Bank Cut-offs: An Historical Report.' Vernon: Columbia Appraisals

– 1990. 'Okanagan Indians Non-Registered: The Reason Why.' *Okanagan Historical Society Report* 54: 77–91

Dickie-Clark, H.D. 1966. *The Marginal Situation: A Sociological Study of a Coloured Group.* London: Routledge and Kegan Paul

Dolby, Elizabeth. 1973. 'The Fur Trade and Culture Change among the Okanagan Indians.' *Okanagan Historical Society Report* 37: 134–51

Douglas Lake Commonage Reserve Report. n.d. I.C.G. Consultants (mimeo)

Duff, Wilson. 1965. *The Impact of the White Man: The Indian History of British Columbia.* Vol. 1. Victoria: Provincial Museum. Memoir 5

Dunning, R.W. 1958. 'Some Implications of Economic Change in Northern Ojibwa Social Structure.' *Canadian Journal of Economic and Political Science* 24 (4): 562–6

– 1959a. 'Ethnic Relations and the Marginal Man in Canada.' *Human Organization* 18: 117–22

– 1959b. *Social and Economic Change among the Northern Ojibwa.* Toronto: University of Toronto Press

– 1962. 'Some Aspects of Governmental Indian Policy and Administration.' *Anthropologica* 4 (n.s.): 209–31

– 1964. 'Some Problems of Reserve Indian Communities: A Case Study.' *Anthropologica* 6 (n.s.): 3–38

Eisenstadt, S.N., and L. Roniger. 1984. *Patrons, Clients, and Friends.* Cambridge, Mass.: Cambridge University Press

Elias, P.D. 1975. *Metropolis and Hinterland in Northern Manitoba.* Winnipeg: Manitoba Museum of Man and Nature

Eliot, T.S. 1962. *Notes towards the Definition of Culture.* London: Faber and Faber

Elmendorf, W.W. 1965. 'Linguistic and Geographical Relations in the Northern Plateau Area.' *Southwestern Journal of Anthropology* 21 (2):63–78

Embree, John F. 1939. *Suye Mura, a Japanese Village.* Chicago: University of Chicago Press

Evans-Pritchard, E.E. 1950. 'Social Anthropology: Past and Present.' *Man* 50 (198): 118–24

Fardon, Richard. 1987. 'History, Ethnicity and Pageantry: The 1987 A.S.A. Conference.' *Anthropology Today* 3 (3): 15–17

Fenton, W.N. 1955. 'Factionalism in American Indian Society.' *Actes du IVe Congrès International des Sciences Anthropologiques et Ethnologiques 1957*. 2: 330–40

Firth, Raymond. 1946. *Malay Fishermen: Their Peasant Economy*. London: Routledge and Kegan Paul

Fisher, Robin. 1971–2. 'Joseph Trutch and Indian Land Policy.' *B.C. Studies* 12: 3–33

– 1975. 'An Exercise in Futility: The Joint Commission on Indian Land in British Columbia, 1875–1880.' *Historical Papers* 1975: 79–94

– 1977. *Contact and Conflict: Indian-European Relations in British Columbia, 1774–1890*. Vancouver: University of British Columbia Press

Fortes, Meyer. 1938. 'Culture Contact as a Dynamic Process.' *Africa*. Supplement

Foster, George M. 1953. 'What Is Folk Culture?' *American Anthropologist* 55: 159–73

– 1960–1. 'Interpersonal Relations in Peasant Society.' *Human Organization* 19: 174–8

Francis, Daniel, and Toby Morantz. 1983. *Partners in Furs: A History of the Fur Trade in Eastern James Bay 1600–1870*. Kingston and Montreal: McGill-Queen's University Press

Frankenberg, R. 1957. *Village on the Border*. London: Cohen and West

Fraser, Paul. 1850–55. 'Thompson's River Journal, 17 August 1850 to 10 June 1855.' Victoria: Public Archives of British Columbia

Gabriel, Theresa. 1958. *Vernon British Columbia: A Brief History*. Vernon: Okanagan Historical Society

Gaffen, Fred. 1985. *Forgotten Soldiers*. Penticton: Theytus Books

Galeski, B. 1971. 'Sociological Problems of the Occupation of Farmers.' In *Peasants and Peasant Societies*, edited by T. Shanin. Harmondsworth: Penguin

– 1972. *Basic Concepts of Rural Sociology*. Manchester: Manchester University Press

Gans, H.J. 1962. *The Urban Villagers: Group and Class in the Life of Italian-Americans*. New York: The Free Press

Gerber, Linda M. 1976. 'Minority Survival: Community Characteristics and Out-migration from Indian Communities across Canada.' University of Toronto, PhD thesis

– 1979. 'The Development of Canadian Indian Communities.' *Canadian Review of Sociology and Anthropology* 16: 404–24

Godelier, Maurice. 1975. 'Modes of Production, Kinship, and Demographic Structures.' In *Marxist Analyses and Social Anthropology*, edited by Maurice Bloch. London: Malaby Press

Gonzalez, Nancie L. 1987. 'Family Labour Strategies in Modern Peasant Societies.'

In *Themes in Ethnology and Culture History;* edited by Leland Donald. Sadar, Meerut (India): Archana Publications

Gordon, Elizabeth. 1988. 'Stress in the Farm Family: Implications for the Rural Human Service Worker.' In *The Political Economy of Agriculture in Western Canada,* edited by G.S. Basran and David A. Hay. Toronto: Garamond Press

Graham, Donald. 1930. 'The Rise and Fall of Grist Milling in the Okanagan Valley.' *Okanagan Historical Society Report* 4: 12–15

Gramsci, Antonio. 1971. *Selection from the Prison Notebooks of Antonio Gramsci,* edited and translated by Quintin Hoare and Geoffrey Nowell Smith. New York: International Publishers

Grant, John Webster. 1984. *Moon of Wintertime: Missionaries and the Indians of Canada in Encounter since 1534.* Toronto: University of Toronto Press

Gulliver, Philip. 1977. 'Networks and Factions: Two Ndendenti Communities.' In *A House Divided? Anthropological Studies of Factionalism'* edited by M. Silverman and R.F. Salisbury. St John's: Memorial University of Newfoundland: Institute of Social and Economic Research

Haines, Francis. 1938. 'The Northward Spread of Horses among the Plains Indians.' *American Anthropologist* 40: 429–37

Hall, Tony. 1990. 'Canada's Bitter Legacy of Injustice.' *Globe and Mail* (Toronto) 16 March

Hansard (Canada). 1917

Hansen, Lise C. 1985. 'Strategies for Development on Nipissing Indian Reserve No. 10.' University of Toronto, PhD thesis

Hatfield, H.R. 1969. 'When Commerce Went Ahorseback.' *Okanagan Historical Society Report* 33: 67–77

Hawthorn, H.B., ed. 1966, 1967. *A Survey of the Contemporary Indians of Canada.* 2 vols. Ottawa: Information Canada

Hawthorn, H.B., C.S. Belshaw, and S.M. Jamieson. 1958. *The Indians of British Columbia: A Study of Contemporary Social Adjustment.* Toronto: University of Toronto Press

Helm, June, ed. 1968. *Essays on the Problem of the Tribe.* Seattle: University of Washington Press. Proceedings of the 1967 annual spring meetings of the American Ethnological Society

Hill-Tout, Charles. 1907. *The Far West: The Home of the Salish and Dene.* British North America I. *The Native British Empire.* Toronto: Copp Clark

– 1911. 'Report on the Ethnology of the Okana'kEn of British Columbia, an Interior Division of the Salish Stock.' *Journal of the Royal Anthropological Institute* 41: 130–61

– 1978. *The Salish People: The Local Contribution of Charles Hill-Tout,* edited by Ralf Maud in 4 vols. Vancouver: Talonbooks

Hirabayashi, Gordon K., and Cecil L. French. 1961. 'Poverty, Poor Acculturation and Apathy: Factors in the Social Status of Some Alberta Metis.' Paper read at the 33rd annual meeting of the Canadian Political Science Association, Montreal

Hoernlé, A.W. 1933. 'New Aims and Methods in Social Anthropology.' *South African Association for the Advancement of Science* 30: 74–92. Reprinted in *The Social Organization of the Nama and Other Essays by Winifred Hoernlé*, edited by Peter Carstens. Johannesburg: University of Witwatersrand Press

Holliday, C.W. 1948. *The Valley of Youth*. Caldwell, Idaho: Caxton Printers Ltd

Homans, G.C. 1951. *The Human Group*. London: Routledge and Kegan Paul

Hudson, Douglas. 1986. 'The Okanagan Indians.' In *Native Peoples: The Canadian Experience*, edited by R. Bruce Morrison and C. Roderick Wilson. Toronto: McClelland and Stewart

Hudson's Bay Company Archives (HBCA)
- B97/a/1, 1822–1823 No. 184f. Thompson's River Journal by James MacMillan and John MacLeod
- B97/a/2, 1826–1827. Journal of Occurrences at Thompson's River by Archibald McDonald
- B97/e/1, 1827. Kamloops Report by Archibald McDonald
- B97/e/2, Kamloops Report
- B97/a/3, 1846. Journal of Alex. C. Anderson of the Hudson's Bay Company
- B97/d/1, 1870–1871. Blotter. Thompson's River District
- B208/a/1, 1822–1823. Spokane District Journal
- B208/e/1, 1822–1823. Spokane House Report by John MacLeod
- D25/7, 1889. Report. Thompson's River District, Kamloops Post by Jas. O. Grahame, Chief Trader and W.H. Adams, Inspecting Officer

Indian Affairs and Northern Development. 1971. *Socio-economic Factors Affecting Land Use in North Okanagan Region*. Kelowna: DIAND Vancouver

Inglis, G.B. 1968. 'An Approach to the Analysis of Reserve Populations as Partial Societies.' Paper presented to the Symposium on the American Reservation System at the 67th Annual Meeting of the American Anthropological Association, Seattle

Isaac, Rhys. 1982. *The Transformation of Virginia 1740–90*. Chapel Hill: University of North Carolina Press

Jacobs, Wilbur R. 1971. 'The Fatal Confrontation: Early Native-White Relations on the Frontiers of Australia, New Guinea and America – A Comparative Study.' *Pacific Historical Review* 40: 283–309

Jakobson, R. 1931. 'Prinzipien der historischen Phonologie.' *Travaux du Cercle Linguistique de Prague*, IV

Jamieson, Kathleen. 1978. *Indian Women and the Law in Canada: Citizens Minus*. Ottawa: Advisory Council on the Status of Women

Jenness, Diamond. 1932. *Indians of Canada*. Ottawa: National Museum of Canada

Johnson, F. Henry. 1937. 'Fur Trading Days at Kamloops.' *B.C. Historical Quarterly* 1: 171–85

Jorgensen, J.G. 1971. 'Indians and the Metropolis.' In *The American Indian in Urban Society*, edited by J.O. Waddell and O.M. Watson. Boston: Little, Brown

Kerr, William, and Associates. 1975. 'Okanagan Band Economic Development Officer Study.' Prepared for the Band and Department of Indian Affairs and Northern Development (mimeo)

Knight, Rolf. 1978. *Indians at Work: An Informal History of Native Indian Labour in British Columbia, 1858–1930*. Vancouver: New Star Books

Kroeber, A.L. 1919. 'On the Principle of Order in Civilization as Exemplified by Changes in Fashion.' *American Anthropologist* 21: 235–63

– 1963 [1939]. *Cultural and Natural Areas of Native North America*. Berkeley: University of California Press

– 1948. *Anthropology*. New York: Harcourt Brace and Co.

Laing, F.W. 1942. 'Some Pioneers of the Cattle Industry.' *British Columbia Historical Quarterly* 6:257–75

Leacock, Eleanor. 1954. *The Montagnais 'Hunting Territory' and the Fur Trade*. American Anthropological Association, Memoir 78. 56 (5), Pt. 2

Lee, R.B. 1979. *The !Kung San: Men, Women, and Work in a Foraging Society*. Cambridge: Cambridge University Press

Lerman, Norman H. 1950–6. 'An Okanagan Winter-Dance.' *Anthropology in B:C.* Nos. 1–5: 35–6

Lévi-Strauss, Claude. 1963. *Structural Anthropology*. New York: Basic Books

Leyton, Elliot. 1975. *The One Blood: Kinship and Class in an Irish Village*. St John's: Memorial University of Newfoundland, Institute of Social and Economic Research

Lithman, Y.G. 1978. *The Community Apart: A Case Study of a Canadian Indian Reserve Community*. Stockholm: University of Stockholm

– 1983. *The Practice of Underdevelopment and the Theory of Development: The Canadian Indian Case*. Stockholm: University of Stockholm

Ludwig, Mary. 1984. 'Friends and Strangers: Social Interaction and Modernization in Central Ireland.' University of Toronto, PhD thesis

Maine, Henry S. 1861. *Ancient Law*. London: J. Murray

– 1871. *Village Communities in the East and West*. London: J. Murray

Manson, Donald. 1841–. Thompson's River Journal. Victoria: Public Archives of British Columbia

Manson, William. 1859–62. Fort Kamloops Journal, January 1859 – November 1862. Victoria: Public Archives of British Columbia

Manuel, G., and M. Poslums, 1974. *The Fourth World: An Indian Reality*. Toronto: Collier-Macmillan Canada

Marais, J.S. 1939. *The Cape Coloured People 1652–1937*. London: Longmans, Green & Co.

Mayer, Philip. 1961. *Townsmen or Tribesmen: Conservatism and the Process of Urbanization in a South African City*. Cape Town: Oxford University Press

– ed. 1980. *Black Villagers in an Industrial Society*. Cape Town: Oxford University Press

Meillassoux, C. 1968. *Urbanization of an African Community*. Seattle: University of Washington Press

Meinig, D.W. 1968. *The Great Columbia Plain: A Historical Geography, 1805–1910*. Seattle: University of Washington Press

Merton, Robert K. 1967. *On Theoretical Sociology*. New York: The Free Press

Miller, Christopher L. 1985. *Prophetic Worlds: Indians and Whites on the Columbia Plateau*. New Brunswick, NJ: Rutgers University Press

Miller, J.R. 1989. *Skyscrapers Hide the Heavens: A History of Indian-White Relations in Canada*. Toronto: University of Toronto Press

Miner, Horace. 1939. *St. Denis: A French-Canadian Parish*. Chicago: University of Chicago Press

Mooney, James. 1928. 'The Aboriginal Population of America North of Mexico.' *Smithsonian Miscellaneous Collections* 80 (7): 1–40

Mooney, Kathleen A. 1979. 'Ethnicity, Economics, the Family Cycle, and Household Composition.' *Canadian Review of Sociology and Anthropology* 16 (4): 387–403

Morantz, Toby. 1982. 'Northern Algonquian Concepts of Status and Leadership Reviewed: A Case Study of the Eighteenth-Century Trading Captain System.' *Canadian Review of Sociology and Anthropology* 19 (4): 482–501

Morice, A.G. 1906. *The History of the Northern Interior of British Columbia. Formerly New Caledonia (1660–1880)*. London: John Lane

– 1910. *History of the Catholic Church in Western Canada*. 2 vols. Toronto: Musson

Mortimore, George E. 1974. 'The Road to Eagle Bay. Structure, Process and Power in a Highly Acculturated Ojibwa Band.' University of Toronto, PhD thesis

– 1975. 'Colonial Transfer: Abandonment or Disguised Domination? A Canadian Indian Reserve Case.' *Anthropologica* 17: 197–203

Mourning Dove. 1976. *Tales of the Okanagans*. Fairfield, Wash.: Ye Galleon Press

McFeat, T. 1983. 'An Affair to Remember: Winoque, 1965.' *Culture* 3 (1): 79–90

McIver, Robert M. and Charles H. Page. 1949. *Society: An Introductory Analysis*. London: Macmillan

McKelvie, B.A. 1949. *Tales of Conflict*. Vancouver: Vancouver Daily Province

McLean, Stan. 1984. *The History of the O'Keefe Ranch*. Edmonton: Uvisco; published by author

Murdock, G.P. 1967. *Ethnographic Atlas*. Pittsburg: University of Pittsburg Press

Nagata, S. 1970. *Modern Transformations of Moenkopi Pueblo*. Chicago: University of Illinois Press

‒ 1971. 'The Reservation Community and the Urban Community.' In *The American Indian in Urban Society*, edited by J.O. Waddell and O.M. Watson. Boston: Little, Brown

National Archives of Canada (NAC)

‒ RG 2, Series 1, Vol. 281. Commonage Reserves (1889)

‒ RG 10, Vol. 1327. 'Sources and Value of Income' (1900)

‒ RG 10, Vol. 3580, File 758. The Death of Inspector Cummiskey (1914)

‒ RG 10, Vol. 3612, File 3756-13. Various Reports and Letters regarding Thomas Greenhow and Cornelius O'Keefe from G.M. Sproat (1877)

‒ RG 10, Vol. 3612, File 3756-16. Joint Indian Reserve Commission. Second Condensed Report by the Joint Commission appointed by the Governments of Canada and British Columbia. (1st December 1877)

‒ RG 10, Vol. 3612, File 3756-22. Confidential letters and Report dealing with the work of the Joint Indian Reserve Commission from G.M. Sproat (1877)

‒ RG 10, Vol. 3635, File 6650. E. Mohun's resignation for 'great pecuniary importance'

‒ RG 10, Vol. 3641, File 7571. Correspondence Joint Indian Reserve Commission, Miscellaneous. July (1877‒)

‒ RG 10, Vol. 8599½. Correspondence. Joint Indian Reserve Commission from Kamloops. July 1877

‒ RG 10, Vol. 3653, File 8701. On the State of Feeling among the Shuswaps and the Okanagan. (August 27, 1877)

‒ RG 10, Vol. 3659, File 9500. Correspondence relating to so-called Chief Tonasket who is not a chief in this country (1877)

‒ RG 10, Vol. 3660, File 9755-5. Joint Indian Reserve Commission. Miscellaneous (1878)

‒ RG 10, Vol. 3663, File 9801. The O'Keefe File. Correspondence and Reports (1877‒9)

‒ RG 10, Vol. 3670, File 10,769. Correspondence ‒ O'Keefe's Land Claim (1877‒8)

‒ RG 10, Vol. 3673, File 11,356. The death of Chief Moses and the election of Chief William (1879)

‒ RG 10, Vol. 3704, File 17,867. Correspondence relating to the Commonage and other Land issues south of the Head of the Lake (1885‒1920)

‒ RG 10, Vol. 3706, File 18,994. Report of E. Mohun on surveying cost etc., and his friendship with Chilahitsa (1880)

‒ RG 10, Vol. 3858, File 81,544 Pt. 1. Interim Report No. 16 of the Royal Commission of Indian Affairs for the Province of B.C. Details on Harris Reserve No. 3 (1913)

- RG 10, Vol. 3858, File 81,544 Pt. 2. Letters from Agent J.W. Mackay making application for extension of certain Indian Reserves in the Okanagan District (1891)
- RG 10, Vol. 3945, File 121,698-64. Okanagan Elections (1912)
- RG 10, Vol. 8588, File 1/1-10-4, Pt. 5
- RG 10, Vol. 10011. Census of Okanagan Tribe (1877)
- RG 10, Vol. 11009. Folios 000977-8. Provincial Government's view that Okanagan Commonages are unnecessary (26 November 1888)

Nicholas, R.W. 1968. 'Factions: A Comparative Analysis.' In *Political Systems and the Distribution of Power*, edited by Michael Banton. London: Tavistock; ASA Monographs 2

Norris, L. 1931. 'The Explorations of Captain Houghton.' *Okanagan Historical Society Report* 5: 30–2

Oblates of Mary Immaculate. Archives. Ottawa

Ogburn, W.F., and M.F. Nimkopf. 1950. *A Handbook of Sociology*. London: Routledge and Kegan Paul

Ogden, Peter Skene. 1853. *Traits of American-Indian Life and Character, by a Fur Trader*. London: Smith, Elder

[The] O'Keefe Historic Ranch 1867–1978. A History. 1978. Vernon: Wayside Press

Ormsby, Margaret A. 1931. 'A Study of the Okanagan Valley of British Columbia.' University of British Columbia, MA thesis

- 1949. 'Captain Houghton's Exploratory Trip 1864.' *Okanagan Historical Society Report* 13: 38–44
- ed. 1976. *A Pioneer Gentlewoman in British Columbia: The Recollections of Susan Allison*. Vancouver: University of British Columbia Press

Osborn, Alan J. 1983. 'Ecological Aspects of Equestrian Adaptations in Aboriginal North America.' *American Anthropologist* 85 (3): 563–91

Ossowski, S. 1956. 'Old Notions and New Problems.' In *Third World Congress of Sociology Proceedings*

- 1963. *Class Structure in the Social Consciousness*. London: Routledge and Kegan Paul

Public Archives of British Columbia (PABC)

- Colonial Secretary's Correspondence 1861–1866
- No ref. number. Letter to Indian Superintendent A.W. Vowell regarding Pere Nequalla (Pierre Machell) dated 8 March 1909
- Document No. 121698-32. Letter to the Superintendent General of Indian Affairs from Chief Pere Nequalla (7 December 1908)
- GR 494. Box 1 File 46. Joint Indian Reserve Commission. Second Condensed Report of the Joint Commissioners appointed by the Governments of Canada and British Columbia (1st December 1877)

- GR 494. Box 2 File 53. Joint Indian Reserve Commission. Second Condensed Report of the Commissioners acting for the Province (1st January 1878)
- GR 494 (2 Boxes). Correspondence and Reports submitted to the Minister regarding the work of the Indian Reserve Commission. 1876–1878
- GR 725. Report of Commissioner C.W. Morrow on the protests against the inclusion or omission of certain people from membership in the band
- GR 725. Correspondence and Reports submitted to the Minister regarding the work of the Indian Reserve Commission
- GR 931. British Columbia. Executive Council. Ditchburn-Clark Report to amend the work of the Commission on Indian Lands and Affairs in general in British Columbia. 1913–1916
- GR 1092. Canada. Department of Indian Affairs. Records of the ... Indian Superintendent of British Columbia. 1897–1905

Pareto, Vilfredo. [1916] 1963. *The Mind and Society*, edited by Arthur Livingston. New York: Dover Publications

Pearson, Patrick. 1986. 'The History and Social Structure of the Rehoboth Baster Community of Namibia.' University of the Witwatersrand, MA thesis

Philpott, Stuart B. 1968. 'Remittance Obligations, Social Networks, and Choice among Montserratian Migrants in Britain.' *Man* (n.s.) 3: 465–76

Pitt-Rivers, J. 1954. *People of Sierra*. London: Weidenfeld and Nicholson
- 1960. 'Social Class in a French Village.' *Anthropological Quarterly* 33 (1): 1–13

Ponting, J.R., and R. Gibbins. 1980. *Out of Irrelevance: A Socio-political Introduction to Indian Affairs in Canada*. Toronto: Butterworths

Porter, John. 1965. *The Vertical Mosaic: An Analysis of Social Class and Power in Canada*. Toronto: University of Toronto Press

Post, Richard H. 1938. 'The Subsistence Quest.' In *The Sinkaietk or Southern Okanogan of Washington* by Walter Cline et al. Menasha: General Series in Anthropology, No. 6

Radcliffe-Brown, A.R. 1952. *Structure and Function in Primitive Society*. London: Cohen and West

Raufer, Sister Maria Ilma. 1966. *Black Robes and Indians on the Last Frontier*. Milwaukee: The Bruce Publishing Company

Ravenhill, Alice. 1938. *The Native Tribes of British Columbia*. Victoria: Charles F. Banfield

Ray, Verne F. 1932. *The Sanpoil and Nespelem: Salishan Peoples of Northeastern Washington*. Seattle: University of Washington Publications in Anthropology Vol. 5
- 1936. 'Native Villages and Groupings of the Columbia Basin.' *Pacific Northwest Quarterly* 27: 99–152

- 1939. *Cultural Relations in the Plateau of Northwestern America.* Los Angeles: Southwestern Museum
- 1974. 'Ethnohistory of the Joseph Band of Nez Perce Indians 1805–1905.' In *Nez Perce Indians,* edited by S.A. Chalfant and V.F. Ray. New York: Garland Publishing Co.
Ray, Verne F., et al. 1938. 'Tribal Distribution in Eastern Oregon and Adjacent Regions.' *American Anthropologist* 40: 384–415
Read, Peter. 1977. 'Preliminary Planning Study, Okanagan Reserves.' Prepared for DIAND and Okanagan Indian Band (mimeo)
Redfield, Robert. 1941. *The Folk Culture of Yucatan.* Chicago: University of Chicago Press
- 1956. *Peasant Society and Culture: An Anthropological Approach to Civilization.* Chicago: University of Chicago Press
- 1960. *The Little Community and Peasant Society and Culture.* Chicago: University of Chicago Press
Redfield, Robert, and Alfonso Villa Rojas. 1934. *Chan Kom: A Maya Village.* Washington: Carnegie Institute of Washington
Reinhart, Herman Francis. 1962. *The Golden Frontier: The Recollections of Herman Francis Reinhart 1851–1869,* edited by D.B. Nunis, Jr. Austin: University of Texas Press
Rich, E.E. 1947. *George Simpson's 1828 Journey to the Columbia.* London: Hudson's Bay Record Society, Vol. 10
- 1959. *The History of the Hudson's Bay Company 1670–1870.* Vol. 2, *1763–1870.* London: Hudson's Bay Record Society
Riches, David. 1984. 'Hunting, Herding and Potlatching: Towards a Sociological Account of Prestige.' *Man* (n.s.) 19: 234–51
Robertson, Heather. 1970. *Reservations Are for Indians.* Toronto: James Lewis and Samuel
Ross, Alexander. 1849. *Adventures of the First Settlers on the Oregon or Columbia River.* London: Smith, Elder, and Company
- 1956 [1855]. *The Fur Hunters of the Far West,* edited by Kenneth A. Spaulding. Norman: University of Oklahoma Press
Ross, D.A. 1960. 'St. Joseph's Jesuit Mission in the Okanagan.' *Okanagan Historical Society Report* 24: 59–61
Rubenstein, Hymie. 1987. *Coping with Poverty: Adaptive Strategies in a Caribbean Village.* Boulder and London: Westview Press
Sahlins, M. 1965. 'On the Sociology of Primitive Exchange.' In *The Relevance of Models in Social Anthropology,* edited by Michael Banton. London: Tavistock; ASA Monographs 1

Saum, Lewis O. 1965. *The Fur Trader and the Indian*. Seattle: University of
Washington Press

Schapera, I. 1947. *Migrant Labour and Tribal Life*. London: Oxford University Press

– 1956. *Government and Politics in Tribal Societies*. London: Watt

Secoy, Frank Raymond. 1953. *Changing Military Patterns on the Great Plains*.
Locust Valley, NY: J.J. Augustin

Shanin, T., ed. 1971. *Peasants and Peasant Societies*. Harmondsworth: Penguin

Shankel, G.E. 1945. 'The Development of Indian Policy in British Columbia.'
University of Washington: PhD thesis

Sharp, J.S. 1980. 'Two Separate Developments: Anthropology in South Africa.'
RAIN 36:4–6

– 1981. 'The Roots of the Development of "Volkekunde" in South Africa.' *Journal
of Southern African Studies* 8 (1): 1–16

Sieciechowicz, Krystyna. 1985. 'Councils and Kitchens: Political Decision-making in
a North-western Ontario Ojibwa-Cree Community.' Paper presented at the 45th
International Congress of Americanists, Bogota, Columbia, 1–9 July

Silverman, M., and R.F. Salisbury, eds. 1977. *A House Divided? Anthropological
Studies of Factionalism*. St John's: Memorial University of Newfoundland,
Institute of Social and Economic Research

Simmel, Georg. 1950. *The Sociology of Georg Simmel*, translated, edited, and with
an Introduction by Kurt H. Wolff. Glencoe: The Free Press

Simpson, George. 1931. *Fur Trade and Empire ... York Factory to Fort George ...
1824–1825*, edited with an Introduction by F. Merk. Cambridge: Harvard
University Press

– 1947. *1828 Journey to the Columbia*, edited by E.E. Rich. London: Champlain
Society for the Hudson's Bay Record Society

Smith, Gavin A. 1984. 'Confederations of Households: Extended Domestic Enterprises in City and Country.' In *Miners, Peasants and Entrepreneurs*, edited by
Norman Long and Bryan Roberts. Cambridge: Cambridge University Press

Smith, Harlan I. 1900. 'Archaeology of the Thompson River Region.' *Memoirs of
the American Museum of Natural History* 2: 401–51

Sorokin, Pitrim A. 1937–41. *Social and Cultural Dynamics*. 4 vols. New York:
American Book Co.

Sorokin, Pitrim A. and C.C. Zimmerman, 1939. *Principles of Rural-Urban Sociology*. New York: H. Holt

Spykman, N.J. 1925. *The Social Theory of Georg Simmel*. Chicago: University of
Chicago Press

Stavenhagen, Rudolfo. 1975. *Social Classes in Agrarian Societies*, translated from
the Spanish edition (1969) by Judy A. Hellman. New York: Doubleday.

Stonequist, E.V. 1937. *The Marginal Man*. New York: Scribner

Surtees, Ursula. 1979. *Sunshine and Butterflies. A Short History of Early Fruit Ranching in Kelowna*. Kelowna: Regatta City Press

Tanner, A., ed. 1983. *The Politics of Indianness*. St John's: Memorial University of Newfoundland, Institute of Social and Economic Research

Teit, James A. 1969 [1898]. *Traditions of the Thompson River Indians of British Columbia*. Boston: Houghton, Mifflin (Kraus Reprint Co.)

– 1900. *The Thompson Indians of British Columbia* edited by Franz Boas. New York: G.E. Stechert Memoir of the American Museum of Natural History

– 1906. *The Lillooet Indians*, edited by Franz Boas. New York: G.E. Stechert; Memoir of the American Museum of Natural History.

– 1909. *The Shuswap*, edited by Franz Boas. New York: G.E. Stechert; Memoir of the American Museum of Natural History.

– 1914. 'Indian Tribes of the Interior of British Columbia.' In *Canada and Its Provinces* 21: 283–312. Toronto: Printed by T. and A. Constable at the University of Edinburgh Press

– 1928. *The Middle Columbia Salish*, edited by Franz Boas, Vol. 2 (4): 83–128. Seattle: University of Washington Publications in Anthropology

– 1930. *The Salishan Tribes of the Western Plateaus*. Forty-Fifth Annual Report of the Bureau of American Ethnology (1927–1928), edited by Franz Boas. Washington, DC: US Government Printing Office

– n.d. 'Salish Ethnographic Notes. Salish Languages. Salish Tribal Names and Distribution.' Letter, Teit to Boas, 4 July 1909. American Philosophical Library Boas Collection (Public Archives of British Columbia. Microfilm: Reel A246, No.61)

Thomas, Robert K. 1966–7. 'Colonialism: Classic and Internal' and 'Powerless Politics,' *New University Thought* 4 (4):37–44, 44–53

Thomson, Duane. 1978. 'Opportunity Lost: A History of Okanagan Reserves in the Colonial Period.' *Okanagan Historical Society Report* 42: 43–52

– 1985. 'A History of the Okanagan.' University of British Columbia, PhD thesis.

– 1986. 'A Problem of Perception: Views of Indians in British Columbia.' Unpublished paper

Tod, John. 1841–1843. Thompson River Journal, 3 August 1841–19 December 1843. Victoria: Public Archives of British Columbia

– n.d. 'History of New Caledonia and the Northwest Coast.' Victoria: Public Archives of British Columbia

Tönnies, Ferdinand. 1955 [1887]. *Community and Association*, translated and supplemented by Charles P. Loomis. London: Routledge and Kegan Paul

Trigger, D.S. 1989. ' "Whitefella Comin": Colonialism, Resistance and Consent in

North Australia.' Paper given at the American Anthropological Association Meeting, Washington, DC

– In press. '"Whitefella Coming" – Colonialism, Resistance and Consent in North Australia.' Cambridge University Press

Upton, Primrose. 1958. *The History of Okanagan Mission*. Okanagan Mission: Centennial Committee

Van Kirk, Sylvia. 1980. *'Many Tender Ties': Women in Fur-Trade Society in Western Canada, 1670–1870*. Winnipeg: Watson and Dwyer

– 1985. 'What if Mama Is an Indian? The Cultural Ambivalence of the Alexander Ross Family.' In *The New Peoples: Being and Becoming a Métis in North America*, edited by Jacqueline Peterson and Jennifer S.H. Brown. Winnipeg: University of Manitoba Press

Vernon British Columbia. Diamond Jubilee (1892–1952). 1952. Vernon: The Vernon News (Souvenir programme)

Vernon News. 1891–1987

Vidich, Arthur J., and Joseph Bensman, 1960. *Small Town and Mass Society: Class, Power and Religion in a Rural Community*. New York: Doubleday

Vogt, Evon. 1960. 'On the Concepts of Structure and Process in Cultural Anthropology.' *American Anthropologist* 62: 18–33

Wakeam, Nadim. 1977. 'Domination, Dependence, and the Marginal Man.' University of Toronto, MA thesis

Ware, Reuben. 1974. *The Lands We Lost: A History of Cut-off Lands and Land Losses from Indian Reserves in British Columbia*. Vancouver: Union of B.C. Indian Chiefs

Warner, W. Lloyd and Paul S. Lunt, 1941. *The Social Life of a Modern Community*. New Haven: Yale University Press

Warner, W. Lloyd, et al. 1949. *Social Class in America: A Manual of Procedure for the Measurement of Social Status*. Chicago: Social Science Research Associates

Watkins, Donald. 1970. 'The Practice of Medicine among the Indians.' *Okanagan Historical Society Report* 34: 30–2

Watkins, Mel, ed. 1977. *Dene Nation – The Colony Within*. Toronto: University of Toronto Press

Weaver, S.M. 1981. *Making Canadian Indian Policy. The Hidden Agenda 1968–1970*. Toronto: University of Toronto Press

Weber, Max. 1968. *Economy and Society*. 3 vols. New York: Bedminister Press

White, Hester. 1940. 'John Carmichael Haynes.' *British Columbia Historical Quarterly* 4 (3): 183–201

Wichern, P.H. 1972. *Political Developments on Indian Reserves*. Winnipeg: University of Manitoba, Centre for Settlement Studies 2, Report No. 11

Williams, Raymond. 1976. *Keywords: A Vocabulary of Culture and Society.* Glasgow: William Collins

Wilson, Monica. 1951. 'Witch Beliefs and Social Structure.' *American Journal of Sociology* 56: 307–13

– 1966. 'Peasant Societies.' In *The Oxford History of South Africa*, edited by Monica Wilson and Leonard Thompson. Oxford: Clarendon Press

Wolf, Eric R. 1955. 'Types of Latin American Peasantry: A Preliminary Discussion.' *American Anthropologist* 57: 452–71

– 1966. *Peasants.* Englewood Cliffs: Prentice-Hall

– 1982. *Europe and the People without History.* Berkeley: University of California Press

Woolliams, Nina G. 1979. *Cattle Ranch: The Story of the Douglas Lake Cattle Company.* Vancouver: Douglas and McIntyre

Worsley, Peter. 1964. 'Bureaucracy and Decolonization: Democracy from the Top.' In *The New Sociology*, edited by Irving L. Horowitz. New York: Oxford University Press

Yakamovitch, Larry. 1966. 'An Historical Interpretation of the Land Utilization and Tenure Patterns in the Vernon Rural Area of the Okanagan Valley, British Columbia.' University of Oregon, MA thesis

Zentner, H. 1972. 'Reservation Social Structure and Anomie.' In *Perspectives on the North American Indians*, edited by M. Nagler. Toronto: McClelland and Stewart

Index

Abel, Mary, Plate 5
Aboriginal rights: Okanagan declaration of, xi, 145
Administrative determinism, 286
Affines, 147–8. *See also* Kinship and marriage; Women
Agencies: establishment of in British Columbia, 87–9
Agents, 88. *See also* Superintendents
Agriculture. *See* Farming
Alcohol: consumption of, 33, 53, 182n, 184, 240, 242, 248–9, 259, 284–5, 287; opening of beer parlours to Indians, 224–5
Alexis, Murray (chief), xiii–xiv, 215–18, 228–9, 231, 232, 246, 252–3, Plate 15; and councillors (1987), Plate 13
Anderson, A.C., 69, 78, 92, 93
Antoine, Jimmy, 216
Arensberg, C.M., 149, 150
Armstrong, Jeannette, C., 174n
Aron, Raymond, xvii

Balf, Mary, 16n, 20, 39, 40, 41, 43, 47

Band: budget, 247; list, 140–2; membership in, 89–90. *See also* Reserves
Band council: affairs and activities of, 239–56; band manager, 227–30, 251–2; chief and councillors, 230–8; Indian Act as amended (1951), 224–7; Indian agent (superintendent), 223–4, 227–9, 231, 233; powers and duties of, 222–38
Bands (traditional), 1–28; as political communities, 15–16
Barman, Jean, 257n
Beals, Alan, 158
Beer. *See* Alcohol
Bensman, Joseph, 275
Berkhofer, Robert F., Jr, 289n
Black, Samuel: murder of, 40
Boas, Franz, 16n, 24
Bock, Philip, 140
Bodemann, Y.M., 190
Boldt, Menno, 233
Bonneau family, 232
Bonneau, Jimmy (chief), 164–5, 214–15, Plate 10